CULTURES OF LAW IN URBAN NORTHERN EUROPE

Drawing together an international team of historians, lawyers and historical sociolinguists, this volume investigates urban cultures of law in Scotland, with a special focus on Aberdeen and its rich civic archive, the Low Countries, Norway, Germany and Poland from c. 1350 to c. 1650.

In these essays, the contributors seek to understand how law works in its cultural and social contexts by focusing specifically on the urban experience and, to a great extent, on urban records. The contributions are concerned with understanding late medieval and early modern legal experts as well as the users of courts and legal services, the languages and records of law, and legal activities occurring inside and outside of official legal fora. This volume considers what the expectations of people at different status levels were for the use of the law, what perceptions of justice and authority existed among different groups, and what their knowledge was of law and legal procedure. By examining how different aspects of legal culture came to be recorded in writing, the contributors reveal how that writing itself then became part of a culture of law.

Cultures of Law in Urban Northern Europe: Scotland and its Neighbours c.1350–c.1650 combines the historical study of law, towns, language and politics in a way that will be accessible and compelling for advanced level undergraduates and post-graduate to postdoctoral researchers and academics in medieval and early modern, urban, legal, political and linguistic history.

Jackson W. Armstrong is a Senior Lecturer in History at the University of Aberdeen, Scotland. He is the author of *England's Northern Frontier: Conflict and Local Society in the Fifteenth-Century Scottish Marches* (2020).

Edda Frankot is Associate Professor in History at Nord University in Bodø, Norway. She specialises in late medieval urban, maritime and legal history. She is the author of *'Of Laws of Ships and Shipmen'. Medieval Maritime Law and its Practice in Urban Northern Europe* (2012).

Themes in Medieval and Early Modern History

Series Editor: Natasha Hodgson, Nottingham Trent University

This is a brand new series which straddles both medieval and early modern worlds, encouraging readers to examine historical change over time as well as promoting understanding of the historical continuity between events in the past, and to challenge perceptions of periodisation. It aims to meet the demand for conceptual or thematic topics which cross a relatively wide chronological span (any period between c. 500–1750), including a broad geographical scope.

Available titles:

Florence in the Early Modern World
Nicholas Baker and Brian Maxson

Dynastic Change
Legitimacy and Gender in Medieval and Early Modern Monarchy
Edited by Ana Maria S. A. Rodrigues, Manuela Santos Silva and Jonathan W. Spangler

The Origins of the Consumer Revolution in England
From Brass Pots to Clocks
Joanne Sear and Ken Sneath

Lived Religion and Gender in Late Medieval and Early Modern Europe
Sari Katajala-Peltomaa and Raisa Maria Toivo

Cultures of Law in Urban Northern Europe
Scotland and its Neighbours c.1350–c.1650
Edited by Jackson W. Armstrong and Edda Frankot

Religion and Conflict in Medieval and Early Modern Worlds
Identities, Communities and Authorities
Edited by Natasha Hodgson, Amy Fuller, John McCallum and Nicholas Morton

For more information about this series, please visit: https://www.routledge.com/Themes-in-Medieval-and-Early-Modern-History/book-series/TMEMH

CULTURES OF LAW IN URBAN NORTHERN EUROPE

Scotland and its Neighbours c. 1350–c. 1650

Edited by
Jackson W. Armstrong and Edda Frankot

Routledge
Taylor & Francis Group
LONDON AND NEW YORK

First published 2021
by Routledge
2 Park Square, Milton Park, Abingdon, Oxon OX14 4RN

and by Routledge
52 Vanderbilt Avenue, New York, NY 10017

Routledge is an imprint of the Taylor & Francis Group, an informa business

British Library Cataloguing-in-Publication Data
A catalogue record for this book is available from the British Library

Library of Congress Cataloging-in-Publication Data
Names: Armstrong, Jackson W. (Jackson Webster),
1978– editor. | Frankot, Edda, editor.
Title: Cultures of law in urban Northern Europe: Scotland and its neighbours c.1350–c.1650 / edited by Jackson W. Armstrong and Edda Frankot.
Description: Milton Park, Abingdon, Oxon; New York, NY: Routledge, 2021. | Includes bibliographical references and index. |
Identifiers: LCCN 2020027957 (print) | LCCN 2020027958 (ebook) | ISBN 9780367206796 (paperback) | ISBN 9780367206802 (hardback) | ISBN 9780429262869 (ebook)
Subjects: LCSH: Law—Scotland—History. | Law—Europe, Northern—History.
Classification: LCC KDC296 .C85 2021 (print) | LCC KDC296 (ebook) | DDC 349.411—dc23
LC record available at https://lccn.loc.gov/2020027957
LC ebook record available at https://lccn.loc.gov/2020027958

ISBN: 978-0-367-20680-2 (hbk)
ISBN: 978-0-367-20679-6 (pbk)
ISBN: 978-0-429-26286-9 (ebk)

Typeset in Bembo
by codeMantra

CONTENTS

ILLUSTRATIONS

Figures

Tables

CONTRIBUTORS

Jackson W. Armstrong is a Senior Lecturer in history at the University of Aberdeen. He was principal investigator in the *Law in the Aberdeen Council Registers* project. His book *England's Northern Frontier: Conflict and Local Society in the Fifteenth-Century Scottish Marches* was published by Cambridge University Press in 2020.

Michael H. Brown is the Professor of Scottish History at the University of St Andrews. His books include *James I* (1994), *The Black Douglases* (1998), *The Wars of Scotland 1214–1371* (2004) and *Disunited Kingdoms: Politics and People in the British Isles 1280–1460* (2013).

Chanelle Delameillieure is a PhD Fellow of the Research Foundation Flanders at KU Leuven. She is completing her PhD thesis on abduction and marriage in fifteenth-century Brabant and Flanders and co-edited *Wijvenwereld* (2019), a book on women's lives in late medieval Low Countries' cities. Her research interests include women's and gender history, family history and the history of law and justice.

David Ditchburn is an Associate Professor of medieval history at Trinity College Dublin, University of Dublin. He is the author of many articles on various aspects of the social and economic history of later medieval Scotland, and of *Scotland and Europe: The medieval Kingdom and its Contacts with Christendom, 1215–1542* (2001).

J.D. Ford is the Professor of Civil Law in the University of Aberdeen. His edition of *Alexander King's Treatise on Maritime Law,* in which use is made of the court records of Aberdeen and other Scottish burghs, appeared in 2018.

Edda Frankot is an Associate Professor in history at the Department of Culture, History and Media at Nord University, Bodø. She was the Project Manager and Editorial Research Fellow on the *Law in the Aberdeen Council Registers* project. She is the author of *'Of Laws of Ships and Shipmen': Medieval Maritime Law in Urban Northern Europe* (2012). Her research focuses on the urban, legal and maritime history of northern Europe in the later middle ages and early modern period.

Jelle Haemers is a Senior Lecturer in medieval history at the University of Leuven (KU Leuven). His research interests include the social and political history of the later middle ages, urban history of the Low Countries and gender history.

Anna D. Havinga is a Lecturer in sociolinguistics in the department of German at the University of Bristol. Her research focuses on historical sociolinguistic processes in German and, more recently, Scots. Her monograph *Invisibilising Austrian German: On the Effect of Linguistic Prescriptions and Educational Reforms on Writing Practices in 18th-century Austria* was published by De Gruyter in 2018. She is also co-editor (with Nils Langer) of *Invisible Languages in the Nineteenth Century,* which was published by Peter Lang in 2015. From 2016 to 2017 she was the Text Enrichment Research Fellow in the *Law in the Aberdeen Council Registers* project (Leverhulme Trust, 2016–2019).

William Hepburn is a Research Fellow on the *Finance, law and the language of governmental practice in late medieval towns: Aberdeen and Augsburg in comparison* project at the University of Aberdeen. He completed a PhD thesis on 'The Household of James IV 1488–1513' at the University of Glasgow. He recently worked as a Research Assistant on the *Law in the Aberdeen Council Registers* project.

Joanna Kopaczyk is a Senior Lecturer in Scots and English at the University of Glasgow. She pioneered new methods of exploring discourse standardisation in historical texts from pragmaphilological and corpus-driven perspectives in *The Legal Language of Scottish Burghs* (Oxford University Press 2013). Her recent co-edited volumes include *Historical Dialectology in the Digital Age* (Edinburgh University Press 2019), *Applications of Pattern-driven Methods in Corpus Linguistics* (John Benjamins 2018) and *Binomials in the History of English* (Cambridge University Press 2017).

Jörg Rogge is a Professor of medieval history in the Johannes Gutenberg-Universität (JGU) Mainz. His research includes the political culture of late medieval cities in the Empire as well as power conflicts in England and Scotland. His publications encompass books and articles on the self-conception of medieval citizens, deviant behaviour, kings and queens and the methods and theories of Cultural History. He serves as Chair of the International Society of Cultural History. He is *inter alia* the editor of *Cultural History in Europe.*

Institutions – Themes – Perspectives (Bielefeld, 2011) and *Recounting Deviance. Forms and Practices of Presenting Divergent Behaviour in the Late Middle Ages and Early Modern Period* (Bielefeld, 2016). He is co-editor (with Martin Kinzinger, Franz Rexroth) of *Gewalt und Widerstand in der politischen Kultur des späten Mittelalters* (Ostfildern, 2015) and co-editor (with Alessandro Arcangeli, Hannu Salmi) of *The Routledge Companion to Cultural History in the Western World* (Abington and New York, 2020).

Andrew R.C. Simpson is the Professor of Scottish Legal History at the University of Edinburgh. He is co-author (with Adelyn Wilson) of *Scottish Legal History Volume One: 1000–1707* (Edinburgh University Press, 2017). He also co-edited *Continuity, Change and Pragmatism in the Law: Essays in Memory of Professor Angelo Forte* (2016) and *Northern Lights: Essays in Private Law in Memory of Professor David Carey Miller* (2018), both published by Aberdeen University Press. He is a co-investigator in the *Law in the Aberdeen Council Registers* project.

Graeme Small is a Professor of medieval history at Durham University, and his published books include *Late Medieval France* (Palgrave Macmillan, 2009) and *Court and Civic Society in the Burgundian Low Countries* (MUP, 2007). He has published on town records in the Southern Low Countries, France and England in the period 1350–1550. He has also published on the Scottish court in the later middle ages in comparative perspective.

Miriam Tveit is an Associate Professor of medieval history at the Department of Culture, History and Media at Nord University, Bodø. Her main field of research is legal history in medieval Europe, especially the legislation processes and legal politics as well as the developments in family law and criminal law. She completed a PhD thesis entitled 'In search of legal transmission – Inheritance and compensation for homicide in medieval secular law' at the University of Tromsø in 2017.

Adelyn L.M. Wilson is a Senior Lecturer in law at the University of Aberdeen. Her principal research interests are in early modern Scottish legal history and legal literature. She is co-author (with Andrew R.C. Simpson) of *Scottish Legal History Volume One: 1000–1707* (Edinburgh University Press, 2017), the first textbook in her discipline. She has held various offices in her research field, including as the Secretary-Treasurer of the Scottish Legal History Group, a Council member of the Stair Society, and the Reviews Editor for the biannual journal *Comparative Legal History*.

Justyna Wubs-Mrozewicz is an Associate Professor of medieval history at the University of Amsterdam. She has published on the Hanse, urban and maritime history of northern Europe, and on the interaction of various mercantile groups in this region. Her recent publications include the edited volume *The*

Routledge Handbook of Maritime Trade Around Europe (2017, with Wim Blockmans and Mikhail Krom) and *Merchants and Commercial Conflicts in Europe, 1250–1600,* special issue of *Continuity and Change,* Volume 32, Issue 1, May 2017 (with Flàvio Miranda). She is currently the PI of the project 'Managing multi-level conflicts in commercial cities in northern Europe (c. 1350–1570)' (Netherlands Organisation for Scientific Research, 2018–2023).

ACKNOWLEDGEMENTS

This volume is one result of several years' collaboration, and it is a pleasure to acknowledge those who have been involved in the steps towards its completion. The Aberdeen Burgh Records Project, housed in the Research Institute of Irish and Scottish Studies (RIISS) at the University of Aberdeen, began as a collaborative partnership in 2012 between the University and the Aberdeen City and Aberdeenshire Archives. Jackson Armstrong, Andrew Mackillop and City Archivist Phil Astley led that initiative which was supported by the RIISS through the Margaret Jones Bequest, which funded an initial pilot project in 2013–2014. Michael P. Brown, then acting director of RIISS, has been a great supporter from those early stages onwards, and Robin Urquhart of the National Records of Scotland, David Ditchburn and Micheál Ó Siochrú, both of Trinity College Dublin, and Siobhán Convery then Head of Special Collections at Aberdeen were also closely involved in the early project with thoughtful and welcome advice.

In 2013 Edda Frankot became formally involved in the first pilot project as researcher, and she subsequently served as a researcher in a related project led by Adam Wyner in 2014. Edda was named as Research Fellow and Project Manager in the Leverhulme Trust research project grant *Law in the Aberdeen Council Registers 1398–1511: Concepts, Practices, Geographies* (LACR), which was led by Jackson Armstrong as Principal Investigator from 2016 to 2019. The LACR project team included co-investigators Andrew Mackillop, Andrew Simpson and Adam Wyner, project partner Phil Astley and the researchers Anna Havinga, Claire Hawes, William Hepburn and Wim Peters, with all of whom it has been a great privilege to work. The LACR project also benefited from the experience and guidance of its advisory board members Steve Boardman, Elizabeth Ewan and Christine Reinle. The Aberdeen Burgh Records Project and the LACR project in particular have only been possible with generous funding from the Leverhulme Trust, the Aberdeen City Council and RIISS, and support from the

University of Aberdeen's Development Trust, Library and Special Collections, Digital and Information Services and the School of Divinity, History and Philosophy. Throughout the life of the LACR project, the wisdom and support of all of the staff of the Aberdeen City and Aberdeenshire Archives has been invaluable.

There are a number of people whose involvement and support along the way has been especially important, including those already named, but among those who particularly stand out are Kelly Anderson, Graeme Benvie, Liz Bowie, Jon Cameron, Lisa Chilton, Judith Cripps, Barney Crockett, Chris Croly, Neil Curtis, Lisa Collinson, Charlotte Farmer, Martin Hall, Brian Henderson, Carol Ince, Katy Kavanagh, Richard Lynch, Aly Macdonald, Andrew Macgregor, Lynsey Macready, Karim Mahmoud, Mike McConnell, June Middleton, Jo Milne, John Morrison, Fiona Musk, Rachel Paterson-Davies, Barry Robertson, Ian Robotham, Margaret Ross, Wendy Rudland, Julie Smart, Radostin Stoyanov, Paula Sweeney, Adelyn Wilson and Ruaraidh Wishart.

Many of the participants in a series of symposia hosted in Aberdeen by the LACR project in 2017 and 2018 are now among the contributors to this book. The input and discussion of all those who were involved was crucial in shaping the development of the present collection, and in particular we wish to appreciate the input of Claire Hawes, Christian Liddy, Andrew Mackillop and Adam Wyner in those sessions. In addition, some of what now appears in the introduction to this volume had the benefit of feedback from audiences at the European Association of Urban History conference in Rome in 2018 (in a panel which also involved Griet Vermeesch and Ans Vervaeke), at the Scottish Records Association conference in 2017 organised by Amy Blakeway and at the RIISS twentieth anniversary conference in Aberdeen in 2019.

We would like to thank the editorial and production team at Routledge, Laura Pilsworth, Lydia de Cruz, Morwenna Scott, Izzy Voice, Emily Irvine, the series editor Natasha Hodgson and all those involved in the production of this book. We are also very grateful to the readers who offered valuable comment on our original publication proposal, and to those who generously offered prompt and constructive critique of the draft submissions to this volume by way of anonymous peer review coordinated by us as the volume editors.

Jackson and Edda would also like to thank each other for an intellectually stimulating and rewarding collaboration throughout all the stages through which this volume has grown. Jackson in particular would like to thank Edda for the enormous patience she showed to her co-editor, especially in the latter stages of this project. Without Edda's diligence, legendary attention to detail and organisation, this volume would have taken a considerably longer time to bring to press. Finally, we would both like to thank our families (and in particular our partners Vicky and Barry) for their support throughout this project, and especially during the challenging circumstances of the 2020 pandemic.

INTRODUCTION

Investigating cultures of law in urban northern Europe

*Jackson W. Armstrong and Edda Frankot**

This book seeks to understand the law in action and in context. To that end the work collected here treats 'the law' in the broad sense of *Recht*, or *le droit*. It is in part a legal history, but one that goes beyond a history of doctrinal change, or even legal-philosophical intellectual endeavours (for instance, the process by which Roman law underwent a 'reception' in medieval and early modern Europe).[1] It is concerned with legal elites and experts but also with wider social categories of users of law, and it draws upon historical research into conflict, dispute and normative frameworks, which remains a flourishing field of study and one in which law is, rightly, a vital feature.[2] In particular, it draws attention to towns and cities as hubs of legal activity, where 'townspeople lived cheek by jowl with the many legal institutions that they used'.[3] To the extent that northern European societies were interconnected through trade, learning, conflict and diplomacy, shared aspects of law and legal change should be identifiable in urban records from the region, and shared questions may be asked of those sources and the languages contained within them. Within the last decade major contributions in this direction have been offered in the study of medieval maritime law and the linguistic framework of law, both taking an important reference point in the Scottish urban context.[4]

In Scotland, the Aberdeen civic archive is of major significance for such an effort. The town's surviving council registers from 1398 to 1511 do suffer a gap (c. 1414–c. 1433), but still more records survive for Aberdeen before 1500 than for all other Scottish towns combined, and these registers received UNESCO UK Memory of the World designation in 2013.[5] Internationally, they invite investigation and comparison with analogous materials from other towns. This was in part the purpose of the project *Law in the Aberdeen Council Registers, 1398–1511: Concepts, Practices, Geographies*. That project concentrated on urban archives as records predominantly of a legal nature, being chiefly records of the business of various courts which exercised jurisdiction in the royal burgh of Aberdeen. This burgh by 1400 boasted a population of no more than a few thousand inhabitants, although it was counted among the four leading towns of Scotland.[6] Many commercial disputes and cases of personal litigation came before the burgh courts, frequently involving merchants and sailors from abroad. These proceedings were almost entirely set down in Latin in 1400, but, by 1500, the use in the registers of Scots (the West Germanic vernacular language of northern Britain, known at the time as 'Inglis') had expanded dramatically. The *Aberdeen Registers Online: 1398–1511* (ARO) is a 1.5-million-word digital edition of the text of these registers, created by the project.[7]

Any investigation of 'the law' meets the wider problem of adequately explaining the context in which law operates. In other words, this prompts a need to examine cultures of law. Unlike 'political culture', which has produced a vast literature concerned with historical as well as present-day contexts,[8] 'legal culture' is much less well developed as a historical subject.[9] One description of legal culture emphasises not change but continuity – seeing it as 'describing relatively stable patterns of legally oriented social behaviour and attitudes'.[10] One of the earliest investigators of legal culture, Lawrence Friedman, defines it as 'the network of values and attitudes [...] which determines when and why and where people turn to law or government or turn away. It is thus the immediate source of legal change, whatever the ultimate source may be'.[11] More recently, Jørn Sunde has set the idea in a historical perspective. In Sunde's approach, legal culture is essentially about how law is understood and applied in practice.[12] He has asserted that 'legal culture represents ideas and expectations of law that are made operational by institutional(-like) practices'.[13] In this assessment, legal culture is shaped simultaneously by institutional and intellectual structures, and Sunde observes the possibility of using the idea either in a narrow sense (being mainly about the law itself) or in a wide sense (as law relates to other aspects of society). According to Harriet Rudolph, the use of this wider sense, taking into account various methodological problems, is necessary in order to deal satisfactorily with the complex relationship between law and society.[14]

In considering all this it is important to distinguish our present particular focus on legal culture from other closely related areas of study. One is the broad academic field of 'law and society' which has existed since the 1950s and which is closely associated with the subject of the sociology of law.[15] The other is the anthropology of law, with a strong legacy of comparative historical treatment which continues to thrive.[16] For our purposes, the problem of legal culture is less about understanding how the social operations of law might be theorised or the ways in which legal ideas can function as conceptual tools, but is more precisely concerned with investigating the ideas, expectations and patterns that shape how law is put to work. Our approach to the topic is partly captured by Steven Winter's observation that 'law is constituted and sustained ... in the forms of life that give meaning to our categories, concepts and values',[17] and is partly grounded in Lawrence Rosen's approach to law as a way in which we order the world and achieve a categorisation of knowledge and the creation of facts.[18] While we do not seek to provide a restrictive definition of legal culture to be rigorously observed in the contributions which follow, our goal is to allow the authors of this volume to open the problem up for interrogation from different perspectives.

The essays gathered here are by no means the first to venture into this territory for the late medieval and early modern periods.[19] Unsurprisingly, given its rich source survival, England has featured prominently in work related to this theme. Anthony Musson, in his important investigation of the growth of legal consciousness in late medieval England, considered the law 'in terms of its interaction with [...] the political, economic, social and religious spheres'.[20] Other studies, especially those concerned with aspects of political culture, have devoted significant attention to the social and cultural use of the law at different social levels.[21] Equally, the relationship between law and literature, a subject of study with a long pedigree, is another possible way into the theme and is well developed in an English context.[22] More generally, law has not been ignored as part of wider 'cultural' historical approaches to the past, for instance, in work that focuses on visual and material sources.[23] And Tom Johnson's new work on late medieval England focuses expressly on legal culture as a problem which in part entails considering 'the ways in which legal meaning was created within everyday life'.[24] The opportunity for this book to examine the topic from the perspective of Scotland and its northern neighbours is thus one which enables a broader set of European comparisons and investigations to be advanced. In doing so we build on a perspective which has proved to be fruitful in other avenues of enquiry in the period.[25]

'Cultures of law' is, then, a topic which invites questions about how law 'works', what the expectations of people at different status levels were for the 'use' of law, what perceptions of justice and authority were among different groups, what their knowledge of law and procedure was (including options to conduct legal transactions and pursue or resolve conflicts out of court) and of course how different aspects of the law at work came to be recorded in writing, and how that writing itself became part of the work of the law. A brief illustration will help to ground what we mean at the outset. It is concerned with how actions could be initiated in Aberdeen's town courts and how the language and quantity of recorded detail changed over time. J.D. Ford's chapter in this volume discusses the Scots term 'borgh' which described, in the early sixteenth century, a document used to initiate a legal action but also the security parties gave to ensure their appearance in court. He notes that in some cases, the first-person assertion given in a written 'borgh' document was copied out into the municipal register.[26] However, the ARO now allows the use of borghs to be traced even deeper in time. In fact, it appears that the earliest known occasion on which such a textual inclusion in the registers occurred was in 1476. In that year one Alexander Rede showed the town magistrates 'that he had strekit ane borch in this maner videlicet I Alexander Rede strekis ane borgh in your hand Alexander of Chaumer [one of the town sergeands] that Johne Androson and Dauid Kyntor' ought to fulfil various obligations to Rede. This borgh closed with the formula 'and wrangis for thai do it nocht And tharto a borgh in your hand Alexander of Chaumer ane of the offisaris forsaidis'.[27] Prior to this entry, the earliest description of the process in the vernacular dates from 1434, when the forespeaker of a merchant of Bruges 'strekit a borch' in the hand of one of Aberdeen's bailies, that his claim should be heard at a court of superior jurisdiction. The entry recorded the rationale, which was

> that the said prufe [offered in the form of witness testimony in favour of his adversary] was of na valu becaus the provarez deponit nocht in fourme of the rolment of the court that the cause was eraste [first] giffin.[28]

This was not quite the inclusion of a first-person assertion in the register, but it was nevertheless the first appearance in the vernacular of the more reticent description of the same process in Latin which is pervasive among entries from earlier decades. Parties might 'porrexit plegium' (1409), 'extendebat plegium' (1406) or respond to a 'plegium super ipsum inuentum' by an opponent (1400).[29] Even so, in 1505 Latin might still be used to record an action initiated with a 'plegium porrectum' by one party upon another.[30]

All these examples raise questions about how linguistic change in the written record (by the increasing use of the vernacular Scots in addition to Latin) might relate to potential change in underlying procedure.[31] For instance, it is unclear whether prior to 1476 in these courts a 'borgh' or 'plegium' was in fact also a written document which recorded a first-person statement. Did such terminology used prior to that date simply record that an oral statement had been made in court to the relevant officer? If so, at what stage, and driven by what relationship between spoken and written language, and between Latin and vernacular language, did these statements come to be written down? When did they first appear as separate documents? In the 1434 example just noted we can see reference made to the 'rolment of the court'; a clear sign, at least, of how litigants used the written record for procedural argumentation. It would seem that the expanding use of the written record across the fifteenth century helped to drive such change, although even in 1317 the court roll was 'inspected and read out in court'.[32] Issues like these touch on the expectations of litigants for the 'use' of law, perceptions of justice and authority (including the authority of language in oral and written forms) and knowledge of law, particularly of procedural law.[33] They also emphasise change over time. However, it is important to keep in mind that legal practices might also emphasise continuities, such as may be seen in the use of chirographs to record acts of voluntary justice in the towns of Picardy, especially Douai. It has been argued that this resulted from the fact that the general populace put more trust in chirographs than in the more efficient practice of recording acts in civic registers, the implementation of which was attempted by the town authorities.[34]

This book also sets out to place its approach to cultures of law within an urban context.[35] We are working under the assumption that urban communities shared a legal culture that was different from, though potentially overlapping with, other legal cultures (for example the legal culture of the surrounding region if the overlord was a regional lord, or the legal culture of a wider polity if a town was subject to royal or princely overlordship).[36] Many towns, though not all – as the contribution by Miriam Tveit on the Norwegian market towns also makes clear – had a more or less autonomous status, having been granted privileges to administer law to its citizens and, potentially, to be exempt from appearing in certain other courts (see also the contribution by Michael Brown). In addition, though town and countryside were everywhere inextricably linked, the urban experience, with its focus on commerce and manufacture, with the close cohabitation of its citizens, and (in a medieval context) with its relatively high share of educated and moneyed – that is, elite – men (and some women), was decidedly different from the rural experience. For one, there were many more legal transactions conducted in a town than there were in the countryside. This was partly a result of the higher concentration of people in a town, but also and especially a consequence of the specific activities in which these people were engaged. In addition, towns were regularly the seat of regional courts such as, for example, the sheriff court of Aberdeenshire which sat in Aberdeen. Through ports and markets, moreover, influences from abroad could enter the urban consciousness. As such, urban legal cultures may also have been more open and susceptible to change than those of other local or regional courts. There certainly existed an urban awareness that laws and legal practice might be different elsewhere.[37] Towns were also points of jurisdictional intersection. In many of the towns of the Low Countries and the German Empire, a single overarching 'national' jurisdiction was not relevant in the middle ages. Instead, there may have been regional dimensions, such as in Flanders and Mecklenburg; the strong influence of a Teutonic overlord, like in Prussia and Livonia; and still other towns were (almost) completely autonomous, like Lübeck and the Dutch town of Kampen. As Musson has stated with regard to England, these jurisdictions may have produced and utilised 'distinct types of law, sometimes competing, occasionally overlapping, invariably invoking different traditions, jurisdictions and modes of operation'.[38]

Another aspect that was specific to the urban experience is that the elite itself was involved in both the promulgation of at least some of its laws and the administration of law, while at the same time being the group that in all probability used the courts most often of all in order to pursue claims, to resolve conflicts or to confirm transactions. As such, it might occur that a person ended up before a court, in which they might also have a function as an official, having gone against a regulation that they themselves had helped create.[39] Overall, members of the urban elite might be highly legally active, even though many of them, at least in the period before c. 1500, did not have a legal education (see the contribution by Andrew Simpson). On the other hand, they might have had relevant experience, which was potentially more valuable, especially when it came to matters of trade and shipping (see the contribution by J.D. Ford). In addition, urban inhabitants on the whole were involved in some sort of legal activity on a more or less regular basis: buying, selling, exchanging, settling disputes, contracting work or marriage, or getting into trouble. These activities were not necessarily conducted in official spaces, but could in principle take place almost anywhere in town, provided there were witnesses (see the contribution by Edda Frankot).

A recent examination of medieval urban culture by Andrew Brown and Jan Dumolyn has taken care to underscore the diversity of towns and cities, that not all were of the same size and status, and that not all regions exhibited similar levels of urbanisation. They argue that urban culture may be defined by its hybridity, amalgamating and adapting various ecclesiastical, noble, princely and rural cultures to urban spaces, and urban forms of social and political interaction.[40] In line with the observation made earlier, political culture has been the subject of a tremendous amount of recent work on late medieval towns.[41] Law and justice in towns have long flourished as an area of historical investigation, one which remains particularly well served in the Italian context, for example in treatments of Bologna and Florence.[42] Nevertheless, towns have had relatively little said about them with an explicit focus on legal culture.[43] Of signal importance as a groundbreaking study of urban legal culture is Daniel Smail's exploration of the language and social structures of emotion, and the publicity of this phenomenon which the tools of the law provided to litigants in medieval Marseille.[44] Relevant too is work on the Hanseatic region and the role of legal rules in urban society.[45] The most explicit and recent treatment, however, is Tom Johnson's investigation of a 'local culture of law' in the English city of Hereford. Johnson argues that the particular 'institutional density' of towns helped to intensify government, such that use of various urban law courts drew inhabitants into relations between authorities. Moreover, he treats urban legal culture as primarily concerned with the 'spatial ordering' of social relations.[46] These points are particularly pertinent to several of the contributions in this book. What the present contributors share is an idea that the study of the late medieval and early modern urban experience adds significantly to the understanding of how law works in society, concerning especially expectations of law, legal knowledge and expertise, and the use of law at different status levels and across different linguistic contexts. What follows by way of illustration of an aspect of legal culture from a northern European town is a short study of practices associated with appeal against judgements in Scotland.

An example of legal culture: falsing the doom in Scottish burghs

One mechanism of legal procedure throughout medieval Scotland, an appeal process known as 'falsing of dooms', serves as a useful illustration of legal culture as a historical problem. Doom falsing was a process whereby litigants could achieve a remedy against judgements ('dooms') pronounced in the 'ordinary' courts of the realm, that is, the courts of barons, sheriffs and burghs ('burgh' being the Scots term for town).[47] This procedure initiated an appeal to a higher jurisdiction. In the case of appeals in burgh courts, a falsed doom went before the royal chamberlain in his itinerant court or 'ayre', and from the ayre the next court of appeal was parliament.[48]

The earliest surviving example of a falsing anywhere in Scotland dates from 1382. This relates to a case heard in the baron court of the bishop of Aberdeen, involving the bishop himself against one John Crab, where a doom in favour of the bishop was falsed by Crab to be taken to the higher jurisdiction of the sheriff's court. That record is in Latin '…si iudicium dici debeat in se putridum est et corruptum…'.[49] The medieval legal treatise *Quoniam Attachiamenta* set out the falsing procedure in baron courts.[50] Various other legal texts of the period also mention the process.[51] In 1430 parliament aimed to regulate doom falsing throughout the kingdom: the unsatisfied party was to say out loud 'that dome is fals, stinkande and rottyn in the self' immediately after judgement was given in court. This is a fair translation into Scots of the Latin expression just noted. Further national legislation on the matter updated procedure in 1504.[52] Falsing was, however, part of an older legal framework. A supposed dissatisfaction with the old ordinary courts – where their administration by officials who were not trained specialists in the law was seen to be ineffective – is understood to have grown in the fifteenth century, a sentiment well expressed by an act of parliament in 1488.[53] That act reversed an experiment in 1487 where a law had been introduced requiring lower ordinary courts to hear cases in the first instance, and so avoid litigants bringing cases directly to parliament or the judicial sessions of the royal council (the precursor of the court of session).[54] At this time the rule also prevailed which required cases concerning feudal tenure of land to be initiated with documents issued by the royal chancery, known as brieves, to be heard in the ordinary courts. This has been understood in the context of litigants' increasing preference in this period for the use of the king's council over the ordinary courts (a step which had been enabled through prior legislation in 1469 and 1471).[55] The effect of the 1487 and 1488 acts may have been to prompt unsatisfied parties to use falsings to seek a hearing in a higher jurisdiction. All the same, one clear finding with regard to Aberdeen's burgh courts is that there is no evident decline in the usage of these tribunals in this period.

Methods of appeal in Aberdeen's courts are a subject worthy of research in their own right,[56] but as for falsing of dooms, there are very few instances to be found between 1398 and 1511, which suggests that falsing was not a familiar process. The earliest is an occurrence in 1399, in *Crab v. Spryng*.[57] Here a doom had been given that Spryng should be restored to real property which his opponent also claimed. A memorandum entirely in Latin recorded that Paul Crab (possibly some relation of John, just noted)[58] had found a *plegium* for the falsed doom to go before the chamberlain ayre. The next occurrence is not until 1444, in *Scherar v. Henrison*, a case initiated with a brieve of right, over possession of a croft situated in Aberdeen's own adjacent rural lands. The defender appears to have waited until the pursuer left the court, and then to have secured a judgement in his own favour. When the pursuer returned to the court, the clerk recorded his spoken statement 'that the dome gefyne […] agaynnis me is fals il and Rotyne in the self and thar to a borch and for this resone / for the balye gif me leve'.[59]

There is no further mention of falsed dooms in Aberdeen until the 1480s, when an entry on 'the falsing of a dewme' in the burgh's so-called Sasine Register occurs alongside other business dated to 1486.[60] This was a regulatory statement on procedure for falsing in different courts, somewhat like the 1430 act of parliament, but not the same.[61] It seems perhaps that this was included because the burgh officials sought to remind themselves of the procedure for falsing around the time of the 1487 and 1488 legislation, necessary given that (apparently) just one falsing had occurred in the burgh courts in nearly nine decades.

A patch of doom falsings then occurs in the main council register series, and at a similar date one can also be found in the court of Dunfermline, another burgh.[62] The first of these was in 1489 in *Eduardson v. Days*.[63] This case concerned the enforcement of a contract for the freight of goods shipped to other northern Scottish ports but unloaded in Aberdeen. This was in the court of the town's bailies and judgement went in favour of Eduardson, a burgess of Edinburgh. His opponent's procurator immediately falsed this doom, saying: 'Jonhe Williamsone dempstar of this courte that dome that thow has gewin aganis me is fals evile ande rottyne in it selff' (and some 53 further words), and found a borgh in the hands of the court sergeand. Some days later the procurator presented his client's 'resonis' (statements of justification) for the falsing which were 'putt in the common kyst to the decision of the saide mater'.[64] In the case of *Murray v. Menzies* (1494), the subject at law was the sum of £80 for the redemption of a share of a fishing on the River Dee.[65] The bailie court's judgement had favoured David Menzies, then provost of the burgh.[66] Some weeks later his opponent appeared in court to false the doom (with some 200 words of speech, and alleging that the doom had been given in an improper court), finding a borgh in the hands of the sergeand and asking for a record of the falsing.[67] On a later date he presented 'certane allegeance and resonis closin vndir his Seill', which the court clerk laid in the 'common kyst'.[68]

The next case was *Gray v. Monrow* (1496). Here one party claimed the other did not procure a dispensation from the papal curia as promised. Doom was given on 11 January in the burgh's head court for Monrow, who also protested for his expenses. Gray falsed the doom in person in the bailie court on 10 February (with some 220 words of speech). Gray found a borgh, and then bound himself 'to the follouing and perseving' of the falsed doom according to law with named witnesses and asked for a record of the falsing.[69] The final occurrence is from 1502, in *Leslie of Warderis and Gordon v. Rutherford*. The matter in dispute was a sum of money which John Leslie of Warderis and his spouse claimed Sir John Rutherford (a former provost) owed them for a share of a fishing on the River Dee. The doom was pronounced in the bailie court and Rutherford's procurator immediately falsed it (with some 69 words of speech).[70] Rutherford found a borgh, then bound himself 'to follow and persew' the falsing according to law. His opponents' procurator asked for 'the Rolment' of the court to be given to his clients and for Rutherford's 'Resounis and lavis' to be given to the chamberlain of Scotland. Eleven days later the procurator presented the court with the 'resounis allegit be him' concerning the falsing on paper closed under his client's seal, but took these documents away with him again.[71]

There is no evidence of these cases actually coming before the chamberlain ayre, although as the last case makes clear this is why 'resonis' were produced and sometimes lodged in the common 'kyst' or chest.[72] These latter cases are few in number, but generally they involved litigants of a high social profile (current or recent provosts, a burgess of Edinburgh, rural landowners) and matters of some weight (shipping contracts, the pursuit of a papal licence and rights in lucrative river fisheries). They give the flavour of a deliberate revival of an older process of falsing in the burgh. However, this was not so much a general innovation as one used for its performative flourish and, one suspects, the rarity of the process served to punctuate a legal challenge. In *Murray v. Menzies* the falser also expressly questioned the authority of the court which had given judgement. The prompt for the resuscitation of falsing may well have been the abortive legislation of 1487–1488, and so we can see in this the manner in which litigants in town courts responded to extra-urban developments.

By contrast to the latter examples, the earliest case of 1399 is recorded in Latin, and this raises the question of the language in which proceedings between Crab and Spryng were conducted. Did Paul Crab false the doom in the vernacular, while the clerk compiling the register set down the memorandum in Latin? By the 1480s any need for such translation had become obsolete due to a significant amount of court business having come in recent decades to be recorded in Scots. While this may appear to be a straightforward demonstration of the rise of the vernacular, it is worth noting that Latin continued to be used for a variety of court business in Aberdeen throughout this period and beyond. The multilingual nature of law even in this one jurisdiction is plain to see (an issue explored by the contributions to this volume by Anna Havinga and Joanna Kopaczyk), but so is the question of the importance of the spoken word. While these cases provide numerous references to written documents used in court, they show clearly that a spoken formula in the vernacular was indeed required for the falsing process itself to be valid. The extent to which recorded speech represents a legal language in its own right, distinct from the written language of legal record, is a topic for future exploration, and one in which the explicit or implicit relationship between Latin and the vernacular needs to be better understood. Was it then acceptable for a speech act to be rendered as a memorandum in the Latin record in the 1390s, whereas, by the 1440s and again in the 1480s and 1490s, a direct written record of vernacular speech had become necessary in these courts? Questions like these are about cultures of law, and are ripe to be considered in comparison with evidence from other towns.[73]

It should perhaps be no surprise that the most prominent members in Aberdeen's local society revived the legal older process of doom falsing. That they did so apparently in response to an external legislative requirement and then to wield it, however infrequently, to draw attention to their prominent disagreements is all the more understandable within the context of the relatively small network of elites who shared in the governance of the burgh. More generally, in this example formulaic practices come into full view as a part of legal behaviour. For falsing it is in the reliance on a required sequence of words spoken in the vernacular – both spoken aloud and recorded in the civic register – to challenge a legal outcome. This underscores the importance of patterned behaviours that served to promote publicity for actions of legal significance. Both doom falsing and similar ceremonies (see Edda Frankot's contribution, commenting on the *wijncoep*) involved a degree of performance by the parties involved, a performance which gained publicity for the underlying act.[74] If the performativity of legal culture in this period requires much better understanding, so also does the question of the spaces where that culture functioned. The extent to which taverns, inns and houses might present both 'public' and 'private' characteristics, and to different degrees allow for the 'publicity' of legal transactions to be achieved is telling of the ways in which legal culture was not confined to the official forum of a law court. Finally, these examples show well how urban archives may also be rich legal records and stand ready for the investigation of aspects of law and its associated cultures.

The present volume

The essays gathered in this collection are drawn from across the fields of history, law and historical sociolinguistics and discuss cultures of law in Scotland (with a special focus on Aberdeen), the Low Countries, Norway, Germany and Poland. The essays had their origins in a series of symposia led by the *Law in the Aberdeen Council Registers* project. In 2017 prospective contributors brought source extracts together for discussion, and they returned in 2018 with draft papers which were pre-circulated and to each of which a respondent was assigned. This proved to be a stimulating and fruitful exercise, not least in bringing the same group together on more than one occasion. That creative process, and the pleasurable task of editing these contributions in 2019–2020, has allowed us to see the interconnections between the various papers, some expected, some unexpected. What has resulted in the final collection of studies has been organised into five parts: Telling Tales; Communication of Law; Jurisdiction and Conflict; Law in Practice, in and out of Court; and Men of Law in Scotland. Although the church, churchmen and canon law do feature in some of what follows, it should be made clear at the outset that the discussion of legal culture in these essays is predominantly conducted with regard to a secular context. That results primarily from our shared focus on records generated by urban governmental administration rather than any intentional exclusion. An acknowledgement that the perspectives raised here may yet be pursued by others with reference to ecclesiastical law and law courts is appropriate. It should also be noted that some of the contributions which have been assembled could easily have been placed into other parts in this book, comfortably touching on two or even three of these themes, and numerous connections may be made between them. Some of the main connections may be briefly highlighted.

First of all, J.D. Ford's contribution on maritime law proposes a way in which medieval and early modern urban court records may be understood in terms of the expected purpose of the legal record for the parties, officials and other contemporary audiences who created and used these records, and in terms of how they may be used by modern historians. In relation to maritime affairs, Ford observes that many entries in the records of Aberdeen's courts in the early sixteenth century appear simply 'to have been attempts to have it put on record that something has happened in the way it should have'.[75] He suggests that, in the resulting accumulation of such 'tales' relating to maritime affairs in the shared record, the legal process generated social awareness of legal norms, without stating them explicitly as legal propositions. For Ford, the task proposed is 'to identify certain broad forms of narrative that came to be considered acceptable, and to examine the presuppositions that made them acceptable'.[76] The insight in this approach to sources is one which we expect readers will appreciate to keep in mind as they proceed through the other contributions in this volume.

Language and the written record are a primary concern in the second part, where the chapters address the theme of 'Communication of Law'. These essays focus on material and linguistic aspects of how law and legal matters were communicated and on the multilingual nature of this communication. William Hepburn and Graeme Small in their contribution focus on the 'common books' of late medieval Aberdeen as the 'central node in the town's documentary network' and a 'physical symbol of burgh authority'.[77] The expansion of writing in this period was part of a Europe-wide development of literacy. Hepburn and Small argue, however, that the common books should not only be understood in terms of literacy; these records also functioned as a powerful symbol of the burgh community, as represented by the urban elite. Joanna Kopaczyk's contribution in this part focuses on multilingualism in a comparative study of Scottish and Polish legal records. She argues that, despite a mixture of Latin and a vernacular apparent in both source sets, such medieval legal texts should be considered to have been written in one linguistic code with a complex structure. It was not the case that the individual languages functioned as separate codes; rather, the single complex multilingual code functioned to exchange information between the 'community of practice' (scribes, notaries, and so on) and the 'text community'.[78] Anna Havinga's chapter examines the process of vernacularisation in the fifteenth-century Aberdeen Council Registers, considering in greater detail the multilingual character of these records and the increasing use over time of vernaculars in relation to Latin. There was no consistent pace to this process in which a mixture of Latin and vernacular languages persisted over time, and Havinga argues that this vernacularisation resulted in more open and transparent legal record-keeping, even as the creation of and access to these sources were controlled by the urban elite. Together these three chapters explore cultures of law by addressing the topic in the wider European context of expanding literacy and vernacular writing, whereby late medieval elites harnessed languages and changing forms of written records and brought them into the service of a range of governing processes among which matters of law were paramount.

Part III presents a series of chapters on jurisdictions and conflicts. These contributions focus on four different regions of northern Europe: Norway, Scotland, Germany and Flanders. The question of jurisdiction can have different implications: who has jurisdiction where, over whom and with regard to what? As Miriam Tveit demonstrates in her chapter on law in Norwegian market towns, those who used law in these towns appear to have relied on the Code of the Realm, despite the existence of a separate town law for the kingdom. As such, the legal culture in these smaller towns reveals 'overlapping and fluid' legal boundaries, rather than overlapping jurisdictions.[79] Michael Brown's treatment of late medieval Peebles shows there was a clash of competing jurisdictions in the Scottish context. Townspeople claimed their autonomy from the crown's officers of adjacent forest jurisdiction. The burgesses of Peebles were able to defend their rights by harnessing their urban privileges, granted by the king, which allowed for the magistrates to have jurisdiction over their own citizens (with some exceptions). Peebles appears to have been much more jurisdictionally minded than the market towns of Norway; nevertheless, both Tveit and Brown show the 'urban' context as the setting for intense legal activity, for example in the convening of courts and the resolution of conflict.

Such heightened legal activity is also recognisable in Germany and Flanders. In his contribution on *Pax Urbana*, Jörg Rogge takes us to Braunschweig, Halle/Saale and Magdeburg. In examining the use of law for the achievement of political goals he focuses on the keeping of the peace, and how citizens and councils created and maintained this peace and sought to protect it from overbearing lords. Citizens also expected the town council to uphold the peace although, as Rogge shows, different groups could have different expectations of what the peace meant, and how it could be maintained, not least in the resolution of disputes. Chanelle Delameillieure and Jelle Haemers turn our attention to gender, age and intergenerational conflicts in their investigation of how the wealthy citizens of Ghent used the law to address disputes between parents and children in matters of marriage. They argue that relatively accessible legal institutions in towns like Ghent provided opportunities for men and women to defend their rights, by reference to law and local custom. In all four contributions in this part different parties' expectations of the law and of the law courts come to the fore, especially concerning the protection of rights that was offered through law, often against external authorities. The extent to which legal culture can be understood helpfully as 'urban', and indeed the extent to which it was a culture dominated by senior male elites, are aspects of the topic opened up in these chapters.

The contributions in part IV examine law in practice, in and out of court, in Aberdeen, Kampen (in the Netherlands) and Danzig. Many surviving urban sources derive from the law as it was put into practice as they record the pursuit or resolution of disputes, legal transactions and contracts, mostly conducted in court or before legal professionals such as notaries. It is more unusual to find sources that concern law in practice outside of official spaces, but one such source is considered by Edda Frankot in her contribution which focuses on private and public houses as spaces of law. In Kampen, Frankot shows, legal culture was not confined to the official fora of law courts but could be enacted through the performance of modest ceremonies, and in non-official spaces where women were also to be found among legal actors. In this part, too, the expectations of the law are pertinent: in how far were rights protected when transactions occurred outside courts and, when conflict arose, in the circumstances required for justice to be served. From the contribution by Justyna Wubs-Mrozewicz on ships and inheritances in Danzig and in the Hanse area, it is clear that there existed expectations that laws and practices were different in the variety of places in which merchants or skippers might be seeking justice, but also that their rights would still be protected, like those of resident burghers. For Wubs-Mrozewicz, urban legal culture in the context of international trade and diplomacy demanded the acceptance of local variation in law and a reliance on flexibility. Looking at the practice of law through the use of particular legal terminology, Armstrong's contribution on 'malice' and motivation for hostility in Aberdeen questions the appearance (and then the demise) of the information that an offender acted out of malice in case entries involving interpersonal violence. Considering the national legislation which shaped this terminology and the local application of those rules in practice (in both Latin and Scots), this chapter argues that what counted most was the registration in the court record of the social relationship of hostility between opponents. Implicit in this is the expectation that personal rights will be better protected in future once the notice of malice is documented and saved for posterity. These expectations are linked to that already noted in relation to Ford's chapter, which is that things should be done in a certain way – an expectation and consensus that was shared between all in a locality. Usages and customs, as noted by both Ford and Wubs-Mrozewicz, are those things that are considered to be normal and customary in a certain place. As such, as Ford argues, legal culture tended to be local: shaped in particular through use of shared linguistic conventions which could describe lawful behaviour and, as such, resulted in the shared expectations of the law. However, this does not mean that one could not also accept that which was considered to be right elsewhere as equally valid. The awareness and acceptance of variations in usages and customs and, as such, of legal cultures is arguably the only characteristic of an overarching northern European urban legal culture in this period.

Part V focuses on 'men of law' in Scotland in the fifteenth, sixteenth and seventeenth centuries. Legal experts and professionals were of vital importance to the character of legal cultures. Their education and training affected what such men thought of the law, of rules and of practices, and, as such, it influenced the use of law and legal sources, legal practices and the recording of business, and the languages used in courts and in written documents. The character of notaries as the most educated legal professionals in fifteenth- and sixteenth-century Scotland is reflected in the practice of noting time in legal documents, as explored by David Ditchburn in his chapter which examines how changing understandings and ways of marking of daily time could come to shape legal events, memories and records. The emergence of recorded time of the clock as a feature of notarial practice is to be explained, according to Ditchburn, by a focus on the usefulness of the practice to those participating as witnesses to legal transactions. Time was thus a cultural tool which was adopted by notaries in their role as 'guardians of private memory'.[80] There is a clear chronological development recognisable between the contributions by Andrew Simpson, exploring the career of Andrew Alanson in the fifteenth century, and by Adelyn Wilson on legal education in Aberdeen in the sixteenth and seventeenth centuries. On the one hand, with the exception of notaries, in late medieval Aberdeen 'men of law' were men without formal legal training but their expertise was derived from experience and familiarity with the operations of the burgh courts. On the other hand, in the seventeenth century legal training was a formal requisite for practice, gained either through university education or through legal apprenticeship. While the importance of the social networks which interlinked legal specialists remained the same in both periods (recalling the points advanced by Kopaczyk on 'communities of practice' and 'text communities'), by the seventeenth century a formal legal community with a professional organisation had grown in Scotland and, as Wilson demonstrates, this was a profession that was very much urban in nature and distributed across different towns of the kingdom.

It has been an enriching exercise working together and with the contributors, and it is our hope that together these essays will help to advance the understanding of historical legal culture, or more precisely the problem of how law worked in urban societies in Scotland and among a number of northern European comparators.

Notes

* We are grateful to Andrew Simpson for his comments on a draft version of this introduction. Any errors are our own.

1 For example, R. Lesaffer, *European Legal History: A Cultural and Political Perspective*, trans. J. Arriens, Cambridge: Cambridge University Press, 2009, pp. 235–88.

2 For example, J. Wubs-Mrozewicz, 'The late medieval and early modern Hanse as an institution of conflict management', *Continuity and Change* 29, 2017, pp. 59–84.

3 T. Johnson, *Law in Common: Legal Cultures in Late-Medieval England,* Oxford: Oxford University Press, 2020, p. 55. See also R. Goddard and T. Phipps (eds) *Town Courts and Urban Society in Late Medieval England, 1250–1500,* Woodbridge: Boydell Press, 2020.

4 E. Frankot, *'Of Laws of Ships and Shipmen': Medieval Maritime Law and its Practice in Urban Northern Europe*, Edinburgh: Edinburgh University Press, 2012 and J. Kopaczyk, *The Legal Language of Scottish Burghs: Standardisation and Lexical Bundles 1380–1560,* Oxford: Oxford University Press, 2013.

5 Modern print editions of some of this material are E. Gemmill (ed.) *Aberdeen Guild Court Records, 1437–1468,* Edinburgh: Scottish History Society, 2005, and W.C. Dickinson (ed.) *Early Records of the Burgh of Aberdeen, 1317. 1398–1407*, Edinburgh: Scottish History Society, 1957.

6 J. Armstrong and A. Mackillop (eds) 'Special section: Communities, courts and scottish towns', *Urban History* 44(3), 2017, pp. 358–423.

7 This project was funded principally by a Leverhulme Trust Research Project Grant, 2016–2019, led by J. Armstrong. Its major digital output is E. Frankot, A. Havinga, C. Hawes, W. Hepburn, W. Peters, J. Armstrong, P. Astley, A. Mackillop, A. Simpson and A. Wyner (eds) *Aberdeen Registers Online: 1398–1511*, Aberdeen: University of Aberdeen, 2019, <https://www.abdn.ac.uk/aro> (accessed 1 January 2020) (hereafter ARO).

8 On medieval 'political culture' as comprising ideas, communication and networks see the overview given in J. Watts, *The Making of Polities: Europe, 1300–1500*, Cambridge: Cambridge University Press, 2009, pp. 129–57. Significant recent work on Scotland, England and the Empire includes: C. Hawes, 'Community and public authority in later fifteenth-century Scotland', unpublished PhD thesis, University of St Andrews, 2015; C.D. Liddy, *Contesting the City: The Politics of Citizenship in English Towns, 1250–1530*, Oxford: Oxford University Press, 2017, and D. Hardy, *Associative Political Culture in the Holy Roman Empire: Upper Germany, 1346–1521*, Oxford: Oxford University Press, 2018.

9 On the 'culturalisation' of various historical disciplines and an overview of scholarship on legal culture, see H. Rudolph, 'Rechtskultur in der Frühen Neuzeit. Perspektive und Erkenntnispotentiale eines modischen Begriffs', *Historische Zeitschrift* 278, 2004, pp. 347–74. Modern legal culture is a more developed discipline; see, for example, V. Gessner, A. Hoeland and C. Varga (eds) *European Legal Cultures*, Aldershot: Dartmouth, 1996, and K. Günther and S. Kadelbach (eds) *Kulturen des Rechts*, Frankfurt am Main: Campus Verlag, 2018.

10 D. Nelken, 'Using the concept of legal culture', *Australian Journal of Legal Philosophy* 29, 2004, pp. 1–26, at p. 1. Nelken in this and other publications has also dealt with criticism of and problems with using the term 'legal culture'. See, for example, 'Thinking about legal culture', *Asian Journal of Law and Society* 1, 2014, pp. 255–74, at pp. 257–67.

11 Friedman goes on: '[legal culture] covers those thoughts and ideas which act as motives or incentives for "legal behaviour"'. L.M. Friedman, *The Republic of Choice. Law, Authority and Culture*, Cambridge, MA: Harvard University Press, 1990, p. 213. Friedman first wrote on the subject in his article 'Legal culture and social development', *Law and Society Review* 4, 1969, pp. 29–44.

12 J.Ø. Sunde, 'Live and let die: An essay concerning legal-cultural understanding', in M. Adams and D. Heirbaut (eds) *The Method and Culture of Comparative Law: Essays in Honour of Mark Van Hoecke*, Oxford: Oxford University Press, 2015, pp. 221–34, at p. 222. See also U. Böker and J.A. Hibbard (eds) *Sites of Discourse – Public and Private Spheres – Legal Culture. Papers from a Conference Held at the Technical University of Dresden, December 2001*, Leiden: Brill, 2002, particularly the chapter by Böker.

13 J.Ø. Sunde, 'Champagne at the funeral: An introduction to legal culture', in J.Ø. Sunde and K.E. Skodvin (eds) *Rendezvous of European Legal Cultures*, Bergen: Fagbokforlaget, 2010, pp. 11–28. Available online at <http://www.uib.no/filearchive/campagne-at-the-funeral-an-introduction-to-legal-culture.pdf>. Quoted text from p. 10 of the online version. This is applied to modern Scottish legal culture in A.R.C. Simpson, 'An introduction to Scottish legal culture', in S. Koch, K. Skodvin, and J. Sunde (eds) *Comparing Legal Cultures*, Bergen: Fagbokforlaget, 2017, pp. 87–130.

14 Rudolph, 'Rechtskultur', p. 361.

15 L. Mather, 'Law and society', in R.E. Goodin (ed.) *The Oxford Handbook of Political Science*, Oxford: Oxford University Press, 2011, via *Oxford Handbooks Online*, <doi:10.1093/oxfordhb/9780199604456.013.0015> (accessed 15 November 2019).

16 The 'Legalism' book series which began with P. Dresch and H. Skoda, *Legalism: Anthropology and History*, Oxford: Oxford University Press, 2012, and now with three further volumes in print, is the leading example of such work.

17 S.L. Winter, *A Clearing in the Forest: Law, Life and Mind*, Chicago, IL: University of Chicago Press, 2001, p. 332.

18 L. Rosen, *Law as Culture*, Princeton, NJ: Princeton University Press, 2006.
19 For example, E. Cohen, *The Crossroads of Justice: Law and Culture in Late Medieval France*, Leiden: Brill, 1993; D. Heirbaut, 'Exploring the law in medieval minds', in A. Musson and C. Stebbing (eds) *Making Legal History: Approaches and Methodologies*, Cambridge: Cambridge University Press, 2012, pp. 118–30.
20 A. Musson, *Medieval Law in Context: The Growth of Legal Consciousness from Magna Carta to the Peasants' Revolt*, Manchester: Manchester University Press, 2001.
21 For instance, E. Powell, *Kingship, Law, and Society: Criminal Justice in the Reign of Henry V*, Oxford: Oxford University Press, 1989; P.C. Maddern, *Violence and Social Order: East Anglia 1422–1442*, Oxford: Oxford University Press, 1992; C.B. Herrup, *The Common Peace: Participation and the Criminal Law in Seventeenth-Century England*, Cambridge: Cambridge University Press, 1987; and M. Gaskill, *Crime and Mentalities in Early Modern England*, Cambridge: Cambridge University Press, 2000.
22 For example, see R.F. Green, 'Medieval literature and law', in D. Wallace (ed.) *The Cambridge History of Medieval English Literature*, Cambridge: Cambridge University Press, 1999, pp. 407–31, and E. Steiner and C. Barrington (eds) *The Letter of the Law: Legal Practice and Literary Production in Medieval England*, Ithaca, NY: Cornell University Press, 2002.
23 P. Raffield, *Images and Cultures of Law in Early Modern England: Justice and Political Power, 1558–1660*, Cambridge: Cambridge University Press, 2004. For a more general cultural history approach to law see E. Conte and L. Mayali (eds) *A Cultural History of Law in the Middle Ages, Volume 2*, London: Bloomsbury, 2019, and P. Goodrich (ed.) *A Cultural History of Law in the Early Modern Age, Volume 3*, London: Bloomsbury, 2019.
24 Johnson, *Law in Common*, p. 7.
25 D. Ditchburn, *Scotland and Europe: The Medieval Kingdom and Its Contacts with Christendom, c. 1214–1545*, East Linton: John Donald, 2001, and E.P. Dennison and G.G. Simpson, 'Scotland', in D.M. Palliser (ed.) *Cambridge Urban History of Britain: Volume 1: 600–1540*, Cambridge: Cambridge University Press, 2000, pp. 715–37.
26 See below, Chapter 1, p. 24, citing among others an entry from 1509 (ARO-8-1036-02).
27 ARO-6-0420-04.
28 ARO-4-0003-06.
29 ARO-2-0025-02 (1409); ARO-1-0277-07 (1406); ARO-1-0171-06 (1400).
30 ARO-8-0455-02.
31 See in the present volume, A. Havinga, 'The vernacularisation of the Aberdeen Council Registers (1398–1511)', esp. pp. 97–8.
32 A.R.C. Simpson and J.W. Armstrong (eds and trans.) 'The roll of the burgh courts of Aberdeen, August–October 1317', in M. Godfrey (ed.) *Miscellany Eight*, Edinburgh: Stair Society, 2020, pp. 57–93, at 84–5. See also in the present volume W. Hepburn and G. Small, 'Common books in Aberdeen, c. 1398–c. 1511', section 'Documentary culture in Aberdeen', pp. 46–8.
33 On these themes see M. Mostert and P.S. Barnwell (eds) *Medieval Legal Process: Physical, Spoken and Written Performance in the Middle Ages*, Turnhout: Brepols, 2011; J. Benham, M. McHaffie and H. Vogt (eds) *Law and Language in the Middle Ages*, Leiden: Brill, 2018. On towns specifically see A. Bartoszewicz, *Urban Literacy in Late Medieval Poland*, Turnhout: Brepols, 2018; M. Mostert and A. Adamska (eds) *Writing and the Administration of Medieval Towns: Medieval Urban Literacy I*, Turnhout: Brepols, 2014; and M. Mostert and A. Adamska (eds) *Uses of the Written Word in Medieval Towns: Medieval Urban Literacy II*, Turnhout: Brepols, 2014.
34 M. Boone, '"Estre le bien commun et general d'icelle preferé au bien privé et particulier". Vrijwillige rechtspraak, stedelijke identiteit en stedelijke diplomatiek', in H. Brand, J. Benders and R. Nip (eds) *Stedelijk verleden in veelvoud. Opstellen over laatmiddeleeuwse stadsgeschiedenis in de Nederlanden*, Hilversum: Verloren, 2011, pp. 197–211, at p. 208.

35 For an overview of the Scottish context see E.P. Dennison, *The Evolution of Scotland's Towns: Creation, Growth and Fragmentation,* Edinburgh: Edinburgh University Press, 2018, pp. 7–46, and J. Armstrong and A. Mackillop (eds) 'Special Issue: Scottish urban archives and histories: Context and a legal historical perspective', *Journal of Irish and Scottish Studies* 9(2), 2018.

36 H.L. MacQueen and W.J. Windram, 'Laws and courts in the burghs', in M. Lynch, M. Spearman and G. Stell (eds) *The Scottish Medieval Town*, Edinburgh: John Donald, 1988, pp. 208–27.

37 See also Frankot, *Medieval Maritime Law*, pp. 145–9.

38 Musson, *Medieval Law in Context*, p. 9.

39 With regard to this, see C. Lansing, *Passion and Order: Restraint of Grief in the Medieval Italian Communes*, Ithaca, NY: Cornell University Press, 2008.

40 A. Brown and J. Dumolyn, 'Medieval urban culture: Conceptual and historiographical problems', in A. Brown and J. Dumolyn (eds) *Medieval Urban Culture*, Turnhout: Brepols, 2017, pp. 1–25, at p. 22. On material culture see E. Gemmill, 'Debt, distraint, display and dead men's treasure: Material culture in late medieval Aberdeen', *Journal of Medieval History* 46, 2020, pp. 350–72 (which appeared just as the present book was being submitted).

41 For instance: E. Hartrich, *Politics and the Urban Sector in Fifteenth-Century England, 1413–1471*, Oxford: Oxford University Press, 2019; Liddy, *Contesting the City*; C. Fletcher, 'News, noise, and the nature of politics in late medieval English provincial towns', *Journal of British Studies* 56, 2017, pp. 250–72, at p. 253; C. Hawes, 'The urban community in fifteenth-century Scotland: Language, law and political practice', in Armstrong and Mackillop (eds) 'Special section: Communities, courts and Scottish towns', pp. 365–80; Hawes, 'Community and public authority', pp. 47–72, 73–105; and P. Lantschner, *The Logic of Political Conflict in Medieval Cities: Italy and the Southern Low Countries, 1370–1440*, Oxford: Oxford University Press, 2015.

42 S.R. Blanshei (ed) *A Companion to Medieval and Renaissance Bologna*, Leiden: Brill, 2018 (especially chapters by De Benedictis, and Blanshei and Cucini); K.J.P. Lowe and T. Dean (eds) *Murder in Renaissance Italy*, Cambridge: Cambridge University Press, 2017; T. Dean, 'Police forces in late medieval Italy: Bologna, 1340–1480', *Social History* 44(2), 2019, pp. 151–72; and L. Armstrong and J. Kirshner (eds) *The Politics of Law in Late Medieval and Renaissance Italy*, Toronto: University of Toronto Press, 2018. See also Lansing, *Passion and Order* and R. Trexler, *Public Life in Renaissance Florence*, Ithaca, NY: Cornell University Press, 1980.

43 On the city court of sixteenth-century Freiberg as record keeper see J. Jordan, 'Rethinking disputes and settlements: How historians can use legal anthropology', in S. Cummins and L. Kounine (eds) *Cultures of Conflict Resolution in Early Modern Europe*, Farnham: Ashgate, 2016, pp. 17–50, at pp. 34–5. On law and cultural networks in Magdeburg see G. Köster, C. Link and H. Lück (eds) *Kulturelle Vernetzung in Europa: Das Magdeburger Recht und seine Städte. Wissenschaftlicher Begleitband zur Ausstellung 'Faszination Stadt'*, Dresden: Sandstein Verlag, 2019.

44 D.L. Smail, *The Consumption of Justice: Emotions, Publicity, and Legal Culture in Marseille, 1264–1423*, Ithaca, NY: Cornell University Press, 2003. Touching on similar themes and with reference to major cities, including Bruges, Ghent, Antwerp and Dijon, see P. Arnade and W. Prevenier, *Honor, Vengeance, and Social Trouble: Pardon Letters in the Burgundian Low Countries*, Ithaca, NY: Cornell University Press, 2015.

45 H. Brand, S. Rabeler, and H. von Seggern (eds) *Gelebte Normen im urbanen Raum? Zur sozial- und kulturgeschichtlichen Analyse rechtlicher Quellen in Städten des Hanseraums (13. bis 16. Jahrhundert)*, Hilversum: Verloren, 2014.

46 Johnson, *Law in Common*, pp. 17, 55–6 (and 55–85 generally).

47 P.J. Hamilton-Grierson, 'Falsing the doom', *Scottish Historical Review* 24, 1997, pp. 1–18. We use the word 'appeal' loosely here, not to imply the technical modern sense. See A.M. Godfrey, *Civil Justice in Renaissance Scotland: The Origins of a Central Court*, Leiden: Brill, 2009, pp. 21–2.

48 On the chamberlain's annual ayre to the burgh courts, see for example H.L. MacQueen, *Common Law and Feudal Society in Medieval Scotland*, Edinburgh: Edinburgh University Press, 1993, pp. 34, 55–66, 247, and W.C. Dickinson, 'The administration of justice in medieval Scotland', *Aberdeen University Review* 34, 1951–1952, pp. 338–51

49 *Registrum Episcopatus Aberdonensis*, ed. C. Innes, 2 vols, Edinburgh: Spalding and Maitland Clubs, 1845, vol. 1, p. 145; MacQueen, *Common Law*, p. 53; and P. Stein, *The Character and Influence of the Roman Civil Law: Historical Essays*, London: Hambledon Press, 1988, p. 301

50 *Quoniam Attachiamenta*, ed. T.D. Fergus, Edinburgh: Stair Society, 1996, pp. 146–7. This text allows 40 days for a party absent from a judgement to make an appeal (i.e. to false the doom).

51 *Scotland under Jus Commune: Census of Manuscripts of Legal Literature in Scotland, Mainly between 1500 and 1660*, ed. G. Dolezalek, 3 vols, Edinburgh: Stair Society, 2010, vol. 1, pp. 151, 153, 174; vol. 2, pp. 70, 92, 322, 332–4; vol. 3, pp. 48, 185, 223, 225, 329, 331–5, 363, 296, 431–3.

52 *The Records of the Parliaments of Scotland to 1707*, ed. K.M. Brown et al., St Andrews, 2007–2020, <www.rps.ac.uk> (accessed 1 January 2020) (hereafter RPS), 1430/8. This was to be done within time to walk 40 paces. Also RPS, 1504/3/65, 1504/3/70; A1504/3/141, A1504/3/146. See Godfrey, *Civil Justice*, pp. 21–2.

53 RPS, 1488/1/25.

54 RPS, 1487/10/14.

55 RPS 1469/16; RPS 1471/5/9; Godfrey, *Civil Justice*, pp. 25, 66, 232; A.R.C. Simpson and A.L.M. Wilson, *Scottish Legal History. Volume 1: 1000–1707*, Edinburgh: Edinburgh University Press, 2017, pp. 109, 118, 121; and Dickinson, 'The administration of justice in medieval Scotland', p. 349.

56 More than 300 mentions of litigants who 'protestit' in court are suggestive of another mechanism for appeal.

57 ARO-1-0016-01 (13 March 1399).

58 On a probable family relation of the Crabs see H.S. Lucas, 'John Crabbe: Flemish pirate, merchant, and adventurer', *Speculum* 20, 1945, pp. 334–50.

59 ARO-4-0369-09 (16 November 1444).

60 Aberdeen City and Aberdeenshire Archives, CA/2/1/1 Sasine Register 1486–1502 (hereafter SR), p. 36.

61 The entry includes the words: 'that dome you has gevin belangand me is evil [and] fals' [and] Rottin in it self for cause it is gevin agan the common law'. The source of the entry has not yet been identified.

62 E. Beveridge (ed.) *The Burgh Records of Dunfermline: Transcribed from the Original Manuscript Volume, Courts, Sasines, etc. 1488–1584*, Edinburgh: Scottish Burgh Records Society, 1917 (at p. 5 of the main text).

63 ARO-7-0138-05 (29 September 1489).

64 ARO-7-0145-03 (9 October 1489).

65 ARO-7-0591-01, 02 (12 December 1494).

66 ARO-7-0585-05 (21 November 1494).

67 ARO-7-0591-02: The speech included the line 'the quhilk dome [...] is evile gevin ande fals in It Self'.

68 ARO-7-0594-02 (23 December 1494).

69 ARO-7-0699-01, 02 (11 January 1496); ARO-7-0705-04 (10 February 1496). The speech included the line 'the quhilk dome [...] is evile and fals in It Self'.

70 ARO-8-0106-01 (2 May 1502). The speech included the line 'that dome [...] Is fals evile and Rottyn in It Self'.

71 ARO-8-0109-02 (13 May 1502).

72 There are numerous mentions of the chamberlain and his ayre throughout the corpus. The latest, however, appears to be from the last case of 1502. The last chamberlain ayre in Scotland was held in 1517 in Edinburgh: A.L. Murray, 'The last chamberlain ayre', *Scottish Historical Review* 39, 1960, p. 85.

73 See, for instance, M.F. Kluge, *Die Macht des Gedächtnisses: Entstehung und Wandel kommunaler Schriftkultur im spätmittelalterlichen Augsburg*, Leiden: Brill, 2014 (especially part IV, concerning 1368–1450).
74 On related points see C. Neville, *Land, Law and People in Medieval Scotland*, Edinburgh: Edinburgh University Press, 2010, pp. 24–30, and Hawes, 'Community and public authority', pp. 23–34, 74–105.
75 See below, p. 24.
76 See below, p. 33.
77 See below, p. 42.
78 See below, p. 62.
79 See below, p. 106.
80 See below, p. 240.

PART I

Telling tales

1

TELLING TALES

Maritime law in Aberdeen in the early sixteenth century

J.D. Ford

Edda Frankot has shown that the burgh records of Aberdeen provide a rich repository of information about maritime trade and its legal regulation in the fifteenth century.[1] In fact, many hundreds of entries relating to the same subject can also be found in the records surviving from the first half of the sixteenth century until they start to thin out in the later 1540s, after the Scottish admiral began to assert an exclusive jurisdiction over seafaring causes.[2] These entries are not merely of great interest for historians intent on tracing the development of maritime law, but actually constitute the single most significant source available for the period. Relevant entries can be found in other burgh records, and seafaring causes were occasionally heard in the central courts, but no other source is as richly informative as the council registers of Aberdeen.[3] However, for scholars used to working on the records of the central courts, as legal historians tend to be, the burgh records are awkward to handle.[4] They are bound to seem both familiar and unfamiliar, and the temptation to focus on the familiar features, while attributing the unfamiliar to curiosities of the recording process, needs to be resisted. The aim of this chapter is not to engage in the task of tracing the development of maritime law in Scotland, which will be attempted elsewhere, but is to consider how such a task might safely be undertaken, which requires examination of the character of the records and of the law found in them.[5] After a preliminary overview is provided of the types of entry examined, in which a change in the procedure followed by litigants comes to light, three possible approaches to the study of the records are considered in turn. It will be seen that the choice between these approaches, which to some extent build upon each other, hinges on the nature of the law referred to in the records and on the sense in which there was a 'culture of law' in Aberdeen in the early sixteenth century.

Court actions and legal remedies

The entries in the records relating to maritime trade are of various types, but they can mostly be divided into three categories. In the first place, many entries simply state that something has happened, such as the delivery of goods from a ship or the payment of freight for the carriage of goods. Although some of these entries may conceivably have been made in the course of disputes that were otherwise unrecorded, they appear usually to have been attempts to have it put on record that something has happened in the way it should have. In the second place, and in sharp contrast, many entries record protestations that something has not happened in the way it should have, for instance (to take the same examples) that goods have not been delivered or that freight has not been paid. Although these entries too may sometimes have been made in the course of disputes, they appear usually to have been made by or at the behest of mariners or merchants who wished to put it on record not only that something had not been done properly, but also that any loss resulting should be borne by another party. In the third place, many entries more clearly record the stages of disputes between parties.[6] They record the making of complaints by mariners and merchants against one another, the summoning of parties to respond to complaints, the setting of dates for hearings, the receipt of arguments or evidence and the delivery of decisions by the bailie court.[7] When decisions were delivered, parties were ordered to deliver goods, to pay freight, to contribute towards losses sustained by others or something similar.

To some extent the entries in the third category resemble those found in the earliest surviving records of the burgh, which date back to the fourteenth century.[8] At the beginning of the sixteenth century defenders were still summoned to answer a 'borgh', of which they were given a copy and of which a copy was sometimes entered in the records.[9] These documents typically opened with an assertion – in the first person – that the pursuer had 'found ane borgh' on the defender, went on to explain that something had happened because of which the defender ought to do something else, 'and wrangis and he do it nocht', and closed with the formula 'and tharto my borgh and ane borgh to follow my borgh'.[10] Although the term 'borgh' was applied to the documents used to initiate actions, it applied more precisely to the security parties were required to provide for their appearance before the court. Borghs were a form of the *attachiamenta* referred to in the opening words of a famous procedural manual that formed part of the 'auld lawes' of Scotland.[11] In accordance with a process widely used in previous centuries, defenders were given four opportunities to appear before the court.[12] If they failed to appear at the fourth hearing, a penalty or 'amerciament' was imposed upon them and the court proceeded to give judgement in their absence. If they did appear, pleas and proofs were received from either party, usually at further hearings, before the court proceeded to deliver its decision.

In the early 1530s, actions started to be initiated in a different way. On 23 February 1531, the bailies assigned further dates to a defender to appear and answer two 'petitions' submitted against him.[13] These petitions were like borghs in complaining that something had been done because of which the defender ought to do something else, 'and wrangs that he dois it nocht', but instead of being addressed to the officer of the court to whom security was given, they begged the judges directly to provide 'remeid of lawe'.[14] For the next fifteen years defenders were often summoned to answer 'petitions' submitted against them.[15] Those copied into the records followed the style of the 1531 petitions, except that they typically opened with a formal address to the court, contained a standardised statement that the defender was acting 'wranguslie and aganes the law' and ended by saying something like 'and this my complent and petitioun to haf the strynth of ane borgh gif neid beis'.[16] As the phrases added at the end indicate, some effort was made to reconcile the use of petitions with the established procedure, though other changes were made at the same time.[17] In the first petition submitted in 1531, the judges were actually asked to provide remeid of law 'conforme to our soverane lords letters direktat to you', which had probably been issued in response to a petition presented to the king.[18] Around the same time, the bailies received letters from the king concerning a ship wrecked on the coast nearby, in relation to which a 'summonds of spulzie' was being raised before 'the lords of counsall'.[19] When a summons was raised before this central court it was in response to a bill of complaint or supplication of a type similar to the petitions coming into use in Aberdeen.[20] Within a decade, local courts throughout the country would be instructed to imitate the procedure favoured by the lords of council.[21] It may be that awareness of how cases were raised in Edinburgh was already encouraging the bailie court of Aberdeen to move in that direction.

Whatever the reason for the move from borghs to petitions may have been, it clarified the purpose of raising actions. Many petitions – resembling again the documents used before the lords of council – spelled out the pursuer's concern that the defender would not do as he should 'without he be compellit be the law'.[22] Of course, whichever form of process was used, all pursuers must have wanted defenders to be subjected to legal compulsion, as is borne out by the recurrence throughout the records of statements that defenders should 'underly the lawe' or 'answer as law will'.[23] The adoption of the standard phrase 'wranguslie and aganes the law' similarly served to clarify the significance of the phrase 'wrangis and he do it nocht' found in the earlier borghs. Both phrases are reminiscent of the technical expression 'wrang et unlaw', which appears in the fourteenth-century records. Historians studying these and other records have observed that lawyers in late medieval Scotland had an opportunity to develop the law by teasing out the meaning of this expression in relation to the cases they handled.[24] Whether or not that actually happened, lawyers appearing before the lords of council certainly did something similar in refining their understanding of various species of wrong like 'spuilzie'.[25] As it happens, while spuilzie is mentioned in the entries examined here, it is always in connection with the practice of the lords of council, yet it may be wondered whether a comparable process of legal abstraction was under way in the bailie court of Aberdeen.[26] As mariners and merchants complained there about 'wrangis' done to them, it may be wondered whether different categories of wrong were carefully distinguished, and whether conditions of liability for each type of wrong were painstakingly specified.

Written pleadings and legal reasoning

On 13 April 1543 an 'obligatioun' was produced before the court by a creditor.[27] A date was set for the debtors named in the document to respond, but their procurator – a university graduate who may possibly have studied law – argued that they need not answer since 'the balze ma nocht decerne bot on wrangs, and thair is na wrang done specifiit in the obligatioun', adding that the debtors 'sould nocht be decernytt to gyf ony answer thairto withtout formaill petitioun and liball war maid thairupoun'.[28] The creditor was informed that he would need to present a petition if he wished to proceed, but whether any need was sensed for a wrong like 'breach of contract' to be specified is doubtful. No petition was presented for the creditor, perhaps because the debtors' procurator had meanwhile presented a successful petition on their behalf, alleging that the creditor had removed their goods from a ship and was refusing to return them 'wrangously and aganes the law'.[29] The wrong was not specified here either, nor was a wrong identified precisely in any of the other petitions entered in the records. There is one petition however that does go further than the rest. On 9 August 1538 it was alleged that certain merchants were refusing to contribute towards losses sustained by others when a ship they shared was plundered of some of its cargo by pirates.[30] What makes the petition exceptional is that it declared their refusal to contribute to be inconsistent with a rule of law established by the 'ald lovabill use lang observit withtin this nobill burght'. This petition at least went beyond alleging vaguely that the merchants were acting wrongfully and against the law by making some attempt to identify the law they were contravening. The court agreed that the merchants were obliged to contribute, 'conforme to the ald lovabill consuetud of this burght'.

If this exceptional petition may be taken to contain a syllogism, in which averments of fact were connected as a minor premiss with a proposition of law as a major premiss, leading to the conclusion that a legal remedy must be granted, the other petitions and borghs may perhaps be regarded as enthymemes, in which the major premiss of the argument was left unstated.[31] There are several reasons why it could have been considered appropriate for the law underpinning pleadings to remain implicit.[32] The applicable law could have been considered too uncontentious to be in need of statement, especially if the dispute centred on the accuracy of factual averments, as it clearly did in many cases. Conversely, where the law did seem contentious, the writers of petitions and borghs could have been reluctant to commit parties to defined positions before argument was engaged in before the court. That legal argument was sometimes expected is suggested by entries recording the willingness of defenders to do whatever 'happennit to be decernit and fundin, other be law or prettike', or to make payments 'gif it wer fundin of law that thai aucht to'.[33] Entries like these are unusual, however, and when they do occur there is rarely any indication of a finding being made, still less of how it was made. It is possible that the clerks who compiled the records preferred not to set down in writing the oral exchanges they heard in the court, but before it is assumed that the task of the legal historian must be to fill in gaps in the records by identifying propositions of law that would have rendered the reasoning in the pleadings coherent, the traces of legal argument that do exist need to be examined carefully.

When parties petitioned the court for 'remeid of law', seeking to have their opponents 'compellit be the law' to do something, and when it was stated that their opponents should appear before the court to 'underly the lawe' or 'answer as law will', the word 'law' was used primarily to signal a desire for disputes to be determined by way of a coercive process.[34] The first of these expressions recurs quite frequently in statements that a party objected to how a case was being handled and 'protestit for remeid of law', meaning that he intended to take any steps he could to challenge the court's ruling.[35] When one party asked the court for copies of depositions received from witnesses, the other party's procurator 'protestit that he gett nocht the same, becaus it is aganis the pratik and styill of court, and for remeid of law gif the bailzeis dois in the contrar'.[36] As parties who protested for 'remeid of law' were making a procedural move, the likelihood is that parties who petitioned for 'remeid of law' were doing the same, and were asking not so much to have their opponents compelled to fulfil their obligations under substantive law as to have them subjected to a process governed by procedural law. It was apparently the procurator who referred to 'the pratik and styill of court' who also complained in a case mentioned earlier about parties being summoned to answer an 'obligatioun'.[37] Given that types of wrong never were specified in petitions, his concern was presumably less with the lack of specification than with the attempt to initiate an action with an obligation instead of a petition. Another common use of the word 'law' was in court orders requiring payments to be made 'within terme of law', which meant that payments were to be made within the period prescribed by procedural law.[38] Accordingly, the point of saying that parties would make payments 'gif it wer fundin of law that thai aucht to' may simply have been that they were prepared to make payments if they were ordered to do so in a court process governed by law, not that they were prepared to make payments if required to do so by substantive law. But what about parties who undertook to do whatever 'happennit to be decernit and fundin, other be law or prettike'? Were they referring to rules directly regulating the activities of mariners and merchants?

A few entries in the records from the 1530s and 1540s are indicative of inquiry into law of a more substantive variety. In one case it was found to be 'the law of the sey' that someone employed as an ordinary sailor on one ship could accept appointment as 'ane bottsman' on another.[39] What exactly was meant by 'the law of the sey' is not apparent, but the idea that sailors should be free to assume more responsible positions on other vessels was broadly consistent with a provision of the maritime code known as the laws of Wisby.[40] In other cases equally vague reference was made to 'the ammarrellis lawis', 'the commont law' or simply 'the law'.[41] When the question was raised 'quhidder gold and silver cumand hayme in ane schip to this realme suld scot and lote witht uther gudis or nocht', the court found that 'all kind of mony, baitht gold and silver, cunzeit and uncunzeit, and als rings, being in ane schip, suld lott and scott witht the uther guds of the said schip'.[42] It is unclear where this answer was found, but it could have been in Justinian's *Digest*, where the same question had been answered in the same way by a Roman jurist.[43] The issue remained controversial in Aberdeen, yet the court's ruling seems to have been remembered by the draftsman of the exceptional petition in which a proposition of law was enunciated, for his complaint related to merchants who carried goods alone; yet the proposition was that if goods were lost, everyone else with 'gudds and money' aboard a ship had to contribute towards the loss sustained.[44] Another exceptional entry contains a protestation that merchants whose goods were stowed in the hold of a ship should not contribute towards losses sustained by those whose goods were stacked above deck, 'conform to the act of parliament maid thairupoune'.[45] Protestations in similar terms were actually quite frequent, but on no other occasion was support drawn from an act of parliament, or for that matter from an ordinance of the burgh council on the same subject.[46]

Maritime practice and legal customs

If an obvious question to ask is why so little interest seems to have been shown in the origins of the rules occasionally applied, there are two equally obvious answers, neither of which is reassuring if the aim is to confirm that more legal reasoning went on than the records reveal. The first is that authoritative sources were not cited in the way they often were by lawyers for the simple reason that lawyers were seldom involved in the handling of cases. As has been seen, procurators with university degrees did occasionally represent parties. Their critical comments on the court's procedure are recorded, but there is no indication that they were particularly prone to rehearsing rules, citing authorities or analysing the terms in which borghs and petitions were expressed.[47] As for the bailies who presided over hearings, they were burgesses, who appeared at other times as parties to actions of a maritime or mercantile nature. In many cases the bailies assembled assizes from among the suitors of the court, whose findings were delivered as the court's decisions, but the suitors were also mariners and merchants, who appeared at other times as litigants.[48] The clerks of the court are identified in one entry as 'notars', and the draftsmen of the borghs and petitions may have been notaries public as well.[49] As has been seen, however, the documents used to initiate actions generally failed to enunciate propositions of law, and while the clerks may be suspected of omitting to record all the arguments advanced orally before the court, it can scarcely be supposed that they prompted parties with arguments they were unable to articulate on their own. Assuming – as we surely must – that the clerks performed a more passive role, the bailie court emerges as a forum in which the affairs of mariners and merchants were subjected to regulation by mariners and merchants themselves.

The second obvious explanation for the absence from the records of references to authoritative sources of law – the laws of Wisby, Justinian's *Digest*, acts of parliament and so on – is that the law was not conceived of in the fashion familiar to lawyers. The exceptional petition already mentioned may have owed something in its composition to written sources, but the rule of law it contained was said to have been established by the 'ald lovable use lang observit withtin this nobill burght'. Similar language is encountered elsewhere. In one case merchants were required to make payments 'eftir the forme of the auld ryte and lovable consuetude usit in this towne a lang tyme bigane'.[50] In several other cases parties were required to make payments in accordance with 'use and wont', 'as use is' or 'as use and wont is amang mariners'.[51] A sailor claimed in one of these cases that, 'be use and custum amang mariners', a skipper ought to reimburse him for expense he had incurred while recovering from an illness contracted on a voyage. Support for this claim could have been drawn from an article in the laws of Wisby, although it is not mentioned in the record.[52] Another article in that code could have been cited to support a claim that a skipper ought to pay for the hire of a lighter required to transfer goods from his ship into an inaccessible harbour, though reference is again made to 'use and custum' alone.[53] Similarly, sailors who wished to terminate their employment on a ship were told that they must first help to complete its unloading, 'conforme to the use of marenellis', although here too reference might have been made to the laws of Wisby.[54] It is of course possible that the clerks failed to record references that were actually made to these articles, but it is also possible, and indeed more likely, that no copy of the code was consulted, that reliance was at most placed on distant recollections of its provisions and that mariners were largely unconscious of any influence the code had exerted on the shaping of their practices.[55] In any case, whether or not the code was cited, and however accurately its provisions may have been remembered, the crucial point is that it would not have contained directly applicable rules if what made behaviour obligatory was its customary observance.

When it was found that 'the law of the sey' permitted an ordinary sailor to withdraw from service on one ship to become an officer on another, the rule was said to have been 'sufficientlie provyne' before the court by 'certane famouse skipperis'.[56] Even if the relevant provision of the laws of Wisby had been cited, what clearly mattered here was the testimony of recognised experts that the practice was known to them.[57] Testimony was taken because to ask what was lawful among mariners was to ask what was normal, and since normative behaviour was thus identified with normal behaviour, there was no sharp distinction, as lawyers would have expected, between questions of law and questions of fact. An assize found in one case that a ship had 'come saifly in the havin of Abirdene and thair was maid fast witht hir anchors and towis, efter the use and custum as maisteris and marenellis usis to lay thair schip'.[58] In another case, a master claimed to have moored his ship in 'the souerast fassoun, be the avyse and sycht of marinars', and asked the bailies to 'sand men of knawlege to se and considder gif the said schipe was soueralie fastnyt'.[59] After a leaking ship was brought into Aberdeen on an earlier occasion, the master had asked the court 'to send downe certane schipmen to se and consider the same'.[60] In these cases, confirmation that standard practice had been adhered to would have amounted to confirmation that obligations had been discharged. There was a normative dimension to an otherwise factual inquiry, and it is not easy to distinguish cases like these from others in which, for example, the issue was whether goods were dry when loaded onto a ship 'it beand considerit be famous merchand men'.[61] The recourse to renowned experts in some of these cases is revealing, but it was not typical. The court was generally able to rely on the expertise of the mariners and merchants assembled in assizes to discover how their affairs were normally conducted.

Even if the more numerous entries in which reference is made to 'use and custum' are added to the handful of entries in which substantive 'law' is mentioned, they still amount to a small proportion of all the entries relating to maritime trade. There are other entries, however, in which questions of law appear to have been brought into focus, albeit without answers being provided. For instance, when evidence presented in one case showed that lint had been wet while being taken in a lighter from a ship into a harbour, the question was raised 'quhidder the awnars of the schip or merchands aucht to pay the skaytht done to the lynt in the forsaid lychtars defalt'.[62] Furthermore, even when no questions were asked, entries often have a repetitive quality that enables regularities of behaviour to be identified with such confidence that it has to be wondered whether things happened as a rule (descriptively) because governed by a rule (prescriptively). If it would be misleading for legal historians to reconstruct the reasoning that might have gone on in the bailie court had lawyers been involved, perhaps it would be possible for them to discover customary norms that offer answers to the questions sometimes raised, or that seem to be implicit in regularities of behaviour discernible elsewhere. As commissions of enquiry were established in many parts of Europe, both before and during the sixteenth century, to investigate and redact the usages and customs considered normative by lay people, and as lawyers, who tended to feature prominently on these commissions, sometimes endeavoured to describe popular customs in books they wrote, there may be some warrant for historians attempting to perform a similar task.[63] Perhaps they could try to identify customary norms in the way contemporary lawyers might have done. Perhaps, although they would need to bear in mind the lessons learned by both historians and anthropologists from study of the codification of legal customs, for what has repeatedly been found is that customary norms tend to change in character when reduced to writing by lawyers.[64] Indeed, even to talk of customary norms may be misleading.[65] For this second approach to be adopted, some way would need to be found of preserving the character of the usages and customs considered normative by mariners and merchants.

Local knowledge and legal cultures

The position reached so far is that although there is some evidence of an ability to think like lawyers among those involved in court cases in Aberdeen in the early sixteenth century, the evidence is too slight to justify an attempt to reconstruct other cases in a way that would make them satisfy the expectations of lawyers. The mariners and merchants who adjudicated on their own affairs would no doubt have agreed with any suggestion put to them that the law consisted of rules, for they did occasionally express their thinking in such terms. For the most part, however, they do not seem to have thought in terms of legal abstractions that could have been related to the facts of cases. The entries in the records in which some semblance of legal reasoning can be found are vastly outnumbered by those in which normative thinking is embedded in factual observations, which is understandable given that the normative appears to have been identified with the normal. The only justification for treating the rare cases in which those involved may have reasoned like lawyers as paradigms for the many in which such reasoning could only be read into the records would be if the records of the majority of cases are unintelligible otherwise. Yet the entries relating to maritime trade can be understood in a different way. A feature common to entries in all three of the categories distinguished earlier is that mariners and merchants were reporting each other's actions to the court, often in the expectation that something would be done about them.[66] They reported one another to the court in much the same way as children tell tales on each other to their parents or teachers. This should not be taken to mean that the mariners and merchants were engaging in some form of puerile behaviour, as if they lacked the sophistication of the trained lawyers who were appearing around the same time in other courts. Just as smart children appreciate that for the tales they tell to be effective they need to resonate with the presuppositions of their parents or teachers, so mariners and merchants must have appreciated that reporting one another to the court would only produce the results they wanted if the court shared their understanding of how things were meant to be done.[67] The tales told had to be tellable tales, and in principle an accumulation of tellable tales may be as effective, extensive and elaborate as an assemblage of applicable rules. If the task of the legal historian is seen as the recovery of tellable tales, or as the investigation of the presuppositions shared by those involved in the court process, then there may be some prospect of an account of the maritime law adhered to in Aberdeen remaining true to the character of the source material available.

Some readers may be reminded of the account of *adat* adjudication in Indonesia originally presented in the Storrs Lectures delivered by Clifford Geertz in 1981.[68] Noting that *adat* was generally perceived to be a kind of custom, Geertz warned that the confusion caused by the concept of custom among anthropologists was exceeded only by the confusion it caused among lawyers. Among anthropologists, custom tended to be reduced to the level of practice, habit or a way of doing things – in other words, to a matter of fact – whereas among lawyers it tended to be turned into abstract generalisations or written rules – in other words, into a kind of law.[69] *Adat*, Geertz insisted, was bound to be misconceived by anyone who thought in terms of a binary opposition between fact and law. As he saw it, *adat* consisted of acceptable representations of reality, or ways of describing the world that were believed to be appropriate. The purpose of adjudication, he believed, was to work towards a consensus on how far something that had happened could be described as something that ought to have happened. Viewed in this way, the legal process was not merely 'functional' but deeply 'cultural', in the sense that it was a means not merely of determining disputes but also of generating social awareness. Geertz famously described people as animals suspended in webs of significance that they themselves had spun, and maintained that the task of the cultural anthropologist was to explain the significance of the webs spun by social groups, not by 'translating' them into supposedly corresponding terms, concepts and symbols drawn from other cultures, but by engaging in a necessarily hermeneutic process of 'interpretation'.[70] Law, he argued in his Storrs Lectures, was one of the types of web people spin, and it needed, if it was to be properly understood, to be interpreted in ways that rendered the thinking of its users intelligible, not simply restated or reworked in keeping with the thinking of external observers.[71] Properly understood, law was intrinsically cultural. The point was not just that the development of a culture could be affected by law, or even that a developed culture could involve expectations of law, but that law was itself a cultural development. As Geertz put it, law needed to be perceived as 'a species of social imagination'.[72]

Geertz also envisaged law as a species of 'local knowledge', by which he appears to have meant two things. The first is that law in a form like *adat* does not consist of abstract generalisations that can be applied logically to separately discovered facts, but is bound up with the facts of circumstantial cases.[73] Knowledge of this type of law is unavoidably localised because it cannot be abstracted from the cases in which it is found without being turned into something it is not. A natural response for some lawyers to make is that 'case law' is a category with which they are all too familiar, and that extracting general rules from particular decisions is what they do best. But could the mariners and merchants who raised cases, served as bailies and sat on assizes in Aberdeen have made the same response? To have been able to extract transferable rules from earlier rulings they would at the very least have required access to those rulings. Written records were obviously being made, and parties frequently asked to be provided with copies of entries affecting them.[74] The existence of these records could have changed the character of the law mentioned, so long as they were used as a source of reference.[75] The reality is, however, that while there were occasions on which earlier rulings were drawn to the court's attention, this only occurred when the rulings had been made at previous stages in the same proceedings.[76] Earlier rulings do not feature anywhere in the entries examined here as what lawyers call 'judicial precedents'. The most that may be suggested is that people involved in litigation sometimes remembered previous cases, which would have given any rules they formulated the fluidity commonly taken to typify the operation of an oral tradition of usage and custom.[77] It has been seen that when a proposition of law was enunciated in one petition, it appeared to build on a decision delivered in a previous case, and the proposal is to treat regularities found in other entries as evidence of legal customs.[78] Different entries related to different cases, distinct from each other in their factual circumstances, yet the entries were often expressed in strikingly similar language. The proposal is not to restate these similarities as abstract generalisations of a kind that could be used to supplement the small number of propositions of law found in the records, but is rather to identify certain broad forms of narrative that came to be considered acceptable and to examine the presuppositions that made them acceptable.

In seeking to examine the presuppositions that made tales tellable, less may perhaps be learned from the methodology of legal historians than from the methodology of intellectual historians, who are used to investigating the linguistic or ideological conventions behind the particular modes of discourse they study.[79] The modes of discourse studied are particular, not simply in the sense that intellectual historians tend to concentrate on specific kinds of thought, but in the crucial sense that they believe thought to be constrained by conventions shared among members of particular linguistic communities.[80] To this extent, they are in agreement with the second thing Geertz had in mind when he remarked that legal knowledge must be local, which is that anything resembling *adat* has to be particular to the community in which it is generated.[81] Law, as a species of social imagination, must be particular to the social group responsible for its development, and it therefore needs to be asked how the group responsible for developing the maritime law adhered to in Aberdeen was defined. In one case, it was argued that the crew of a foreign ship should not be required to make a payment, 'becaus it is nocht the use of thair cuntra', but the court concluded that they ought to pay, 'conforme to the auld use observit withtin this guid towne past memour of man'.[82] As has been seen already, reference was made in other cases to the custom 'usit in this towne' or 'withtin this nobill burght'.[83] When the latter phrase was used in the exceptional petition in which a proposition of law was enunciated, reference was initially made to the custom of the 'realm', possibly because account was being taken of a ruling in an earlier case, for in that case advice had been sought from 'the towne of Edinburgh'.[84] However, the court insisted on the petition being 'correctit' and 'reformit', and the word 'realm' was excised and replaced with 'burght', a firm indication that the court believed its concern to be with its local law.[85] Adherence to its own law – to the development of a shared understanding of how maritime trade should be regulated or to the generation of a culture of law – was one of the ways in which the urban community defined itself.[86] It may be illuminating to search for the origins of the burgh's law, which may reveal the extent to which it was open to external influences, but however cosmopolitan these influences may turn out to have been, it was ultimately the usages and customs of the burgh that were given effect.[87]

Conclusion: urban discourse and legal constraints

It now seems clear that the study of language must be central to any attempt to trace the development of maritime law in the early sixteenth century, not just for the obvious reason that our knowledge of the subject has to be drawn from what is said about it in written records, but also because lawful behaviour appears to have been conceived of as behaviour susceptible to acceptable description.[88] As intellectual historians have shown, linguistic conventions constrain both the ways in which behaviour can be justified and the range of behaviour people can indulge in when they may need to provide justifications for their actions.[89] Aware that they might have to appear before the bailie court to defend themselves, mariners and merchants had to be mindful of the tales that might be told there and to act accordingly. On the one hand, these tales described established practices, yet on the other hand, the practices had come to be established because there were tales that could be told about them. It was the approbatory description of standard ways of doing things, or more accurately the availability of approbatory descriptions, that gave normal practice its normative dimension. Sometimes, inevitably, practices were raised for discussion before they were fully established, and it was on these occasions that resort was taken to what looks more like the reasoning of lawyers. Propositions of law were remembered – and possibility remains that they were recited from written sources – yet even then law does not appear to have been regarded as something distinct from the factual situations to which it might be applied. However clearly propositions of law may have been recalled, what made them binding was not their origin in authoritative sources but their absorption into the usage and custom of the burgh. Recalling propositions of law formed part of the process of negotiating acceptance of new tales. These moments of uncertainty, when a degree of innovation occurred, are especially interesting for historians intent on tracing the development of the law, but they should not be allowed to give a false impression of the nature of the law that was being developed.

Notes

1 E. Frankot, 'Maritime law and practice in late medieval Aberdeen', *Scottish Historical Review* 89, 2010, pp. 136–52 and E. Frankot, *'Of Laws of Ships and Shipmen': Medieval Maritime Law and Its Practice in Urban Northern Europe*, Edinburgh: Edinburgh University Press, 2012.

2 The change in jurisdiction is briefly outlined in J.D. Ford (ed.) *Alexander King's Treatise on Maritime Law*, Edinburgh: Stair Society, 2018, pp. lxxi–vii.

3 Aberdeen City and Aberdeenshire Archives (hereafter ACAA), CA1/1 Aberdeen Council, Baillie and Guild Court Registers (hereafter ACR). As is explained in the chapter of this volume by William Hepburn and Graeme Small, 'council registers' may be a misleading description of these varied records.

4 This chapter is written for the benefit of 'legal historians' in the broad sense of scholars committed to tracing the development of law and thinking about law. There is of course much in the records examined that should be of interest to social, economic and other historians as well, but these aspects are only touched on in passing.

5 A first attempt to pursue the approach proposed, in which some of the entries discussed here are explored more fully, will appear soon under the title 'General Average in Scotland during the Sixteenth Century' in a collection of essays on The History of Insurance Law edited by Guido Rossi and Phillip Hellwege.
6 As well as thinning out generally in the later 1540s, the entries relating to maritime trade by then fall mainly into the first two categories.
7 In most of the relevant entries in the council register parties were generally said to have appeared before the *curia ballivorum burgi*, though sometimes the provost sat along with the bailies in this court and sometimes maritime matters were considered elsewhere.
8 W.C. Dickinson (ed.) *Early Records of the Burgh of Aberdeen, 1317 and 1398–1407*, Edinburgh: Scottish History Society, 1957.
9 ACAA, ACR, vol. 9, p. 543, vol. 10, p. 211, and vol. 12/2, p. 520.
10 ACAA, ACR, vol. 8, p. 1036, vol. 11, p. 636, vol. 12/1, pp. 16, 164, 278, 286, and vol. 12/2, pp. 520, 701, 753, 773.
11 T.D. Fergus (ed.) *Quoniam Attachiamenta*, Edinburgh: Stair Society, 1996, pp. 116–7; see too C. Innes and R. Renwick (eds) *The Ancient Laws and Customs of the Burghs of Scotland*, 2 vols, Edinburgh: Burgh Record Society, 1868–1910, vol. 1, pp. 27, 36–7, 54, 57.
12 P.J. Hamilton-Grierson (ed.) *Habakkuk Bisset's Rolment of Courtis*, 3 vols, Edinburgh: Scottish Text Society, 1920–1926, vol. 3, pp. 29–84.
13 ACAA, ACR, vol. 13, p. 95.
14 ACAA, ACR, vol. 13, pp. 96–7.
15 Although it is possible that petitions were already in use in other types of cases, a more comprehensive search through the two parts of ACAA, ACR, vol. 12, has revealed that they contain as many as forty borghs but not a single petition. Similarly, in the first 95 pages of ACR, vol. 13, five borghs have been found but no petitions.
16 ACAA, ACR, vol. 13, p. 303; ACR, vol. 14, pp. 256–7, 260, 587–8; ACR, vol. 15, pp. 286, 298, 334–5, 368–9, 445, 653–5, 662, 665, 682–3, 736–7; ACR, vol. 16, pp. 90–1, 122, 189, 452, 454, 467, 521–2, 561–2, 611, 711–2, 741, 760, 794, 855; ACR, vol. 17, pp. 440–1; ACR, vol. 18, p. 248; and ACR, vol. 19, pp. 4, 98, 123–4.
17 Instead of court officers receiving borghs from defenders, for example, defenders were increasingly required to provide the bailies themselves with security in the form of 'caution', which could be both *de iudicio sisti et iudicatum solvi* (that is, a guarantee both that they would appear before the court to hear sentence given and that any award of damages the court made would be satisfied).
18 The study of petitions as a direct link between rulers and ruled has of course become a growth industry in recent years (see, for example, K. Bowie, 'From customary to constitutional right: The right to petition in Scotland before the 1707 act of union', *Parliaments, Estates and Representation* 38, 2018, pp. 279–92). The essential element in the 1531 case is that those in authority were being begged to intervene in a dispute.
19 ACAA, ACR, vol. 13, pp. 15–23, 103, 115–7, 134–9, 143–4.
20 A.B. Calderwood (ed.) *Acts of the Lords of Council, 1501–1503*, Edinburgh: HM Stationary Office, 1993, p. xxv.
21 *The Records of the Parliaments of Scotland to 1707*, ed. K.M. Brown et al., St Andrews, 2007–2020, <www.rps.ac.uk> (hereafter RPS), 1540/12/14.
22 ACAA, ACR, vol. 14, pp. 587–8; ACR, vol. 15, pp. 286, 298, 334–5, 368–9, 445, 655, 662, 665, 736–7; ACR, vol. 16, pp. 90–1, 122, 452, 454, 467, 521–2, 561–2, 611, 627–8, 760, 855; and ACR, vol. 19, pp. 123–4.
23 ACAA, ACR, vol. 8, pp. 798, 830; ACR, vol. 10, pp. 29, 115, 167, 169, 277, 366; ACR, vol. 11, pp. 521, 636; ACR, vol. 12/1, pp. 126, 261–3; ACR, vol. 12/2, pp. 522, 666, 700–1, 710–1, 753–4; ACR, vol. 13, pp. 172, 180, 506, 508; ACR, vol. 14, pp. 254, 256, 259, 264–5, 266–7, 536, 545, 620; ACR, vol. 15, pp. 33–5, 48, 55, 108, 110, 167, 204, 294, 387, 445, 448; ACR, vol. 16, pp. 104–5, 131, 155, 375; ACR, vol. 18, p. 243; and ACR, vol. 19, pp. 310, 316–7, 394.

24 A. Harding, 'Rights, wrongs and remedies in late medieval English and Scots law', in H.L. MacQueen (ed.) *Miscellany Four*, Edinburgh: Stair Society, 2002, pp. 1–8 and H.L. MacQueen, 'Some notes on wrang and unlaw', in H.L. MacQueen (ed.) *Miscellany Five*, Edinburgh: Stair Society, 2006, pp. 13–26.

25 A.M. Godfrey, *Civil Justice in Renaissance Scotland: The Origins of a Central Court*, Leiden: Brill, 2009, pp. 239–47.

26 ACAA, ACR, vol. 14, pp. 566–8, 570–2, ACR, vol. 15, pp. 485–6, and ACR, vol. 18, p. 241. Actions for spuilzie can be found in D. Littlejohn (ed.) *Records of the Sheriff Court of Aberdeenshire*, 3 vols, Aberdeen: New Spalding Club, 1904–1907, vol. 1, pp. 47–63, 149–63, 255–6, and they may well be found elsewhere in the burgh records, though Edda Frankot has found that the term 'spuilzie' is absent from the volumes up to 1511.

27 ACAA, ACR, vol. 17, pp. 434–6.

28 ACAA, ACR, vol. 17, p. 440.

29 ACAA, ACR, vol. 17, pp. 441, 446, 450, 453, 463, 571.

30 ACAA, ACR, vol. 15, pp. 711–2.

31 For the later use of this Aristotelian distinction by Scots lawyers, see J.D. Ford, *Law and Opinion in Scotland during the Seventeenth Century*, Oxford: Hart Publishing, 2007, pp. 513–5.

32 J.G.H. Hudson, 'Court cases and legal arguments in England, c. 1066–1166', *Transactions of the Royal Historical Society* 10, 2000, pp. 91–116, explains why this may have happened and how historians may respond in dealing with truncated pleadings.

33 ACAA, ACR, vol. 9, p. 399 and ACR, vol. 11, p. 535.

34 The process was backed up with recurring threats of seizure of property (poinding) or person (warding), and occasionally with other threats too.

35 A particularly instructive example can be found at ACAA, ACR, vol. 16, pp. 632, 637.

36 ACAA, ACR, vol. 16, p. 617.

37 See again the quotations in note 28.

38 This expression is equiparated with the equally common 'within thre tydis' in ACAA, ACR, vol. 12/2, p. 672.

39 ACAA, ACR, vol. 14, p. 413.

40 T. Twiss (ed.) *The Black Book of the Admiralty*, 4 vols, London: Longman, 1871–1876, vol. 4, p. 283.

41 ACAA, ACR, vol. 13, pp. 403–4 and ACR, vol. 12/2, pp. 675, 689–90.

42 ACAA, ACR, vol. 13, pp. 410, 425.

43 A. Watson (ed.) *The Digest of Justinian*, 4 vols, Philadelphia: University of Pennsylvania Press, 1985, vol. 1, p. 419.

44 ACAA, ACR, vol. 13, pp. 465, 506–9, 511–3; ACR, vol. 14, pp. 139–40; and ACR, vol. 15, pp. 711–2.

45 ACAA, ACR, vol. 16, p. 784.

46 For the protestations, see ACAA, ACR, vol. 8, pp. 1029–30; ACR, vol. 9, p. 732; ACR, vol. 12/1, pp. 407–8; ACR, vol. 12/2, p. 529; ACR, vol. 15, pp. 89–90, 94, 96, 118, 278; for the legislation see RPS, 1467/1/4, ratified in 1487/10/19, and ACAA, ACR, vol. 9, p. 398. It is this particular topic and these particular entries that are examined more fully in the essay referred to in note 5. The significance of the expression 'lott and scott' will be explained there.

47 For a persuasive explanation of the involvement of lawyers in an unusual episode, see A.R.C. Simpson, 'Spuilzie and shipwreck in the burgh records', *Journal of Irish and Scottish Studies* 9, 2018, pp. 70–92.

48 *Cf.* Dickinson, *Early Records of the Burgh of Aberdeen*, pp. cxxviii–ix.

49 ACAA, ACR, vol. 13, p. 18.

50 ACAA, ACR, vol. 13, pp. 157–8. Another entry in which similar language is used will be returned to below.

51 ACAA, ACR, vol. 13, p. 502; ACR, vol. 15, p. 230; ACR, vol. 16, p. 205; ACR, vol. 17, pp. 573–4, 579–80; and ACR, vol. 19, p. 4.

52 Twiss, *Black Book of the Admiralty*, vol. 4, p. 270. The corresponding article in the laws of Oleron (*Black Book of the Admiralty*, vol. 1, pp. 94–7) was less supportive.

53 ACAA, ACR, vol. 12/2, p. 672 and Twiss, *Black Book of the Admiralty*, vol. 4, p. 281.

54 ACAA, ACR, vol. 19, p. 401 and Twiss, *Black Book of the Admiralty*, vol. 4, p. 280.

55 None of the findings listed matches the terms of the code exactly. Frankot, '*Of Laws of Ships and Shipmen*', pp. 154–7, 195, found not only that the code was unknown in the fifteenth century but also that rulings then were influenced in the same vague and probably indirect way by the laws of Oleron. She is presumably correct in suggesting that legislation informing the laws of Wisby is more likely to have been known about earlier in the sixteenth century than the code itself. Essentially, though, mariners and merchants in Scotland are less likely to have consulted written statements of the law at any stage than to have remembered conversations they had been engaged in with mariners and merchants from overseas.

56 ACAA, ACR, vol. 14, p. 413.

57 Again, the practice was not covered exactly by the terms of the provision in the code.

58 ACAA, ACR, vol. 20, p. 24.

59 ACAA, ACR, vol. 12/2, p. 865.

60 ACAA, ACR, vol. 12/1, p. 245.

61 ACAA, ACR, vol. 12/1, p. 293.

62 ACAA, ACR, vol. 16, p. 389. For the hard of Scots, 'skaytht' means loss or harm.

63 D. Heirbaut, 'Exploring the law in medieval minds: The duty of the legal historian to write the books of non-written law', in A. Musson and C. Stebbings (eds) *Making Legal History: Approaches and Methodologies*, Cambridge: Cambridge University Press, 2012, pp. 118–30, recommends such an approach.

64 See, for example, E. Kadens, 'Custom's past', in C.A. Bradley (ed.) *Custom's Future: International Law in a Changing World*, Cambridge: Cambridge University Press, 2016, pp. 11–33.

65 As Heirbaut points out, German historians distinguish between legal customs of the kind found in Aberdeen (*Rechtsgewohnheiten*) and the customary laws reconstructed from them by lawyers (*Gewohnheitsrechten*). The precise significance of these terms tends to vary from one historian to another, but the crucial point is that lay people and trained lawyers tended to view customs in different ways.

66 Even when the aim was to record satisfaction with something that had been done, the expectation generally was that the person responsible would be released from an obligation.

67 This is not a roundabout way of saying that children need to know the rules of the game, although some of them may think in these terms. On this point much can, of course, be learned from the later Wittgenstein.

68 Clifford Geertz, *Local Knowledge: Further Essays in Interpretive Anthropology*, London: Fontana, 1993, pp. 167–234.

69 On the reworking of *adat* by legal scholars, see, for instance, Z.Z. Mutaqin, 'Indonesian customary law and European colonialism: A comparative analysis on *adat* law', *Journal of East Asia and International Law* 4, 2011, pp. 351–76.

70 *The Interpretation of Cultures: Selected Essays*, New York: Basic Books, 1973, pp. 3–30.

71 Whether this is generally true of all law, as Geertz suggested, need not be considered here.

72 Geertz, *Local Knowledge*, p. 232.

73 See too Geertz, *Available Light: Anthropological Reflections on Philosophical Topics*, Princeton, NJ: Princeton University Press, 2000, pp. 133–40.

74 ACAA, ACR, vol. 12/1, pp. 170, 173, 216, 351; ACR, vol. 12/2, pp. 477, 480–1, 526, 674, 697–701, 711; ACR, vol. 13, pp. 15–23, 134–9, 143–4, 406, 410–3, 415–8, 421–5, 495–8, 513; ACR, vol. 14, pp. 141, 191, 215, 429, 546–7, 589; ACR, vol. 15,

pp. 20, 36, 47, 70, 87, 167, 408, 485; ACR, vol. 16, pp. 67, 83, 175, 195, 256, 271, 316, 391, 452, 462, 465, 474, 487, 604, 612, 632, 653, 744; ACR, vol. 17, pp. 573–4; ACR, vol. 18, pp. 235, 251, 364, 373, 512, 529, 579; and ACR, vol. 19, pp. 104, 291, 301, 303, 310, 324, 412, 418.

75 Interesting questions are raised in S. Teuscher, 'Document collections, mobilized regulations and the making of customary law at the end of the middle ages', *Archival Science* 10, 2010, pp. 211–29.

76 ACAA, ACR, vol. 12/1, pp. 216–7, 228; ACR, vol. 14, p. 360; ACR, vol. 17, p. 575; and ACR, vol. 18, p. 415.

77 The relevant literature is reviewed with characteristic insight in J. Goody, *The Logic of Writing and the Organisation of Society*, Cambridge: Cambridge University Press, 1986, pp. 127–70.

78 To be clear, it has been seen that the draftsman of a petition may have remembered a previous ruling, which is not the same thing as citing a previous ruling as if it provided some sort of authority for a rule. There is evidence in the records of other burghs during the sixteenth century that court decisions were sometimes expected to have an effect on legal development, but not as what lawyers would now call precedents.

79 Something could perhaps be learned from the varied contributions made in recent years to 'legal narratology' (see, for example, G. van Niekerk, 'Indigenous law and narrative: Rethinking methodology', *Comparative and International Law Journal of South Africa* 32, 1999, pp. 208–27). But there is a difference between attending to the stories people sometimes tell about the law and recognising that some law sometimes consists in the stories people tell.

80 See, for example, A. Brett, 'What is intellectual history now?', in D. Cannadine (ed.) *What Is History Now?* Basingstoke: Palgrave Macmillan, 2003, pp. 113–31.

81 The connection is formed by a shared debt to linguistic philosophy.

82 ACAA, ACR, vol. 15, pp. 167–8. For what may have been a different view of the law applicable to prize-taking, a matter generally left to the admiralty courts, see ACAA, ACR, vol. 20, p. 120.

83 ACAA, ACR, vol. 13, pp. 157–8 and ACR, vol. 15, p. 716.

84 ACAA, ACR, vol. 13, p. 425.

85 The entries involving maritime law may be compared with ACAA, ACR, vol. 19, pp. 341–2, where a case about customs dues was taken to be governed by the 'use and prattik of the burrowis of the realme'. Whether the attitudes encountered in Aberdeen in the early sixteenth century were widespread throughout the country and century needs further investigation.

86 *Cf.* C. Hawes, 'The urban community in fifteenth century Scotland: Language, law and political practice', *Urban History* 44, 2017, pp. 365–80.

87 T. Johnson, 'Law, space and local knowledge in late medieval England', unpublished PhD thesis, Birkbeck, University of London, 2014, deals with law as local knowledge in this sense.

88 The fundamental importance to work in this area of J. Kopaczyk, *The Legal Language of Scottish Burghs: Standardization and Lexical Bundles, 1380–1560*, Oxford: Oxford University Press, 2013, will be apparent.

89 The classic study remains Q. Skinner, 'The principles and practice of opposition: The case of Bolingbroke versus Walpole', in N. McKendrick (ed.) *Historical Perspectives: Studies in English thought and Society in Honour of J. H. Plumb*, London: Europa, 1974, pp. 93–128.

PART II

Communication of law

2

COMMON BOOKS IN ABERDEEN, c. 1398–c. 1511

William Hepburn and Graeme Small

The Aberdeen Council Registers survive almost in their entirety from 1398, offering by far the most complete example of such a record from any Scottish town before the sixteenth century.[1] These registers were often called 'common books' by contemporaries. That historical term is perhaps also a helpful one for modern historians to adopt in place of other descriptions such as 'court book' or 'council register' because it acknowledges that the use of these books was broad, consisting primarily of records of the process and decisions of the burgh courts but also including statutes and ordinances laid down by the burgh council, records of the admission of burgesses, records of the elections of burgh officials and copies of other documents such as letters from the king.[2] The term 'common books' also invokes the idea of community which was central in the political culture of the burgh. Claire Hawes argues that

> the Scottish medieval burgh community could be thought of as a location, a legal construct and a group of people [and] the overlap between these elements provided a conceptual space which could be appropriated by those in authority in order to legitimise political decisions and actions.[3]

All usages of the term 'community' in the context of the burgh had the function of describing a given group of people as a corporate body united by legal privileges tied to a particular place. It could be attached to the shared property of the burgh community through terms such as common rental, common work, common purse and common good.[4] Community was a term that legitimised the political power of a governing elite by characterising them as a group acting in the interests of the many.[5] It underlined the political necessity for those in power to serve the people of the burgh more broadly, while allowing control over this broader group of people.

Aberdeen's government was dominated by a small merchant elite. This elite was remarkably stable over multiple generations and showed continuing interest in the written word. They came primarily from a small number of families who controlled politics in fifteenth- and sixteenth-century Aberdeen.[6] Through the language and ideology of community, they associated their prosperity with that of the town.[7] As written records became more widespread and their uses more widely recognised, it appears a member of this merchant elite, William Chalmer, initiated a new way of using writing to represent the burgh – common books.[8] In 1486 his great-grandson William Chalmer took over the office of town clerk, showing that the family remained at the heart of civic government and documentary practice.

This chapter will argue that the common books of Aberdeen can be situated in a European story of increasing literacy and the proliferation of writing but, just as community was not the inclusive and egalitarian idea it might appear to modern eyes, these common books should not be primarily understood as a means of increasing access to the law and engagement with the written word. [9] Rather, they were another tool for the established elite of medieval Aberdeen to entrench their civic power – an ever more effective tool as people increasingly understood their world through writing and documents.[10]

This chapter will first explore the genesis of these surviving records and how they changed in their first 100 years or so of use. It will argue that they were a product of a growing emphasis – closely associated, in Scotland, with notaries public – upon the value of writing as a way to represent the world, demonstrated in everything from legal documents to literary texts to the non-literate use of documents in ritual. While tracing part of a similar story to Michael Clanchy's account of medieval England's journey from memory to written records, this argument asserts, with similar emphasis to Daniel Lord Smail's work on Marseille, that a clear division between oral and written culture cannot be sustained. Instead it aims to encompass the full range of engagements with the written word, literate and non-literate.[11] As such, this chapter will explore how these records were a central node in the town's documentary network and a physical symbol of burgh authority, showing how they were useful to the burgh's elite in both literate and non-literate contexts. Finally, it will demonstrate that the authority of these records was fiercely defended by the burgh administration and the elite that controlled it.

Documentary practice in the century following 1398

1398 marked the date of a new initiative in civic record-keeping, at least according to a description made of Aberdeen's archives by its town clerk, Thomas Mollisone, in 1591. Mollisone wrote that the first register to be kept in Aberdeen was probably the book beginning in 1398. That there was no book before this, he argued, was proven by the existence of scrolls on parchment containing the courts of the burgh for many years – one scroll to a year – which ended when the earliest register began.[12] One such roll, dating from 1317, is still preserved, and it is the earliest surviving local court record from anywhere in Scotland.[13] Thus 1398 marked a change in the physical media of the civic records, from parchment to paper and from rolls to books, but there was also continuity. Comparison of the 1317 roll with the earliest book does not suggest a dramatic change in the subject matter or manner of what was recorded, although in the 1590s Mollisone found the content of the rolls limited compared with the records to which he was accustomed. He found in them 'Na action nor maner of consequence therein nor yit any ordinanceis statutis or constitutiouns bot onlie Simpill actiouns for annuellis and convictionis of wemen and mannis wyffis for brewing'.[14]

Mollisone also describes the earliest books – from the late fourteenth and early fifteenth centuries – as being bound one book to a year. The internal evidence in the first two volumes of the Aberdeen Council Registers as they survive today supports this, for the pages recording the proceedings of the Michaelmas head court often state 'here begins the book of the community' and often have decorated initials, suggesting that they were once the first pages of separate gatherings.[15] Mollisone's account indicates that material from 1434 onwards existed in bindings covering multi-year periods which sometimes differed from the periods covered by the present-day bindings.[16] At any rate, information recorded in this way could be bound into large volumes covering longer periods of time. This facilitated consultation and invited more elaborate exposition in an expandable format.[17]

Across the fifteenth century the way the common books were created continued to change and new forms of record-keeping emerged to complement the registers. One of the most significant changes was a great increase in the amount of writing in the registers from the beginning of the fifteenth century to the end. Anna Havinga's research shows that the average number of language tokens per year in the first volume of the register, covering 1398–1407, is 10,791, whereas the average per year by the seventh volume, covering 1487–1501, is 33,106. This suggests either that more business was being recorded in the city, or that what was recorded was now set down in greater detail. There is also an increase in the number of records in Scots. Havinga's calculations show that in volume one 0.24 per cent of entries are in Scots. In volume four (1433–1447) this rises to 5.57 per cent. By volume six (1468–1486) about one-third of entries are in Scots, rising to 63.89 per cent in volume eight (1501–1511).[18]

The near-complete survival of the common books of the fifteenth century also allows developments in the deployment of scribal apparatus to be traced. A major change in this area came in the use of marginal notes to highlight the contents of adjacent entries. In the earlier pages of volume four (1433–1447) there are few marginal additions. Occasionally a *manicula* or the word *nota* appears to highlight a particular entry or the name of an individual referred to in the entry. There is no clear pattern to the use of these additions and they appear either to have been added by the clerk as he worked to entries he deemed noteworthy (such as a series of abbreviated *nota* additions next to several statutes) or perhaps added later when a specific case was being consulted, as when '*nota* alexander coupar' appears next to an entry about Alexander Coupar on one page and 'alexander coupar' next to another entry about him on the next page.[19]

By the end of volume four and into volume five (part one) (1448–1466) names were used as marginal notes more systematically. They appeared next to entries which recorded legal cases that lasted for more than one sitting.[20] A common reason for cases stretching over several days was that parties being summoned to court did not attend. For each non-attendance they were subject to a fine. Highlighting these entries would have made it easy to find the stages of a particular legal process quickly, and to calculate the fine to be paid by someone who had been absent on one or more occasion. It is also in such entries that by far the most common usage of Arabic numerals occurs in these records. Arabic numerals are used to record the day of the process (first, second, third or fourth), whereas number words (e.g. 'three') are generally used when numbers are written elsewhere in the records.[21] This appears to be a further effort to make it easy to refer back to stages in such a case. A reader could thus scan the margin for a name, and then more quickly be able to identify what day of the process it was if they could also scan across for Arabic numerals rather than looking for a word in the flow of the entry text. From early in volume seven (1487–1501) marginal headings were used for almost every entry recorded as part of a court, rather than just for entries that were given a numbered day to refer to their place in an ongoing legal suit. These were evidently part of a systematic structuring of the register. Moreover, unlike the sporadic insertion of *nota*, *maniculae* and names in the margin next to entries highlighted for some particular reason after the point at which they were originally written, these headings were now apparently written before the main text of the entry itself. There are pages where the marginal headings are wrongly aligned to the entry they describe as well as cases where a marginal heading is given but no entry has been provided, clearly suggesting that the structure of marginal references was set up before the entries themselves were added.[22]

There are also signs of experimentation within the common books, which led to the creation of separate books for certain categories of information. Volume four includes the earliest known appearance of guild court records among those of the burgh, before they emerged into a specialised book of their own in the form of the guild court book covering the years 1441–1468.[23] It can be argued that the documentary change reflected the response of the burgh executive to the political instability that wracked the north-east of Scotland in this period, arising first from the murder of James I in 1437, and later from the civil conflict between James II and the Douglases in the 1450s.[24] For some reason, however, this specialisation appears to have been abandoned after 1468, and guild court records appeared once again in the main series of common books, albeit in far lower numbers than had occurred in the separate guild court book.[25] The later fifteenth century saw the creation of another specialised book, designated as a sasine register in archival catalogues, covering 1484–1502. It primarily consists of copies of land conveyances.[26] Other types of material also appear sporadically in this book, such as letters, a written version of an oath and records relating to various courts, including the sheriff court. This varied material suggests further ad hoc, experimental approaches to record-keeping were provoked by this new book.[27]

More was being written and much of it was in the vernacular.[28] What was written was made easier to consult, and careful choices were being made about what should be recorded and where. From the rolls of the fourteenth century to the increasingly voluminous and vernacular common books and the further specialised volumes that grew out of them, it seems clear that civic record-keeping in Aberdeen expanded considerably in the later middle ages, and particularly in the second half of the fifteenth century. An increasing volume of written material was consolidated into a form that was more physically compact and accessible than rolls.

Literate culture

The creation and development of Aberdeen's common books converged with several other developments across this period that served to increase engagement with the written word. Grant Simpson has argued that a 'silent revolution in lay literacy' took place in Scotland in the latter half of the fifteenth century. Roger Mason has linked this 'revolution' to the increasing availability of education through the new collegiate churches and universities of the period, the increasing involvement of laymen as legal practitioners and the reading and learning inherent in the humanist focus on classical texts. There was an increasing demand for access to the law, which Mark Godfrey has identified as crucial to the formation of a 'central' court of session and which, it is reasonable to assume, led to an increase in demand for legal writing. Written records in Scots began to appear from the late fourteenth century, and by the late fifteenth and early sixteenth century Scotland was experiencing what has been called the 'Aureate Age' of Scots literature, in the work of writers in the vernacular such as Robert Henryson and William Dunbar. Literary works in Scots were amongst the output of Scotland's first printing press, set up by Walter Chepman and Andrew Myllar in 1508.[29]

At the heart of many of these developments were notaries. Notaries were officers created by imperial, papal or royal authority to write legally binding documents. John Durkan and W.W. Scott have noted a substantial increase in evidence of notarial practice from the latter decades of the fourteenth century.[30] In relation to Aberdeen, Harold Booton observed that there was an increasing demand in the later middle ages for literate men to deal with often complex documents, in response to which a class of professional notaries developed to serve Aberdeen's burgesses and, to a lesser extent, local landed society. Some of them also served in burgh administration such as Sir John Stirling and Master David Nicholson as town clerks.[31] The rise of notaries symbolised growing faith in the written word and these men were gatekeepers to its official power and authority.

In a different way, town clerks also served this function, making that post a natural role for notaries to take on. The interest of such men in the written word extended beyond its use for the legal documents that formed the bulk of their day-to-day work. Aberdeen notary Andrew Cadiou translated Alain Chartier's *Bréviaire des nobles* into Scots in 1508 and one of Scotland's 'makars', Robert Henryson, is thought to have been a Dunfermline notary.[32] Indeed, Aberdeen and its immediate surroundings appear to have had a distinctive literate culture. The earliest surviving work of literature in Scots, John Barbour's *Bruce*, was written by an archdeacon of Aberdeen. The *Aberdeen Breviary*, compiled in the early sixteenth century, was completed under the supervision of William Elphinstone, bishop of Aberdeen. Saints related to Aberdeen and the north-east of Scotland made up the largest regional grouping of Scottish saints in the book.[33]

The link between literacy, literature and documentary practice has been attested elsewhere in this period. Sarah Rees Jones has highlighted how Thomas More's *Utopia* drew on More's familiarity with urban records as a magistrate of London, while Andy Wood has demonstrated that the contents of the Yarmouth Hutch formed the basis of two histories of the town in the late-sixteenth and early seventeenth centuries.[34] Aberdeen's medieval records do not appear to have been used directly in this way, but those who wrote and kept them certainly had literary interests, as demonstrated by the poems copied into the so-called sasine register of 1484–1502.[35] One anonymous poem in the register directly addresses the power and reach of the written word with the following metaphor:

> And al the wode in to the warld' at growis
> Wer crafty pennis convenient to write
> An al the sey undir the hevin at flowis
> Wer changite in Ink and wer' so infinite
> And al the erd' wer' plesand papir quhite[36]

All of this suggests that the keeping of common books was in part born of, and contributed to, a growing trend among Scots to understand the world through writing. In this light, the Aberdeen common books can be viewed as part of a late medieval European trend towards increased use of written records which, alongside developments such as print technology, laid the foundations for a major growth in literacy in the early modern period.[37]

Documentary culture in Aberdeen

By the later middle ages, written records were in regular use in Aberdeen. In the common books, there is evidence of the burgh administration archiving documents going back hundreds of years. Written on the front and back of a folded page in the part of volume seven dated to 1492 is an inventory of the town's muniments, including charters from William I, Robert I, James III and other kings, at least some of which still survive in the city's collections.[38] As well as holding royal documents confirming burgh privileges, the burgh administration created and kept records of its own. It employed town clerks. The common books offer by far the most substantial extant evidence of these clerks' work, but the burgh administration was represented by other forms of writing, from letters to account books, written by town clerks and others.[39]

Records were also created and kept in the burgh beyond the confines of the burgh administration. Such were the accumulations of written material by some residents of Aberdeen that they appear to have assembled substantial personal archives of documents recording their rights. An entry from Aberdeen in 1465 refers to certain charters of John of Mar and his nephew which were 'tane away fra him vnwittandely'. When he openly asked about them in the kirk, this led to John Blinseile coming forward to admit that he had the charters and to explain how they had come into his possession.[40] There is also evidence of individuals within the town creating their own records. One Andrew Winton was asked in 1492 to provide evidence from his own 'cownt buk' (account book) to show how much he was owed by Mathew Toschow.[41]

Evidence from within the common books illustrates how they interacted with the wider documentary culture of the town as well as the world beyond its boundaries. One such interaction was the appearance of other documents copied into the books. These include incoming documents, such as letters from the king, and outgoing documents, such as a written assurance given to French merchants by the burgh authorities in 1495.[42] These are distinct from written acts entered directly into the books rather than as copies. For instance, a record of an agreement between an Aberdeen burgess and a merchant of Lille made in 1463 refers to its own writing, noting that the agreement was 'ackyt in the commone buke of Aberdeen with the common clerkis hande' and 'signyt with his signe manuale', which appears below it.[43]

The bulk of what was written in the common books consisted of the ongoing records of burgh administration rather than copies or original acts and, leaving aside the probability that such records were copied from notes or drafts, they were written up especially for these books. Nevertheless, the books often referred to other written records brought forward in the court and incorporated information from these other records. An entry from October 1488 outlines complex proceedings concerning the rights of land in the burgh disputed by Will Moir and his nephew John Moir. The entry contains frequent references to other documents and the actions performed with them. It notes that Sir John Rutherfurd, acting as procurator to John Moir, 'producit' an instrument of procuratory and an instrument of sasine breaking, and that these instruments were 'opinly rede'. The court then asked for the 'richtis' of both parties. Rutherfurd produced those for the nephew, but the uncle disobeyed and left the court. It was decided that Rutherfurd was thus to remain in control of the lands in the name of John Moir until more 'richtis', presumably those asked of Will Moir, were shown to the court.[44] This entry illustrates the density of other written documentation that often lay behind the information recorded in the common books.

Of course, 'richtis' and 'evidencis' called upon in court proceedings recorded in the common books could be from earlier records in the books themselves. The record of a legal action from February 1471 stipulated that the judgement depended on earlier evidence from the registers. To resolve a dispute over a barrel of salmon and some hides between William Vokat and William Anderson, Vokat was asked to show an act to support his case from the common book and, if he could, William Anderson would have to fulfil his obligation as stated in the act.[45] If he could not find such an act it would be judged that Anderson had already fulfilled his obligations. Another entry, from April 1498, makes reference to an earlier record in the books. It notes that William Anderson – possibly the same person as in the previous example – had been paid by Thomas Raneir on behalf of his brother John Anderson and states that the payment was made in accordance with a record of the debt 'contenit in this book'.[46] A search of the books appears to reveal the earlier entry to which the 1498 entry referred, which occurred three and a half years earlier in September 1494.[47] Searches of the records could be more extensive than this. In a dispute over fishings in Aberdeen in 1504 an attempt was made to find a jury (in Scots called an assize) that both parties agreed was impartial. This effort was unsuccessful and the record states that the case was then delayed for eight days 'quhile the ald bukis be secht for the declaracioun of the verite'.[48]

These examples show how deeply networked the information in the common books was, and how they formed part of an expanding use of records in the burgh as a whole, at least for those wealthy, influential or – in records such as those recording punishments or fines – unfortunate enough to have business that needed recording. As well as increasing the volume of written documentation produced and kept in Aberdeen, the registers supplied context which linked other documents to each other as well as with original information in the register. Moreover, different records within the register linked to each other across days, weeks, months and even years. The books, then, acted like a switchboard in a wider network of written records, and perhaps emphasised the value of making and keeping written records to town dwellers and others who came into contact with the burgh administration. More directly, it gave those who controlled the burgh's administration an increasingly useful tool with which to navigate knowledge about power and property in the burgh's past and present, knowledge which they could employ to inform and justify their decisions.

Documents as objects

The common books and their relationship to other documents should not be understood purely in terms of literacy, however. Brian Stock has written that 'literacy is not textuality. One can be literate without the overt use of texts, and one can use texts extensively without evidencing literacy'[49]. Andy Wood, writing of memory and custom in early modern England noted that the sensory or material was intertwined with the cerebral or literate.[50] Richard Firth Green found that in late medieval England, 'written documents might still be regarded as potent artifacts' and the written word 'objectified, fetishised and demonised'.[51] Much of what is written in the common books concerns rituals that governed aspects of life in the town such as the punishment of transgressors or the transfer of lands within the town. For example, people found guilty of crimes could be made to process with candles they paid for as fines and prostrate themselves barefooted and bareheaded, wearing only a gown, before their victims at the high altar in St Nicholas parish church, sometimes offering up the knife with which they had committed the crime.[52] 'Earth and stone' were presented before the court as part of the ritual involved in recovering burgage lands for which rent had not been paid.[53] Kathryn Reyerson has described such rituals as 'rituals of medieval business'. They were not like the dramatic rituals of royal entries or coronations, but rather 'repeated actions and gestures of a formal nature' which provided assurance and asserted legitimacy.[54]

Written records not only described such rituals, they could be used in them. The power invested in ritual involving written documents is suggested by records of a court case in Aberdeen involving John of Kintore, Robert Boyd and Henry Hartwitson in 1468.[55] The case centred around a dispute over barrels of salmon. According to the depositions of witnesses, Henry Hartwitson was owed two barrels each from both John and Robert. Robert had given two barrels to Henry. The dispute arose because Robert said these had been paid to settle John's debt, whereas Henry insisted that they had settled Robert's own debt. Why this distinction was so crucial to these people is not clear, but most relevant for the present argument is the testimony of Isabell, Robert Boyd's wife.[56] What she appears to have said is that Henry brought Robert's 'obligation' (that is, the document that acted as a receipt of the debt and which was to be returned when the debt was cleared) to Robert but that Robert asked for John's obligation instead because this was the debt he believed to have been paid. An argument seems to have developed as Robert refused to take the obligation for his own debt which Henry had brought. Henry then apparently tried to throw the obligation into the hands of Isabell but her husband told her not to take it. At this point, Henry picked up the obligation and threw it into the fire, and in response Robert took it 'apon his sawle' that Henry had been paid of two barrels of John's salmon. The emphasis placed on physical contact with the record of debt in this case, and the inclusion of the detailed narrative of these events in legal proceedings, illustrates the potent materiality of written records and echoes Firth Green's observation of late medieval England that 'documents were sometimes still thought of as somehow symbolizing, rather than merely recording, the legal facts to which they attested'.[57]

The civic archives that encompassed the common books also functioned as a focus for ritual under the control of the burgh government. Indeed, the origins of the common books closely coincided with the building of a new tolbooth, the centre of administrative ritual in civic government. This major change to the burgh was initiated in 1393 when Robert III issued a charter granting Aberdeen the right to build a new tolbooth. Tolbooths, among other functions, provided sites for civic archives. Sarah Rees Jones has argued that 'leaps forward' in civic record-keeping in medieval England coincided with periods of significant change to the civic landscape.[58] Within the tolbooth, it is likely that in the fifteenth century, common books, in whatever physical form they existed at the time, were kept in the 'common kyst' (common chest). This was a forerunner to the extant 'meikle kist' (great chest) which was ordered in 1591 at the time Thomas Mollisone made an inventory of the burgh's records.[59] Recent work on the Yarmouth Hutch gives an indication of how such chests were used. The Hutch, which had existed since at least 1542, held a diverse collection of records of the town's rights. By the late sixteenth century it comprised 'an iron-bound oaken trunk and an array of boxes, compartments and shelves' and there was a Hutch book which recorded loans of documents and new additions to the collection.[60] Evidence for Aberdeen's 'common kyst' from the Aberdeen Council Registers shows that documents were placed in and produced from the kist; that financial calculations were made on it; that the common clerk appears to have been responsible for looking after it; and that it was furnished with some kind of enclosure.[61] One entry also reveals its use as the focal point of a ritual of forgiveness of the type which usually took place in St Nicholas Kirk. In 1488, William Portar was found guilty of a breach of the peace at the burgh's bailies' court and, to make amends, he was asked to come to the tolbooth door and then come before the common kist bareheaded to beseech the alderman and the council to ask Andrew Branch, the bailie, to remit the offence Portar had done to him, after which Portar was to sit down on one knee and ask Branch's forgiveness.[62] This substituted the tolbooth for the church and the kist for the altar, with the enclosure around the kist further suggesting this physical and conceptual parallel.

The common books, too, had power as objects which went beyond the strictly literate use of their contents. The keeping of these records in a form, which meant many years' worth of judgements and ordinances laid down by the burgh authorities could be contained in a single object, meant that the registers could function as a powerful symbol of the authority of the burgh community. In April 1474 David Collison was given the special privilege of being allowed to be the first to present someone to become a burgess after a year when no burgesses were to be made except for sons of burgesses. The reason he was given this privilege was that he had secured the return, presumably by making a payment on behalf of the burgh, of a common book which had been given as a guarantee to John of Mar.[63] The value of the book in this case was presumably not the inherent value of its materials or the information within it, but its value as a symbol of the burgh community and its good faith. As Mar appears to have been an active participant in Aberdeen's burgh government, this example shows the symbolic value of the book only in the context of the burgh community rather than to an outside party.[64] Even so, the common books, much like the tolbooth and the common seals, were functional objects but also symbols that legitimised the rule of the town elite as representatives of 'the communite of the burgh'.[65]

Access and control

Written records, then, were widely used in late medieval Aberdeen, both within and beyond the civic administration. The creation of common books offered a new and powerful means of gathering information and linking that information internally within the books and externally to other documents. At least some members of the burgh community were able to request to see, or have copies made of, records within the common books. Challenge to the records could be considered a significant offence. In 1505, Sir John Stirling, notary and common clerk, protested in the burgh's bailie court about a complaint that had been made against him by Matthew Branch. He noted that Branch had taken issue with

> ane act of the saide court buk … sayande he sulde preiwe the saide act fals in four of fiwe poyntis to the gret Infamite ande dishonor to the saide bailyeis sittande as Jugez ande hyme that wrait the saide act [John Stirling].[66]

Despite his denial that he had ever made the complaint, Branch was found guilty and made to

> sit one his kneis and ask the saide ser Johne forgefnes Ande thareftir the said Mathou deponit the gret aitht that the saide ser Johne was leile faithfule and trewe man and notor in ale his dowingis Ande hed med the said act Ande ale ponntis contenit in It Ande that the saide was leile and treue in ale ponntis contenit in It Alsua the said Mathou askit the saide bailyeis and notor forgefnes,

as well as paying a stone of wax to the holy blood shrine of the parish church and £20 to the building's upkeep.[67] This was the kind of punishment given to those who had committed acts of violence and it is telling of the extent to which the authority of the common books was guarded by the civic administration.

As we have seen, the internal evidence of the common books suggests they were used increasingly across the fifteenth century, just as a range of other developments increased engagement with the written word. As the heart of a network of documents these books – and the civic archive of which they were a substantial part – must have been recognised for their potential as a means of reinforcing and maintaining the position of magistrate dynasties for which the continued prosperity of the burgh community was not an abstract ideal, but a means of ensuring the hegemony of their family and name in the generations to come. While the books presented an 'institutional possibility' that may have fed into wider changes in the consumption of law, it was a possibility introduced primarily for the small elite that dominated Aberdeen's civic institutions, and one which helped enforce their social and political control of the town.[68] The marriage of civic leadership with writing and archival practices was literally embodied by the sixteenth-century Menzies family which came to hold the office of provost (alderman) and town clerk simultaneously in the person of Thomas Menzies.[69]

Conclusion

Aberdeen's common books grew in size and sophistication concurrently with developments across Europe that made written records an increasingly common feature of everyday life. In a town with an already active documentary culture, they became a hub that acted as a reference point for a wider hinterland of documents. A side effect of this may have been to stimulate the wider use of written records, but the real purpose of the common books, born of the recognition of the power of written records by the town's governing elite, was to put writing in their service rather than to create a resource to benefit the population of the town more broadly. This is not to say that the wider population did not have opportunities to benefit from the existence of common books – as we have seen, the ideology of community held by the civic elite was that what was good for them was good for the community as a whole and to retain its power this idea must at least sometimes have accorded with reality. Nevertheless, these books offered the entrenched oligarchy of Aberdeen ways of buttressing their power and control over the town's memory and resistance to this hegemony could be met with strong punishments. The common books, like other objects at the focus of civic ritual such as the common kist and the tolbooth, were at the administrative nexus of an urban culture of law. They reinforced an urban ideology of community in which the needs of a wealthy elite were made synonymous with the needs of the many even as they formed part of a European documentary revolution that would ultimately open up the power of the written word up to many more people.[70]

Notes

1 These registers survive as a near-complete series from 1398 up to the present day, with the only significant gap occurring between 1414 and 1433. For further comment on this missing material and surviving excerpts from it, see 'Uncovering Scotland's "UNESCO heritage"', 22 November 2016, available at <https://www.abdn.ac.uk/news/10171/> (accessed 10 December 2019). The transcriptions of the first eight volumes of these registers are now available digitally as E. Frankot, A.D. Havinga, C. Hawes, W. Hepburn, W. Peters, J. Armstrong, P. Astley, A. Mackillop, A.R.C. Simpson and A. Wyner (eds) *Aberdeen Registers Online: 1398–1511*, Aberdeen: University of Aberdeen, 2019, <www.abdn.ac.uk/aro> (accessed 21 December 2019) (hereafter ARO entry ID). For descriptions of surviving burgh records across Scotland, see D. Robertson, 'Burgh court records, 1319–1834' in *An Introductory Survey of the Sources and Literature of Scots Law* (Edinburgh: Stair Society, 1936), pp. 98–110 and A. Murray, 'Whatever happened to the Scottish burgh records?', *Journal of Irish and Scottish Studies* 9(2), 2018 (special issue: 'Scottish urban archives and histories: Context and a legal historical perspective', J.W. Armstrong and A. Mackillop (eds)), pp. 10–28.

2 The books fit into a genre of records that are often called town books, though this term is not used in Aberdeen. For instance, from the 1350s Swedish laws stated that all judicial proceedings in the town should be recorded in the *stadens bok* (town book) which was kept by the town scribe. Inger Larsson argues that while in the 1350s *stadens bok* may have referred to a single book, by the early fifteenth century *stadens bok* was a legal term which encompassed a range of specialised registers; Inger Larsson, 'Producing, using, and keeping records in medieval Swedish towns' in M. Mostert and A. Adamska (eds) *Writing and the Administration of Medieval Towns*, Turnhout: Brepols, 2014, pp. 13–30, at 23.

3 C. Hawes, 'The urban community in fifteenth-century Scotland: Language, law and political practice', *Urban History* 44(3), 2017 (special section: 'Communities, courts and Scottish towns', J.W. Armstrong and A. Mackillop (eds)), pp. 365–80, at p. 369; the malleable use of 'community' in late medieval Scotland is discussed further in Claire Hawes, 'Community and public authority in later fifteenth-century Scotland', unpublished PhD thesis, University of St Andrews, 2015, particularly at pp. 50–8.

4 Hawes, 'The urban community', p. 14.

5 For E.P. Dennison, medieval Scottish burghs and the power associated with them, despite perhaps having a greater sense of 'oneness' than their English counterparts, epitomised inequality through their stratification of urban society; E. Patricia Dennison, 'Power to the people? The Myth of the medieval burgh community', in S. Foster, A. Macinnes and R. Macinnes (eds) *Scottish Power Centres from the Early Middle Ages to the Twentieth Century*, Glasgow: Cruithne, 1998, pp. 100–31, at pp. 112–8.

6 Harold Booton identifies the 11 elite families of late medieval Aberdeen as the Blinseiles, the Chalmers, the Cullens, the Collisons, the Fichets, the Mars, the Menzies, the Rutherfurds and the Prats (H. Booton, 'Burgesses and landed men in north-east Scotland in the later middle ages', unpublished PhD thesis, University of Aberdeen, 1987, p. 105).

7 Hawes, 'Community and public authority', p. 58.

8 This is discussed in a forthcoming article by the authors; G. Small and W. Hepburn, 'Reading the social history of the archive outside-in: Writing and power, c. 1400–1600'.

9 This essay will refer to these books as common books except when referring to their modern bindings and archival classification as part of the Aberdeen Council Registers series: Aberdeen City & Aberdeenshire Archives (hereafter ACAA), CA/1/1, Aberdeen Council, Baillie, and Guild Court Registers.

10 Under the influence of Michel Foucault, power has been a key theme in the 'archival turn': A. Walsham, K. Peters and L. Corens, 'Introduction: Archives and information in the early modern world', in L. Corens, K. Peters and A. Walsham (eds) *Archives and Information in the Early Modern World*, Oxford: Oxford University Press, 2018, pp. 1–25, at p. 3. In contrast, it has been argued that the parish registers of early modern England were intended to service parishioners' needs (Andrew Gordon, 'The paper parish: The parish register and the reformation of parish memory in early modern London', *Memory Studies* 11(1), 2018, pp. 51–68, at p. 53).

11 M. Clanchy, *From Memory to Written Record: England 1066–1307*, Chichester: Wiley-Blackwell, 2013, and D.L. Smail, *The Consumption of Justice: Emotions, Publicity and Legal Culture in Marseille, 1264–1423*, London: Cornell University Press, 2003, p. 213.

12 J.A. Cripps, 'Report to City of Aberdeen District Council on Missing Register of Council, 26 June 1981'; J. Stuart, 'The editor's preface', in *Miscellany of the Spalding Club*, vol. 5, Aberdeen: Spalding Club, 1852, p. 9. The earliest version of Mollisone's inventory, though less detailed than some of the later versions discussed by Cripps, can be found in L.B. Taylor (ed. and trans.) *Aberdeen Council Letters*, vol. 1, 1552–1633, London: Oxford University Press, 1942, pp. 47–50.

13 ACAA, CA/5/6, the 'Burgh Court Roll'; A.R.C. Simpson and J.W. Armstrong (eds and trans.) 'The roll of the burgh courts of Aberdeen, August–October 1317', in M. Godfrey (ed.) *Miscellany Eight*, Edinburgh: Stair Society, 2020, pp. 57–93.

14 Cripps, 'Report'; W.C. Dickinson (ed.) *Early Records of the Burgh of Aberdeen, 1317. 1398–1407*, Edinburgh: Scottish History Society, 1957, p. vi and ACAA, CA/3/A2/67, 'Catalogue of the Registers and Court Books of Aberdeen'.

15 For example, ARO-1-0071-01 (6 October 1399) and ARO-2-0101-03 (6 October 1410).

16 For instance, the inventory describes a book covering 1434–1460, whereas the current volume starting in 1434 runs only to 1447 (Cripps, 'Report'). Project volunteer John Corral has recently identified a reference to the rebinding of the registers, which appears to refer to the earliest form of bindings which still survive in the present day: ACAA, CA/1/1/61, p. 88 (22 October 1742).

17 For the advantages of books over rolls, see Clanchy, *From Memory to Written Record*, pp. 118, 135–44.
18 A. Havinga, 'The vernacularisation of the Aberdeen Council Registers (1398–1511)', in this volume.
19 For example, ARO-4-0033-05 (February 1435); ARO-4-0030-10 (13 December 1434) and ARO-4-0031-02 (16 December 1434).
20 For example, ARO-5-0323-03 (28 November 1457).
21 For example, The use of 'three' in ARO-5-0119-06 (17 May 1451). The 'process of the four courts' is described in Dickinson, *Early Records*, pp. cxxxi–ii.
22 For example, ARO-7-0192-03 (25 August 1490).
23 This book has been transcribed in a modern edition: Elizabeth Gemmill (ed.) *Aberdeen Guild Court Records, 1437–1468*, Edinburgh: Scottish History Society, 2005.
24 Small and Hepburn, 'Reading the social history of the archive outside-in'; Stephen Boardman, 'The burgh and the realm: Medieval politics, c. 1100–1500', in E.P. Dennison, D. Ditchburn and M. Lynch (eds) *Aberdeen Before 1800: A New History*, East Linton: Tuckwell, 2002, pp. 203–23, at pp. 213–9.
25 Gemmill, *Aberdeen Guild Court*, pp. 1–2.
26 ACAA, CA/2/1/1.
27 This book is discussed further in Edda Frankot's contribution to this volume, in which she questions the use of the term 'sasine register' to describe it.
28 It should be noted that the Sasine Register was almost entirely in Latin.
29 G.G. Simpson, *Scottish Handwriting, 1150–1650: An Introduction to the Reading of Documents*, Edinburgh: Bratton, 1973, p. 12. Simpson highlights a record from Dundee in 1476 which 'casually reveals' a merchant having produced a legal deed in his own handwriting (p. 11); R. Mason, '"Regnum et Imperium": Humanism and political culture in early renaissance Scotland', in R. Mason (ed.) *Kingship and the Commonweal: Political Thought in Renaissance and Reformation Scotland*, East Linton: Tuckwell, 1998, pp. 104–38; and A.M. Godfrey, *Civil Justice in Renaissance Scotland: The Origins of a Central Court*, Leiden: Brill, 2009. The term 'Aureate Age' was used by Ranald Nicholson to describe the flourishing cultural activity of Scotland in the late fifteenth and early sixteenth centuries (R. Nicholson, *Scotland: The Later Middle Ages*, Edinburgh: Oliver and Boyd, 1974, pp. 576–606). There was a marked increase in the use of paper in Europe in the later middle ages, and the significance of this to Aberdeen's record-keeping practices is discussed in Small and Hepburn, 'Reading the social history of the archive outside-in'.
30 J. Durkan, 'The early Scottish notary', in I. Cowan and D. Shaw (eds) *The Renaissance and Reformation in Scotland*, Edinburgh: Scottish Academic Press, 1983, pp. 22–40, at p. 23 and W.W. Scott, 'William Cranston, notary public c. 1395–1425, and some contemporaries', in H.L. Macqueen (ed.) *Miscellany Seven*, Edinburgh: Stair Society, 2015, pp. 125–32.
31 Booton, 'Burgesses and landed men', p. 8.
32 H. Booton, 'John and Andrew Cadiou: Aberdeen notaries of the fifteenth and early sixteenth centuries', *Northern Scotland* 9, 1989, pp. 17–20, at p. 19; E.P.D. Torrie, 'The guild in fifteenth-century Dunfermline', in M. Lynch, M. Spearman and G. Stell (eds) *The Scottish Medieval Town*, Edinburgh: John Donald, 1988, pp. 245–60, at p. 260, n. 40; and see also A.R.C. Simpson, 'Andrew Alanson: Man of law in the Aberdeen Council Register, c. 1440–c. 1475?', in this volume. *Makar*, broadly meaning 'maker' in Middle Scots, was used for authors of literary works. In modern times, the term is applied to three poets of the fifteenth and sixteenth centuries in particular: Gavin Douglas, William Dunbar and Robert Henryson.
33 T. Turpie, 'North-Eastern Scottish saints in the Aberdeen Breviary and the *Historia Gentis Scotorum* of Hector Boece: Liturgy, history and religious practice in late medieval Scotland', in J. Geddes (ed.) *Medieval Art, Architecture and Archaeology in the Dioceses of Aberdeen and Moray*, Abingdon: Routledge, 2016, pp. 239–47, at pp. 239–40, and

N. Royan, 'Aberdeen and St Andrews', in D. Wallace (ed.) *Europe: A Literary History, 1348–1418*, vol. 1, Oxford: Oxford University Press, 2016, pp. 363–76.

34 S. Rees Jones, 'Thomas More's Utopia and medieval London', in R. Horrox and S. Rees Jones (eds) *Pragmatic Utopias: Ideals and Communities, 1200–1630*, Cambridge: Cambridge University Press, 2001, pp. 117–35, and A. Wood, 'Tales from the "Yarmouth Hutch": Civic identities and hidden histories in an urban archive', *Past and Present* 230, Supplement 11, 2016, pp. 213–30.

35 In the later sixteenth century, Walter Cullen, 'reader and later vicar of Aberdeen', blended genres of writing in what is known as the *Aberdeen Chronicle*, which Sebastiaan Verweij has described as 'a generically confused mass of materials: part parish register, part family history, part commonplace book, part verse miscellany' (S. Verweij, *The Literary Culture of Early Modern Scotland: Manuscript Production and Transmission, 1560–1625*, Oxford: Oxford University Press, 2016, p. 132). Priscilla Bawcutt has argued that much older Scots poetry would have been lost were it not for the tendency of clerks to copy them into official documents on which they were working (P. Bawcutt, 'The earliest texts of Dunbar', in F. Riddy (ed.) *Regionalism in Late Medieval Manuscripts and Texts*, Cambridge: Brewer, 1991, pp. 183–98, at p. 185).

36 ACAA, CA/2/1/1, p. 172 (u/v spellings modernised); H.M. Shire and A. Fenton. 'The sweepings of parnassus: Four poems transcribed from the record books of the burgh sasines of Aberdeen', *Aberdeen University Review* 36(1), 1955, pp. 43–54.

37 See for example the work of E. Ketelaar: 'Records out and archives in: Early modern cities as creators of records and as communities of archives', *Archival Science* 10, 2010, pp. 201–10, and E. Ketelaar, 'Muniments as monuments. The dawn of archives as cultural patrimony', *Archival Science* 7, 2007, pp. 343–57.

38 ARO-7-0365-01 (date uncertain); the creation of this inventory may have been related to the burgh's defence of long-held rights to the forest of Stocket, which were threatened by several grants of rights in and around the burgh made to the king's servant and sea captain Andrew Wood in the 1490s (Boardman, 'The burgh and the realm', pp. 206–7).

39 For instance, an entry from 13 July 1498 shows the alderman John Rutherford submitting a written financial account (ARO-7-0884-04).

40 ARO-5-0547-07 (7 May 1465).

41 ARO-7-0360-01 (27 October 1492).

42 ARO-7-0696-03 (24 December 1495).

43 ARO-5-0483-05 (20 March 1464).

44 ARO-7-0080-05 (6 October 1488).

45 ARO-6-0137-07 (4 February 1471).

46 ARO-7-0872-02 (10 April 1497).

47 ARO-7-0562-03 (12 September 1494).

48 ARO-8-0357-03 (12 July 1504).

49 B. Stock, *The Implications of Literacy: Written Language and Models of Interpretation in the Eleventh and Twelfth Centuries*, Princeton, NJ: Princeton University Press, 1983, p. 7; Stock's work forms part of a wider debate about the interaction between orality and literacy framed by scholars such as Jack Goody and Walter Ong.

50 A. Wood, *The Memory of the People: Custom and Popular Senses of the Past in Early Modern England*, Cambridge: Cambridge University Press, 2013, p. 252. See generally, A. Walsham, 'The social history of the archive: Record-keeping in early modern Europe', *Past and Present* 230, Supplement 11, 2016, pp. 9–48.

51 R.F. Green, *A Crisis of Truth: Literature and Law in Ricardian England*, Philadelphia: University of Pennsylvania Press, 2002, pp. 249, 251. Green highlights the presence of the written word in medieval Christian iconography, such as the 'the widespread image of the suffering Christ as a crucified charter or book spread our upon the writing desk of the cross and lettered with the ink of his blood', as evidence of the treatment of the written word with 'awe and mystery' (pp. 259–63).

52 For example, ARO-6-0416-01 (16 January 1476).

53 For example, ARO-6-0133-03 (7 January 1471), which refers to earth and stone being presented in a bag; Dickinson, *Early Records*, p. cxx.

54 K. Reyerson, 'Rituals in medieval business', in J. Rollo-Koster (ed.) *Medieval and Early Modern Ritual: Formalized Behaviour in Europe, China and Japan*, Leiden: Brill, 2002, pp. 81–103.

55 ARO-6-0006-03 (date uncertain).

56 Isabell's surname is not given.

57 Green, *A Crisis of Truth*, p. 275.

58 ACAA, CA/3/A1/24; S. Rees Jones, 'Civic literacy in later medieval England', in M. Mostert and A. Adamska (eds) *Writing and the Administration of Medieval Towns*, Turnhout: Brepols, 2014, pp. 219–30, at p. 224.

59 Cripps, 'Report'; The 'meikle kist' can be viewed today in Aberdeen's Tolbooth Museum and its key is in the collections of Aberdeen Art Gallery and Museums; 'Meikle Kist Key', *Aberdeen Art Gallery and Museums*, online, available at <http://www.aagm.co.uk/theCollections/objects/object/Meikle-Kist-Key> (accessed 6 December 2019).

60 Wood, 'Yarmouth Hutch', p. 216.

61 ARO-7-0145-03 (9 October 1489); ARO-7-1051-04 (8 May 1500); ARO-7-0454-06 (9 August 1493); ARO-6-0976-01 (13 November 1486); and ARO-7-0880-06 (15 June 1498).

62 ARO-7-0090-04 (14 November 1488).

63 ARO-6-0295-08 (27 April 1474): this may be the same John of Mar as in the entry from 1465 mentioned earlier; the town's seals too were symbols of the burgh community's authority and a record from 1447 tells us that the town paid off a debt it owed to Thomas Bernwale of London to ensure the return of the common seal, which had apparently been given as a guarantee of the debt: ARO-5-0723-01 (24 October 1447).

64 See, for instance, a John of Mar listed as part of a group of men chosen by the council in August 1474 to assess who still had to pay two recent taxes or owed any rents on burgh properties: ARO-6-0309-01 (26 August 1474).

65 A snapshot of part of this group in 1480 can be seen in the record of the receipt of a letter from the king to the alderman, council and community of Aberdeen: ARO-6-0609-09 (18 January 1480).

66 ARO-8-0462-01 (14 June 1505); translation:

> … an act of the said court book … saying he would prove the said act false in four or five of its points, to the great infamy and dishonour of the said bailies sitting as judges and he that wrote the said act [John Stirling].

67 ARO-8-0476-05 (4 August 1505); translation:

> … sit on his knees and ask the said Sir John forgiveness. And thereafter the said Matthew deposed under the great oath that said Sir John was a just, faithful and honest man and notary in all his doings and had made the said act and all points contained in it and that the said act was just and honest in all points contained in it. Also, the said Matthew asked the said bailies and notary for forgiveness.

68 David Nelken contends, drawing on Lawrence Friedman and others, that insisting on this dichotomy between 'external' (i.e. related to wider range of social groups that interact with the law; 'demand for law') and 'internal' (i.e. related to legal profession; 'supply of law') legal culture is likely to obscure more than it reveals and that access to the law depends on the institutional possibilities provided: D. Nelken, 'Using the concept of legal culture', *Australian Journal of Legal Philosophy* 29, 2004, pp. 1–26, at pp. 8–9.

69 The sixteenth-century Menzies family are covered at length in A. White, 'Religion, politics and society in Aberdeen, 1543–1593', unpublished PhD thesis, University of Edinburgh, 1985.

70 See now R. Head, *Making Archives in Early Modern Europe. Proof, Information, and Political Record-keeping, 1400–1700*, Cambridge: Cambridge University Press, 2019 and M. Friedrich, *The Birth of the Archive: A History of Knowledge*, trans. J.N. Dillon, Ann Arbor: University of Michigan Press, 2018.

3

THE LANGUAGE OF MEDIEVAL LEGAL RECORD AS A COMPLEX MULTILINGUAL CODE

Joanna Kopaczyk

Introduction

The language of legal record in late medieval urban cultures was multilingual at its core. Latin was still the main written language but the local languages were being incorporated into legal discourse all over Europe. Some authors interpret that linguistic situation as *diglossia*, with Latin acting as the more prestigious 'high' language and the local language having a lower status.[1] Some others talk about a competition between languages, as if they were in a struggle to dominate the written record.[2] I would like to argue that the interactions and hierarchies of linguistic ingredients are more nuanced and stem from the choices made by the multilingual scribe who wrote in a specific local context. Such simultaneous employment of multiple languages should be analysed in a systematic way in order to understand its impact on the overall tenor of the documents. This chapter offers a structural framework designed to pinpoint switches between languages on all levels of linguistic complexity in a communicative event, and illustrates this complexity with examples from fourteenth- and fifteenth-century documents. To showcase the interplay of Latin and the local language in a broader European perspective, the discussion draws on two geographically distant legal cultures of medieval Europe: Scotland and Poland.[3] Illustrative examples come from two roughly contemporary sources: the *Linguistic Atlas of Older Scots (1380–1500)* (henceforth LAOS),[4] whose underlying database comprises diplomatic transcripts of legal and administrative texts from medieval Scotland, and the *Electronic Repository of Greater Poland Oaths (1386–1448)* (henceforth eRO-ThA), which contains diplomatic transcripts of Old Polish oaths – the earliest extant record of that language outside the religious context – embedded in Latin land court books.[5] I start by introducing the notion of *code* as applied to human communication and ask how this term relates to situations involving more than one language, with emphasis on historical contexts. After summarising the current research on historical multilingualism, the discussion moves on to consider why legal register can be treated as a single code composed of more than one linguistic resource. The core of this argument rests on the roles of the writers and audiences involved, their cognitive abilities and engagement with the text. Against this background, I present a detailed illustration of the interplay between Latin and the vernaculars – Scots[6] and Polish[7] – and (sub)code-switching on various levels of linguistic structure: from macrogenres to the level of spelling units. I also point out the significance of the presence – or absence – of visual cues for the switch. The multilingual code of medieval administrative record is then showcased in a single mid-fifteenth century text from the protocol book of the notary James Young, where the roles and forms of Latin and Scots are observed and related to the framework introduced earlier. The chapter closes with overall reflections on the cultural implications of multilingualism in the medieval northern European legal context.

Languages as codes

Code is usually perceived as something secret, shared by a closed group of people, but also as something of significance to that group or to those who stay on the outside. Language is essentially a system of arbitrary signs,[8] while meaning can be *en*coded and *de*coded by humans who are equipped with the necessary cognitive and interpretative abilities. This is why individual languages are conceptualised in linguistic research as separate codes. If two or more languages are encountered within the same communicative event – the same text, the same manuscript, the same dialogue – the shift from one language to the other can be conceptualised as *code-switching*, in line with Haugen's classic definition of this phenomenon as an 'alternate use of two languages'.[9]

In this chapter I argue that despite the mixture of Latin and the vernacular in medieval legal texts, we still deal with a single code. This code has a complex structure – it is composed of multilingual ingredients which are used in a range of functions and whose proportions and forms vary across time. What is crucial for the legal culture using this code is that the code remains accessible and flexible for the community involved in local administrative and legal proceedings.[10]

Even though much linguistic work on code-switching originated in the context of spoken language,[11] of special importance for this study is the more recent recognition of the multilingual nature of *written* texts, which demand an analytical framework suited to their communicative characteristics and a broader cultural context.[12] For historical linguistics, which relies on written record, it is important not to dismiss writing as a somehow deficient version of 'language', or treat it only as an opaque window onto the elusive spoken communication of the past. Much has been done to acknowledge the systemic nature of writing in its own right, especially in the last two decades on the wave of historical sociolinguistics and pragmatics (pragmaphilology) as well as in the study of semiotics of code-switching in a written text.[13] These publications as well as the present chapter share the conviction that 'the material expression of the text is always significant; it is a separately variable semiotic frame'.[14] Within this frame, conventionally agreed linguistic signs – morphemes, words, phrases – interact according to systematic rules; their arrangement becomes significant to those who understand these rules.

The choice of the system of signs, together with its conventional associations, carries meaning in its own right; some systems may, for instance, be more prestigious than others; some may require specialist knowledge or cultural experience to unpack. Socially oriented semiotic approaches to language use set out to understand which codes were selected for which purpose and how these choices related to a given culture. They also ask what the codes tell us about the participants of that culture.[15] In the medieval context, formulaic language was framed in different (sub)codes, Latin and the vernacular, each working within a set of associated conventions: those for Latin accumulated through centuries of legal practices[16] and those for the vernacular beginning to emerge.[17]

More than one language, more than one code?

Linguistic approaches to historical multilingualism

Due to the preoccupation of modern linguistics with speech, the theoretical and data-driven approaches to code-switching until the 2000s were devised on the basis of spoken exchanges.[18] A notable exception to this trend as well as a springboard for later work on historical multilingualism can be seen in the early work on mixed-language texts, including the so-called macaronic texts (e.g. sermons or verse mixing Latin grammar and vernacular words), and on multilingualism in Middle English literature.[19] For the study of historical multilingual communication, the analytical framework for code-switching had to be adapted to the medium, and this conceptual and practical work is ongoing.

In the collection which lay the groundwork for the current study of historical code-switching, Herbert Schendl and Laura Wright reviewed earlier scholarship and put forward several areas for further linguistic empirical investigation and fine-tuned conceptualisations: exploring a broader range of genres, registers and contexts (linguistic, social, geographical, cultural), creating digital resources and linguistic corpora which do not dismiss the multilingual character of communication and tracing patterns of multilingual language use systematically across time and space.[20] These themes have been pursued in business writing,[21] medical genres,[22] religious writing (sermons in particular),[23] in cultural contexts other than the so-far predominant English-focussed perspective[24] and in the recent questioning of the monolingual nature of linguistic corpora.[25] In search of a broader framework to capture this diversity of contexts, the latest proposal is to extend the outlook on code-switching and talk about multilingual practices[26] in general, bringing to the fore the social and individual factors which influence linguistic repertoires. The complex written code, which is argued for here in the context of medieval urban legal cultures, can certainly be seen as an example of multilingual practice.

Legal register as a complex multilingual code

In the past, the multilingual nature of legal culture was the norm, involving Latin and the vernacular.[27] Latin was omnipresent and indispensable, but, as intimated earlier, its status as the 'higher language', understood in terms of a typical diglossic situation, should not be taken for granted. To see Latin in a diglossic relationship with the vernacular is to assume that it was authoritative and privileged, while the vernacular served lower-profile roles.[28] However, if one takes the situation in late medieval Scotland as an example, two problems arise with adopting this approach. First, the vernacular linguistic fabric was present to varying degrees in legal texts from the beginning of the written record. Place names, personal names[29] and terms of legal importance which were lacking from civil and canon law (e.g. *kirseth*[30] or *blaa and blodi*; see examples below),[31] occur in legal Latin as code-switches to the vernacular on the lexical level (see 'The level of lexicon' section). These were not negligible ingredients of legal discourse, which was otherwise overwhelmingly Latin. Quite the contrary, names and other linguistic items of local importance are indexical,[32] so in terms of legal significance one could argue that the vernacular could be employed for the most important functions, while Latin was a blueprint, a formulaic construct passed on as a set of practices from one generation of clerks to the next (see 'Writers and audiences' section). Second, in the later middle ages, Scots performed the same functions as Latin – the case study at the end of the chapter illustrates it well – and the difference between the languages was perhaps more one of proportion rather than status.[33] The shift towards the vernacular was gradual, but it could only happen because the vernacular had achieved a status on a par with Latin, the traditional written vehicle of law. Administrative discourse in fifteenth-century Scotland operated within a well-established and fine-grained textual framework[34] and utilised larger and smaller formulaic strings to carry the most important meanings.[35] This is good evidence for textual standardisation, which indicates a high degree of specialisation and stylistic sophistication of the vernacular in the local legal culture. It is thus problematic to see the relationship between Latin and Scots as strictly hierarchical.

In a wider European perspective, important insights on multilingual communication in urban contexts have emerged from the Medieval Urban Literacy project at the University of Utrecht.[36] These concern, for example, the shared properties of local customary laws committed to writing and the pivotal role of chanceries in the construction of the written record and the local government. Across Europe, the linguistic fabric of urban administration could include multiple local languages alongside Latin, with Middle Low German asserting itself, for example, as the language of the Hanseatic League.[37] In the central European context, the administrative record was mainly kept in Latin, but recent scholarship has argued for the recognition of the role of and mutual complementary relationships between varieties of Polish, Czech, Hungarian and German.[38] Scholars working on medieval Romance languages and Latin also see '"multilingualism" [as] more appropriate to the complex linguistic relationships that could be observed in medieval Europe', as opposed to diglossia.[39] Thus, in the context of urban administration, rather than separate languages performing their communicative functions in isolation, we witness a complex code built on the same principles and recognisable across Europe. It was composed of subcodes, Latin and vernacular languages, which complemented each other and drew on each other to carry specific local and global meanings. The scribes had to be able to access both subcodes simultaneously and switch between them on different levels of linguistic complexity. The audiences who engaged with legal discourse were certainly exposed to its multilingual character, but their engagement with the overall code depended on their level of literacy.

Writers and audiences

Administrative records reveal the central role of burgh courts in the day-to-day management of community life in a medieval Scottish town.[40] On closer inspection, there existed two communities which exchanged information: the first organised the administrative practices and gave authority to the texts as a reflection and a record of legal events, while the other was *constructed* by these events – its members recognised themselves through the text (labels, frames of reference, roles captured in the vernacular and in Latin).[41] Thus, the notaries, scribes and clerks in a Scottish burgh formed the first community. It can be conceptualised as a 'community of practice',[42] which is characterised by mutual engagement, a shared joint enterprise and a particular linguistic repertoire – the familiarity with multilingual legal discourse, its structures and ingredients.[43] The form and the content of administrative record had to be accessible not only to the scribes and current participants of the communicative event, but also those who might have wanted to use the record in the future. In fact, more often than not, the intended audience of the legal record was distant in time from the moment of writing, so the linguistic fabric of the record had to be transparent and trustworthy.[44] The changeable nature of a living language could have been perceived as a threat to the stability and transparency of the record. As a community of practice, the scribes and notaries overcame this problem by developing, learning, sustaining and transmitting the 'way of doing things' or, in other words, they worked towards standardising legal discourse which would create an authoritative and binding legal record.

The recipients of these texts – the burgesses and other people involved in legal proceedings, including the scribes themselves – can be perceived as the other community, a 'text community'.[45] It is the text (previously oral, memorised and, presumably, vernacular, now written down in a register-specific code) that becomes a fixed and authoritative point of reference for their roles, obligations and

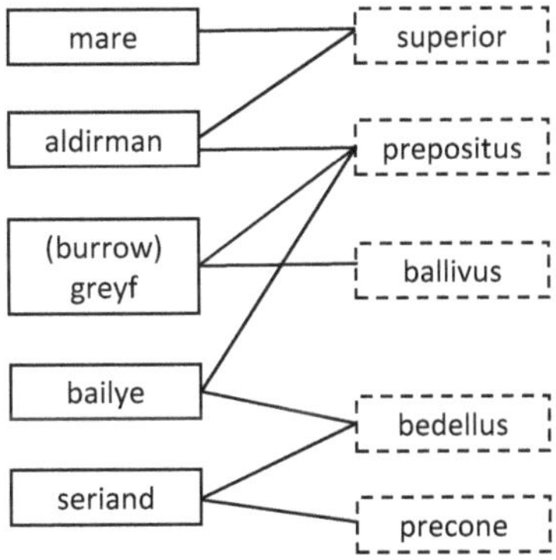

FIGURE 3.1 Administrative roles and term overlaps in Scots (solid outline) and Latin (dashed outline) in *Leges Burgorum*.[46]

rights in the burgh. The ability to recognise these text-external consequences relied on the ability to interpret a multilingual code. Consider Figure 3.1, which presents a network of translational equivalents for the terms for the most important administrative roles in a Scottish burgh, as captured in the Latin and Scots versions of the *Leges Burgorum*, the collection of laws pertaining to Scottish royal burghs, compiled in Latin and later in Scots.[47]

The terms in Latin and in Scots do not match neatly one-to-one; they create a gradient scale of near-synonyms, shading into each other through reinterpretation in the other language. Yet, the terms define roles which on a given occasion would not be subject to a loose interpretation. The people of the burgh, both the literate multilingual writers and the illiterate (possibly monoglot) audiences, would know what to expect of an *aldirman*, perhaps more than of a *prepositus*.[48] What this situation suggests is that certain local vernacular practices may not have been easily rendered by a single Latin term, steeped in a more generic legal culture. Conversely, the conventional Latin terms may have been too rigid to capture what a given person actually did in a burgh.[49] Nevertheless, as a text community, the people of the burgh had to be able to recognise the meanings embedded in the multilingual documents. Admittedly, meanings carried through this complex code bear implications which go beyond the active consumers of the administrative record and concern broader communities, if not societies and nations.

Switching (sub)codes in medieval legal discourse: a structural approach

Switching codes may happen on all levels of linguistic structure and be visually marked or unmarked on all these levels by means of an array of visual cues.[50] In the context of legal discourse, as suggested earlier, one complex code is employed to achieve the communicative goals, which means that any switches between

Latin and the vernacular should be conceptualised as switches between subcodes. Before the discussion moves on to a single case study, I illustrate the similarities in multilingual practice in the urban legal cultures of fifteenth-century Scotland and Poland. In both locations, the complex code can incorporate items from different languages on various structural levels, from macro (the manuscript) to micro (spelling choices) levels.

The level of macrogenre

Various genres may function within a larger collection of texts, which in itself becomes a macrogenre.[51] Some medieval manuscripts are compiled out of different genres gathered by a scribe, as is the case with *Sammelhandschriften*,[52] or they consist of loose parts bound together by a collector. Miscellanies and medieval cartularies are good examples of such collections.[53] Other administrative records may be interpreted as multi-genre, depending on how fine-grained a typology of the forms of legal writing one adopts. In any case, the code-switching may be present on the level of the whole collection, for example, where some genres have Latin as the main language, while some others have the vernacular. In my primary material, the eROThA corpus can be said to have been written wholesale in Latin; it is not the case that one entry is in Latin and an adjacent one is in Old Polish. Switches to the vernacular happen on deeper structural levels. For LAOS it is hard to tell, as the corpus is purposefully made of texts identified as Scots, which may have been part of larger multilingual compilations.

The level of discourse

Thus, going deeper into the textual fabric of a genre, one encounters particular discourse units, for instance, rubrics, incipits and explicits, reported speech passages, lists of names and so on. Switching from Latin to the vernacular for oath-taking is the primary focus of the eROThA digitisation project, whose tagging procedures have enabled tracing the switches in a systematic way.[54]

Example (1) Latin to Polish, Kalisz Land Court Book 2, f.115, R. 407 (1413), <https://rotha.ehum.psnc.pl/breeze/Ka.407>[55]

Testes ducit Jutka de Bobri contra Halscam filiam suam: primus Johannes de Cirnino, qui fuit fideiussor pro dotalicio, secundus Staszek Rzekta, tercius Janussius de Cotarbi, quartus Thomas de ibidem, quintus Laurencius de Crosznino, sextus Albertus de ibidem.

Rotha
Jaco czoſm ranczil za hal iutką halſcze
ſzecznadcze grziwen poſſagu to geſt

yeg zaplaczono *Ceteri ad testimonium*: Jaco
halſcze zaplaczono etc.

Translation: 'Witnesses presented by Jutka of Bobry against his daughter, Halszka: first Jan of Czernino, who is a guarantor of the dowry, second Staszek Rzekta, third Janusz of Kotarby, fourth Tomasz thereof, fifth Wawrzyniec of Krosznino, sixth Albert thereof. Oath. That I have guaranteed on Jutka's behalf for Halszka sixteen marcs in dowry which has been paid to her. *Ceteri ad testimonium* [Others testify accordingly]: That Halszka was paid etc.'

Figure 3.2 presents the manuscript image of the text in Example (1) to illustrate the point about visual cues for code-switching and changes in discourse units. Notice that the multilingual text is written by the same scribe who chose to introduce line breaks between the Latin preamble, the code-switch and discourse trigger *Rotha*, and the text of the oath. In addition, on closer inspection, the oath contains a visually unmarked switch to Latin on the level of the clause (*ceteri ad testimonium*), embedded in the Polish discourse unit.

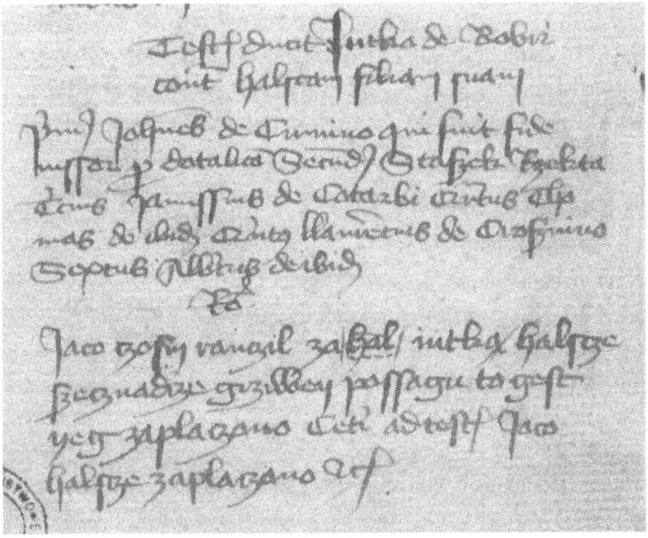

FIGURE 3.2 Kalisz Land Court Book 2, f.115, R. 407 (1413). Copyright State Archive in Poznań (Archiwum Państwowe w Poznaniu).

The level of syntax

In medieval legal record, Latin and the vernacular can swap within larger discourse units on the level of sentence or even within a sentence. We have already seen this earlier in the Polish oath in Example (1), where the additional testimonies are introduced by an unmediated Latin clause.[56] Consider also the switch from Scots to Latin at the level of the clause unit in the following example:

Example (2) Scots to Latin, National Records of Scotland B22/22/2, f. 52v, notarial protocol book (1488), LAOS file #785

...in the maist strait stile And sekerest forme of obligacioune yat[57] can be deuisit but fraud or gile Renunciand al preuilege of law Ciuile or Canone actis statutis of parliament or generale counsale maid or to be maid letterez of supersedere Respitt the terme contenit in the law *de pecunia non immunata* And al vtheris Remedis yat may be proponit in contrare...

Translation: 'In the straightest style and most secure form of obligation that can be devised without fraud or deceit, renouncing all privilege of civil or canon law, acts, statutes of parliaments or General Council made or to be made the letters of superseder [an agreement among creditors to postpone action] to delay the term contained in the law *de pecunia non immunata*. And all other remedies that may be proposed to the contrary...'

The reference to the specific legal provision concerning financial matters is done by means of a switch to Latin (*de pecunia...*) within a longer Scots passage and back again. In fact, that switch does not contain a self-standing verb (which is implicit), so it can also illustrate the interaction of languages within the clause on a lower structural level.

The level of lexicon

Smaller linguistic units from a different language can also be incorporated into longer passages in the main language. In such cases the issue of how to distinguish between borrowing and code-switching comes to the fore.[58] In general, there are several factors to consider: the frequency across the linguistic record for a given period, the inclusion in dictionaries, morphological productivity – or the ability to adapt into the grammatical structure of the main language, e.g. by attaching inflectional endings, and spelling adaptation. The examples below illustrate code-switching on the lexical level – it would be difficult to argue that the switched items were borrowings and had already entered the recipient language and blended in with the rest of its lexicon.

Example (3) Latin to Scots: example from *Leges Burgorum*, chapter xxxi:[59]

L: *Et est retinendum quod in placitis burgorum utitur* Twertnay *in defensionibus defendando* wrang and unlawe
Sc: And it is to wyt that in borow mutis thar is hantyd and oysyt thuertnay in defendande wrang and unlawe

Translation: 'And it is to be known that at the burgh moots [formal meetings] the custom of twertnay [a flat denial] is used in defence if accused of wrongdoings...'

Example (4) Latin to Polish, Gniezno Land Court Book 3, f. 19v, R. 310 (1424), https://rotha.ehum.psnc.pl/breeze/Gn.310

… *infra meridiem, vulgariter* dopoludnya

Translation: 'before noon, in the local language before noon'

It is often the case that one-off word-level switches are flagged in the main language of the passage, as illustrated in (4) where the Latin *vulgariter* prepares the reader for the switch to the vernacular.

The level of morphology

On this level, we look inside the word structure. There are cases in the medieval records where one linguistic system provides inflections to be attached to lexical items from another linguistic system. This phenomenon can be conceptualised as going even deeper into the levels of linguistic structural complexity – a code-switch on the level of morphology. Consider the Latin inflection (third declension, masculine) on the Polish first name *Jaszko* in (5).

Example (5) Polish to Latin, Poznań Land Court Book 1, f. 112, R. 164 (1393), https://rotha.ehum.psnc.pl/breeze/Pn.164

Item Pelka tenetur 6 penas non comparentes et 2 pokupna *et super suo patre contra* Jaszko*nem* Szoboczszky …

Translation: 'Next Pelka has six different fines and two damage fees on his father's behalf against Jaszko[+Lat.infl] Szoboczszky...'

This is a frequent practice in administrative record; interestingly, last names are not prone to code-switching on this level, cf. *Szoboczszky*, which remains uninflected.[60]

Example (6) Scots to Latin (?), National Records of Scotland, MS 34.4.3, f. 77r, arbitration (1437), LAOS file #250

… s(er) Jamys of ogyluy and ye remanent of ye Jug(is) arbitror(is) (con)tenit Jn ye fyrst (com)p(ro)misß…

Translation: 'sir James of Ogilvy and the remaining judges arbitrators mentioned in the first settlement'

In this example from a Scots register, the inflectional endings and other parts of words were abbreviated – the traditional expansions of particular abbreviations are provided in parentheses in (6). The question arises whether these symbolic representations of some underlying linguistic content take the Scots grammar as the point of reference, or perhaps imply the switch to Latin, which is ultimately the source of the abbreviating system in Scots. Such ambiguous forms, copiously encountered in Anglo-Norman business writing, have been labelled *visual diamorphs*.[61] These can potentially be code-switches on the level of a morpheme, marked visually by means of an ambiguous symbol.

The level of orthography

A respelling of a word in a different orthographic system can also be seen as code-switching, this time on the level of spelling. For instance, in order to fit it into a Latin administrative record, a person's name may be respelled according to Latin conventions, regardless of having its own written form in the vernacular. In a way, the word stays in the vernacular (and would be read out as such, if required) but its representation on the page is rendered through another language's spelling conventions. To use an example from the Polish land courts, the same Polish diminutive name appears in the record as *Jasek*, *Jaszko* (see Example 5) or *Jasco*, but the last version is a Latin respelling to fit it into the surrounding context (7).

Example (7) Poznań Land Court Cook 1, f. 185, R. 339 (1397), https://rotha.ehum.psnc.pl/breeze/Pn.339

Jaco *Jaſek* przi jal [...] y wſøl mego cloueka y ſzelaſa *Item Jasco iurabit*: Czo ...

Translation: 'That *Jaszek* arrived [...] and captured my man and my iron plough Next *Jasco* will testify: As ...'

In the Scots material, the opposite direction of an orthographic switch can be discerned. Some scribes respelled the Latin formula confirming the notary's identity, *in manu propria*, according to the Scots spelling convention. In Older Scots, the sequence <ew> can stand for the vowel /u/, as in *blue* spelled <blew> or *virtue* spelled <virtew>, so using this convention within a Latin word is an instance of code-switching to the vernacular on the level of spelling, see (8) and (9).

Example (8) National Library of Scotland CH 1494, Spottiswoode Papers (1490), obligation, LAOS file #189

The ȝere of god J^{m} iiij^{c} and Nyntj ȝer(is) alexand(er) fulfurt MANEW p(ro)p(ri)a

Translation: 'The year of God 1490 years Alexander Fulfurt in his own hand'

Example (9) National Records of Scotland, B20/10/1, p.52.

Ye quhylk day it is funde be ane inquest y^{t} a(n)d(er)o fowlar burges(s) of du(n) fermlyne Js nerest & lachfull ayr to s(s) Jhon terwat hys eme wmquhyll cwret off Du(n)fermlyne
Archybalde stewart baylȝe <u>manw p(ro)p(ri)a</u>

Translation: 'The which day it is found by an inquest that Andrew Fowler burgess of Dunfermline is the nearest and lawful heir to sir John Terwart his uncle, the late curate of Dunfermline, Archibald Stewart baillie <u>in his own hand</u>'

It is also possible to mark the orthographic switch visually by the change of hand or script,[62] which implies awareness of the change between linguistic systems on the part of the scribe. In the examples listed earlier, there was no visible change in the script when switching to the spelling conventions of the other language.

Visual aspects of code-switching on the page

The earlier discussion has already highlighted several cases where code-switching was marked visually on the page. Visual cues may be very diverse: ink/colour change, letter size, line breaks, the choice to use the margin, orientation, hands, pointers, and so on. Various typologies have been suggested within the field of manuscript studies and the 'pragmatics of the page'.[63] In such cases, the interaction of the two languages, the two (sub)codes making up the complex multilingual legal code, is made explicit and brought to the fore. The function of visual marking should be best considered on a case-by-case basis but it seems to be related to the awareness of the scribe and to the processing capabilities of the audience, who might welcome the convenience of a visual prompt to decode the message. At the same time, the absence of visual cues for code-switching, quite prominent in the material consulted, indicates a closely integrated linguistic repertoire – a complex multilingual code – which draws on the available languages without drawing attention to the ingredients.

A multilingual code in practice: a case study

The text in the Appendix concerns a neighbourly dispute, settled in court on 13 August 1459 and entered in James Young's notarial protocol book.[64] The jury passed a verdict reconciling two parties: William Forton and his wife Margaret Nairn on the one hand, and Thomas Scot on the other hand. Thomas had dismantled a *gavil* (a front wall, a gable) between their properties in Canongate, which was found to have been unlawful. Thomas was fined 30 shillings and required to reconstruct the *gavil* without any cost to the injured party.

The entry in the notarial protocol book starts and finishes in Latin, which by this token can be seen as the main language of the passage. After the details of the case are laid out in Latin, the verdict is recorded first in Latin and then in the vernacular, after an explicit flag *in wlgari* 'in the local language', which signals both the code-switch and the new discourse element (see 'Legal register as a complex multilingual code' section). The respective Latin and Scots parts are not, however, monolingual. In the Latin preamble, there are several kinds of borrowings from the Germanic languages as well as instances of lexical code-switching. The words *burgensis* 'burgess' or *burgo* 'burgh, town', for instance, are early Germanic loanwords. Even the Latin *gabello*, describing the part of the house which is being disputed, is etymologically linked to the Old Norse term *gafl* 'a gable'. These lexical items have already been incorporated into the grammatical fabric of Latin, so they can be considered borrowings. But there are also items taken over wholesale from Scots, importantly people's surnames and names of landmarks, in this case the name of the street *leichwind*. These are code-switches on the lexical level, since they had not been adjusted to the Latin grammar or spelling, as was sometimes the case with first names (see 'The level of lexicon' section). The choice on the part of the scribe to inflect and Latinise first names but leave the surnames in their vernacular form goes hand in hand with a characteristic practice in administrative Latin-based multilingualism (see 'The level of morphology' section).[65] This practice is perhaps taken for granted by those familiar with it, but it merits a separate reflection in another study.

In the Scots part, there are plentiful Romance borrowings, ultimately from Latin but mediated through Old French and incorporated into the grammatical system of Scots and its orthography, e.g. *debat*, *oblist* or *decret*. There are a few items in that section, however, whose form strongly resembles the preceding Latin part of the same text, as in *arbitro(uris) & amicable (com)po(n)itovr(is)*, which corresponds with *arbit(ri)cintor(um) siue amicabili(um) (com)po(n)itoru(m)*. It seems that the compiler of this text was switching back to his comfortable Latin subcode for these specific terms. The adaptation to the vernacular lies mainly in adding an abbreviated ending to the words, which in itself can be treated as a visual diamorph since the abbreviations could have had both a Latin and a native interpretation (see 'The level of morphology' section).

All in all, this entry in the protocol book is a good example of a complex multilingual code at work, in which the notary was clearly fluent. He used Latin to begin and close off the entry but sprinkled the Latin with indispensable local references. The repetition of the verdict in both languages may indicate that the notary was anxious about the transparency of the record and chose to write it down again in Scots for his intended audience. His Scots, however, was filled with Latinate borrowings and switches so the two (sub)codes of legal discourse could not be easily disentangled.

Conclusions

Legal discourse in northern European urban contexts was at least bilingual, so by extension, multilingual. Latin and the vernacular were present in the record to different degrees and their functional relationship changed over time: from more clearly separated functions characteristic of each language – Latin for the formulaic record and the local language for local reference – to overlapping and ultimately competing competencies. At the point when both could carry the same functions and meanings, their relationship can no longer be seen as a hierarchical diglossic situation. If anything, the prestigious and authoritative legal code is multilingual in its own right; it is expected and interpretable by the community of practice by which it is constructed, and by the text community which it, in turn, creates. As Armstrong and Mackillop point out in the context of Scottish towns, medieval urban centres functioned as 'hubs for the mixing of legal (and political) cultures and vocabularies',[66] and were engaged in and defined by multilingual repertoires and practices of their administrators.

The structural framework presented in this chapter helps to unpack the intricate interplay of Latin and the vernacular within the complex multilingual code in a systematic manner, and allows for the reflection on the material characteristics of historical multilingual communication. The analytical tools work in various contexts; here we have presented similar code-switching strategies in legal and administrative records composed in medieval Scotland and Poland. The proportions of linguistic ingredients in the code may fluctuate over time due to external cultural pressures which differ from place to place. Indeed, the Polish oaths gradually disappear from the land court books,[67] while the Scots vernacular takes over from Latin to a great degree,[68] on the wave of administrative vernacularisation happening across Europe during the early modern period. The language of medieval legal and administrative texts, however, is still very much multilingual, looking back to the European *Latinitas* and the common cultural, religious and educational Latin benchmark, but at the same time bearing a testimony to the growing functional capacity of local forms of communication. The scribes and notaries across northern European urban cultures navigated both worlds and both codes, and constructed the record in a robust multilingual manner.

Appendix

Protocol book of James Young, 13 August 1495, Edinburgh, National Records of Scotland, HM General Register House B22/22/6, ff. 99v-100r, transcribed by Keith Williamson for the *Linguistic Atlas of Older Scots* (LAOS, file #832)

Notes to the text

Abbreviations expanded in parentheses (except a raised <t> which is kept as in the manuscript), line divisions preserved, capitalisation and punctuation as in the manuscript, insertions in square brackets, Scots text in regular font in black, *Latin text in italics*, Germanic and Celtic borrowings in Latin in grey, **Latin borrowings in the Scots text (with various degrees of adaptation) in bold** and borrowings into Scots from Old French underlined, according to etymologies given in the *Dictionary of the Scots Language*.

[f. 99v]

'Pro Thoma Scot *tinctor(e)'*
xiij^{o} *die me(n)s(is) augustj Anno &c(etera) lxxxxv*^{to} *jndict(i)o(n)e xiij*^{a}
t(er)cia pont(ifica)t(us) pape Alex(and)ri sextj Anno quarto p(er)sonalit(er) (con)sti
tutj willi(elm)us fortone *burgens(is) de* Edinburgh *& m(ar)g(ar)eta*
narne *eius sponsa ex p(ar)te vna Et thomas* scot *tinctor* burgens(is) burgj *vicj cano(n)icoru(m)*
mo(na)st(er)ij s(anc)tecruc(is) p(ro)pe Edi(n)
burgh *ex p(ar)te alt(er)a ex suis c(er)tis scie(n)ciis & spo(n)taneis vo*
lu(n)tatibus ad s(anc)ta dej ewa(n)gelia Juraueru(n)t star(e) de
creto Laudo (con)silio & deliberac(i)o(n)i Jstoru(m) viroru(m) subsc(ri)ptor(um)
vi(delicet) Joh(ann)is Johnesone *georgij* kincaid *Joha(n)nis* glene, *pat(ri)cij*
stawis *& thome* wallas *lathanoru(m) Judicu(m) abit(ri)cintor(um)*
siue amicabiliu(m) (com)po(n)itoru(m) int(er) d(ic)tas p(ar)tes co(m)meru(n)t elector(um)
penes edificacione(m) facta(m) & fienda(m) & p(er) ips(i)u(m) thoma(m) in gabello *orie(n)*
tali dom(us) D(ic)toru(m) will(ielm)i & m(ar)garete eius sponse iuxta
t(er)ra(m) d(ic)ti thome, Que t(er)re (con)tigne Jacent in & D & burgo
vicj cano(n)icoru(m) d(ic)tj mo(na)st(er)ij ex p(ar)te boreali vicj regij eiusd(em)
ad capud venelle dict(e) leichwind *Jnt(er) d(ic)tam venella(m)*
ex p(ar)te occidentali ex p(ar)te vna & t(er)ra(m) quond(am) dauid
ramsay *ex p(ar)te orie(n)tali ex p(ar)te & vn & altera Que Judi*
ces arbitratores sup(ra)sc(ri)ptj bene & matur(e) auisatj eoru(m) decretu(m) & deliberacione(m)
in sc(ri)ptis int(er) d(ic)tas p(ar)tes p(ro)ut sequit(ur) in wlgari fulminaueru(n)t & dederu(n)t

we Johne Johnesone george of kincaid Johnne of
glene pat(ri)k stallis & thomas wallas masonis Jug(is)
arbitro(uris) & **amicable (com)po(n)itovr(is)** betuex willia(m) forton
& m(ar)g(ar)et narne his spous on ye ta p(ar)t & thomas
scot litstar on ye toy(er) p(ar)t ane(n)t ye debat of ane
gavill betuex yar twa land(is) liand i(n) ye cano(n)
gat at ye hed of leich wind Thai beand oblist & suorne be ye fachis & treuchis i(n) yar bodeis to
stand & abid at our decret & **deliu(er)ans** but **Jmpe**
dime(n)t

[f. 100r]
or agai(n)callin in tyme to cu(m) we w^{t} yar allegacio(n)is
beand riply avisit havand god befor E yus we decret
deliu(er)is ordanis & gevis for sente(n)s arbitrale That be

cauß we find y^{t} ye said thomas has done p(ar)t of wrang
in ye dovne taki(n) of a p(ar)t of ye said gavill & putti(n) of
p(ar)t of Robert(is) y(ar) intill That y(ar)for ye said thomas sall (con)tent
& pay now i(n) hand to ye said(is) willia(m) & m(ar)garet his spous
ye sovme of threttj s gud & vsuale mone of scotland
For ye quhilk ye said thomas sall haf all his nedful
asiame(n)t(is) i(n) ye said gavill Ande sall haf leiff to
tak done ye p(ar)tis yarof Ande sall ger lay ye sa(m)my(n)
agai(n) And big vp ye said gavill alß hech as he plesß
kepand ye said willia(m) & his wiff [ska^{t}les] thevy(n)nais
y^{t} ar in ye said gavill ska^{t}les y(ar)thro^{u} quhilk thewy(n)na
is ye said thomas sall ger led to ye hech & big yai(m)
on his cost sufficiandlie as effer(is) *Sup(er) p(re)miss(is) d(ic)t(us)*
thomas scot petiit Jnstr(umentu)m Act(a) erant hec infra b(ur)gu(m)
de Edinburgh *in bocha ant(er)iori* malcolmi kincaid
ho(ra) octaua ante m(er)edie(m) vel eoc(ir)ca Sub a(n)no &c(etera) p(rese)ntib(us)
Jbidem p(ro)uid(is) vir(is) vi(delicet) Ricardo faffyngton *Andrea*
kincaid *testibus ad p(re)missa vocat(is)*

Notes

1 Acknowledgements: The work on this paper was supported by the National Science Centre in Poland (Narodowe Centrum Nauki; 2014/13/B/HS2/00644) and the eROThA project. On *diglossia* see, for example, T.W. Machan, 'Language contact in *Piers Plowman*', *Speculum* 69, 1994, pp. 359–85, at pp. 360–1; W.J. Ong, 'Orality, literacy, and medieval textualization', *New Literary History* 16(1), 1984, pp. 1–12, at pp. 4–5. For an overview of the mutual relationships between Latin and European vernaculars between AD 500 and 1500 and a useful bibiography, see M.W. Herren, 'Latin and the vernacular languages', in F.A.C. Mantello and A.G. Rigg (eds) *Medieval Latin: An Introduction and Bibliographical Guide*, Washington, DC: Catholic University of America Press, 1996, pp. 122–9. Latin has also been perceived as a standard language in opposition to the un-standardised local languages; see for example the section entitled 'The Latin language as a standard and its relation to the vernacular', in M. Goyens and W. Verbeke (eds) *The Dawn of the Written Vernacular in Western Europe*, Leuven: Leuven University Press, 2003, pp. 1–145, with chapters on the linguistic situation in France, the Low Countries and Switzerland.

2 For example, M.T. Clanchy notices that people in England in the twelfth and thirteenth centuries had a choice between English, French and Latin, but '[no] one language could serve all the diverse purposes required because their struggle for dominance was still undecided', in *From Memory to Written Record. England 1066–1307*, Cambridge, MA: Harvard University Press, 1979, p. 154.

3 The inclusion of the Polish material in a volume on northern European legal cultures is justified – Polish towns were typically founded on Magdeburg law, which had resonance across Northern and Central Europe, while the towns along the Baltic coast, including Polish towns, were often granted Lübeck law (I am grateful to Edda Frankot for this observation). See for example D. Nicholas, *The Growth of the Medieval City. From Late Antiquity to the Early Fourteenth Century*, London/New York: Routledge, 1997, pp. 154–5, 202.

4 *Linguistic Atlas of Older Scots* (LAOS) 2008. Phase 1: 1380–1500, ed. K. Williamson, University of Edinburgh, <http://www.lel.ed.ac.uk/ihd/laos1/laos1.html> (accessed 25 April 2019).

5 See the project's website: *Electronic Repository of Greater Poland Oaths* <https://rotha.ehum.psnc.pl/> (accessed 26 April 2019) and J. Kopaczyk, M. Włodarczyk and E. Adamczyk, 'Medieval multilingualism in Poland: Creating a corpus of Greater Poland Court Oaths (Rotha)', *Studia Anglica Posnaniensia* 51(3), 2016, pp. 9–35. The project's short title, eROThA, is based on *rota*, the Polish word for 'an oath', which in the Latin parts of the record and in the transitions between Latin and Polish often appears as *rot(h)a* (or in various abbreviated forms, see M. Włodarczyk and E. Adamczyk, 'Metalinguistic and visual cues to the co-occurrence of Latin and Old Polish in the *Electronic Repository of Greater Poland Oaths*, 1386–1446 (*eROThA*)', in preparation).

6 For the most comprehensive treatments of the history of Scots to date, see C. Macafee and A.J. Aitken, 'A history of Scots to 1700', in *A Dictionary of the Older Scottish Tongue*, vol. XII, Oxford: Oxford University Press, 2002, pp. xxix–clvii. Online <https://dsl.ac.uk/about-scots/history-of-scots/>, as well as C. Jones (ed.) *The Edinburgh History of the Scots Language*, Edinburgh: Edinburgh University Press, 1997.

7 To my knowledge, there is no single-volume history of Polish available in English. There are several publications in German; see W. Kuraszkiewicz, *Historische Grammatik der Polnischen Sprache*, Munich: Otto Sagner, 1972, and J. Mazur, *Geschichte der Polnischen Sprache*, Frankfurt am Main: Peter Lang, 1993. For a detailed account of the history of the language and linguistic developments in Polish, see K. Długosz-Kurczabowa and S. Dubisz, *Gramatyka historyczna języka polskiego* [*A Historical Grammar of Polish*], 2nd edn, Warsaw: Wydawnictwa Uniwersytetu Warszawskiego, 2001.

8 R. Jakobson, 'Linguistics in relation to other sciences', in R. Jakobson, *On Language* (eds. Linda R. Waugh and Monique Monville-Burston), Cambridge, MA: Harvard University Press, [1970] 1990, pp. 451–88, at p. 455.

9 E. Haugen, 'Bilingualism, language contact and immigrant languages in the United States: A research report. 1956–70', in T. Sebeok (ed.) *Current Trends in Linguistics*, vol. 10, The Hague: Mouton, 1973, pp. 505–91, at p. 521.

10 A similar idea for spoken code-switching as an '*alloy* of two or more speech varieties' was put forward by C. Alvarez-Cáccamo in 'From "switching code" to "code-switching": Towards a reconceptualisation of communicative codes', in P. Auer (ed.) *Code-Switching in Conversation. Language, Interaction and Identity*, London/New York: Routledge, 1998, pp. 29–48, at p. 39, emphasis original. He noticed that in a communicative situation which draws on multiple linguistic resources '[e]ach utterance, turn or entire discourse [...] produces a compound communicative effect and it may be effectively interpreted by participants as a coherent whole on the basis of a coherent code' (ibid., pp. 39–40). More recently, the concept of translanguaging has emerged as a way to capture the 'trans-semiotic system with many meaning-making signs, primarily linguistic ones that combine to make up a person's semiotic repertoire', in response to the 'complex interactions of the 21st century'; O. García and Li Wei, *Translanguaging: Language, Bilingualism and Education*. Basingstoke: Palgrave Macmillan, 2014. pp. 42–3.

11 Early approaches to the modern study of language saw linguistic signs predominantly as an arbitrary relationship between the concept and the sound and were very dismissive of writing; see F. de Saussure, *Course in General Linguistics* (trans. R. Harris), London: Bloomsbury, [1916/1967] 2013, p. 140. Jakobson, even though he was a structuralist, understood the importance of writing as a vehicle for language and meaning, 'Linguistics in relation to other sciences', pp. 455–6. See also literature review in Alvarez-Cáccamo, 'From "switching code" to "code-switching"', pp. 30–6.

12 The medium of communication is 'charged with cultural signification'; U. Eco, *A Theory of Semiotics*. Bloomington: Indiana University Press, 1976, p. 267.

13 For the pragmaphilological turn in historical linguistics, see A.H. Jucker (ed.) *Historical Pragmatics*, Amsterdam: John Benjamins, 1995; I. Taavitsainen and S. Fitzmaurice, 'Historical pragmatics: What it is and how to do it', in S. Fitzmaurice and I. Taavitsainen (eds) *Methods in Historical Pragmatics*, Berlin: De Gruyter, 2007, pp. 11–36; M. Sebba, 'Sociolinguistic approaches to writing systems research', *Writing Systems Research* 1(1), 2009, pp. 35–49; for multilingualism in written texts, see chapters in M. Sebba, S. Mahootian and C. Jonsson (eds) *Language Mixing and Code-Switching in Writing. Approaches to Mixed-Language Written Discourse*, London: Routledge, 2012.

14 G. Kress and T. van Leeuwen, *Reading Images. The Grammar of Visual Design*, London: Routledge, 1996, p. 231.

15 'Every text is a system of signs organised according to codes and subcodes which reflect certain values, attitudes, beliefs, assumptions and practices. Codes transcend single texts, linking them together in an interpretive framework which is used by their producers and interpreters. In creating texts we select and combine signs in relation to the codes with which we are familiar', D. Chandler, *Semiotics. The basics*, 2nd edn, London/New York: Routledge, 2007, p. 157.

16 B. Bedos-Rezak, 'Secular administration', in F.A.C. Mantello and A.G. Rigg (eds) *Medieval Latin: An Introduction and Bibliographical Guide*, Washington, DC: Catholic University of America Press, 1996, pp. 195–229.

17 For the standardisation of administrative discourse in medieval Lowland Scotland, see J. Kopaczyk, *The Legal Language of Scottish Burghs. Standardisation and Lexical Bundles, 1380–1560*, Oxford: Oxford University Press, 2013.

18 See, for example, L. Milroy and P. Muysken (eds) *One Speaker, Two Languages: Cross-Disciplinary Perspectives on Code-Switching*, Cambridge: Cambridge University Press, 1995, and P. Garnder-Chloros, *Code-Switching*, Cambridge: Cambridge University Press, 2009. A recent handbook of linguistic code-switching concentrates solely on processes and forms of code-switching in speech, with some attention paid to internet communication; see B.E. Bullock and A.J. Toribio (eds) *The Cambridge Handbook of Linguistic Code-Switching*, Cambridge: Cambridge University Press, 2009.

19 L. Wright, 'Macaronic writing in a London archive, 1380–1480', in M. Rissanen et al. (eds) *History of Englishes. New Methods and Interpretations in Historical Linguistics*, Berlin: Mouton de Gruyter, 1992, pp. 762–70; L. Wright, 'Early Modern London business English', in D. Kastovsky (ed.) *Studies in Early Modern English*, Berlin: Mouton de Gruyter, 1994, pp. 449–65; Machan, 'Language contact in *Piers Plowman*'; L. Wright, 'A hypothesis on the structure of macaronic business writing', in J. Fisiak (ed.) *Medieval Dialectology*, Berlin: Mouton de Gruyter, 1995, pp. 309–21; H. Schendl, 'Text types and code-switching in medieval and Early Modern English', *Vienna English Working Papers* 5, 1996, pp. 50–62; H.-J. Diller, 'Code-switching in medieval English drama', *Comparative Drama* 31, 1997/98, pp. 500–37; H. Schendl, '"To London fro Kent/Sunt predia depopulantes": Code-switching and medieval English macaronic poems', *Vienna English Working Papers* 6(1), 1997, pp. 52–66; H. Schendl, 'Linguistic aspects of code-switching in medieval English texts', in D.A. Trotter (ed.) *Multilingualism in Later Medieval Britain*, Cambridge: D.S. Brewer, 2000, pp. 77–92; H. Schendl, 'Code-choice and code-switching in some early fifteenth-century letters', in P.J. Lucas and A. Lucas (eds) *Middle English from Tongue to Text*, Bern: Peter Lang, 2002, pp. 247–62; and L. Wright, 'Models of language mixing: Code-switching versus semicommunication in medieval Latin and Middle English accounts', in D. Kastovsky and A. Mettinger (eds) *Language Contact in the History of English*, Frankfurt: Peter Lang, 2001, pp. 363–76.

20 H. Schendl and L. Wright, 'Code switching in early English: Historical background and methodological and theoretical issues', in H. Schendl and L. Wright (eds) *Code-Switching in Early English*, Berlin: Walter de Gruyter, 2011, pp. 15–45. For further general overviews of the field, see H. Schendl, 'Multilingualism, code-switching, and language contact in historical sociolinguistics', in J.M. Hernandez-Campoy and J.C. Conde-Silvestre (eds) *The Handbook of Historical Sociolinguistics*, Oxford: Blackwell,

2010, pp. 520–33, and P. Pahta, 'Code-switching in English of the middle ages', in T. Nevalainen and E.C. Traugott (eds) *The Oxford Handbook of the History of English*, New York: Oxford University Press, 2012, pp. 528–37. New is M. Keller, *Code-switching. Unifying Contemporary and Historical Perspectives*, Cham: Palgrave Macmillan, 2020.

21 L. Wright, 'On variation in medieval mixed-language business writing', in Schendl and Wright (eds) *Code-Switching in Early English*, pp. 191–218.

22 P. Pahta, 'Code-switching in medieval medical writing', in I. Taavitsainen and P. Pahta (eds) *Medical and Scientific Writing in Late Medieval English*, Cambridge: Cambridge University Press, 2004, pp. 73–99, and P. Pahta, 'Code-switching in Early Modern English medical writing', in I. Taavitsainen and P. Pahta (eds) *Medical Writing in Early Modern English*, Cambridge: Cambridge University Press, 2011, pp. 115–32.

23 H Johnson, *The Grammar of Good Friday: Macaronic Sermons of Late Medieval England*, Turnhout: Brepols, 2012; H. Schendl, 'Code-switching in late medieval macaronic sermons', in J.A. Jefferson and A. Putter (eds) *Multilingualism in Medieval Britain (c.1066–1520): Sources and Analyses*, Turnhout: Brepols, 2013, pp. 153–69; and H. Halmari, 'Language switching and alliteration in Oxford, MS Bodley 649', in A. Classen (ed.) *Multilingualism in the Middle Ages and Early Modern Age: Communication and Miscommunication in the Premodern World*, Berlin: Walter de Gruyter, 2016, pp. 313–28.

24 N. McLelland, 'A historical study of codeswitching in writing: German and Latin in Schottelius' *Ausführliche Arbeit von der Teutschen Haubtsprache* (1663)', *International Journal of Bilingualism* 8, 2004, pp. 499–523; J. Kopaczyk, 'Code-switching in the records of a Scottish brotherhood in early modern Poland-Lithuania', *Poznań Studies in Contemporary Linguistics* 49(3), 2013, pp. 281–319; and Kopaczyk, Włodarczyk and Adamczyk, 'Medieval multilingualism in Poland'.

25 A. Nurmi, T. Rütten and P. Pahta, *Challenging the Myth of Monolongual Corpora*, Leiden: Brill/Rodopi, 2017.

26 P. Pahta, J. Skaffari and L. Wright (eds) *Multilingual Practices in Language History*, Boston/Berlin: Mouton, 2018.

27 For an overview of the administrative system, record-keeping and the roles and forms of Latin in medieval European administration, see Bedos-Rezak, 'Secular administration'.

28 C.A. Fergusson, 'Diglossia', *Word* 15, 1959, pp. 325–40.

29 For a comprehensive database of Scottish personal names found in over 8,600 documents, see A. Beam, J. Bradley, D. Broun, J.R. Davies, M. Hammond, M. Pasin (with others), *The People of Medieval Scotland, 1093–1314*, online, Glasgow and London, 2012, <https://www.poms.ac.uk/> (accessed 27 April 2019).

30 Dictionary of the Scots Language: *kirseth* n. Temporary exemption from payment of dues granted to a new settler in a burgh.

31 For more examples, see J. Kopaczyk, 'Latin and Scots versions of Scottish medieval burgh laws (*Leges Burgorum*)', *Scottish Language* 30, 2011, pp. 1–17.

32 *indexical* – of

> "an expression whose extension [applicability] is relative to a specific context, in which a specific person speaks to a specific other or others, in a specific place, and so on. E.g. *here* is an indexical expression, whose application, as in *Mary lives here*, varies from one use to another," in P.H. Matthews (ed.) *The Concise Oxford Dictionary of Linguistics*, 3rd edn, Oxford: Oxford University Press, 2014.

33 The topic of genre vernacularisation is explored by Anna Havinga in this volume.

34 Scots documents drew on Latin models, as visible in the vernacular styles outlining the authoritative formulation of particular legal documents. See for example P. Gouldesbrough, *Formulary of Old Scots Legal Documents*, Edinburgh: Stair Society, 1985. However, they also contained their own linguistic strategies and phraseology. A systematic comparison of the two traditions has not been undertaken yet (to the best of my knowledge).

35 Kopaczyk, *The Legal Language of Scottish burghs*.

36 G. Declercq, M. Mostert, W. Ysebaert and A. Adamska (eds) *New Approaches to Medieval Urban Literacy*, Brussels: Koninklijke Vlaamse Academie van België voor Wetenschappen en Kunsten, 2013; M. Mostert and A. Adamska (eds) *Writing and the Administration of Medieval Towns: Medieval Urban Literacy*, vol. I, Turnhout: Brepols, 2014; M. Mostert and A. Adamska (eds) *Uses of the Written Word in Medieval Towns: Medieval Urban Literacy*, vol. II, Turnhout: Brepols, 2014. For a comprehensive bibliography on urban literacy listing more than 6,700 titles, see M. Mostert, *A Bibliography of Works on Medieval Communication*, Turnhout: Brepols, 2012.

37 R. Peters, 'Das Mittelniederdeutsche als Sprache der Hanse', in P.S. Ureland (ed.) *Sprachkontakt in der Hanse*, Tübingen: Niemeyer, 1987, pp. 65–88.

38 A. Adamska, 'Latin and three vernaculars in East Central Europe from the point of view of the history of social communication', in M. Garrison, A.P. Orbán and M. Mostert (eds) *Spoken and Written Language. Relations between Latin and the Vernacular Languages in the Earlier Middle Ages*, Turnhout: Brepols, pp. 325–64.

39 Garrison, Orbán and Mostert, *Spoken and Written Language*, p. ix.

40 J.W. Armstrong and A. Mackillop, 'Introduction: Communities, courts and Scottish towns', *Urban History* 44(3), 2017 (special section: 'Communities, courts and Scottish towns', J.W. Armstrong and A. Mackillop (eds)), pp. 358–64.

41 For an overview of research on the concept of a community from a historian's perspective, see C. Hawes, 'The urban community in fifteenth-century Scotland: Language, law and political practice', *Urban History* 44(3), 2017 (special section: 'Communities, courts and Scottish towns', J.W. Armstrong and A. Mackillop (eds)), pp. 365–80.

42 This notion originates in the psychological work on 'situated learning'; J. Lave and E. Wenger, *Situated Learning: Legitimate Peripheral Participation*, Cambridge: Cambridge University Press, 1991, and E. Wenger, *Communities of Practice: Learning, Meaning and Identity*. New York: Cambridge University Press, 1998. It has been applied in sociolinguistics; see J. Holmes and M. Meyerhoff, 'The community of practice: Theories and methodologies in language and gender research', *Language in Society* 28, 1999, pp. 173–83 and more recently adapted to historical sociolinguistics and pragmatics, see A.H. Jucker and J. Kopaczyk, 'Communities of practice as a locus of language change', in J. Kopaczyk and A.H. Jucker (eds) *Communities of Practice in the History of English*, Amsterdam: John Benjamins, 2013, pp. 1–13.

43 Michael Richter mentions Swansea burghers who shared a pool of idioms to refer to time measurements in concrete physical terms; see 'Trace elements of obliterated vernacular languages in Latin texts', in: Garrison, Orbán, and Mostert (eds) *Spoken and Written Language*, pp. 1–9, at p. 8.

44 For the emergence of discourse standardisation in the administrative record in Scotland, see Kopaczyk, *The Legal Language of Scottish Burghs*. For the discussion of how the written word gained the trust of medieval communities, see Clanchy, *From Memory to Written Record*, pp. 231–57.

45 Andrew Butcher extends the more established sociolinguistic concept of a speech community to a text community in his analysis of the administrative records of Hythe, one of the Cinque Ports, 'The functions of script in the speech community of a late medieval town, c. 1300–1550', in J.C. Crick and A. Walsham (eds) *The Uses of Script and Print*, Cambridge: Cambridge university Press, 2004, pp. 157–70. This notion was applied in the Scottish context and supported with textual data extracted by corpus-linguistic methods in J. Kopaczyk, 'How a community of practice creates a text community: Middle Scots legal and administrative discourse', in Kopaczyk and Jucker (eds) *Communities of Practice*, pp. 225–50.

46 On the relationship between the Latin and Scots versions of the *Leges*, see Kopaczyk, 'Latin and Scots versions of Scottish medieval burgh laws', and recent work by the same author: J. Kopaczyk, 'Textual standardisation of legal Scots vis a vis Latin', in L. Wright (ed.) *The Multilingual Origins of Standard English*, Berlin: Mouton de Gruyter, 2020.

47 The parallel versions of the laws were consulted in *The Acts of the Parliaments of Scotland* (hereafter *APS*), vol. I, ed. Cosmo Innes and Thomas Thomson, Edinburgh: Record Commission, 1844. It is noteworthy that *provost* does not appear in the edition as a vernacular counterpart of *prepositus*. The editors of the *APS* claim to have followed the Berne MS (National Records of Scotland) for the Latin version (the empirical degree-of-difference test I carried out also suggests it; see J. Kopaczyk, 'Textual standardisation of legal Scots *vis a vis* Latin', in Wright (ed.) *The Multilingual Origins of Standard English*, Figure 2) but it is not clear which vernacular manuscript or manuscripts served as the basis of the parallel Scots version of the *Leges*. For comment on this and related manuscripts, see now A. Taylor, *The Laws of Medieval Scotland: Legal Compilations from the Thirteenth and Fourteenth Centuries*, Edinburgh: Stair Society, 2019. Pryde suggests that the term *provost* for the head of the local government started to be used after 1450, first in Glasgow, then Edinburgh, and in the Acts of the Parliament in 1503/4 (G.S. Pryde, 'Introduction', *Ayr Burgh Accounts, 1534–1624*, Edinburgh: Scottish History Society, 1937, pp. xxii–xxiii). Contemporary records compiled directly in the burghs seem to be using *provost* regularly, albeit in combinations reflecting the broader community, as in *provost and balzeis; provost, balzeis and consail; provost, baizeis, consail* and *comonite*; see Kopaczyk, 'How a community of practice creates a text community', p. 234. To establish the network of Latin and Scots nomenclature counterparts across all witnesses of burgh laws in both languages would be a major project, which falls outside the scope of this chapter. It is also worth noting that the nomenclature seems to have been different in the records compiled directly in the burghs.

48 As Andrew R.C. Simpson's chapter in this volume demonstrates, a similar network of Latin and vernacular labels could be constructed for the various roles of the men of law in medieval Scotland.

49 For various outlooks on medieval urban communities from the perspective of individuals, see, for example, Elizabeth Ewan on communal rights and privileges as a unifying force in *Townlife in Fourteenth-Century Scotland*, Edinburgh: Edinburgh University Press, 1990; conversely, on the hierarchies precluding a sense of community, see E.P. Dennison, 'Power to the people? The myth of the medieval burgh community', in S.M. Foster, A.I. Macinnes, and R. MacInnes (eds) *Scottish Power Centres*. Glasgow: Cruithne, 1998, pp. 100–31 and Hawes, 'The urban community in fifteenth-century Scotland'.

50 I put forward a comprehensive framework designed to capture this complexity in a systematic manner; J. Kopaczyk, 'Administrative multilingualism on the page in early modern Poland: In search of a framework for written code-switching', in: Pahta, Skaffari, and Wright (eds) *Multilingual Practices in Language History*, pp. 275–98.

51 Other examples of a macrogenre would be a textbook, a newspaper or a conversation, each forming a whole but with discernible individual genres within it such as a report, a declaration, a story, a joke, and others.

52 P.D. Kurtz and L.E. Voigts, 'The significance of now-dispersed Bute 13: A mixed-language scientific manuscript', in P. Pahta and A.H. Jucker (eds) *Communicating Early English Manuscripts*, Cambridge: Cambridge University Press, 2011, pp. 38–54 and D. Schipor, 'A study of multilingualism in the late medieval material of the Hampshire Record Office', unpublished PhD thesis, University of Stavanger, 2017.

53 M. Connolly and R. Radulescu (eds), *Insular Books: Vernacular Manuscript Miscellanies in Late Medieval Britain*, Oxford, 2015, and J. Tucker, *Reading and Shaping Medieval Cartularies. Multi-Scribe Manuscripts and their Patterns of Growth. A Study of the Earliest Cartularies of Glasgow Cathedral and Lindores Abbey*, Woodbridge: Boydell & Brewer, 2020.

54 M. Włodarczyk, J. Kopaczyk and M. Kozak, 'Multilingualism in Greater Poland court records (1386–1448): Tagging discourse boundaries and code-switching', *Corpora*, forthcoming.

55 Latin abbreviations have been silently expanded; compare the facsimile in Figure 3.2.

56 Some scholars distinguish between code-switching and language mixing to capture switching from one language to another between and within sentences, e.g. R. Ingham, 'Mixing languages on the manor', *Medium Aevum* 78(1), 2009, pp. 80–97. Sociolinguistic and psycholinguistic research on spoken code-switching refers to inter- and intra-sentential code-switching, respectively; see C. Myers-Scotton, 'Comparing codeswitching and borrowing', in C.M. Eastman (ed.) *Codeswitching*, Clevedon: Multilingual Matters, 1992, pp. 19–39.

57 There were two ways of spelling /ð/, the first sound of *that*, in Middle Scots: with a <y> which had initially been a thorn but in time became indistinguishable from the <y> used for vowels, as in <yat> 'that' >, and with a <th> as in <vtheris> 'others'. The first variant was becoming the norm for word-initial contexts while the second was found in middle and final positions, until Anglicisation eradicated that distinction. For details, see B. Molineaux, J. Kopaczyk, R. Alcorn, W. Maguire, V. Karaiskos and B. Los, 'Phonotactics, graphotactics and contrast: The history of Scots dental fricative spellings', *English Language and Linguistics*, 2020.

58 L. Voigts, 'What's the word? Bilingualism in late-medieval England', *Speculum* 71, 1996, pp. 813–26.

59 Kopaczyk, 'Latin and Scots versions of Scottish medieval burgh laws', p. 11. This example comes from the *APS*, vol. 1.

60 Kopaczyk discussed this phenomenon in more detail in 'Code-switching in the records of a Scottish brotherhood', pp. 289–91.

61 Wright, 'On variation in medieval mixed-language business writing'.

62 S. Kaislaniemi, 'Code-switching, script-switching, and typeface-switching in early modern English manuscript letters and printed tracts', in M. Peikola, A. Mäkilähde, H. Salmi, M.-L. Varila and J. Skaffari, *Verbal and Visual Communication in Early English Texts*, Turnhout: Brepols, 2017, pp. 165–200.

63 This conceptualisation was proposed by R. Carrol, M. Peikola, H. Salmi, M.-L. Varila, J. Skaffari and R. Hiltunen, 'Pragmatics on the page. Visual text in late medieval English books', *European Journal of English Studies* 17(1), 2013, pp. 54–71. Earlier similar approaches include T.W. Machan, 'The visual pragmatics of code-switching in late Middle English literature', in Schendl and Wright (eds) *Code-Switching in Early English*, pp. 303–33; more recently, the eROThA project has incorporated work on visual aspects of code-switching: M. Włodarczyk, J. Kopaczyk and E. Adamczyk, 'Visual code-switching in the electronic repository of Greater Poland Oaths 1386–1444 (ROThA)', paper presented at Monolingual Histories – Multilingual Practices. Issues in Historical Language Contact, University of Ghent, 2017.

64 James Young was a notary of Canongate; see H. Paton, 'Introduction', in G. Donaldson (ed.) *The Protocol Book of James Young 1485–1515*, Edinburgh: Scottish Records Society, p. v. The transcription comes from the LAOS files. The original is kept at the National Records of Scotland; see Appendix for details.

65 See, for example, J. Armstrong, 'Concepts of kinship in Lancastrian Westmorland', in B. Thompson and J. Watts (eds) *Political Society in Later Medieval England: A Festschrift for Christine Carpenter*, Woodbridge: Boydell Press, 2015, pp. 146–65, at pp. 153–4.

66 Armstrong and Mackillop, 'Introduction: Communities, courts and Scottish towns', p. 363.

67 For Latinisation in particular locations covered by the eROThA project, see H. Kowalewicz and W. Kuraszkiewicz (eds) *Wielkopolskie roty sądowe XIV–XV wieku* [*The Greater Poland Court Oaths of the 14th–15th century*], Warszawa, Poznań, Wrocław, Kraków and Gdańsk: Państwowe Wydawnictwo Naukowe, vol. 1, *Roty poznańskie* [*The Poznań oaths*], 1959, p. 10; vol. 2, *Roty pyzdrskie* [*The Pyzdry oaths*], 1960, p. 6; vol. 5, A, *Roty gnieźnieńskie* [*The Gniezno oaths*], 1981, p. 7.

68 See, for example, A. Havinga's chapter in this volume.

4

THE VERNACULARISATION OF THE ABERDEEN COUNCIL REGISTERS (1398–1511)

*Anna D. Havinga**

Introduction: vernacularisation

Latin was the lingua franca in the middle ages and beyond, enabling communication across different language communities. Despite obvious advantages, a gradual shift from Latin to the vernaculars in written texts took place all over Europe. Schendl as well as Pahta and Taavitsainen use the term *vernacularisation* to refer to the expanding range of vernaculars in comparison to Latin.[1] This term encompasses both the writing of original texts in the vernacular and the translation of Latin texts into the vernacular. Depending on the domain and region, this vernacularisation can be observed before and after two major extra-linguistic developments: the invention of printing with moveable type in the mid-fifteenth century, and the Reformation, beginning in the early sixteenth century. Burke notes that in the domain of administration, for example, 'Latin was replaced by some vernaculars in the early fifteenth century [...], in the fourteenth century, or even, in the case of the chancery of Castile, in the thirteenth century'.[2] Based on research by Voigts of scientific and medical codices from England, Pahta and Taavitsainen state that a 'first phase of vernacularisation seems to have been largely completed by 1475'.[3] Middle English recipes, in contrast, were vernacularised in the fourteenth century, according to Carroll.[4] This small selection of conclusions shows that the shift from Latin to a vernacular was by no means a consistent process, with different text types being vernacularised at different times, even in different centuries. Definite conclusions about the timeline of vernacularisation in a particular region are, therefore, difficult to reach and researchers need to look at different text types in order to gain an accurate picture of these processes. Building on in-depth analyses of certain text types, we can look at the bigger picture and try to understand why Latin was replaced by vernaculars.

While such in-depth analyses exist for certain text types (see earlier point as well as Stenroos, who works on vernacularisation in local administrative writing from England), research on this topic has focused on English, with Scots remaining under-researched with regard to vernacularisation.[5] Both English and Scots descended from the Anglian dialect of Old English and both were certainly used in speech prior to any preserved records written in these languages.[6] For Scots, Smith notes that this period (up to 1375) is generally referred to as 'pre-literary' Scots.[7] Before 1375, 'the only evidence [of the use of Scots] of any significance is to be found in place-names and in occasional glosses on Latin material', according to Smith.[8] This does, of course, not mean that no texts were written in Scots prior to 1375. In the Early Scots (1375–1450) and Early Middle Scots periods (1450–1550), Scots developed into what Smith calls an '*elaborated* language, i.e. a variety that could be used in more than one register, including writing as well as speech'.[9] Görlach illustrates this development for the Lowlands in a number of graphs, which show the language choices (Latin, Scots, Scottish English) in different text types (religion and administration, scholarly texts, literature, conversation).[10] The graph for 'religion, administration' suggests that Scots was the dominant language in these domains by 1400, with Latin gradually declining from 1400 to the end of the 1600s. Scots, on the other hand, started to decline in the second half of the 1400s at the expense of Scottish English, which had completely replaced Scots in the domains of 'religion, administration' by about 1650, according to Görlach's graphs. It seems, however, problematic to combine the domains of religion and administration in one graph. Also, neither the specific sources nor the method used for these graphs is mentioned and the graphs are described as a 'rough survey' by Görlach himself.[11] To achieve a better and more accurate understanding of vernacularisation processes, a careful analysis of one particular register, such as legal writing, may be more appropriate. With regard to this register, Corbett et al. state that the proceedings in the Scottish Parliament began to be recorded in Scots in 1390, with Scots becoming the more dominant language in the records of parliament after 1425 when the earlier Latin Acts were translated into the vernacular.[12] This happened during the reign of King James I, who composed original poetry in Scots[13] and who seems to have advocated the use of Scots in legal sources. This move from Latin to Scots in legal writing must, however, also be seen in the wider context of late medieval Europe – a time when multilingualism was the norm and when vernaculars across Europe were used in an increasing number of functions and domains.[14]

While Görlach's graphs and the findings about language choice in the proceedings of the Scottish Parliament provide first insights into the vernacularisation of Scottish legal writing, a comprehensive diachronic study of vernacularisation processes in one particular documentary legal source from Scotland, as carried out here, has not been undertaken yet. It can be argued that the vernacularisation of legal texts results in more open and transparent legal records that can be consulted by the populace. At the same time, the vernacularisation of legal texts indicates a shift in the political worldviews of an influential elite, which broadened access to the law through vernacularisation, thus changing or modifying 'cultures of law'. In this chapter, processes of vernacularisation are analysed in the first eight volumes (1398–1511) of Scotland's oldest and most complete run of civic records, the Aberdeen Council Registers.[15] Given their long run, these sources are particularly suited for linguistic research on changes in language use.

Vernacularisation in the Aberdeen Council Registers: a quantitative analysis

The corpus and method

The Law in the Aberdeen Council Registers (LACR) project team fully transcribed volumes one to eight of the registers (excluding the material written between 1414 and 1433, which is missing). This forms the publication *Aberdeen Registers Online: 1398–1511 (ARO)*.[16] The results presented here are based upon an examination of the corpus as it stood during its period of creation. At the time of study, the majority of the initial transcriptions, which can be described as semi-diplomatic, were edited and their TEI-compliant annotations checked.[17] Table 4.1 specifies the size of the overall corpus and the individual volumes. At the time of study, the corpus contained 34,077 entries, which made up 1,805,670 tokens.[18] Not every volume covers the same number of administrative years. The average number of entries and tokens per administrative year in Table 4.1 reveals an overall increase in how much was written down over the years, with the highest average in volume eight (518 entries and 33,106 tokens per administrative year). This may either indicate that recording burgh business became increasingly important or that more issues arose in the burgh that needed to be recorded.

TABLE 4.1 The Aberdeen Council Registers corpus

Volume	*Time period*	*Number of entries*	*Number of tokens*	*Average number of entries per admin. year*	*Average number of tokens per admin. year*[a]
Vol. 1	1398–1407	2,528	86,326	316	10,791
Vol. 2	1408–1414	1,490	44,611	248	7,435
Vol. 4	1433–1448	3,755	150,996	250	10,066
Vol. 5.1	1448–1468	4,418	207,601	210	9,886
Vol. 5.2	1441–1471	1,052	44,157	38	1,577
Vol. 6	1466–1486	9,047	556,506	431	26,500
Vol. 7	1487–1501	6,606	384,411	440	25,627
Vol. 8	1501–1511	5,181	331,062	518	33,106
Total	**1398–1511**	**34,077**	**1,805,670**		

a The administrative years 1403/1404 and 1404/1405 are not recorded in volume one. The few entries that were dated 1405 (without a specific date) are here included in the administrative year 1405/1406.

As Table 4.1 indicates, volume five part two (5.2) overlaps with volumes four, five part one (5.1) and six. This is because volume 5.2 contains the guild court records, which were separated from other burgh business between 1441 and 1472.[19] Initially, all volumes were treated as separate entities in the quantitative analyses, in order to detect any differences in language use between the guild court and other burgh business. In the final calculations, the figures of this overlapping period were, however, combined in order to trace the vernacularisation process consistently across the volumes (see sections 'Quantitative analysis of the matrix language of entries', 'Quantitative analysis of the number of words in Scots as opposed to Latin' and 'Comparisons and explanations').

The quantitative analyses were carried out on the prototype of the LACR online search platform, which was only accessible to the research team at the time of writing. The platform, which is now freely available online, serves as a repository for the images of the original documents and the *ARO* transcriptions.[20] The search platform allows users to query the transcriptions in various ways.[21] Search terms can be specified by time periods, volumes, language and other factors.

For the analyses presented here, XQuery was used to quantify the number of entries with Scots and with Latin as the matrix language as well as the number of words in Scots or Latin. The 'matrix language' is here defined as the dominant language of an entry.[22] This generally means that if the majority of words in an entry were Scots, then the entry was annotated as Scots.[23] The initial annotations applied by the transcribers were checked automatically by a tool developed by Wim Peters. This tool matched all words in each entry to a lookup list of Latin words compiled from Latin entries in the Aberdeen Council Registers. Using a probability threshold of 0.5, any entry that was marked up as Latin but with the number of Latin words being below this threshold was flagged for the editor, Edda Frankot, to review. This tool thus guaranteed the consistent assignment of languages to individual entries. In most cases, the matrix language was easy to determine. For some entries, however, it was not possible to determine a matrix language based on the 'dominance' approach (particularly in lists of names with Latinised first names but with Scots surnames). In these instances, the attribute "mul" for 'multiple languages' was used in the language tags.

The XQuery searches were divided into administrative years, running from the first Monday after Michaelmas (29 September) to the following year. The administrative years were determined manually by going through the dates of individual entries in the transcriptions and noting the entry IDs of the first and last entries of each administrative year. One issue here is that the entries are not always in diachronic order, particularly between 1466 and 1472, the period covered at the beginning of volume six. In this particular case, the entries were listed in a time period (1466–1472), rather than individual administrative years. There are also copies of letters, dated with their original date, that were incorporated into an entry under the date of the entry rather than when the original letter was written. The dates of these original letters were not taken into account in the quantitative analyses described below.

After determining the administrative years manually, XQuery was used to determine the number of entries with Scots/Latin/Dutch/multiple languages as the matrix language (see Appendix, XQuery 1). The query provided in the appendix finds and lists all entries annotated as Scots for the administrative year 1433/1434, which spans from the first entry on page 1 of volume four to (and including) the first entry on page 23 of volume four. The same query was then used for Latin, Dutch and entries with multiple languages by replacing the language attribute "sco" with "lat", "nld" and "mul", respectively, and all results were recorded in a spreadsheet. The entry identification numbers (xml:id) were then changed for the specific administrative years and the query was run again. To count tokens in Scots, Latin, Dutch and multiple languages, a more complex query was used (see Appendix, XQuery 2). This query tokenised words annotated as Scots, Latin, Dutch and multiple languages per administrative year, which was again expressed by the range of xml:id (in the query provided in the appendix it is 1433/1434), in monolingual as well as multilingual entries. In other words, it did not just count the words in each Scots entry but also the Scots words within Latin entries. Words were defined as a string of letters or numbers (0–9, a–z, A–Z), so that punctuation marks were not counted as separate words.

It has to be pointed out that these queries rely on the quality of annotations. The editing process carried out by the project team during and after the research presented here may result in slight differences in the findings if the same analyses were carried out again. Furthermore, it is not always possible to identify a word as Scots or Latin due to abbreviations. The abbreviation *barrell'*, for example, could stand for a Latin or Scots word, and the ampersand, which was expanded silently in the transcriptions, could stand for *et* or *and*. It is also problematic to determine when a borrowed Latin word has become a naturalised part of Scots. This distinction between borrowing and code-switching, the latter defined here as 'the use of more than one language in the course of a single communicative episode',[24] is a much-discussed topic in linguistic research.[25] Matras points out that these two phenomena can either be considered as two distinct phenomena or, and this is the view taken in this chapter, as 'related points on a continuum'.[26] For example, the word *item*, one of the most frequently used words in the corpus, could be categorised as Latin or it could be seen as a word that had become Scots by the fifteenth century. The *Dictionary of the Scots Language* lists examples of *item* being used in Scottish documents from 1397, suggesting that *item* can be considered a naturalised Scots word in fifteenth-century records.[27] However, even attestations in dictionaries are not always a reliable source for determining whether a word has become naturalised, and therefore constitutes borrowing rather than single-word code-switching.[28] Due to these issues, Trotter urges researchers to take a multilingual approach when working on late medieval Britain.[29] During this time, 'for the educated at least, monolingualism was the exception and not the norm'.[30] Working with XML annotations does not make it easy to take such a multilingual approach as it forces the transcriber to categorise entries and words into certain languages. This does, however, not mean that the same word can only be read as a Latin *or* Scots word. Returning to *item*, this word was annotated as Latin when occurring in a Latin context, i.e. when the preceding and/or following words were clearly Latin, and as Scots in a Scots context.

While the categorisation of individual words into specific languages remains problematic, the matrix languages of entries in the Aberdeen Council Registers are in the majority of cases clear. The quantitative analysis of the matrix language of entries and the use of the 'multiple languages' attribute surpass the problem of categorising individual words to some extent. However, an analysis of the matrix language ignores instances of language mixing and code-switching within individual entries. The 'Code-switching in the Aberdeen Council Registers' section is dedicated to some of these instances. Furthermore, a quantitative analysis of the words in Scots as opposed to Latin was carried out to illustrate that Scots did occur in administrative years where no entries with Scots as the matrix language were found (see year 1438/1439). Although specific numbers are presented in the 'Quantitative analysis of the number of words in Scots as opposed to Latin' section, the figures have to be seen as approximations due to the issues of annotating words in a specific language described earlier.

Quantitative analysis of the matrix language of entries

In this section, the quantitative analysis of the matrix language, i.e. the dominant language, of entries is presented, before moving on to the number of words in Scots as opposed to Latin in the following section. The findings of these analyses are then compared in the 'Comparisons and explanations' section.

As Table 4.2 shows, Scots and Latin are not the only languages used in the Aberdeen Council Registers. In volume 5.2, a letter in Middle Dutch from Antwerp is copied into the council registers (see entry ARO-5-0714-02), with another, albeit very short entry in Middle Dutch, in volume six (entry ARO-6-0691-04). These two entries point to the close trading relationships between

TABLE 4.2 Matrix languages of entries in the Aberdeen Council Registers (1398–1511)

Volume	*Time period*	*Number of entries*	*Scots*		*Latin*		*Dutch*		*Multiple*	
			n	*%*	*n*	*%*	*n*	*%*	*n*	*%*
Vol. 1	1398–1407	2,528	6	0.24	2,508	99.21	0	0	14	0.55
Vol. 2	1408–1414	1,490	9	0.60	1,467	98.46	0	0	14	0.94
Vol. 4	1433–1448	3,755	209	5.57	3,540	94.27	0	0	6	0.16
Vol. 5.1	1448–1468	4,418	317	7.18	4,092	92.62	0	0	9	0.20
Vol. 5.2	1441–1471	1,052	226	21.48	823	78.23	1	0.10	2	0.19
Vol. 6	1466–1486	9,047	2,958	32.70	6,087	67.28	1	0.01	1	0.01
Vol. 7	1487–1501	6,606	3,601	54.51	3,004	45.47	0	0	1	0.02
Vol. 8	1501–1511	5,181	3,310	63.89	1,870	36.09	0	0	1	0.02

Aberdeen and the Low Countries, which cannot be discussed in more detail here.[31] Table 4.2 also provides the number of entries with 'multiple languages', i.e. entries without a 'dominant' language. One of these entries will be discussed further in the 'Code-switching in the Aberdeen Council Registers' section. This section will instead focus on the vernacularisation in volumes one to eight of the Aberdeen Council Registers.

The quantitative analysis of the council registers revealed a considerable diachronic increase in the number of entries with Scots as the matrix language (see Table 4.2 and Figure 4.1). The number of entries with Scots as the matrix language remains under 1 per cent in the first two volumes (six entries in volume one and nine entries in volume two). It can be assumed but not proven that this percentage is higher in the material written between 1414 and 1433, which is missing. Given that merely 5.6 per cent of entries, i.e. 209 entries, had Scots as the matrix language in volume four and 7.2 per cent in volume 5.1 (317 entries), it is unlikely that the percentage of Scots entries in the material written between 1414 and 1433 is higher than 7 per cent. While this needs to remain as speculation, a clear increase in the use of Scots can be seen between volumes four and eight, with Scots gradually becoming the more dominant language at the expense of Latin, which decreases from 94.3 per cent in volume four to 36.1 per cent in volume eight. Of interest is also the difference between volume 5.1, in which 7.2 per cent of entries have Scots as the matrix language, and volume 5.2, in which considerably more entries with Scots as the matrix language can be found, namely 21.5 per cent. Given that volume 5.2 deals with the guild court business, this difference indicates that the content of the entries was one of the factors for language choice, with Scots being used more frequently for guild court business than for other burgh business recorded in volume 5.1. The entries in volume 5.2 are, however, not as regular as the ones in 5.1, which leads to divergent percentages in individual administrative years in volume 5.2. For example, in the year 1460/1461, only one entry was recorded. This entry was written in Latin, which means that in this particular year, 100 per cent of entries had Latin as the matrix language. Due to these discrepancies, the calculations of volume 5.2 were incorporated into the numbers from volumes four, five and six for the individual administrative years. The diachronic development across volumes four to eight, divided into the administrative years, is shown in Figure 4.1.[32]

The dotted polynomial trend line in Figure 4.1 illustrates a relatively gradual increase in the use of Scots between 1433 and 1511. The continuous black line indicates, however, that there is a particular strong increase of Scots in 1443/1444, in which the entries with Scots as the matrix language reach over the 10 per cent mark for the first time (16.2 per cent, i.e. 59 entries, in 1443/1444 and 18.1 per cent, i.e. 95 entries, in 1444/1445). The next time such a high percentage of entries with Scots as the matrix language is reached is 20 years later, in 1464/1465 (16.0 per cent, i.e. 45 entries). From 1466/1467 onwards, the percentage of entries with Scots as the matrix language remains above 10 per cent, with further

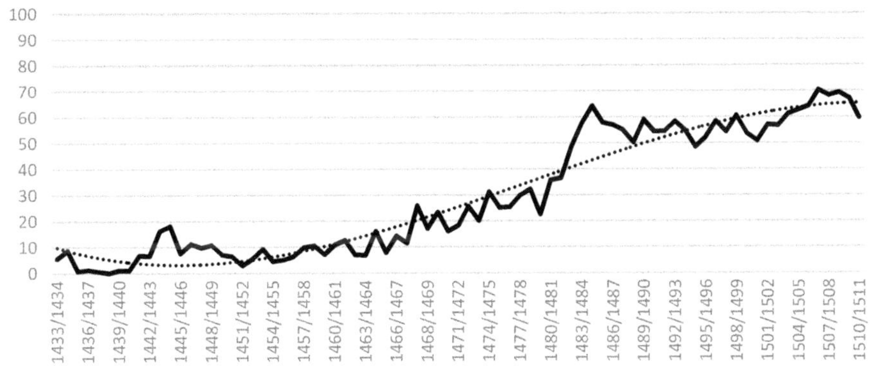

FIGURE 4.1 Percentage of entries with Scots as the matrix language in the Aberdeen Council Registers (1433–1511).

increases to 25.7 per cent in 1472/1473 (211 entries) and to 31.2 per cent in 1474/1475 (197 entries). Further considerable increases can then be detected between 1481/1482 and 1484/1485, the latter year being the one with the highest percentage of entries with Scots as the matrix language in the fifteenth century. During these four administrative years, the percentage increased from 36.5 per cent in 1481/1482 to 64.2 per cent in 1484/1485. The year before that constitutes the first year where Scots entries outnumber Latin ones, with 57.5 per cent of entries having Scots as the matrix language. After the peak in 1484/1485, a relatively balanced use of Scots and Latin can be observed, when considering the matrix language of entries. A further increase follows in the sixteenth century, during which Scots is consistently used in more entries than Latin. The highest percentage of entries with Scots as the dominant language can be found in 1506/1507 (70.3 per cent). After that, the percentage drops below the 70 per cent mark again. We can, therefore, conclude that the Aberdeen Council Registers were not fully vernacularised by 1511, with Latin remaining to be used as the matrix language in a considerable number of entries. The following section will report on the number of Scots as opposed to Latin words in the same period of time, before providing explanations for the increasing use of Scots in the council registers.

Quantitative analysis of the number of words in Scots as opposed to Latin

It is, of course, no surprise that the increase in the number of words in Scots runs parallel to the increase of entries with Scots as the matrix language. However, the percentages of Scots words are higher than the percentages of Scots entries in each of the volumes. This can be explained by the length of individual entries

TABLE 4.3 Number of tokens in different languages in the Aberdeen Council Registers (1398–1511)

Volume	*Time period*	*Number of tokens*	*Scots*		*Latin*		*Dutch*		*Multiple*	
			n	*%*	*n*	*%*	*n*	*%*	*n*	*%*
Vol. 1	1398–1407	86,326	1,122	1.30	83,064	96.22	0	0	2,140	2.48
Vol. 2	1408–1414	44,611	585	1.31	40,656	91.13	0	0	3,370	7.55
Vol. 4	1433–1448	150,996	14,072	9.32	135,267	89.58	0	0	1,657	1.10
Vol. 5.1	1448–1468	207,601	41,967	20.22	157,582	75.91	0	0	8,052	3.88
Vol. 5.2	1441–1471	44,157	18,068	40.92	25,843	58.53	89	0.20	157	0.36
Vol. 6	1466–1486	556,506	283,108	50.87	273,364	49.12	18	0.00	16	0.00
Vol. 7	1487–1501	384,411	260,758	67.83	123,617	32.16	0	0	36	0.01
Vol. 8	1501–1511	331,062	236,387	71.40	94,550	28.56	3	0.00	122	0.04

with some Latin entries (such as the admission of the burgesses) being very short and the use of Scots within entries with Latin as the matrix language (see the 'Code-switching in the Aberdeen Council Registers' section).

As Table 4.3 shows, the percentage of Scots words remains equally low in volumes one and two (1.3 per cent). Entries with multiple languages are, however, more common in volume two. Rather than categorising individual words into Latin and Scots in these entries, the words were annotated as 'multiple', with 7.6 per cent of 'multiple language words' in volume two and 2.5 per cent in volume one. This lowered the percentage of Latin words from 96.2 per cent in volume one to 91.1 per cent in volume 2. In volume four, 9.3 per cent of tokens, i.e. 14,072 words, were annotated as Scots. This percentage increases to 20.2 per cent (41,967 tokens) in volume 5.1 and to 40.9 per cent (18,068 tokens) in volume 5.2. In volume six, slightly more words are annotated as Scots (283,108 tokens, 50.9 per cent) than as Latin (273,364 tokens, 49.1 per cent) and in volume seven, Scots is the dominant language, with 260,758 tokens, which equates to 67.8 per cent. A further increase in the percentage of Scots words can be seen in volume eight, with 71.4 per cent of words being annotated as Scots.

Figure 4.2 illustrates the increase of tokens annotated as Scots between 1433 and 1511. While specific numbers are presented in Table 4.3 and were used as the basis for the graph below, these numbers do not fully account for the fact that it is not always possible to strictly categorise words as Latin or Scots, even if some words are marked as appearing in entries with 'multiple languages'. For example, the word 'item' (see earlier point), used at the beginning of many entries, was annotated as Latin when the matrix language of the rest of the entry was Latin but as Scots when the matrix language was Scots. The fuzziness of the line graph below highlights this issue, with exact numbers being difficult if not impossible to determine. This graph merely approximates the number of tokens that *can* be

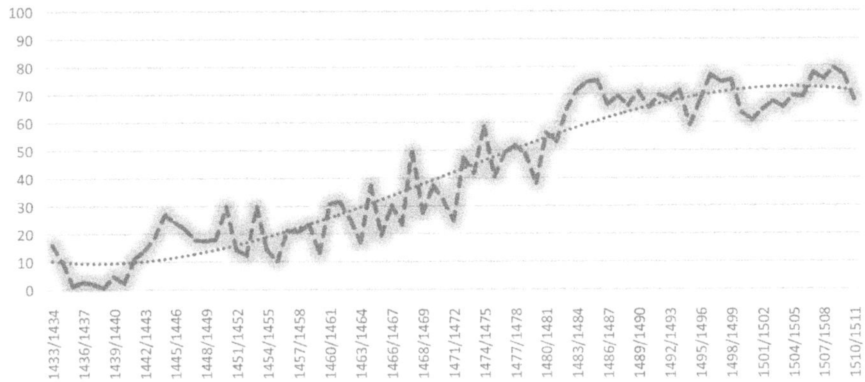

FIGURE 4.2 Percentage of tokens annotated as Scots in the Aberdeen Council Registers (1433–1511).

classified as 'Scots' and the increasing vernacularisation over time. In order to avoid evoking an unrealistic image of an entirely clear distinction between Latin and Scots, the Latin numbers are not represented in the graph. As Trotter points out:

> [n]either for the modern lexicographer nor for the user of the languages of Britain in the middle ages can clear-cut distinctions between vernaculars, or between vernacular and Latin, be considered an accurate representation of linguistic and social reality. Glossators and writers alike show scant regard for watertight divisions between languages.[33]

The fact that the Aberdeen Council Registers are multilingual in nature needs to be kept in mind and is discussed in more detail in the 'Code-switching in the Aberdeen Council Registers' section.

Despite the issues surrounding the categorisation of individual words as Scots, a clear increase in the use of Scots can be observed in the period under investigation (see polynomial trend line in Figure 4.2). With the exception of the first administrative year (1433–1434), the number of words annotated as Scots remains below 10 per cent until 1441/1442. After that, a drastic increase of Scots can be observed between 1441/1442 and 1445/1446, with the percentage of words annotated as Scots rising from approximately 10 per cent to over 25 per cent. In 1464/1465, more than every third word can be considered Scots, with further increases in the 1470s. The year 1474/1475 is the first in which more words are annotated as Scots (58.5 per cent) than as Latin (41.5 per cent). Scots can be considered the dominant language in the Aberdeen Council Registers from the early 1480s onwards, with percentages of Scots words ranging from 53 per cent in 1481/1482 to almost 75 per cent in 1485/1486 in the 1480s. The highest percentage of words annotated as Scots can be found in 1508/1509 (79.3 per cent). However, as pointed out in the previous section, Latin clearly remains to be used throughout the period under investigation, indicating its continuous importance in legal writing.

Despite the problematic issue of categorising words into Latin or Scots, it is worth quantifying the number of Scots words as it allows us to uncover Scots words used within Latin entries and thus complements the quantitative analysis of the matrix language of entries. In the following section, the differences between the results of these analyses are discussed, before providing some explanations for the vernacularisation developments in the council registers.

Comparisons and explanations

In order to show vernacularisation processes in the Aberdeen Council Registers more clearly, the period covered by volumes four to eight was divided into 16 intervals of five administrative years each (see Figure 4.3).[34] In the first two of these intervals (1433/1434–1442/1443), the percentage of Scots entries and words remains below the 10 per cent mark. After that, the numbers for Scots words diverge from the numbers for entries with Scots as the matrix language. In the third interval (1443/1444–1447/1448), there is a difference of almost 10 per cent between them (Scots entries: 13.1 per cent, Scots words: 22.3 per cent). After the rather drastic increase in the use of Scots between the first two and the third interval, the process continues more gradually between 1448/1449 and 1481/1482, with a difference between the percentage of Scots entries and Scots words ranging from 11.4 per cent in 1448/1449–1452/1453 to 22.8 per cent in 1472/1473–1476/1477. After another considerable increase between 1481/1482 and 1486/1487, the number of Scots entries and words remains fairly stable between 1487/1488 and 1501/1502. A further increase in the use of Scots can be seen in the final two intervals, with the percentage of Scots words staying above the percentage of Scots entries. A comparison of the two graphs plotted in Figure 4.3 illustrates that solely counting the matrix language of entries or the dominant language of texts (which seems to be the preferred research method currently employed) does not provide a full and accurate picture of vernacularisation processes. While the categorisation of individual words into distinct languages remains problematic, the method employed here highlights the fact that the vernacular may have been used more widely earlier on than previously thought.

The particularly drastic increase between 1481 and 1482, when 36.5 per cent of entries and 53 per cent of words were annotated as Scots, and the following three administrative years[35] partly coincides with the beginning of the so-called Sasine Register of Aberdeen (1484–1502), one of the only Scottish burgh protocol books surviving from the fifteenth century.[36] Frankot explains that the misleading term ‘sasine’, which refers to the transfer of ownership of property, was added later. In fact, this register includes entries relating to the sheriff court in Scotland, copies of legal documents and various legal entries,

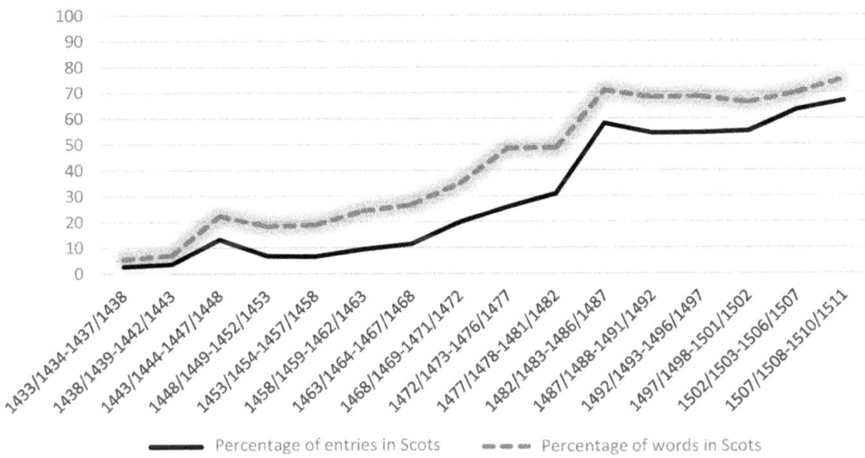

FIGURE 4.3 Diachronic development of the use of Scots in the Aberdeen Council Registers in per cent (1433–1511).

many but not all of which concern property. Frankot speculates that some of the business recorded in Latin in the Aberdeen Council Registers was transferred to the Sasine Registers in 1484, which would explain the relative drastic decrease of Latin in that year. The Sasine Register itself is mostly written in Latin.[37]

The fact that Scots became the more dominant language in the records of parliament after 1425 (see 'Introduction') and the fact that the vernacular was used almost exclusively in other Scottish burgh records, such as the Burgh Court Book (1457–1479) from Newburgh in Fife, by 1480[38] points to a more local rather than a national development in the vernacularisation of the Aberdeen Council Registers. This raises questions about the spread of the vernacular in legal records of different Scottish burghs, which cannot be addressed here. It also highlights the point made in the 'Introduction': vernacularisation processes happened at different times in different regions and in different records, making it difficult to determine a general timeline of vernacularisation. It can, however, be generally assumed that all legal records in Scotland were multilingual in the fifteenth century, with code-switching and language mixing occurring frequently. The following section will discuss the multilingual nature of the Aberdeen Council Registers, focussing on instances of code-switching, before moving on to more general conclusions.

Code-switching in the Aberdeen Council Registers

As the earlier analyses show, Scots and Latin are used in each of the first eight volumes of the Aberdeen Council Registers. In the TEI-compliant transcriptions of the Aberdeen Council Registers, Scots words within Latin entries and Latin words within Scots entries were annotated with the tag <foreign>, which makes it easy to quantify the number of code-switches (CS) into Latin and Scots in the records. As mentioned earlier, code-switching is here defined as 'the use of more than one language in the course of a single communicative episode'.[39] Table 4.4 lists the number of these CS, separated into volumes. The normalised frequency of these CS (Scots and Latin together) is also provided to compare the relative frequency of the CS per 1,000 entries in the eight volumes (as explained earlier, relying on data compiled at the time of study).

Schendl comments on the chronological correlation between vernacularisation and the use of code-switching, but concedes that further research into this correlation is necessary.[40] Some conclusions concerning the link between code-switching and vernacularisation can be drawn from Table 4.4. The number of CS into Scots is naturally higher in the volumes where more Latin is used, i.e. volumes one to six. In volumes seven and eight, on the other hand, CS into Latin outnumber those into Scots, which is not particularly surprising given that more than half the entries are in Scots in these two volumes. What is striking is the relatively low number of CS in volume two (62.4 CS per 1,000 entries) and volume six (67.2 CS per 1,000 entries). The three highest relative numbers of CS can be found in volumes four (90.8), 5.1 (118.8) and 5.2 (127.4), i.e. at the beginning of the increase of Scots. While these figures neither take the length or the nature of the CS nor entries with 'multiple languages' into account, they suggest that the number of CS is higher at the beginning of the vernacularisation process. However, statistical tests indicate that there is no statistically significant correlation between the decrease of Latin entries and the number of CS in the first eight volumes of the Aberdeen Council Registers.[41] The number of entries with Latin as the matrix language decreases steadily, while there is a spike in CS in volumes 4–5.2. The spike in CS into Scots may be due to scribes starting to consider Scots as a language that was appropriate to use in legal contexts or even necessary to

TABLE 4.4 Number of code-switches in the Aberdeen Council Registers (1398–1511)

Volume	*Time period*	*Number of entries*	*Number of tokens*	*CS into Scots*	*CS into Latin*	*Total number of CS*	*Normalised CS per 1,000 entries*	*% of entries annotated as 'Scots'*
Vol. 1	1398–1407	2,528	86,326	187	28	215	85.05	0.24
Vol. 2	1408–1414	1,490	44,611	92	1	93	62.42	0.60
Vol. 4	1433–1448	3,755	150,996	307	34	341	90.81	5.57
Vol. 5.1	1448–1468	4,418	207,601	402	123	525	118.83	7.18
Vol. 5.2	1441–1471	1,052	44,157	88	46	134	127.38	21.58
Vol. 6	1466–1486	9,047	556,506	325	283	608	67.20	32.70
Vol. 7	1487–1501	6,606	384,411	167	376	543	82.20	54.51
Vol. 8	1501–1511	5,181	331,062	135	279	414	79.91	63.89

aid comprehension (see below). CS into Latin, on the other hand, may have been used in Scots entries to stick to the traditional structure and conventions of the registers, which may have been considered more important in the earlier volumes than when Scots was fairly well established as a written legal language. Without a careful qualitative analysis of the nature of the CS in all volumes of the council registers, these possibilities remain speculations. The following analysis of CS in volume 5.2, in which the highest relative number of CS can be observed, does, however, support some of these suggestions.

Table 4.4 shows that 46 CS are into Latin and 88 CS into Scots in volume 5.2. These CS can be divided into (a) intrasentential CS, i.e. switches between or within sentence constituents, and (b) intersentential CS, i.e. switches between sentences or independent clauses.[42] The majority of CS in volume 5.2 are intrasentential (34 into Latin and 87 into Scots). Intersentential code-switching is more common in switches into Latin because Latin is sometimes used for the heading and/or date at the beginning of entries. Entry ARO-5-0782-01, for example, starts with the date in Latin before continuing in Scots, as the following transcription and image show (Figure 4.4):

The image illustrates that there is no difference in the scribe's handwriting between the Latin beginning and the Scots continuation of this entry. In fact, no change in handwriting was detected for any of the CS in volume 5.2. There are, however, other visual cues in entries that switch between Scots and Latin, such as line breaks. Kopaczyk's model for conceptualising code-switching on different levels takes such visual cues into account and highlights the interaction between these cues and instances of code-switching.[43] In this model, CS can be categorised on six different levels: (a) macrogenre: the switch of codes between different genres (i.e. what Voigts refers to as intertextual level),[44] (b) discourse: CS beyond the sentence level (i.e. for 'larger, functionally and textually coherent passages' such as reported speech), (c) clause: CS between complete clausal units (i.e. intersentential code-switching), (d) word: CS for a single phrase or word (i.e. intrasentential code-switching), (e) morpheme: the use of a different code for single morphemes (e.g. for the root and for inflections), and (f) orthography: when words are spelled 'according to orthographic conventions taken from another code'.[45] The model then allows researchers to specify whether the

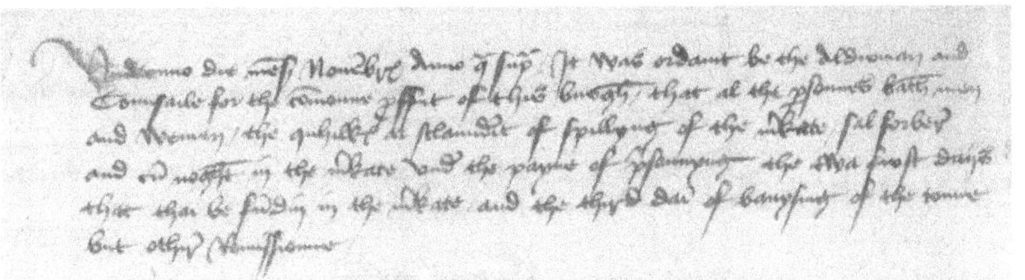

FIGURE 4.4 Entry ARO-5-0782-01 of the Aberdeen Council Registers, dated 11 November 1454. By permission of Aberdeen City and Aberdeenshire Archives.

scribe used visual cues for these CS. Applied to volume 5.2, CS in the Aberdeen Council Registers can be described in the following way based on Kopaczyk's model. Since the entries included in the council registers can be considered to constitute one text genre (legal texts), there are no CS on the macrogenre level. Code-switching can, however, be observed on the discourse, clause, word and morpheme levels.[46] There are no visual cues for CS on the word and morpheme level. On the discourse and clause level, on the other hand, the scribes do use visual cues in the form of line breaks. This is, however, not always the case, as the example of the Latin date earlier shows.

Dates constitute only one part of the CS into Latin, as Figure 4.5 illustrates. Most CS into Latin are modifications of names, such as *pater* (father) or *filius* (son). After dates, the next most frequent use of code-switching into Latin are Latinised names, such as *Willelmus* for 'William', which can be considered CS on the morpheme level. There is also some legal terminology for which Latin is used, e.g. 'transeat de villa' for '[s/he may/must] pass through the town'. As mentioned before, Latin is also used in headings and marginalia. The copy of a letter in Middle Dutch is, for example, introduced in Latin: 'Copia obligacionis Walteri michaelis de Andwarpia' (ARO-5-0714-02). Similarly, Latin is used as a structuring element and as a cohesion marker, with expressions such as 'in primis' or 'videlicet'.

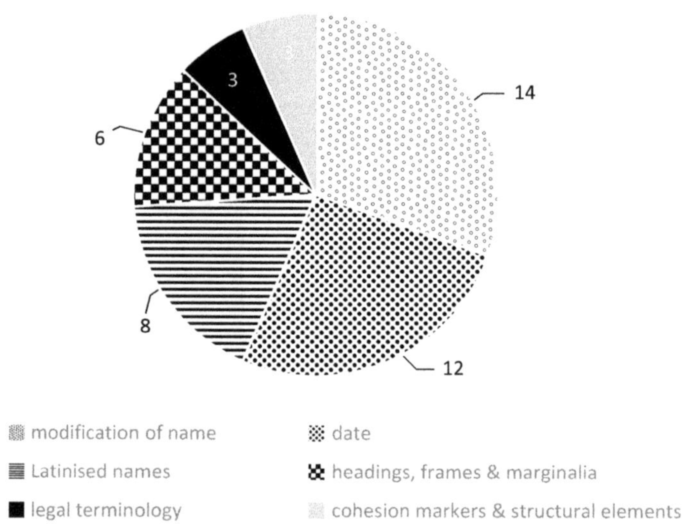

FIGURE 4.5 Code-Switches (CS) into Latin in volume 5.2 (1441–1472).

In summary, CS into Latin are mainly used for specific legal writing practices, such as modifiers after names, and to structure the text through dates, headings and other structural elements. CS into Scots, on the other hand, seem to be used when there is no Latin equivalent, when the Latin equivalent is unknown or

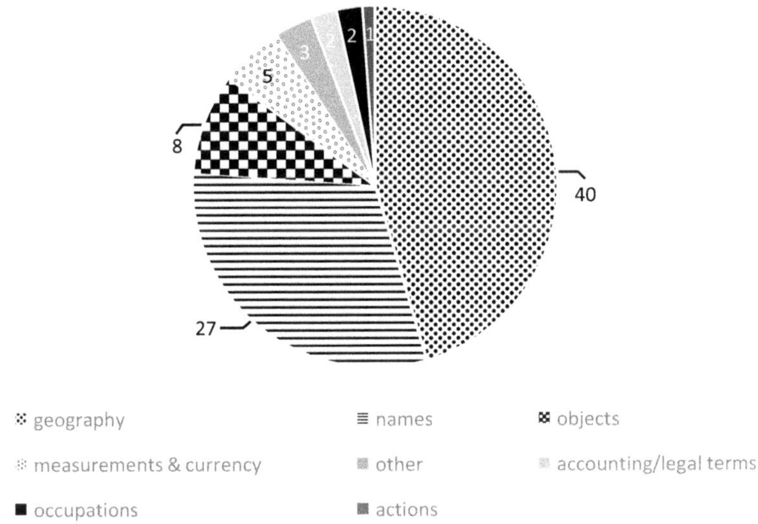

FIGURE 4.6 Code-Switches (CS) into Scots in volume 5.2 (1441–1472).

much rarer than the Scots term, or to ensure understanding. Figure 4.6, which shows the CS into Scots divided into different functions, illustrates these points.

In contrast to the CS into Latin, most CS into Scots refer to locations or geographical features, particularly place names, names of streets, crofts and rivers. To provide just one of the 40 examples, entry ARO-5-0699-01 reads 'Jacentem ex parte occidentali de ly schipraw inter terram Johannis Rede [...]', with 'ly schipraw' referring to a street name in Aberdeen that is still in use today, albeit in its English form 'shiprow'. This is a typical example of intrasentential CS. The Scots form of this particularly street name was, however, not always used. In fact, the Latin equivalent ('Vico Nauium') occurs more frequently than 'schipraw', but only in entries with Latin as the matrix language (in 179 entries). Overall, the Scots form is used in 21 Latin and 41 Scots entries, and is particularly frequent in volumes six and seven of the council registers. However, no particular development in the use of the Latin as opposed to Scots form emerges from this data. Geographical terms, like street names, and Scots surnames together account for about three quarters of all CS into Scots. While first names are often Latinised, surnames usually remain in their Scots form, such as 'alexander of kintor' in entry ARO-5-0652-04. Furthermore, some objects (for example, 'ly barge') as well as some measurements and currency (such as 'mitez', i.e. a small copper coin) appear in Scots.

As these examples show, the Scots terms are often introduced with the definite article 'ly', which was borrowed from Anglo-Norman. The *Dictionary of the Scots Language* explains that 'ly' (also spelled *le, lie* or *lee*) was used 'when citing, in Latin contexts, appellative place-names in the vernacular which idiomatically required the definite article', and possibly subsequently was 'applied also to any vernacular designation in a Latin context' and was similarly used in medieval English materials.[47] The use of the Anglo-Norman article shows that Scots was influenced by a variety of languages, many of which were used in a legal context, demonstrating the multilingual nature of this text type.

A few CS into Scots can also be found for accounting and legal terms (e.g. 'ly tollis', which refers to tax paid to a landowner), occupations (such as 'baxter' for 'baker') and actions (e.g. 'Johannes Richardson grauntis plukkyng of schorlingis' for 'John Richardson grants the gathering of sheep skin'). Other CS into Scots were difficult to categorise (see 'other' category). Sometimes an entry starts in Latin but ends in Scots, as the following transcription of entry ARO-5-0676-01, which deals with fish trade, illustrates. This entry was annotated with the attribute "mul" for multiple languages, as it is difficult to determine the dominant language of this entry. Therefore, no 'foreign' annotations are used here, even though the scribe clearly switches between Latin and Scots. Where exactly these CS start and end is, however, not always easy to determine. The abbreviation *barrell'* could, for example, be interpreted as Latin or Scots. Indeed, it remains unknown if the scribe himself consciously distinguished between these two languages (see Trotter's earlier statement). There is certainly no indication in the handwriting that suggests that the two languages were strictly divided (see Figure 4.7). This kind of mixing of languages is not unusual in late medieval Britain and can be observed in various text types. Wright, for example, illustrates that the abbreviations in late medieval business writing in England can simultaneously be interpreted as both English and Latin.[48]

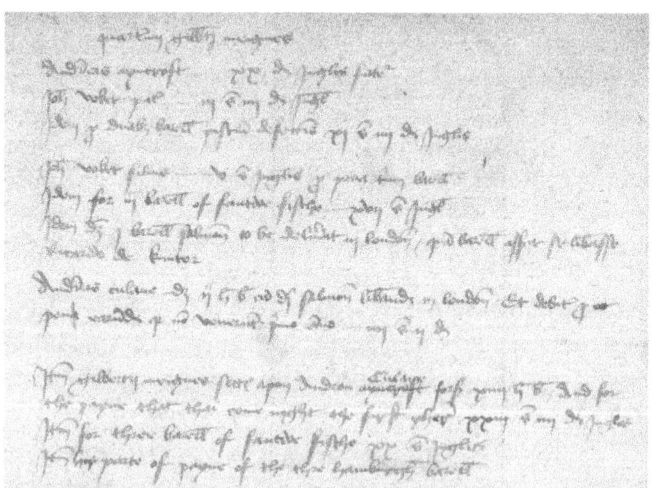

FIGURE 4.7 Entry ARO-5-0676-01 of the Aberdeen Council Registers, dated 9 March 1444. By permission of Aberdeen City and Aberdeenshire Archives.

Particularly interesting in the previous entry is that the scribe translates a Latin phrase into Scots: *Et debit' p[ro] pena earu[n]d[em] q[uod] no[n] veneru[n]t p[ri] mo a[n]no* to *And for the payne that thai come noght the first yher'*. This shows that there was a Latin equivalent to the Scots phrase and that the scribe was happy and ready to use it. It can, therefore, be assumed that this translation is meant to aid comprehension for the readers of the records.

The previous entry demonstrates the multilingual nature of the council registers. Of course, these records are no exception to the use of various languages in other texts. Amongst others, Wright, Schendl and Kopaczyk have illustrated that multilingualism was the norm in late medieval and early modern texts.[49] The potential correlation between vernacularisation and CS, however, remains under-researched. The quantitative analyses presented here suggest that CS is more common at the beginning of the vernacularisation process. While the data from the Aberdeen Council Registers do not provide evidence for a statistically significant correlation, the results still indicate that the scribes switched between languages more frequently when they started to use Scots as the matrix language in entries more often. To fully understand why this is the case, instances of CS in all eight volumes of the registers would have to be analysed qualitatively, which needs to remain a topic for further research at this stage. There are, however, other conclusions that can be drawn from the results presented here.

Conclusions

This chapter highlights the significance of the Aberdeen Council Registers for linguistic research on vernacularisation and multilingualism in late medieval texts. Due to their almost continuous run from 1398, these records are particularly suitable to investigating diachronic changes in language use. The quantitative analyses allow us to trace the increasing vernacularisation of the Aberdeen Council Registers, concluding that Scots can be considered the dominant language in these records from the early 1480s onwards (at least with regard to the number of Scots words). Nevertheless, Latin remained in constant use during the period under investigation (1398–1511). This is particularly interesting in the later volumes: scribes did not use Scots consistently, despite accepting it as a suitable language for legal discourse. Latin remains visible in the records and thus maintains its role as language of law, albeit alongside the vernacular.

The coexistence of Latin and Scots in the records can be seen as constituting 'a complex multilingual code', which was used by the scribes to convey meaning.[50] The use of abbreviations that could be either read as Latin or Scots suggests that scribes did not distinguish rigidly between the two languages. Nevertheless, clear instances of code-switching can be found in the registers. These seem to be more common at the beginning of the vernacularisation process and, as the analysis of volume 5.2 showed, were used for different purposes. CS into Latin mainly occur for formulaic parts, such as dates or structural elements, or specific writing conventions (e.g. *filius* after a name). Some of the CS into Scots, on the other hand, seem to aid comprehension, suggesting that not all readers were able to understand Latin. This raises questions about how audiences engaged or were expected to engage with the records, which is an aspect that needs to be investigated further.

The multilingual nature of the Aberdeen Council Registers presents some problems for the quantitative analyses presented here. A strict categorisation into Latin and Scots words is not always possible due to frequent abbreviations and suspension marks used by scribes. The TEI-compliant annotations in the transcriptions of the council registers can point to these problems to some extent (e.g. by annotating entries with multiple languages and frequent CS with "mul"). One point to stress here is that the main aim of creating the Aberdeen Council Registers transcriptions, the *ARO*, was to build an open basis for further investigation from various disciplinary perspectives (including the historical, legal, linguistic, palaeographical) rather than to construct a corpus richly annotated for linguistic research. Furthermore, the transcriptions should be comprehensible to non-academics. Therefore, Scots abbreviations were expanded and annotated with the <expan> tag, while Latin expansions remain unmarked, also due to the time constraints of the LACR project. Wright stresses the problem of silent expansions in transcriptions of medieval texts and their role in neutralising the language.[51] In the transcriptions of the Aberdeen Council Registers, this problem can only be overcome by a rather time-consuming process of adding specific annotations to the expanded words, but that is possible given that the resource is open for reuse. Despite these issues, the analyses presented here are a worthwhile exercise, showing the multilingual nature of the Aberdeen Council Registers and the increasing vernacularisation between 1398 and 1511. The results highlight the point that different records were vernacularised at different times and/or at a different pace in different regions. In-depth analyses of individual records are, therefore, necessary to gain an accurate picture of vernacularisation processes in Scotland and elsewhere.

The vernacularisation of legal texts more generally has to be seen in the context of a changing legal culture. The use of the vernacular allowed more people to access legal contents, even if this access was controlled and not necessarily direct. At the same time, the elite could use these legal texts to diffuse certain knowledge, as Hepburn and Small point out.[52] It would be interesting to investigate what kind of 'knowledge' was disseminated via the vernacular. While we know that certain legal contents remained to be expressed in Latin, such as property transfers or the admissions of the burgesses of guild, it remains to be seen to what extent the contents of an entry influenced a scribe's language choice and whether the scribes were 'free to choose' between languages. Such research on the choices made by the people directly involved in writing legal texts, i.e. by the community of practice, would provide further insights into how 'cultures of law' developed over time. The Aberdeen Council Registers would certainly be a suitable source to research this topic.

Appendix

XQuery 1:

```
for $i in //ns:div[@xml:lang="sco"] [@xml:id >"ARO-4-0001-00"]
[@xml:id <"ARO-4-0023-02"] return $i
```

XQuery 2:

```
for $lang in ("lat", "sco", "nld", "mul")
return (concat("Words annotated as ", $lang, ": ",
count(for $j in (
for $i in //ns:div[@xml:lang = $lang ][@xml:id >"ARO-4-0001-
00"][@xml:id <"ARO-4-0023-02"]//*
return if (not($i/@xml:lang) or $i/@xml:lang = $lang) then (
tokenize(normalize-space(string-join($i/text(), ' ')), ' ')
) else ()
)
where matches($j, '[0-9a-zA-Z]')
return $j
)
+
count(for $j in (
for $i in //ns:div[@xml:lang!= $lang][@xml:id >"ARO-4-0001-
00"][@xml:id <"ARO-4-0023-02"]//*
return if ($i/@xml:lang = $lang) then (
tokenize(normalize-space(string-join($i/text(), ' ')), ' ')
) else ()
)
where matches($j, '[0-9a-zA-Z]')
return $j
)))
```

Notes

* I thank the editors and the anonymous reviewer for their feedback and helpful suggestions for improvement. I also thank Radostin Stoyanov (University of Cambridge) for his help with XQuery and Dr Song Liu (University of Bristol) for his help with the Pearson correlation text.

1 H. Schendl, 'Mixed-language texts as data and evidence in English historical linguistics', in D. Minkova and R. Stockwell (eds) *Studies in the History of the English Language: A Millennial Perspective*, Berlin: Mouton de Gruyter, 2002, pp. 51–78; P. Pahta and I. Taavitsainen, 'Vernacularisation of scientific and medical writing in its sociohistorical context', in I. Taavitsainen and P. Pahta (eds) *Medical and Scientific*

Writing in Late Medieval English, Cambridge: Cambridge University Press, 2004, pp. 1–22.
2 P. Burke, *Languages and Communities in Early Modern Europe*, Cambridge: Cambridge University Press, 2004, p. 10.
3 Pahta and Taavitsainen, 'Vernacularisation', p. 12.
4 R. Carroll, 'Middle English recipes: Vernacularisation of a text-type', in Taavitsainen and Pahta (eds) *Medical and Scientific Writing*, pp. 174–91.
5 M. Stenroos, 'The "vernacularisation" and "standardisation" of local administrative writing in late and post-medieval England', in L. Wright (ed.) *The Multilingual Origins of Standard English*, Berlin: De Gruyter Mouton, 2020, pp. 39–86.
6 C. Macafee, 'Scots', in *Encyclopedia of Language and Linguistics*, 2nd edn, Boston: Elsevier, 2006, pp. 33–6, at p. 34.
7 J. Smith, *Older Scots. A Linguistic Reader*, Edinburgh: The Scottish Text Society, 2012, p. 6.
8 Ibid.
9 Ibid., p. 8. Original italicisation.
10 M. Görlach, *A textual history of Scots*, Heidelberg: Winter, 2002, p. 26.
11 Ibid.
12 J. Corbett, J.D. McClure and J. Stuart-Smith, 'A brief history of Scots', in J. Corbett, J.D. McClure and J. Stuart-Smith (eds) *The Edinburgh Companion to Scots*, Edinburgh: Edinburgh University Press, 2003, pp. 1–16, at p. 8.
13 J. Kopaczyk, *The Legal Language of Scottish Burghs. Standardization and Lexical Bundles (1380–1560)*, Oxford: Oxford University Press, 2013, p. 89.
14 H. Schendl, 'Multilingualism, code-switching, and language contact in historical sociolinguistics', in J.M. Hernández-Campoy and J.C. Conde-Silvestre (eds) *The Handbook of Historical Sociolinguistics*, Oxford: Wiley-Blackwell, 2010, pp. 520–33, p. 521, and Burke, *Languages and Communities*.
15 See the introduction to this volume for details on the Aberdeen Council Registers.
16 E. Frankot, A. Havinga, C. Hawes, W. Hepburn, W. Peters, J. Armstrong, P. Astley, A. Mackillop, A. Simpson and A. Wyner (eds) *Aberdeen Registers Online: 1398–1511* (hereafter *ARO*), Aberdeen: University of Aberdeen, 2019, <https://www.abdn.ac.uk/aro> (accessed 29 August 2019).
17 For further details, see A.D. Havinga and A.Z. Wyner, 'The Aberdeen burgh records of 1398–1531 and the semantic web', *Journal of Catalan Intellectual History*, 2018, pp. 151–7.
18 These figures are based on calculations carried out on and prior to 7 January 2019 and are subject to slight changes due to the continuing editing process at the time of writing.
19 See E. Gemmill, *Aberdeen Guild Court Records 1437–1468*, Edinburgh: Scottish History Society, 2005, who provides a transcription of volume 5.2 in book form, for more information on this particular volume.
20 University of Aberdeen, *Search Aberdeen Registers*, n.d., <https://sar.abdn.ac.uk> (accessed 31 August 2019). This platform is based on the application created under the supervision of A. Wyner by R. Stoyanov, M. Zak, C. Beck, J. Burn and J. Siemaszko, published in 2017 at GitHub.
21 For details, see Havinga and Wyner, 'The Aberdeen burgh records'.
22 Cf. C. Myers-Scotton, *Contact Linguistics*, Oxford: Oxford University Press, 2002, and P. Auer and R. Muhamedova, '"Embedded language" and "matrix language" in insertional language mixing: Some problematic cases', *Journal of Italian Linguistics* 17(1), 2005, pp. 35–54.
23 There are, however, cases of entries that start and end with a passage in Latin, with a larger Scots section in between. These entries were annotated as Latin, even though the number of Scots words may have exceeded the number of Latin words in the entry. The quantitative analysis based on word counts (see the 'Quantitative analysis of the number of words in Scots as opposed to Latin' section) takes these cases into account.

24 M. Heller, 'Introduction', in M. Heller (ed.) *Codeswitching. Anthropological and Linguistic Perspectives*, Berlin: Mouton de Gruyter, 1988, pp. 1–24, at p. 1.
25 Cf. H. Schendl, 'Code-switching in Anglo-Saxon England: A corpus-based approach', in P. Pahta, J. Skaffari and L. Wright (eds) *Multilingual Practices in Language History: English and Beyond,* Berlin: De Gruyter Mouton, 2017, pp. 39–60.
26 Y. Matras, *Language Contact*, Cambridge: Cambridge University Press, 2009, p. 110.
27 Scottish Language Dictionaries, 'item', *Dictionary of the Scots Language*, online, n.d., <http://www.dsl.ac.uk/entry/dost/item> (accessed 4 May 2018).
28 Cf. R.Q. de Barros, 'Twentieth-century Romance loans: Code-switching in the Oxford English Dictionary?', in Pahta, Skaffari and Wright (eds) *Multilingual Practices in Language History*, pp. 61–76.
29 D.A. Trotter, 'Multilingualism in later medieval Britain: Introduction', in D.A. Trotter (ed.) *Multilingualism in Later Medieval Britain*, Cambridge: D.S. Brewer, 2000, pp. 1–5, at p. 3.
30 Ibid.
31 Cf. A.D. Havinga, 'Assessing the intensity of language contact between Middle Dutch and Scots in late medieval Aberdeen', in J. Kopaczyk and R. Millar (eds) *Language on the Move across Contexts and Communities*, Aberdeen: Publications of the Forum for Research on the Languages of Scotland and Ulster, in press.
32 Volumes one and two are not included in this figure since, as Table 4.2 shows, the percentage of entries with Scots as the matrix language is very low in these two volumes.
33 D.A. Trotter, 'Language contact and lexicography: The case of Anglo-Norman', in H.F. Nielsen and L. Schøsler (eds) *The Origins and Development of Emigrant Languages*, Proceedings from the Second Rasmus Rask Colloquium, Odense University, November 1994, Odense: Odense University Press, 1996, pp. 21–39, at p. 21.
34 The last interval contains only four years (1507/1508–1510/1511).
35 In 1482/1483: 48.5 per cent of entries and 64.6 per cent of words annotated as Scots; 1483 /1484: 57.5 per cent of entries and 71.5 per cent of words annotated as Scots; 1484 /1485: 64.2 per cent of entries and 74.5 per cent of words annotated as Scots.
36 E. Frankot, 'Manslaughter in 1480s Aberdeen: Notes from another fifteenth-century register', *Aberdeen Registers*, Aberdeen, 2017, <https://aberdeenregisters.org/blog/> (accessed 29 March 2018).
37 Ibid.
38 An analysis of the matrix language of entries in the Newburgh Burgh Court Book, which was transcribed by Dr William Hepburn, shows that 98.3 per cent of the entries have Scots as the matrix language between 1457 and 1479 compared to 20.9 per cent of entries during the same period in the Aberdeen Council Registers. The Newburgh burgh records are held at the University of St Andrews Library Department of Special Collections, reference number B54, <https://encore.st-andrews.ac.uk/iii/encore/record/C__Rx1867012> (accessed 30 March 2018).
39 Heller, 'Introduction', p. 1.
40 Schendl, 'Mixed-language texts', p. 70.
41 The Pearson correlation test resulted in a coefficient (r) of 0.173, with a p-value of 0.682 (threshold for p-value = 0.05), which means that there is no statistically significant correlation between the percentage of entries in Latin and the normalised number of CS in volumes one to eight of the ACR. The same test was carried out for volumes 1–5.2 with the percentage of entries in Scots, which resulted in a higher coefficient (r) of 0.828, which means that there is a positive correlation between the increase of Scots entries and the rise in the relative number of CS, but it also did not show a statistically significant correlation (p = 0.083).
42 S. Romaine, *Bilingualism*, Oxford: Basil Blackwell, 1989, p. 112–3, and H. Schendl, 'Beyond boundaries: Code-switching in the leases of Oswald of Worcester', in H. Schendl and L. Wright (eds) *Code-Switching in Early English*, Berlin: de Gruyter, 2011, pp. 47–94, at p. 69.

43 J. Kopaczyk, 'Administrative multilingualism on the page in early modern Poland: In search of a framework for written code-switching', in Pahta, Skaffari and Wright (eds) *Multilingual Practices in Language History*, pp. 262–84.
44 L.E. Voigts, 'What's the word? Bilingualism in late-medieval England', *Speculum* 71, 1996, pp. 813–26.
45 Kopaczyk, 'Administrative multilingualism', p. 276. See J. Kopaczyk, 'The language of medieval legal record as a complex multilingual code' in this volume for examples of code-switching on these different levels.
46 The orthographic level needs to be investigated further. Instances of orthographic code-switching, assuming that these can be found in the Aberdeen Council Registers, were not annotated as 'foreign' in the transcriptions, so they would have to be analysed manually.
47 Scottish Language Dictionaries, 'le *def. art.*', *Dictionary of the Scots Language*, online, n.d., <http://www.dsl.ac.uk/entry/dost/le_def_art> (accessed 7 May 2018).
48 L. Wright, 'Bills, accounts, inventories: Everyday trilingual activities in the business world of later medieval England', in Trotter (ed.) *Multilingualism in Later Medieval Britain*, pp. 149–56.
49 L. Wright, 'Mixed-language business writing: Five hundred years of code-switching', in E.H. Jahr (ed.) *Language Change: Advances in Historical Sociolinguistics*, Berlin: Mouton de Gruyter, 1998, pp. 99–118; Schendl, 'Mixed-language texts'; Schendl, 'Multilingualism'; Kopaczyk, 'Administrative multilingualism'; cf. Trotter, *Multilingualism*; and Schendl and Wright (eds) *Code-Switching in Early English*.
50 Kopaczyk, 'The language of medieval legal record as a complex multilingual code', in this volume.
51 L. Wright, 'On variation in medieval mixed-language business writing', in Schendl and Wright (eds) *Code-Switching in Early English*, pp. 191–218.
52 W. Hepburn and G. Small, 'Common books in Aberdeen, c. 1398–c. 1511', in this volume.

PART III
Jurisdiction and conflict

5

URBAN LAW IN NORWEGIAN MARKET TOWNS

Legal culture in a long fourteenth century

Miriam Tveit

Like many Scottish towns, most Scandinavian medieval towns were small in terms of population, size and financial volume.[1] In contrast with the majority of other continental and insular regions, the number of urban settlements was also few, particularly in Norway. Despite the relative lack of urbanisation in the middle ages, extensive scholarship exists on Norwegian urban politics and culture.[2] What has been studied to a lesser degree are the subjects of towns as environments of legal activity and the legal culture that developed in these urban spaces. Due to a lack of town records surviving from the central middle ages, and few and incomplete sources from the late middle ages, much of our knowledge of Norwegian urban life comes from archaeological work.[3] Relevant studies have yielded information on spatial divisions within towns and the demarcations of urban and rural space – or rather, the lack of such demarcations. However, the legal space within the town has not yet been analysed, even if the extent of those legal boundaries has been a topic of discussion.[4]

Following the definition of Jørn Øyrehagen Sunde, this study mainly stays within the *narrow* sense of the concept of legal culture, which concentrates on how the law is expected to work.[5] That focus is nevertheless not exclusive of legal culture in its *wider* sense, in which it is 'more closely tied to other fields of society'.[6] In the context of studying urban legal culture, this chapter seeks to explore how law worked in the smaller towns of Norway and to identify the expectations that inhabitants had of the legal system in these market towns. This is to understand more fully the urban element in the legal system of the Norwegian kingdom in a European context.

When discussing the impact of urban law, it is of interest to define the parameters of this law. In the European context, there was often a sharp distinction between the urban sphere – thus the jurisdiction of urban law – and the surrounding land. The late medieval Norwegian town was not as distinct from its surroundings as most European towns with a twelfth-century genesis.[7] The boundaries between the urban legal space, called *takmark*, and surrounding rural space may appear blurred to modern historians.[8] Likewise, it would be overly simplistic to think that a town law clearly distinguished a town from its surroundings.[9] Today, scholars are less receptive to the idea of clear-cut legal jurisdictions in the middle ages and more aware of how principles of accessibility and sensibility played a role in both the comprehension of law and the execution of justice. Legal boundaries were overlapping and fluid, and that should be our point of departure when trying to understand legal culture within Norwegian market towns.[10]

After a code was issued for Norway in 1274 by King Magnús Hákonarson (1263–1280), a new Town Law was promulgated in 1276.[11] The Town Law was originally designed for the major export town of Bergen, but it was gradually adapted for the other larger towns of Oslo, Niðaros (Trondheim) and Tønsberg. The status of this new law regarding its use in legal practice in other towns has not been studied in full. Understanding the impact of the new Town Law on the market towns requires a close reading of the arguments and resolutions in the surviving documents, which consist mainly of charters. The material that could be termed 'case law' is, however, neither systematic in terms of registering cases from town courts, nor abundant enough to permit anything more than suggestive conclusions to be drawn regarding the urban legal culture of either the market towns or Norwegian towns in general. Many of the known written documents relating to Norway in the middle ages have been transcribed and published in the continuing collection *Diplomatarium Norvegicum* (hereafter *DN*) instituted in 1847.[12] This collection does not comprise town records as such, but relevant documents demonstrate how law worked in an urban context in Norway. Although substantially more charters survive from 1300 onwards, written sources touching on medieval legal culture in general and Norwegian urban life in particular are still scarce. The material can at best offer glimpses into the legal culture that had developed in Norwegian urban settlements, but it can possibly also provide information as to whether an 'urban' legal culture can be said to have developed in parallel to a 'rural' legal culture.[13] Around 1300, market towns like Vágar and Skien flourished (see below), but several of them had declined in importance by the early fifteenth century. The long fourteenth century has therefore been chosen as the scope for this study. In what follows, the legal charters from this period will be examined with particular regard to the participants in urban legal activity and the question of where legal proceedings took place within the market towns.

Understanding Norwegian urbanisation

Norwegian urbanisation did not produce the hierarchical networks and diversification of trade or production that were characteristic of the urban landscape elsewhere (for instance in England).[14]

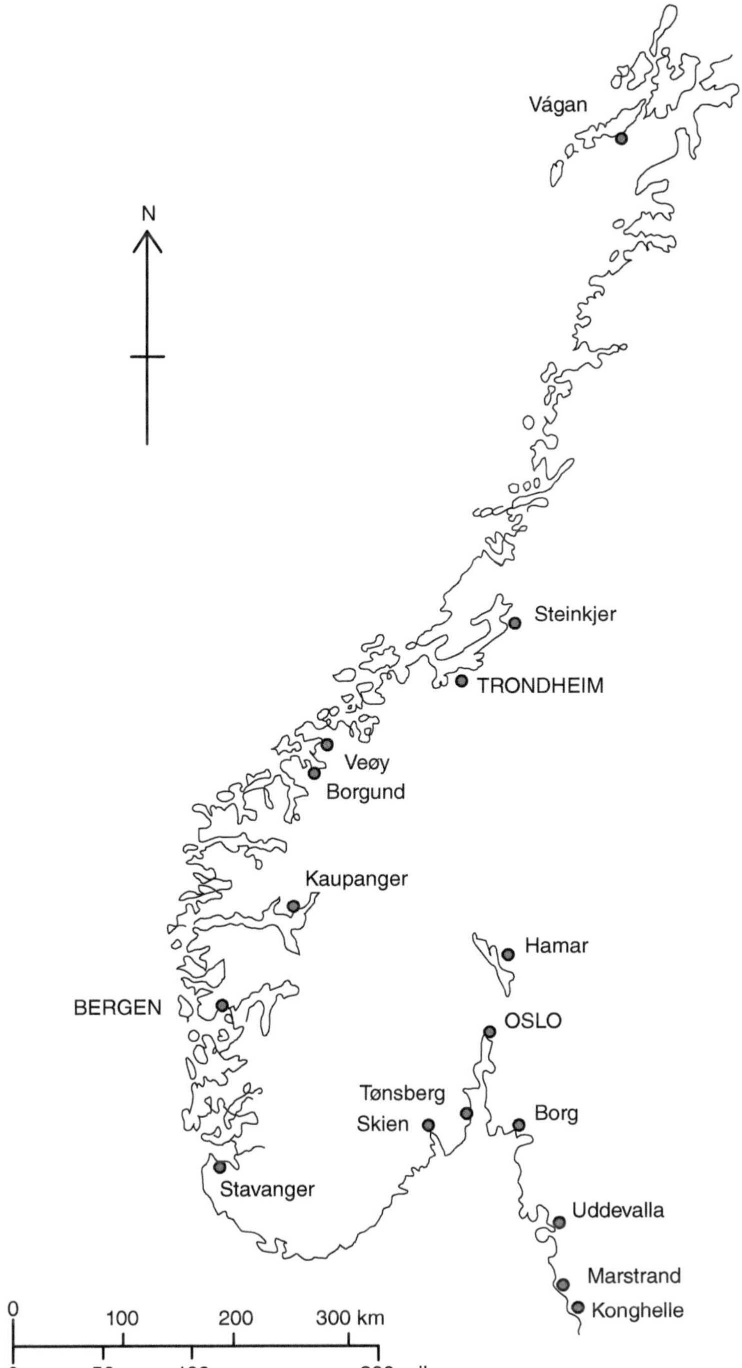

FIGURE 5.1 Map of medieval Norway's towns.

Source: Richard Holt, 'What if the sea were different? Urbanization in medieval Norway', *Past & Present* 195, Issue suppl 2, 2007, pp. 132–147 <https://doi.org/10.1093/pastj/gtm026>, at p. 134.

These differences have spurred a scholarly debate in Norway on what constitutes a town and which urban sites could justly be defined as such in the middle ages. To tackle the discrepancy, scholars have sought to highlight the functional, topographical and administrative-legal qualities of urban settlements as qualifiers to classify them as towns.[15] In some instances, scholars have been reluctant to put a settlement in any urban category and have instead suggested several non-urban labels, such as 'fishing station' or 'densely populated area'.[16] The pre-eminent Norwegian historian in the field, Knut Helle, used expressions such as 'townlike place' (*bylignende sted*) when describing one of these sites.[17] Norwegian scholarship customarily divides urban sites into towns; small towns; and markets, some with permanent settlements. Terminology in the source material from the twelfth to the fifteenth centuries justifies this division to some degree, with *kaupstadir* ('town'), *smaar kaupstader* ('small town') and *kaupstefna* ('marketplace or centre of commerce').[18] The latter two categories signify what in this chapter are termed 'market towns', on the basis that they should be studied as part of the Norwegian urban landscape, being understood in a sense as 'urban' by medieval spectators. Other terms signifying 'town' include *kaupang*[19] and *bæ*.[20] Helle, together with Arnved Nedkvitne, suggested in 1977 that a useful approach when studying Norwegian towns is to follow the medieval notion of what was urban.[21] Even so, Skien, which survived as a town into the modern age, only received its town privileges in 1358, even if the same royal letter granting those privileges described the customs *j bynom j Skidu* ('in the town of Skien'), confirming that it was already considered to be a town before this date.[22] Privileges were not a necessary criteria for what constituted a town in medieval Norway. Moreover, the medieval and the modern ideas of what constitutes a town do not necessarily correspond. A traditional definition is that a town is the densely populated hub of a larger area that has specialised functions for its surroundings and a continuous existence.[23] In a publication on the multifaceted nature of Norwegian town history, archaeologist Reidar Bertelsen argued that the status of an urban site in Norway was not comparable with that of insular or continental towns.[24] Pointing to the functions of Norway's northernmost medieval urban site, Vágar, Bertelsen rejected the distinctions in status made by historians such as Helle between those places earning the status of 'town' and those found to be too small and short-lived.[25] All these urban locations meet the definition of a town, according to Bertelsen. The termination of a town's existence at a later point should not exclude it from a historical discussion of urbanisation. Helle also admitted the constraints of using a narrow town definition when studying the medieval urban history of Norway.[26] Following Bertelsen's approach, this chapter seeks to analyse the sources of urban legal culture in Norway's smaller towns. Their relative lack of size, and the length of time for which they existed, make the legal culture within them an interesting object of study, because they represent the intrinsic urban development in Norway. When determining the status of a town one should consider of first importance its function within its own lifetime rather than its continuity through time.

Even in Scandinavian terms Norway was not very urbanised. From 1319 to 1343, Norway and Sweden entered into a bilateral union, and in 1380, Norway fell under the Danish crown. All three kingdoms entered into the Kalmar Union in 1397, which created an uneasy political situation throughout the fifteenth century. The union between Norway and Sweden did not produce legal unification other than that the administrations of their legislative enterprises mutually inspired each other.[27] Nevertheless, the development of law and of urbanisation in Sweden was comparable to the urban-legal development in Norway. In or around the late 1340s, King Magnus Eiriksson (1319–1364) issued the Code of the Realm for Sweden and afterwards, in the 1350s, he similarly promulgated a Town Law for the realm.[28] The Swedish realm counted 42 towns in the middle ages, according to Hans Andersson.[29] By contrast, the Danish experience to a large degree followed the continental urbanisation process in the middle ages, and Denmark had approximately 110 towns, with somewhat fewer at the beginning of the sixteenth century.[30] The Norwegian towns of any notable size were Niðaros, Bergen, Stavanger, Tønsberg, Oslo and Hamar. The documented market towns in the late middle ages were also few in number. Listed from north to south, the market towns that existed in the fourteenth century were Vágar, Veøy,[31] Borgund,[32] Kaupanger,[33] Skien,[34] Sarpsborg, Oddevold, Konghelle and Marstrand, the latter three of which are now part of modern-day Sweden.[35] All the Norwegian towns but Hamar were situated along the coast with access to the sea shipping.[36] The four market towns north of Bergen had strong connections with this major export town as suppliers of goods such as stockfish and other marine products, together with iron and stone.[37] Exchange relied on trade networks comprising elite families holding properties in both Bergen and a northern town. The importance of the supplies coming into Bergen is revealed in the privilege granted to the Hanseatic towns in 1294: it forbade foreign merchants from sailing *ultra Bergas uersus partes boreales* ('beyond Bergen to the northern parts') as part of a general policy to control trade.[38] Only domestic traders were allowed to collect domestic products, which possibly also reduced direct foreign influence through trade on the local legal culture in the market towns.

Urban law in Scandinavia

Written laws first emerged in Scandinavia in the twelfth and thirteenth centuries. These laws applied to larger jurisdictions, or legal provinces, and are therefore called 'provincial laws' today. Designated town laws originated in the same period and were called *Bærkoyar rettr* or *Bjarkeyjarréttr*.[39] The extant manuscripts of the Norwegian *Bærkoyar rettr* were dedicated to Niðaros, a royal town and the episcopal seat, but more general versions were valid in other towns and commercial sites.[40] From the mid-thirteenth century, major legal reforms began in Norway, and in 1274, King Magnús Hákonson, nicknamed *lagabætir* ('the Lawmender'), issued the Norwegian Code of the Realm.[41] This was a little earlier than the assumed date of origin of the Scottish *Regiam Maiestatem* and *Quoniam*

Attachiamenta, which in contrast were not codifications.[42] The king issued a separate Town Law for Bergen in 1276.[43] Similar to how the *Leges Burgorum* constituted a national framework for the Scottish burghs, the new Town Law became a general law for Norwegian Towns during the fourteenth century. The new Town Law in the same manner was built on the old *Bærkoyar rettr*, which it replaced. However, whereas the *Bærkoyar rettr* is comparable with the compilation of burgh laws of the Scottish *Leges Burgorum*,[44] the new Town Law was consciously constructed and published as part of the legal reform of the second half of the thirteenth century. Adapted versions of the new Town Law were introduced to the other three main towns of Niðaros, Tønsberg and Oslo within a few decades, and the law was generally distributed and in use among Norwegian towns throughout the fourteenth century.[45] Little is known about how this process developed exactly, for example, how fast the Town Law was disseminated or to what degree the small towns made use of it. The *Bærkoyar rettr* itself stated that it was valid also in fishing stations and with regard to trading ventures.[46] This claim was copied into the *farmanna logh*, a book regulating sea travel and trade that accompanied the new Town Law in many of the surviving manuscripts.

Most of the surviving manuscripts of the new Town Law are copies of the version made for Bergen. Therefore, much of its known content was adapted to fit Bergen's circumstances. In her analysis of two Niðaros manuscript versions of the Town Law, Grethe Blom suggested that, like Bergen, the main towns of Niðaros, Tønsberg and Oslo had already developed sufficient administrative power by the 1270s to be able to enforce the new Town Law.[47] While this is true, few legal historians today adhere to such a distinct definition regarding the enforceability of written law. The current view is that the distribution of medieval law tended to be based on practicality rather than that a law was used only in the jurisdiction for which it was written. Towns were increasingly important hubs for tax administration and, of course, trade. The Crown took great interest in maintaining trade and trade privileges within the towns, as demonstrated by a legal amendment postdating the new Town Law.[48] This Town Law, as well as the Code of the Realm, remained valid over the next three centuries, although the Dano-Norwegian administration increasingly struggled to understand the Old Norse language it was written in.[49] Copies of these codes were still included in legal collections in the sixteenth century, and they were also excerpted in late medieval documents.[50]

The contents of the new Town Law in Norway did not deviate substantially from the Code of the Realm. In effect, the Norwegian Town Law followed the Code of the Realm while incorporating adjustments to account for an urban setting. Jørn Øyrehagen Sunde estimates that 30–50 per cent of the contents of the Code of the Realm were changed, with the sections either adjusted or new, in the new Town Law.[51] Only a few paragraphs (concerning, for instance, protection from fire) are not to be found in the earlier law at all.[52] In comparison, according to linguist Bo Wendt, exactly 50 per cent of the paragraphs of the Swedish Town Law were parallel with the Swedish Code of the Realm and 50 per cent were exclusive to that corpus.[53] As a product of the same administration that had produced the Norwegian Code of the Realm, similar influences can be seen to be at work in King Magnús' new Town Law. The members of the royal administration that formulated the Code of the Realm were educated within the context of the European intellectual legal school of law, and neo-Roman and canonical legal thought can be traced in the law of 1274.[54] Nevertheless, the contents of the Code of the Realm, and therefore also the new Town Law, were adapted to local conditions.[55]

All the same, when analysing how the law worked in the market towns, it is to be noted that the surviving evidence of law in practice rarely, if ever, cites the new Town Law, or any other law for that matter. On rare occasions, medieval Norwegian charters referred to actions being taken 'according to custom', using terms for 'custom' such as *vane*, *sedhwane*[56] or 'done legally', making use of the Old Norse terms for 'law' (*lagh* or *lof*) or the more Danified versions (*loug* and *lov*).[57] One of the few examples is from one of Norway's larger towns, Oslo, where in 1498, peasants were fined 'according to the law [*lagh*] of Norway as old custom [*sedhwane*] has been in this country'.[58] A fine resolved this case, in which the peasants themselves had summoned the commoners for a town assembly (*mót*) without permission from the authorities. The lack of a direct reference to written law should be viewed as a matter of formulation and legal cultural language rather than as a lack of knowledge of the law or a refusal to use it. The use of law will be addressed in the following section.

Urban legal culture and the practice of law

Turning to the legal practice in Norwegian medieval market towns, a brief comment on the Scandinavian legal system as it had developed up to the late thirteenth century will be helpful. The traditional medieval lawscape in the Old Norse world was the *þing*, a representative assembly, which was held outdoors in a designated and preferably neutral place.[59] Provincial assemblies, called the *lǫgþing*, were the highest organ of justice in the kingdom, presided over by the *lǫgmaðr/lagman* (lawman) who sat together with a jury, but assemblies were regularly held for smaller regional entities such as a county (*fylki*) or farthing (*fjórðungr*) as well as in each local community. The Nordic institution of the *þing* was also part of town life, although the town assembly was usually termed a *mót* ('meeting').[60] In the late thirteenth century, however, a number of the provincial assemblies were moved from their original rural sites to the leading town in the province.[61] For example, the county assembly (*fylkisþing*) was held in the market town of Veøy in 1439.[62] Town assemblies were originally held outdoors but came to be held within a town house beginning in the fourteenth century.[63]

The written law codes in Norway set out a very detailed regulation of the legal system. However, there were several alternatives to judicial solutions, including out of court settlement or vengeance and, in any case, it was not a given that parties would want to or would be able to involve the courts in a conflict.

Although authorities encouraged an official administration of justice in towns and countryside, it was not necessarily the favoured option of any of the parties involved. However, as written records became the norm, some actions, such as transactions of property, must have made the services of the law court desirable, including for those living in or around the market towns. The Code of the Realm and the Town Law also came with a provision that demanded the parties 'to make a letter' (*gera bref*) after a sale.[64] Accordingly, a substantial proportion of the charters concern transactions of property and privileges.[65] When a man called Josepper in 1356 sold a large property in Sunvin (western province) to one Þronde for the value of 36 cows, he had the transaction witnessed in writing in the town of Kaupanger.[66] Although the parties might not have lived in the town themselves, they may have sought the services of the town officials to record their agreement. It would seem that the two men's legal expectation for their transaction was for it to be recorded in writing. The same charter (or diploma) includes a highly specific description of the timing and contents of the two instalments already paid by the buyer and those agreed upon for the future. The procedures between Josepper and Þronde are in accordance with the instructions for disposing of property in Code of the Realm, which makes sense as the property sold was situated in the rural area.[67] This is one of the few cases that can be followed until its resolution: three years later, the lawman of the provincial assembly wrote a charter to state that he had witnessed the pair transacting again, now in Oslo, on the other side of the country from Kaupanger.[68] And in 1360, it was recorded that Josepper had received the full payment from Þronde. The dominance of provincial property in the diplomas suggests that the small towns were largely meeting places for rural activities.

The issue of location leads to the question of what constituted the spaces of law in a market town. Where did the parties meet the representatives of the law to have their cases heard and transactions witnessed? It appears that during the fourteenth century, a court of justice with an official representative gradually replaced the *mót* as the active judicial institution. Little evidence exists of attempts to systemise legal proceedings, as opposed to the law itself, leaving few clues regarding any common understanding of what constituted the typical court site in a town. Legal charters from the Norwegian market towns rarely disclose where a case was heard. The sparse and diverse evidence from the sources may provide an accurate representation of the inconsistent realities of urban justice. The physical space of law may well have taken diverse forms in the market towns, and practical considerations rather than standardised concepts may have dictated where the town's court of justice was held. It is not certain that the market towns had a specific town hall in this period, or any public buildings at all. Most of the charters from market towns were witnessed in town houses, possibly the homes of the officials. For example, one mention of the physical judicial space is found in a diploma from Kaupanger, where a settlement of an inheritance in 1337 was conducted 'in the common room of the Brasi house' (*i stofuni i Brasa garðe*).[69] Although the location of the Brasi house is unknown, it was likely one of the town houses in Kaupanger. From Sarpsborg, we learn that the legal recording of one transaction of 1367 took place 'in the common room of the priest's house' (*j stofuonne a præs gardenom*).[70] Priests were literate and belonged to the social elite, a further indication of legal affairs conducted in spaces controlled by governing officials. The lawman of Skien (*Skiðu/Skidu*) stated that he heard cases in the *gestgardenom*, the guesthouse, in March and May 1341.[71] This building was possibly a public house in which he lodged and exercised his office while in town. At some point, the assembly in Skien was moved to a permanent building, and the settlement of a fishing rights dispute from 1400 mentions the hearing taking place in its common room (*gaardszstufunne*).[72] The number of witnesses, as recorded in the charters from market towns, further suggests that these cases were smaller, more confined events, which were not held in front of the town population like a *mót*. Some larger towns may have had designated buildings for judicial activity, but the market towns most likely combined judicial activity with other meetings involving the king's ombudsman. As a result, they used a room or building suitable for this purpose.

In addition to the question of where the space of law was or was expected to be in the towns, one may ask who performed justice in the market towns and to which level of society those seeking and executing justice belonged. The witnesses and validators appearing in the charters usually belonged to the regional elite. In cases from the larger towns, we can typically find prominent figures imposing determinations. In the above-mentioned case from Oslo, in which the peasants were fined for summoning individuals to a town assembly themselves, the fine was witnessed by the lawman, the bishop, the archpriest, the mayor and seven members of the Oslo city council.[73] This was a very high-ranking group of men in what we must assume was a momentous and high-profile case. We find high-ranking judges in the market towns as well: from Konghelle, we have nothing but documents of royal origin or concerning conflicts and agreements within the royal administration.[74]

The regular cases involving property transactions in market towns often involved the elite as well. A charter concerning land rent from 1321 written in the northernmost town in Norway, the market town of Vágar, was witnessed by the lawman of the province of Hálogaland together with the priest of the powerful *Þrondarnes* church.[75] While the land in question, Sandtorg, was under the *Þrondarnes* canonry, it was not part of the church's land but owned by the equally prominent Erling Viðkunnsson, a prominent estate holder in the region and, two years later, the high steward of Norway.[76] This diploma of land rent written in Vágar thus involved three of the highest-ranking men in the region. In these cases, it was apparently not the idea of a liberating *stadtluft* or the impact of the new Town Law that caused the transaction to be recorded in the market town instead of elsewhere. On the contrary, the town was merely the location where high-ranking officials stayed and executed their office; it did not serve as a particular sphere of jurisdiction. Regarding the medieval Scottish burghs, Hector MacQueen and William Windram have asserted that modern historians have stressed the distinction between the law of the burghs and the law of the realm more than medieval subjects would have done.[77] It is evident that the distinction was similarly blurred in the Norwegian market towns as the rural cases dominate the surviving charters originating in them. The relatively weak urbanisation of Norway seemingly upheld the value of landed, rural property over urban property. Although the market towns could be remote in a Norwegian or European sense, the wealth of the political and economic elite that lived in them could be significant, as demonstrated by a dowry list from a wedding in Vágar in 1335.[78] The bride, Jngibiarghar, was the daughter of Jwar the lawman. The groom, Þorlæifr, was the son of Sigurðr, who had the byname *bonde*, indicating that they were estate holders with *oðal* (allodial land).[79] The dowry consisted, in addition to property and fish products, of 74 items, valued at 10 marks gold, representing the full extent of the northern networks, with an English wool carpet, four high-quality items of German cloth, a coffer with German ironwork and fine pelt work. In return, the bride received a counter-gift. The rich dowry identified Jngibiarghar and Þorlæifr as being among those who would be considered elite in any part of Europe, and the regional town of Vágar was a suitable location in which to record this marital transaction.[80] The above-mentioned inheritance distribution heard in the Brasi house in Kaupanger included three prominent local men: *Sira* (priest) Hauk, Thorstein Skolle and Erp Björnssön were witnesses in November 1337 in an agreement regarding an inheritance involving three farmsteads.[81] The precise status of the latter two men is unknown, but they both testified with seals which is an indication of their aristocratic status.[82] The parties that were involved, Ordrek with his nephews and Endride Botolfssön with his paternal grandmother, are also thought to have belonged to the aristocracy.[83] The case was therefore a transfer of property within the land-based elite of Kaupanger's hinterland, witnessed by their peers.

Private legal contracts without prominent figures among witnesses can also be found. One example is a letter from Borgund dated 1338 proving a sale from a certain Karl to a certain Simun of a property with the value of two months' rent in kind (*manaða mata læigu*), making it a very modest property.[84] The property belonged to Karl's wife Gyrid and, we learn, it had previously been parcelled out from a larger property belonging to Gyrid's aunt. The contents of the Town Law relied on the Code of the Realm for sorting out inheritance and agricultural questions.[85] In market towns, these two topics frequently arose in matters of law. An equally humble sale was registered in Sarpsborg in 1367, when three parts of a farmstead further south were sold by a married couple to one Hallæ Dyra, who had already acquired one and a half parts from the wife's former husband, and had transferred the first down payment.[86] These registered transactions bear witness to an existing legal culture among the parties which consisted of a shared knowledge of law and common expectations and traditions with regards to legal practices. Furthermore, the parties seemed to have possessed a perception of justice that was in accordance with written procedures, but that more likely reflects an understanding of common legal standards that had been recorded in the Code of the Realm. The latter two cases also demonstrate that people outside the elite in society had insight into the legal procedures that were relevant to be able to function within their own economic boundaries, although this insight was not necessarily based on first-hand knowledge of the written law, but rather on an understanding of existing laws. In the cases from both 1338 and 1367, the parties had made arrangements following common legal standards before setting out to register their agreements. The documents do not oppose the instructions from the Code of the Realm, although they do not quote them.[87] Those involved knew the ideas behind the law, if not the law itself. We also see in these examples an expectation by the parties involved that both the transaction and the agreed-upon proceedings would be recorded and witnessed by official legal specialists, such as the lawman and town magistrates. Although the cases were embedded within a legal culture, they do not provide evidence of a particular urban legal culture having emerged in Norwegian society. The only 'urban' element in these cases is the fact that they were recorded within towns. There are similar examples of legal transactions in this period taking place outside the few urban settlements. The town was probably used as the site of the transaction because of its convenience; it was where the legal officials held office.

Several studies have illustrated that the body of legal officials was sometimes mobile, visiting some of the important local assembly sites or commercial emporia of their region.[88] Nevertheless, in the early fourteenth century, the administration seems to have established itself in the urban settlements, with the rural population present or represented in the town. One example is when Þorer, baron and district governor in the town of Skien, registered a statement that he had heard testimony in a disputed property sale case while traveling in the province.[89] The Code of the Realm describes a procedure of producing witnesses and presenting them before the court in disputed sales.[90] Therefore, the legal activity in the towns touched upon the rural assemblies, which means that it is impossible to consider the legal spaces of town and province as having been strictly separate. It is similarly impossible to identify two distinct legal cultures, one with urban and one with rural qualities.

Although most documents concern the friendly transfer of property, we also find disputes being settled in market towns, such as the above-mentioned conflict over fishing rights in Skien in 1400.[91] Furthermore, some cases involved 'criminal' matters. Again in Skien, a murder case was reported to the king in 1325 by district governor Hakon, son of the above-mentioned Þorer.[92] In 1341, another murder case was presented to the lawman Thord Thorgilssön and ombudsman Björgulf Astasön, again in Skien.[93] In this case, the two administrators attested to having heard *prov* (proof) regarding Tholf who had killed Olaf. On this point, the Town Law followed the Code of the Realm, which stated that no one other than the one guilty of homicide should pay compensation and fines and that the victim's closest heir should be the recipient.[94] In this way, the law released both families from any involvement. The revisions of King Magnús ('the Lawmender') saw changes to procedure that brought the Code of the Realm into line with European developments in legal thought and procedures, with a clearer divide being made in general terms between homicide in the first and second degree: murder would be punished with exile and/or death while homicide would be amended through the payment of fines and a compensation. The law included procedural innovations in the case of homicide. Rules on investigation were added; in the so-called *prov*, an oral testimony with a description of the events was to be recorded.[95] The 'proof-taking' that we see in these two cases was only one part of the investigation. The investigation was then used to determine what verdict should be given to the guilty party through an exploration of the graveness of the action. The king was himself invested with the right to show mercy to the accused. The fact that the proof-taking was done in Skien may have been coincidental. Ombudsman Björgulf similarly attested to a homicide testimony having been given in 1337, but then in Mærden, just north of the town, possibly at the site of the homicide.[96] Notably, a large portion of the charters concerning *prov* originate from Skien and its province.[97]

From the town Borgund, a charter from 1421 reveals a serious incident of name-calling.[98] Insults, libel and defamation were crimes according to most European written laws including the Scandinavian legal tradition. In this *prov*, we learn that Haluard Erlendzsson had called Joon Sæmundasson a 'damned son of a whore and a queer scoundrel' (*fendans skækeson oc arghan hieransson*), and witnesses swore full oaths thereupon.[99] Insult is one of the crimes addressed in the Norwegian Town Law, with a fixed compensation to the insulted party of four silver marks.[100] The crime, resolution and sum are not exclusive features of the Town Law, though they are borrowed almost verbatim from the Code of the Realm, which itself had copied the punishment of insults from earlier provincial laws.[101] The difference between the new Town Law and the Code of the Realm from the 1270s and the earlier provincial laws was that insults were one of the few crimes that continued to be settled through monetary compensation, while the possibility to redress with money for other crimes such as homicide, adultery and theft was restricted or abolished.[102] While the new laws described insults and libel in general terms, the older provincial law *Gulaþingslog* included a short list of examples of verbal offences, including saying that a man had been sexually penetrated or that he was a prostitute or any of several animals of the female sex.[103] Attacking an individual's manliness was a grave crime according to many European laws, and the *Gulaþingslog* even gave victims the right to kill someone for such an offence. The Code of the Realm had superseded the old provincial law of *Gulaþing* for some 150 years by the time the case of Haluard and Joon came along. The case was referred to the provincial assembly of *Gulaþing*, held in the town of Bergen later in the year of 1421.[104] There, the lawman awarded Joon compensation of five cows from Haluard, which was the equivalent of approximately four silver marks in the fifteenth century.[105] Thus the fine both complied with the current law and reflected the older regional legal culture.

The Norwegian market towns of Borgund, Veøy and Vágar diminished in prominence during the fifteenth century. The protracted process of deterioration is only attested to by a letter from King Olaf in 1384 demanding that trade be conducted in these market towns and not in the fjords and the fishing stations, reflecting a concern that the market towns were falling into disuse.[106] Their decline is traditionally explained in the context of the economic devastation in the wake of the plague that struck Norway in the late 1340s.[107] The fact that legal letters were issued in these market towns at this time indicates that the fundamental legal and commercial functions of the market towns were nevertheless maintained during this process of decline. The weak urban tradition in Norway possibly intensified the de-urbanisation process in the provinces. During the fifteenth century, the northernmost provincial assemblies were moved from Vágar to the rural estate of Engeley across the fjord, and then permanently situated there.

Concluding remarks

The cases examined here from Norway's market towns only yield fragments of an existing legal culture; they only provide examples of laypeople encountering the law through cases they brought before officials or to which they were summoned, but do not clarify whether and how they might have come into contact with the law in other contexts. Nevertheless, the examination of charters from the market towns has shed light on a lesser-known side of the medieval urban experience. This analysis has shown that there was no distinct urban legal culture in the Norwegian small towns, and that legal affairs in these towns are difficult to distinguish from the legal affairs of the surrounding province. The market towns functioned as judicial hubs for their areas without, it seems, any particular 'urban' tasks. The results demonstrate that the legal apparatus of the market town dealt with the same types of cases that the rural assemblies did and in many ways served as a substitute rural assembly. The market towns served as assembly places within a legal context, just as they were sites for administration and the distribution of goods. The royal policy of unification of the legal system seemingly led to a coordination, which meant that representatives of the authorities and those subjects interested in the services of the legal officials met in these urban locations.

This study has revealed that people had knowledge of how to make use of the law and the possibilities that the legal system provided. Property transactions predominate in the source material, which is also mainly concerned with the legal activity of those at higher levels of society. Thus, to a large degree, what is revealed is the social elite's knowledge of law and legal procedures. However, some transactions also provide insight into the legal behaviour of ordinary people, suggesting that they too had expectations for the use of the legal system for their own interest.

We have seen strong indications that the promulgation of the new Town Law had little direct impact on the use of law in Norwegian market towns. Still, as this study has revealed, the participants did abide by legal norms – it was just that these corresponded with those of the non-urban Code of the Realm. The legal culture of late medieval Norwegian market towns was furthermore grounded in the law in a conceptual way; that is, the legal practice worked from an *idea* of law and not necessarily from the written law itself.

Notes

1 E.P. Dennison and G.G. Simpson, 'Scotland', in D.M. Palliser (ed.) *Cambridge Urban History of Britain*, vol. I, Cambridge/New York: Cambridge University Press, 2000, pp. 715–37, at pp. 722–31.

2 Notable examples of multi-authored works are G.A. Blom (ed.) *Urbaniseringsprosessen i Norden. Del 1. Middelaldersteder. Det XVII. nordiske historikermøte*, Trondheim: Universitetsforlaget, 1977; K. Helle, 'Fra opphavet til omkring 1500', in K. Helle, F.-E. Eliassen, J.E. Myhre and O.S. Stugu (eds) *Norsk byhistorie: urbanisering gjennom 1300 år*, Oslo: Pax, 2006, pp. 23–142; H. Andersson, G. Hansen and I. Øye (eds) *De første 200 årene – nytt blikk på 27 skandinaviske middelalderbyer*, UBAS Nordisk 5, Bergen: Universitetet i Bergen, 2005; and F.-E. Eliassen and T. Gansum (eds) *Den urbane underskog, Strandsteder, utvekslingssteder og småbyer i vikingtid, middelalder og tidlig nytid*, Oslo: Novus Forlag, 2009.

3 For the market towns: B. Solli, 'Veøyas arkeologi', in *Veøyboka*, Molde: Romsdalsmuseet, 1999, pp. 8–100; S. Myrvoll, *Handelstorget in Skien: A Study of Activity on an Early Medieval Site*, Bergen: Riksantikvaren, Utgravningskontoret for Bergen, 1992; R. Bertelsen et al., 'The Storvågan Project 1985–86', *Norwegian Archeological Review* 20(1), 1987, pp. 51–5; K.E. Lind, 'Arkeologisk innsikt i Vågans rolle fra høymiddelalder til seinmiddelalder', *Gunneria* 64, 1991, pp. 135–45; and A.J. Larsen, 'Borgund på Sunnmøre: de eldste konstruksjonene', in Andersson, Hansen and Øye (eds) *De første 200 årene*, pp. 41–56. For a general discussion of urbanity and space, see A. Christophersen, 'Performing towns. Steps towards an understanding of medieval urban communities as social practice', *Archaeological Dialogues* 22, 2015, pp. 109–32.

4 Helle, 'Fra opphavet til omkring 1500', pp. 92–3, and J. Hagland, 'Town Law versus County Law: On the Kristindómsbálkr (Church Law) of Niðaróss Bjarkeyjarréttr and Frostuþingslög', in S. Brink and L. Collinson (eds) *New Approaches to Early Law in Scandinavia*, Acta Scandinavica 3, Turnhout: Brepols, 2014, pp. 57–66.

5 J. Sunde, 'Champagne at the funeral – An introduction to legal culture', in J. Sunde and K. Skodvin (eds) *Rendezvous of European Legal Cultures*, Bergen: Fagbokforlaget, 2010, pp. 3–17.

6 Sunde, 'Champagne at the funeral', p. 9.

7 Helle, 'Fra opphavet til omkring 1500', p. 92.

8 A contemporary use from 1294: Archiv der Hansestadt Lübeck, Urkundenb I. 561–3. Definition and demarcation of *takmark* for Bergen: K. Helle, *Kongssete og kjøpstad til 1536, Bergen bys historie*, vol. I, Oslo: Universitetsforlaget, 1982, pp. 259–73.

9 Hagland, 'Town Law versus County Law', pp. 57–66.

10 See, for instance, A. Musson, 'Introduction', in A. Musson (ed.) *Boundaries of the Law: Geography, Gender and Jurisdiction in Medieval and Early Modern Europe*, Aldershot: Ashgate, 2005, pp. 1–6, and D. Heirbaut, 'Rules for solving conflicts in the middle ages: Part of the solution, part of the problem', in Musson (ed.) *Boundaries of the Law*, pp. 118–29.

11 The Norwegian code can be found in M. Rindal and B. Dale Spørck, *Kong Magnus Håkonsson Lagabøtes landslov, Norrøn tekst med fullstendig variantsapparat*, 2 vols, Oslo: Arkivverket, 2018. Also in Norges gamle Love (hereafter NgL): R. Keyser et al., *Norges gamle Love indtil 1387*, vol. II, Kristiania: Gröndahl, 1848, pp. 7–178. The new Town Law is found in Ibid., pp. 187–290.

12 *Diplomatarium Norvegicum, Oldbreve til Kundskab om Norges indre og ydre Forhold, Sprog, Slægter, Sæder, Lovgivning og Rettergang i Middelalderen*, 23 vols, Christiania/Oslo: various publishers, 1847–2011.

13 On the development of legal culture in medieval Norway, see J.Ø. Sunde, 'Daughters of God and counsellors of the judges of men: Changes in the legal culture of the Norwegian realm in the high middle ages', in Brink and Collinson (eds) *New Approaches to Early Law in Scandinavia*, pp. 131–83.
14 R. Holt, 'What if the sea were different? Urbanization in medieval Norway', *Past & Present* 195, Issue suppl 2, 2007, pp. 132–47.
15 H. Andersson, 'Sverige. En forskningsöversikt', in Blom (ed.) *Urbaniseringsprosessen i Norden*, pp. 91–146, at pp. 92–4; K. Helle, 'Byen som historisk fenomen', in Helle, Eliassen, Myhre and Stugu (eds) *Norsk byhistorie*, pp. 9–19, at p. 16; and T. Gansum, 'Rurale strukturer, urbane funksjoner og definisjonsdiskurser', in Brendalsmo, Eliassen and Gansum (eds) *Den urbane underskog*, pp. 19–40.
16 See, for instance, Larsen, 'Borgund på Sunnmøre', p. 55.
17 See, for instance, Helle, 'Fra opphavet til omkring 1500', p. 68.
18 *NgL III* (R. Keyser et al., *NgL indtil 1387*, vol. 3, Kristiania: Gröndahl, 1849), p. 222: King Olaf's amendment on trade in northern Norway from 1384.
19 Hákonar saga Hákonarsonar, nos. 56, 183, and 215.
20 Mangús lagabætir's Town Law III.18, *NgL II*, p. 209. See also I.2, *NgL* II, p. 188 (*bearens*) and n. 9 (*biar*). *DN I* no. 51, p. 38, dated 1226x1254, presents 'the town Stavanger itself' (*bœen sialvan Stafangr*) as a gift to the church of St. Svitun. From Hákonar saga Hákonarsonar, we have *bœiarmenn* ('townsmen') no. 46 and bęiar ('of town') no. 69.
21 K. Helle and A. Nedkvitne, 'Norge. Sentrumsdannelser og byutvikling i norsk middelalder', in Blom (ed.) *Urbaniseringsprosessen i Norden*, pp. 189–278, at p. 192.
22 *DN XV* no. 20, pp. 21–2.
23 Helle and Nedkvitne, 'Norge', pp. 190–2.
24 R. Bertelsen, 'Vágar, en kortlevd by eller et urbant fiskevær?', in Brendalsmo, Eliassen and Gansum (eds) *Den urbane underskog*, pp. 199–211.
25 Bertelsen, 'Vágar, en kortlevd by', pp. 201–9.
26 K. Helle, 'Etterord: Underskogen i et samlende perspektiv', in Brendalsmo, Eliassen and Gansum (eds) *Den urbane underskog*, pp. 247–59, at p. 247–8.
27 M. Tveit, *In Search of Legal Transmission, Inheritance and Compensation for Homicide in Medieval Secular Law*, Tromsø: University of Tromsø, 2016, pp. 49–50, 186–8 and 294–7.
28 The dating of the Swedish Code of the Realm and Town Law has proven to be difficult. See Å. Holmbäck, 'Innledning', in Å. Holmbäck and E. Wessén (eds) *Magnus Erikssons Landslag i nusvensk tolkning*, Stockholm: Awe/Gebers, 1962, pp. xiii–lxix, at pp. xxx–xxxi. Göran Dahlbäck has suggested that the Swedish Code of the Realm and the Town Law met the high standards of medieval European legal ideology, which demanded consistency and formality in legislation. G. Dahlbäck, 'Svensk stadslagstiftning under medeltiden', in A. Dybdahl and J. Sandnes (eds) *Nordiske middelalderlover: tekst og kontekst: rapport fra seminar ved Senter for middelalderstudier*, Trondheim: Tapir, 1997, pp. 103–15, at p. 107. Influence from the Norwegian Town Law and the Code of the Realm has also been suggested. Sofia Gustafsson has recently given a more nuanced interpretation of the Swedish Town Law, suggesting it includes legislation that is far more independent; see S. Gustafsson, 'Sale of goods around the Baltic Sea in the middle ages', in J. Wubs-Mrozewicz and S. Jenks (eds) *The Hanse in Medieval and Early Modern Europe*, The Northern World 60, Leiden: Brill, 2013, pp. 129–48.
29 Andersson, 'Sverige. En forskningsöversikt', pp. 91–146. These included Viborg in modern Russia and a number of towns in modern Finland.
30 A. Andrèn, *Den urbana scenen: städer och samhälle i det medeltida Danmark*, Acta archaeologica Lundensia: Series in 8o, vol. 13, Malmö: Liber Förlag, 1985.
31 B. Solli, 'Kjøpstedet på Veøya i Romsdal', in Andersson, Hansen, and Øye (eds) *De første 200 årene*, pp. 109–24.

32 A.J. Larsen, 'Borgund på Sunnmøre'.
33 I. Øye, 'Kaupangen i Sogn i komparativ belysning', *Viking* 52, 1989, pp. 144–65.
34 S. Myrvoll, *Handelstorget in Skien*, passim.
35 Steinkjer is usually listed among towns from the central middle ages. Oddevold (Uddevalla) received town privileges from the Swedish king in 1490; see *Svensk Diplomatariums hovudkartotek över medeltidsbreven* (*SDHK*) no. 32436, <riksarkivet.se/sdhk> (accessed 15 April 2020). Charters issued in Oddevold from the Swedish material date between 1517 and 1529: *SDHK* nos. 38033, 38167, 38612 and 38890. The Norwegian charters date between 1495 and 1556: *DN VII* no. 708, *VIII* no. 605, *IX* no. 422, *X* no. 747, *XII* no. 300 and *XXII* no. 117.
36 Myrvoll, *Handelstorget i Skien*, pp. 248, 272–5.
37 Bertelsen, 'Vágar, en kortlevd by', p. 201, and Helle, 'Fra opphavet til omkring 1500', pp. 72–3.
38 The letter is preserved in the Archiv der Hansestadt Lübeck, Urkundenb I. 561–3, Norvagica 022, 022a bis 022c, 07.1–3/21 – Norwegen (Norvagica), and Kontor zu Bergen, 07.1–3 Auswärtige Beziehungen (Externa).
39 *NgL I* (R. Keyser et al., *NgL indtil 1387*, vol. 1, Kristiania: Gröndahl, 1846), p. 303.
40 N. Bjørgo, 'Vågastemna i mellomalderen' in *Hamarspor–Eit festskrift til Lars Hamre 1912–1982*, Oslo: Universitetsforlaget, 1982, p. 50; J R. Hagland and J. Sandnes, *Bjarkøyretten – Nidaros eldste bylov*, Gjøvik: Samlaget, 1997, pp. xx–xxxxviii; and Dahlbäck, 'Svensk stadslagstiftning under medeltiden', pp. 109–11.
41 Found in *NgL II*, pp. 2–178, and A. Taranger, *Magnus Lagabøters Landslov*, Oslo: Universitetsforlaget, 1979 [1915].
42 A.R. Simpson and A.L. Wilson, *Scottish Legal History*, vol. 1, Edinburgh: Edinburgh University Press, 2017, pp. 60–2.
43 *NgL II*, pp. 181–290.
44 H.L. MacQueen and W.J. Windram, 'Laws and courts in the burghs', in M. Lynch, M. Spearman and G. Stell (eds) *The Scottish Medieval Town*, Edinburgh: John Donald, 1988, pp. 208–27, and Simpson and Wilson, *Scottish Legal History*, p. 61.
45 G.A. Blom, 'Magnus Lagabøters bylov og Trondheim, med en innledning om Bergen bylovs overføring til rikets øvrige kjøpsteder', *Trondhjemske samlinger* 9(2), 1974, pp. 99–145, at p. 104–6, and Helle and Nedkvitne, 'Norge', p. 264. See the versions for unspecified towns in *NgL II*, p. 182–3.
46 *Bærkoyar rettr* no. 42, in *NgL I*, pp. 312–3, and Magnús lagabætir's Town Law IX.19.3, *NgL II*, p. 284.
47 Blom, 'Magnus Lagabøters bylov og Trondheim', p. 102.
48 For instance, the amendment 'Um torg fyrir hvers mannz ðyrr' (1299), *NgL III*, no. 12, p. 42.
49 F. Scheel, *Lagmann og skriver. Rettsliv i Norge i det 16de og 17de århundre*, Kristiania, 1923, pp. 72–3, and G. Storm, *NgL indtil 1387*, vol. 4, Kristiania: Gröndahl, 1885, p. 758.
50 M. Tveit, 'The introduction of a law of the realm in northern Norway', in S. Imsen (ed.) *Legislation and State Formation, Norway and Its Neighbours in the Middle Ages*, Trondheim: Akademika (2013), pp. 41–54.
51 J.Ø. Sunde (6 June 2018), 'Magnus Lagabøters Landslov', in *Store Norske Leksikon*, <https://snl.no/Magnus_Lagab%C3%B8tes_landslov> (accessed 15 April 2020).
52 For details, see K. Robberstad, *Magnus Lagabøters bylov*, Kristiania: Cammermeyer, 1923, pp. 2–76.
53 B.-A. Wendt, 'Magnus Erikssons stadslag – en lagspråkets särling?', *Arkiv för nordisk filologi* 111, 1996, pp. 89–111, at p. 91. Of a total of 312 paragraphs, 156 are unique.
54 Tveit, *In Search of Legal Transmission*, pp. 285, 294–5.
55 See, for instance, Tveit, *In Search of Legal Transmission*, p. 173 on *óðal*.
56 *DN I* no. 993, p. 717.
57 See, for instance, *DN I* no. 790, p. 574 (1444); *DN II* no. 691, pp. 515–6; *DN XI* no. 108, p. 93; *DN XXI* no. 581, p. 476; and *DN XXI* no. 617, p. 469.

58 *DN I* no. 993. '[...] effther Noriges lagh som gamall sedhwane haffuer warit her i landet.'
59 A. Bugge, 'Tingsteder, gilder og andre gamle mittpunkter i de norske bygder?', *Norsk historisk tidskrift* 25, 1920, pp. 195–252.
60 Magnús lagabætir's Town Law, VI 1, *NgL II*, p. 240, and G. Storm, *Sigurd Ranessøns Proces*, Kristiania: Det Mallingske bogtrykkeri, 1877, p. 8 *mot* [sic] (110) and p. 34 *mót* (11).
61 J.A. Seip, *Lagmann og lagting i senmiddelalderen og det 16de århundre*, Dybwad, 1934, p. 16, and S. Imsen, *Norsk bondekommunalisme. Fra Magnus Lagabøte til Kristian Kvart*, vol. I, Trondheim: Tapir, 1990, p. 88.
62 *DN X* no. 167, p. 128–9. For an earlier example, see Helle, 'Fra opphavet til omkring 1500', p. 72.
63 Also in the versions of the legal texts, see Magnús lagabætir's Town Law, I.1, *NgL II*, p. 187 and n. 14.
64 The Code of the Realm VIII.11, *NgL II*, p. 157, and Magnús lagabætir's Town Law VII.17, *NgL II*, p. 261.
65 EA-5965 Riksarkivets diplomsamling, <arkivverket.no/>.
66 *DN I* no. 348.
67 The Code of the Realm VI.12; Disposal of property in the Town Law: Magnús lagabætir's Town Law VI.5.
68 DN V no. 234.
69 *DN I* no. 248, p. 199.
70 *DN I* no. 393, p. 301–2. The connection between clergy and administration of justice is pointed out by Steinar Imsen: Imsen, *Norsk bondekommunalisme*, vol. I, pp. 50 and 70.
71 *DN I* no. 269 and 270, pp. 214–5.
72 *DN XXI* no. 219, p. 169. The surviving charter is a translation from 1680. Imsen, *Norsk bondekommunalisme*, vol. I, p. 50.
73 *DN I* no. 993. '[...]konung haffuer hwar serdeless forlent her i righet hørige och lyduge i alle mathe oc giffue oc gielde them [. . .] alth thet som them bøør vt at giffwe oppa wor naduge herre konungx wegne' *DN V* nos. 21 and 22, pp. 21–2.
74 See *DN IV* no. 65, p. 68; *DN V* no. 42, pp. 40–1; and *DN VII* no. 42, p. 39 and nos. 117–8, pp. 132–3.
75 *DN I* no. 163, p. 142.
76 K. Helle, 'Erling Vidkunnsson', in *Norsk biografisk leksikon*, <nbl.snl.no/Erling_vidkunnsson> (accessed 15 April 2020).
77 MacQueen and Windram, 'Laws and courts in the burghs', pp. 215–21.
78 *DN IV* no. 217, pp. 190–1.
79 K. Robberstad et al., 'Odelsrett', in *Kulturhistorisk Leksikon for Nordisk Middelalder*, vol. 12, Copenhagen: Rosenkilde og Bagger, 1967, pp. 493–503.
80 R. Bertelsen, 'Periferi og periferidannelse fra førhistorisk til historisk tid', *Gunneria* 64, 1991, pp. 51–71, at p. 59, and Lind, 'Arkeologisk innsikt i Vågans rolle', p. 140.
81 *DN I* no. 248, p. 199. The farmsteads were Drifdal, Holsete and Lomheim in the rural areas north of Kaupanger.
82 O.E. Haugen, 'Høgmellomalderen 1050–1350', in H. Sandøy and A. Nesse (eds) *Tidslinjer*, vol. 4, Bergen: University of Bergen, 2017, p. 41.
83 J.R. Ugulen, *'... alle the knaber ther inde och sædescwenne...': ei undersøking i den sosiale samansetjinga av den jordeigande eliten på Vestlandet i mellomalderen*, Bergen: University of Bergen, 2007, pp. 315–8.
84 *DN I* no. 250, p. 200. On the classification of estates, see A.W. Brøgger and A.S. Steinnes, *Gammel mål og vekt i Norge*, Oslo: Kildeforlaget, 1982, pp. 75–6.
85 Compare Magnús lagabætir's Town Law V.1–24 to the Norwegian Code of the Realm V.1–25 and Magnus Eriksson's Town Law to the Swedish Code of the Realm, Inheritance Section.

86 *DN I* no. 393, pp. 301–2.
87 The Code of the Realm VI.12; Magnús lagabætir's Town Law VI.5.
88 M. Njåstad, 'The eastern realm: The king of Norway and the border province Jemtland', in S. Imsen (ed.) *Rex Insularum: The King of Norway and His 'Skattlands' as a Political System c. 1260–1450*, Bergen: Fagbokforlaget, 2014, pp. 337–8; Tveit, 'The introduction of a law of the realm in northern Norway', pp. 45–6; and R.B. Wærdahl, 'Norges konges rike og hans skattland: Kongemakt og statsutvikling i den norrøne verden i middeladleren', unpublished PhD thesis, Norwegian University of Science and Technology, 2006, p. 146.
89 *DN I* no. 95, pp. 87–8 and N. Bjørgo, 'Tore Håkonsson Biskopsson', in *Norsk biografisk leksikon*, 2009, <https://nbl.snl.no/Tore_H%C3%A5konsson_Biskopsson> (accessed 15 April 2020).
90 The Code of the Realm VIII.10–12, *NgL II*, pp. 155–7.
91 *DN XXI* no. 219, p. 169.
92 *DN II* no. 156, p. 133.
93 *DN I* no. 269, p. 214.
94 The Norwegian Code of the Realm, IV.13, X.1.2, X.2.5. Several copies of the Code of the Realm had reinstated the old compensation system.
95 Magnús lagabætir's Town Law, IV.18–19, *NgL II*, pp. 220–1; The Code of the Realm, IV.17–18, *NgL II*, pp. 62–3; and S. Imsen, 'Den gammelnorske drapsprosessen', *Historisk Tidsskrift* 88, 2009, pp. 185–229, at p. 206.
96 *DN I* no. 245, p. 196. Responsibilities to report a homicide in Magnús lagabætir's Town Law, IV.2, *NgL II*, pp. 210–1, and IV.12 *NgL II*, pp. 216–7; and The Code of the Realm IV.2, *NgL II*, p. 49 and IV.11, *NgL II*, p. 56.
97 Imsen, 'Den gammelnorske drapsprosessen', p. 189.
98 *DN II* no. 661, p. 492.
99 *Arghan* from ON *argr*, with the meanings 'female', 'cowardly' or 'the passive one in male homosexual intercourse'. For further information, see W.R. Dynes (ed.) *Encyclopedia of homosexuality*, vol. 2. Oxfordshire: Routledge, 2016.
100 Magnús lagabætir's Town Law IV.23–25. *NgL II*, pp. 224–5. However, IV.23 only exists in one of the extant manuscripts; see Robberstad, *Magnus Lagabøters bylov*, p. 19.
101 Norwegian Code of the Realm IV.23–25, *NgL II*, pp. 68–70.
102 Tveit, *In Search of Legal Transmission*, pp. 284–5.
103 Mare, bitch, and 'other bearing animals', in *Gulaþingslog* ch. 196, *NgL 1*, p. 70.
104 *DN II* no. 662, pp. 492–3.
105 Brøgger and Steinnes, *Gammel mål og vekt i Norge*, p. 65. However, at this point, Joon also sued one Asbjorn Sigurdasson, who had to pay 10 cows and the partial rent of a property.
106 *NgL III*, p. 222: King Olaf's amendment on trade in northern Norway from 1384.
107 Solli, 'Veøyas arkeologi', pp. 98–9, and A.T. Falkanger, *Lagmann og Lagting i Hålogaland gjennom 1000 år*, Oslo: Universitetsforlaget, 2007, p. 64.

6

THE BURGH AND THE FOREST

Burgesses and officers in fifteenth-century Scotland

Michael H. Brown

The urban communities of medieval Scotland were defined by law as much as economics. The oldest of these burghs dated from the twelfth century and were founded by charters from the king or other lords which conferred legal rights on the new town. These rights extended, not just within the burgh but over a surrounding liberty or trading monopoly, while burgesses could demand that when facing less serious accusations beyond their burgh, they could be judged before their burgess court. From the start, then, burghs were self-conscious legal communities distinct from other parts of the kingdom.[1] They were also places in which law, not simply burgh law, was enforced. To take the atypical example of St Andrews, the burgh and its environs housed courts of the bishop, the prior and the canons of St Mary's, as well as that of the burgesses.[2] On some level, this intensity of legal activity was a feature of most of the kingdom's towns.

The urban history of medieval Scotland has, not surprisingly, been drawn to the kingdom's largest towns. Whilst small by the standards of the main continental urban centres, Edinburgh, Aberdeen, Perth and, before 1296, Berwick-upon-Tweed were demonstrably important in the development of Scotland.[3] As well as being considered as special legal communities, the role which these large burghs played as the key points of contact between Scotland and the wider world, especially as the ports through which wool, hides and other goods were exported and finished goods imported, has given them a central place in discussions of economic change between 1100 and 1550. They have, moreover, provided the best case studies of local religious affiliations and lay piety in the later middle ages.[4] Yet the centres which have attracted most attention, those mentioned earlier plus the ecclesiastical burgh of St Andrews, were atypical in their size and national importance.[5] The majority of Scotland's urban communities, including the 20 or so founded between 1424 and 1488, were small settlements whose significance, economically and administratively, was generally local. The experience of these burghs was not the same as that of major urban centres like Aberdeen and Edinburgh and has received less attention. By looking at the experience of one such burgh during a period of major change in the later fifteenth century, this article explores how such smaller towns fitted into frameworks of landholding, justice and authority.

The burgh of Peebles in southern Scotland provides an example of a well-established but relatively small urban community in fifteenth-century Scotland. Peebles was founded by King David I in the first half of the twelfth century. Like that king's other foundations, Peebles's role was to provide an economic and administrative hub to the new sheriffdom established around it. It was located on the banks of the upper River Tweed and the alternative name for its sheriffdom was Tweeddale. The royal burgh was laid out alongside a small royal castle, the high street running down from the castle gate in a plan typical of twelfth-century foundations in Scotland. While the castle had never been large and by the fifteenth century seems to have had no military value, the castle mount remained a feature in burgh documents. The site also contained buildings which may have been used by the sheriff of Peebles as the location for his court.[6] Unusually the parish church was located away from the main street of the burgh on a site across the small Eddleston Water to the west. This suggests the site of a settlement which was older than the burgh. By the fifteenth century religious foundations around the burgh included a chapel to the Virgin, a hospital dedicated to St Lawrence to the east of the burgh and the Cross Kirk, a house of friars on the site where an ancient stone cross had been discovered. This cluster of religious institutions suggests the significance of Peebles, both as the centre of a deanery of the diocese of Glasgow and of ecclesiastical patronage from the surrounding area.

Peebles's economic value to the crown was, however, limited. Its inland location meant that Peebles produced no customs revenue derived from the export of wool and hides. Its financial contribution to the crown was the payment of its burgh ferme or rent of £9 6s 8d each year, as specified in the burgh's charter.[7] Evidence suggests that much of the burgesses' wealth derived from their own use of the town's lands for pasture and cultivation. Peebles's role in trade was presumably as a market for goods from its hinterland to be purchased and dispatched for export via Edinburgh. Though this would have included wool and hides, the most important product was probably salmon, whose export to England and the continent was a lucrative source of income for Scottish merchants. The significance of this trade for Peebles is suggested by the salmon on the burgh's coat of arms and a royal charter of 1441 to the burgesses in which the initial letter 'J' of the king's name was rendered in the form of a leaping salmon.[8]

The burgh's location was dictated by various routeways. By the 1460s there was a stone bridge over the River Tweed at the burgh's southern boundary which the burgesses maintained.[9] The king's itinerant justices used established ways to travel on from Selkirk to hold their court in Peebles (known as the justice ayre). Their route then took them west across the watershed between the Tweed and Clyde valleys to Lanark, following what must have been a key road from east to west in southern Scotland.[10] A similarly easy 22-mile journey existed for travellers from Peebles to Edinburgh both for the burgh's goods and for local men attending the king's courts which were increasingly fixed there. However, the burgh's experiences were also defined by its position in the marches of the kingdom towards England. Though about 40 miles from the Anglo-Scottish border the dangers of this position to property and status in the burgh were reflected by a royal charter of 1452. In this, King James II narrated that 'by the hazards of war and fire' the charters and certain deeds conveying property to the burgh had been 'destroyed, burned and annulled'. These losses had been suffered 'in times long past', probably meaning periods of relatively intense warfare in the Borders during the 1380s or 1400s, but they show the potential vulnerability of urban records.[11] The threats had not departed in the fifteenth century. In November 1463 the 11-year-old James III had been brought 'at a time of great peril' to Peebles to stiffen the resolve of his troops against an enemy incursion.[12] Moreover, as we will see, the nature of society in the marches and the dramatic changes in this part of Scotland from the 1450s would have a significant effect on the position of the burgh. The responses of the burgesses provide examples of a legal corporation operating effectively in a shifting jurisdictional environment.

In the summer of 1478 the burgesses of this small, but locally significant, settlement faced a direct challenge to their legal rights. At five o'clock in the afternoon on 11 June 1478 at the gate of a house in Peebles, a group of men witnessed the drawing up of a legal instrument. The document narrated the events which had occurred in the burgh that day.[13] It recorded that Thomas Yellowlock had entered the burgh on the orders of James Pringle. Pringle was the currour of the ward of Tweed, the local official of one of the divisions of the great lordship of Ettrick Forest, which had been in royal hands since 1455. The instrument stated the 'town of Peebles is situated within the boundaries or borders of the forest of Ettrick', though it actually stood just beyond its north-western edge. Thomas Yellowlock had come to enforce the authority of the currour within this lordship. Yellowlock carried 'his little book of paper unsealed', which contained the names of 'certain burgesses' of Peebles. These individuals had been judged to owe money within the Forest by the currour's court and Yellowlock intended to 'levy distraint' on their property in the burgh, seizing goods to cover the sums owed, taking them from any who would not 'surrender'.[14] He was answered by Patrick Dixon and Thomas Haw, the bailies of the burgh, the officials responsible for holding the burgh court and for rendering the accounts of the community at the royal exchequer.[15] They responded to Yellowlock's action by producing a royal letter bearing the privy seal of the king.

The text of this letter which had been written four years earlier in 1473 was included in the instrument. In the letter, King James III of Scotland discharged the burgesses and inhabitants of Peebles from answering in the 'bounde courtis' of the Forest. Should burgesses trespass in the Forest or take green wood from within its boundaries, their cases would be heard not by local officers but considered when the king's justices held their court at Peebles whilst on their justice ayre. The king ordered the officers of the Forest not to compel the burgesses to answer in their courts under the threat of heavy punishment. Citing this letter, the bailies ordered Thomas Yellowlock to 'cease from the taking of the said distraints when none should be given by anyone to him in this manner'. Pressing on, Yellowlock then entered the house of one John Clerk and took some wax 'in the name of said distraint as he said himself'. The bailies refused to accept even the symbolic display of the officer's authority. They and their companions

> … took back the said wax from him and lifted it from his hands, not in contempt nor in deforcement, as it was said, but for the saving of their liberties and privileges given to them by our said supreme lord king as is manifestly shown in the said letter.

As a means of recording and justifying their actions, the bailies and community had the event recorded by a notary at the gates of John Clerk's house.[16]

The events of June 1478 were not an isolated clash between the burgesses and the officers of the Forest. The letter which was read out by the bailies in Yellowlock's face had been issued by the king in October 1473. Its firm instructions to the officials not to call or compel the burgesses of Peebles to appear in their courts strongly indicate that a similar summons had occurred in the recent past.[17] Tellingly, in the isolated account of the royal treasurer which survives for 1473–1474, payment was made to a messenger for taking the king's letter to David Pringle. David was the father of James Pringle and had himself held the office of currour of Tweed in the previous decade. The letter was sent on 6 September and may have related to an initial complaint from the burgesses about the Pringles' actions.[18] The financial accounts presented at the exchequer by James Pringle as currour of the ward of Tweed suggest a further background to the events of 1478. They show that in the year ending in June 1478, Pringle had held 'le bondecourt' of the Forest in Peebles raising a profit of £88 10s 4d. A group of individuals were named as being fined in the *curia bondarum* for taking green wood in the forest, the crime specifically named in the king's letter. They were released from payment, as they had also been fined during the justice ayre. This again provides a connection to the right granted to the burgesses to answer only before the royal justices.[19] The following year, though the profits of justice were not itemised in Pringle's account, the sum of £62 was noted as pending from the fines from one *bondecourt* concerning the inhabitants of Peebles.[20]

The rebuff given to Yellowlock in September 1478 may explain the non-payment of fines recorded in this entry, but it did not end the matter. Two years later, in August 1480, James III issued a further letter, this time with the full authority of the great seal. This stated that the king had heard 'the mournful relation and complaint' of the burgesses of Peebles, that 'in diverse times past and lately' some of them had been made to appear before the Forest courts. Whether these complaints referred to the charges brought in 1478 or fresh arrests made since then is not clear, but, prompted by the petition, the king ordered his officials to refrain from making such efforts again. Once more King James asserted that the only court to which the burgesses could be called to answer such charges outside of the burgh liberty was during the justice ayre when it sat in Peebles.[21]

It is not surprising that these local events have received no attention from historians of fifteenth-century Scotland. In a decade which witnessed James III's assumption of personal authority, apparent moves towards peace with England, the sentence of forfeiture passed on the earldom of Ross, the king's clash with his brothers and the beginning of the crisis of war and political dissension which lasted from 1479 to 1489, the complaints of the Peebles burgesses seem minute.[22] However, in terms of the issues raised and their context with regard to local relationships, they represent a useful case study of the changing nature of Scottish government, society and legal culture in the later fifteenth century. In the first place they supply an example of interaction and conflict between an urban community and officers with jurisdiction over an adjacent area, revealing the ways in which burgesses articulated and defended their corporate legal rights. The events also display the significance of major shifts in structures of local administration and society which occurred during the mid-fifteenth century. Though the largest changes happened beyond their bounds, burghs like Peebles were also deeply affected by the alterations to established frameworks of lordship and justice. Finally, it provides an example of the way in which the role of the king and royal government extended and became more complex as a consequence of the increased territorial and jurisdictional presence of the crown up to the 1470s.

The events of 11 June 1478 were the climax of ongoing tensions between the burgesses of Peebles and the officials of the Forest. These disputes may have owed something to the lack of ancient proofs of their liberties on the part of the burgesses. The absence of clear evidence of their freedom from the courts of the Forest may have given the currours the belief that they could compel the burgesses to answer for any actions undertaken within their jurisdiction. However, tensions can also be linked to wider changes in government and society in the region and the kingdom. For Peebles, these related most immediately to the status and government of the Forest itself. This area of over 250 square miles of upland moor and wood had been established in the twelfth century as a royal hunting preserve. During the 1320s King Robert I had turned it into a private lordship for his trusted adherent, James lord of Douglas.[23] For the next 130 years, Ettrick and Selkirk Forest was held by the Douglases (created as earls of Douglas in 1358 and known as the Black Douglases) as one of their principal estates. Their rights of justice over this lordship were not always clear. In the famous emerald charter of 1324, King Robert allowed Douglas to possess his major estates free from royal exactions and from royal justice but reserved crimes of manslaughter to the crown.[24] In 1354, however, Robert's son, David II, granted William lord (and later earl) of Douglas his lands, including the lordship of Ettrick and Selkirk Forest, in regality, implying full regal rights over the exercise of justice.[25] There remained debates about the extent of Douglas's rights of regality in the Forest relative to the crown in the mid-fifteenth century.[26]

Although Ettrick Forest was turned from a royal hunting preserve into a private regality, forest law continued to apply there. The Douglases also retained the right to administer forest law via its special courts. In 1446 William earl of Douglas had exempted Melrose Abbey from appearing 'at our courts of the bounds of our forest of Ettrick'.[27] This was the court whose authority over them was being contested by the burgesses of Peebles in 1478.[28] The bound court dealt specifically with breaches of forest law by individuals from outside the Forest who broke its law. In 1499, in the major reorganisation of the administration of Ettrick Forest undertaken by James IV, it was said that 'it is complained that the neighbours and inhabitants within the boundaries around the said forest destroy the wood and deer greatly' and that, to prevent this, the bound court needed to be held each year.[29] The taking of green wood, the offence levelled against the burgesses in Yellowlock's book, which reduced the cover for game, and the killing of deer were two of the main offences within forest law. The third was the cultivating of ground, growing 'ony maner of corne', and building dikes or fences to prevent grazing. The efforts by the currours to enforce the law by holding their court and distraining the burgesses lay behind the friction of the 1470s but had been a feature of local jurisdiction since the thirteenth century.[30]

It is hard to assess the character of Douglas lordship in the Forest.[31] However, the wider evidence and reputation of the earls make it difficult to imagine that they did not press their rights up to, and even beyond, their legal limits. What this meant for Peebles is unclear, though the timing of the request for a fresh charter in the midst of tense relations between King James II and the Douglas earl in early 1452 is suggestive of the burgh's involvement in this developing conflict.[32] Three years later, in 1455, tensions came to a climax with several months of warfare between the king's forces and the Black Douglases. Both sides passed through Peebles. In early February, James earl of Douglas had issued a charter from the burgh as he withdrew from Clydesdale into the Borders.[33] Six weeks later, in late March, the king took the submission of at least one local lord, James Tweedie, in Peebles.[34] The struggle ended with the defeat and exile of Earl James to England and his forfeiture of property and legal rights in parliament in June.[35] The Forest passed into the king's hands and, in August, it was permanently annexed to the crown.[36] The fall of the earl of Douglas was the defining moment in fifteenth-century Scottish politics and one of a series of royal forfeitures of great magnate dynasties between 1425 and 1483. These altered the character of Scotland's political society and, in many regions, caused a fundamental shift in local government and social structure. Ettrick Forest and the neighbouring districts, including Peebles and upper Tweeddale, provide a clear example of this.

The removal of the earl of Douglas and the royal annexation of the Forest meant that its officials changed from being the local servants of a great noble to being royal agents directly answerable to the king. The evidence suggests that most of these officials survived the transition from the Douglases to royal lordship. The chief official in the Forest was the bailie, who was responsible for leasing the lands of the Forest to the tenants and holding the courts which dealt with normal justice in the lordship. After 1455 the position was held by a local lord, Thomas Cranstoun of that ilk, whose family had been tenants and councillors of the Douglas earls. Thomas probably inherited the office from his father in the 1440s and it would pass to his own son in 1471–1473.[37] The same continuity is likely amongst the currours of the wards of Tweed, Ettrick and Yarrow. As the events of 1478 demonstrated, these officers were 'the backbone of the administration' in the Forest.[38] Each ward had two officials, a currour and a master currour, who were responsible for collecting the fermes and renders paid by the tenants and answering for them at the royal exchequer. They also held the courts which enforced the forest law and collected the fines levied for offences. A reluctance to disturb local structures encouraged the crown to retain existing officials. This is clear in the Yarrow ward. In 1425 Archibald, fifth earl of Douglas, had issued letters granting William and George Middlemast the mastership of the ward of Yarrow 'wythin our saide forest' for life.[39] From 1455 the Middlemast family would continue to hold office in Yarrow ward and it is likely that the other officials, the Pringles in the ward of Tweed and the Scotts in the Ettrick ward, retained positions held under the Douglases.[40]

However, this apparent continuity of office holding occurred alongside a major change in the leadership of local political society in the area around the Forest. The forfeiture of 1455 removed the established focus of political and social life in the middle march. In place of the earl of Douglas, leading roles passed to a more diffuse group of magnates and lesser nobles. Potentially the most important of these nobles was the branch of the Douglas family which held the earldom of Angus, the so-called Red Douglases. James II had given George Douglas, earl of Angus, lands near Selkirk and relied on him as warden of the eastern and middle marches to defend the region against efforts by the English and Black Douglases to reverse the outcome of 1455.[41] However, George's death in 1463, during the minority of King James III, left an underage son and heir and restricted his family's influence at a critical time. George's younger brother, William Douglas of Cluny, initially stepped into his role. In early 1464 William received the office of march warden vacated by his brother and benefited from a grant of lands near Peebles.[42]

The 15 years between 1463 and 1478 witnessed a growing connection between local patronage and influence at the royal court which had implications for the running of the Forest. Lands and offices in the area were assigned to individuals from outside the region like the young James III's guardian, Robert lord Boyd, in the later 1460s and the king's uncle, James, earl of Buchan, from 1470.[43] For local families like the Pringles this development had significant consequences. Their monopoly of the offices of currour and master currour in the 1450s ended during the next decade. William Douglas of Cluny was appointed master currour by 1470 and was succeeded in the office by a royal councillor, David Crichton of Cranstoun.[44] Crichton's appointment indicated the way that local families had increasingly to compete for key positions with individuals better positioned to secure royal favour. Though the Pringles retained the lesser position of currour, they were no longer the senior figures in the Tweed ward.[45] The effect on the Pringles of this loss of a post they had held until 1469, and which they probably felt they had a right to hold, is hard to judge. It is possible that it had an effect on the way they performed the role. James Pringle's forceful approach to the burgesses of Peebles in the summer of 1473 and the more fully described incident of August 1478 could have been the actions of a local official who was keen to maximise the profits of his court.

This reading of the events of June 1478 in Peebles creates an impression of the burgesses being confronted by the demands of an assertive local noble armed with the authority of office. This image feeds into a wider sense of the place of the burghs in the government and political society of fifteenth-century Scotland. In many political studies, towns have tended to figure as passive settings for events, the king's courts, parliament and occasionally episodes of violence. The assassination of James I in the Blackfriars monastery of Perth was an event in which the local burgesses were involved, a small number as participants but most as a community caught up in a major political crisis.[46] In the same way, the burgh of Stirling's destruction at the hands of the Black Douglases in 1452 was an act of vengeance for King James II's killing of William, earl of Douglas, in the neighbouring castle. The treatment of the undefended urban space became an easy way to symbolise and react to the king's act of violence within the enclosed royal castle. James II's compensation of the burgh for 'fire-raisings, robberies and depredations, barbarously and most cruelly done by our rebels and traitors' with a grant of the rights to the hospital of St James by Stirling bridge confirmed the sense that, like ecclesiastical institutions, burghs lacked the ability to defend their rights and property and required active royal protection.[47] The evidence from Perth, Edinburgh, Aberdeen and elsewhere, of burgh communities making efforts to safeguard and strengthen their boundaries, provides evidence of collective action by burgesses in this regard.[48] However, they are countered by examples of burghs forming relationships with local nobles which suggest a degree of dependency on them. Aberdeen's relations with the earls of Mar and of Huntly in 1463 clearly reflected the influence of these magnates in the burgh.[49] On a smaller scale, the frequent examples of Aberdeen giving burgess status to individuals at the request of significant figures from outside the burgh indicate a more low-level type of influence. In 1440 Aberdeen even appointed a local lord, Alexander Irvine, as their captain and although they determined never to repeat this experiment five years later, other burghs can similarly be seen to have existed under the strong influence of a magnate.[50] In St Andrews, for example, the provost regularly came from the family connections of the bishop and combined the role with custody of the bishop's castle.[51] During the 1440s the chancellor, William Crichton, based himself in Edinburgh Castle. The fact that his deputy in the castle, William Cranstoun, was also provost of Edinburgh and that on Crichton's temporary eclipse in 1445, Cranstoun was replaced as provost by Patrick Cockburn, a partisan of the Crichton's enemies, strongly suggests the link between urban office and wider politics in the largest burgh in the realm.[52]

However, there also exist clear examples of urban communities in fifteenth-century Scotland asserting their rights against the demands of royal officials. A number of these revolved around the efforts of burgh officials to defend their rights over fairs, special markets held once or twice a year on set dates. Perth was involved in a long-running dispute with the sheriffs of Perth about the jurisdiction of the latter over the burgh's midsummer fair. As the burgh had been given the right to appoint its own sheriff, responsible for dealing with local royal justice within the burgh, in 1394, the burgesses clearly regarded this freedom from the jurisdiction of the wider sheriffdom as extending to their fair.[53] However, in 1441 the sheriff, John Ruthven of that ilk, a near neighbour of the burgh, had made 'questionis and demande' at the fair, clearly exerting his judicial authority over the market.[54] In response, just before midsummer 1442, the burgesses secured letters from King James II confirming their freedom from Ruthven's jurisdiction. This did not end the dispute and in June 1443 an arbitration again confirmed the burgh's full right over the fair and its court.[55] A final attempt by Ruthven to impose his justice on the occasion in 1444, by taking a thief at the fair, led to an armed clash in which 20 men were reportedly killed.[56] The whole episode demonstrated the readiness of the burgesses to defend their rights forcefully by a range of means.

A parallel dispute between the burgh and the sheriff of Ayr which began in the later 1450s indicates that the Perth example was not a one-off. In 1458 James II had granted the burgesses of Ayr the right to hold a second fair at Michaelmas (29 September).[57] The charter included the grant of all the privileges associated with fairs but did not itemise them. In the absence of an unequivocal statement, as at Perth, the local sheriff sought to take over 'the keeping of the fair' with its associated judicial profits. This provoked the burgh officials into action. They secured a letter from James II dated 7 July 1459 in which he ordered the sheriff, George Campbell of Loudon, and his deputies to 'sesse and desist' from the breaking of the fair and collection of unjust exactions from those present.[58] On the day before the fair in 1460, the provost, John Multrar, accompanied by the bailies and with the assent of the community, came to the market cross and had the letter read out. This public assertion of the burgh liberties was designed to forestall any breach of the fair the following day.[59] Instead, on Michaelmas Day, Campbell's deputy, John Dalrymple, came to Ayr and demanded that the provost and bailies find pledges (guarantors) for their appearance at the sheriff's court on the day after the fair. As at Peebles, this demand was met with a firm response. The provost asked for the sheriff's warrant for his actions to be shown and, when Dalrymple did not produce this, Multrar asserted that the fair was held by royal letters which had been publically proclaimed and which gave the whole jurisdiction to the burgesses and prevented the sheriff from interfering.[60] Again, like the burgesses of Peebles, the provost of Ayr had both the proclamation of the king's letters and the burgh's response to the sheriff's man carefully recorded in notarised instruments. Instead of the sheriff's court, the dispute was rapidly brought before the Lords of Council in early October. With the king recently dead, having been fatally injured at the siege of Roxburgh Castle in August, the burgesses received a less supportive response to their claims. The councillors judged that the burgesses could produce no evidence that they had 'keping, rewling na govirnance' of the fair (apparently setting aside the old king's letter). Instead these duties and rights pertained to the sheriff. However, the sheriff was forbidden from exacting unlaws (judicial fines) or other monetary duties from the fair.[61]

The matter of the fair was bound up with a second area of dispute between the burgh of Ayr and the sheriff. In another letter written two days after he had dealt with the issue of the fair, James II responded to another complaint by the burgesses. The king stated that the burgesses had informed him that the neighbouring barony of Alloway belonged to the burgh. However, the tenants had been required by the king's officials to appear as witnesses in the courts of the sheriff, justiciars and chamberlain. This was against the terms of the burgh's own charters which required the tenants only to appear in the burgh courts. The king confirmed this exemption.[62] However, over a decade later in September 1471, the burgesses complained to James III that the same practice was continuing. They clearly presented the king with his father's letter from 1459 as this was referred to in a new statement of the burgh's rights. James III wrote that the tenants of Alloway were 'daily summoned by our letters and officers to appear in Edinburgh and other places to sit upon assizes and are compelled by our sheriff of Ayr and his deputes to sit upon inquests and assizes in our sheriff courts of Ayr'. He ordered his officials not to arrest the tenants or the burgesses or to insist that they attended courts other than that of the burgh.[63] Although the dispute would re-emerge in the following century, James III, like his father, had given unequivocal support to the freedom of the burgh's tenants from his own officials.

There are striking parallels between the behaviour of the burgesses of Ayr and those of Peebles. Both responded to what they regarded as intrusions on their rights by royal officials by holding public demonstrations of those liberties. In Ayr, the burgesses proclaimed the king's letter, which gave the burgesses the right to run their fair, on the day before it opened. The timing was a direct challenge to the sheriff to assert or abandon his claims. In Peebles, the initiative came from the currour, James Pringle. He sent his servant, Thomas Yellowlock, into the burgh either to secure the surrender of those burgesses charged with offences in the bound court, or to distrain (seize) goods to cover their fines. The burgesses responded in a similar way to those of Ayr. They pointed out that Yellowlock brought his indictments in a small unsealed book, perhaps indicating the absence of a formal legal summons. By contrast, the bailies and community had the notary bring out the letter 'sealed with the privy seal of our supreme lord king' and 'narrated (it) by reading and in public form, laying out the liberties and discharges, as it appears, from the said distraints'.[64] The text of the letter was later included in the notarised instrument which described the whole event. When Yellowlock tried to ignore the reading of the letter and entered John Clerk's property to take a lump of wax as a symbolic display of his ability to distrain goods within the burgh, the burgesses 'took back the said wax from him'. They did so not 'in deforcement', as an act of violence, but to prevent harm being done to their liberties. The wax from John Clerk's house may have acted as a symbol of the burgh's right to be exempt from the bound court of the Forest. Had Yellowlock removed it from the burgh's own boundaries, both he and the burgesses would have seen it as a demonstration of the currour's ability to impose his judgement and his jurisdiction on the burgesses for acts done within his ward of the Forest.[65]

The awareness of the importance of such complex public narrations and physical demonstrations of legal rights form part of the environment identified so effectively by Claire Hawes. In particular she stressed the value of making open and public statements concerning legal decisions or claims as a way of validating them against future challenges. Hawes also demonstrated how in the context of fifteenth-century Scottish burghs a special significance was attached to the expression of corporate unity behind a particular position, both internally and in negotiation with external players.[66] This is evident in the earlier case studies. Stress was placed on the collective action of 'alderman, bailies, council and community' of the burgh, binding in the whole burgess body to the actions of their officials. As Hawes also identified, urban liberties were held for the 'common good' of the burgh and thus their maintenance and defence was to be undertaken by the whole community.

Underlying all these examples of legal activity involving burgesses and officials has been the clash of competing rights and jurisdictions. The issues have not been identical. The burgesses of Ayr were pressing for the territorial extent of their special legal rights to encompass both the temporary occasion of their Michaelmas Fair and their tenants in Alloway. They sought these exemptions from the reach of normal royal justice as exercised primarily by the sheriff, but also other royal officials such as the chamberlain, justiciar and lords of the king's council. The inhabitants of Peebles pressed for the activities of burgesses beyond the burgh (and in the king's forest) to be covered by the exemption of this group from courts with jurisdiction outside the burgh except that of the justiciar and his court of the justice ayre. However, in both these cases, the disputes also reflected a changing judicial environment from the 1450s onwards. It is striking, for example, that, while in the 1450s the Ayr burgesses had complained their tenants were being called to attend the sheriff courts, in 1471 the grievance was that this group 'are daily summoned by our letters and officers to appear in Edinburgh' (or other places).[67] The stress on daily summons to Edinburgh sounds like a reflection of the increasing flow of cases to the king's council mentioned in legislation of the period. In a different way, as has been discussed, the royal annexation of Ettrick Forest changed the nature of local administration and political society. It meant that the dispute between the burgh and the currour was not between a royal burgh and the agent of a great magnate but between a royal burgh and an officer of the king. James III was ultimately responsible for the exercise of the law of the Forest and, as the burgh's lord, for the workings of the laws of the burgesses. The ultimate decision in the dispute to hear the cases involving the acts of burgesses in Ettrick Forest before the justiciars on their ayre simply moved the decision into another royal forum. Such a shift merely illustrates the primacy of royal justice by the 1470s and may have been to the advantage of a burgh like Peebles. In his letter sent to the burgesses in 1474 confirming their exemption from the Forest courts, James III wrote

> James by the grace of God king of Scots, to all and sundry our lieges and subjects to whose knowledge these our letters shall come, greetings. Know that our burgh of Peebles is an old, free burgh of our realm infeft and founded by our progenitors of most noble mind with liberties, privileges and free burgage, like other burghs so privileged in times past ...[68]

Royal burghs were foundations with privileges and freedoms which were both ancient and guaranteed by the crown. The king had obligations towards these products of his ancestors' patronage and lordship, and in the fifteenth century, such burghs were frequently able to call upon these ties in their interest. Though, as Ayr discovered in 1460 (perhaps significantly, just after the death of their royal protector, James II), this did not guarantee that their claims would be upheld against other plaintiffs, officers or other neighbours, it did confer a significant advantage on appeals for royal support.

The success of the burgesses of Peebles in securing repeated statements of the king's support for their liberties surely indicates that their burgh was neither politically passive nor important only in a purely local frame of reference. Equally it is important to recognise the burgh as an assertive entity within its own frame. Within three years of the defence of the burgh's rights against the currour, the burgesses were embroiled in another dispute before the king's justices. This time the case was brought by two neighbouring landowners who accused the burgesses of occupying Cademuir, which lay on the hills across the Tweed from their burgh, cultivating it and denying access to the herds of their neighbours. It seems that the burgh was stepping beyond the liberties defined in the royal charter of 1452.[69] This had allowed the burgesses the right to pasture their animals but no more. The plaintiffs, Thomas Lowis of Manor and John Gledstanes of that ilk, claimed that the evidence they presented to the justices and the inquest in Peebles had been ignored and that those involved had exceeded their powers in ruling for the burgesses.[70] After a delay, in late March 1482 the lords of the council ruled that the case should be heard again in the next justice ayre at Peebles. In the event, and possibly because of the rolling crisis which developed from mid-1482, it was not until February 1485 that judgement was given.[71] In his court in the tolbooth of Peebles, the justiciar-depute, William Lord Borthwick, from the deliberation of a new inquest, found that the burgh possessed the right of possession and sowing on Cademuir.[72] The verdict provided only a temporary resolution. Friction with the Gledstanes family continued into the next century over the rights to these lands.[73] It is probably mistaken to look for any echoes of the age-old tension between rancher and farmer in this episode, but the occupation of new land and the vigorous defence of their position in the king's courts confirms that, rather than peaceful citizens imposed upon by rough 'upland men', fifteenth-century Scottish burgesses could be difficult, pushy neighbours.

The events of 11 June 1478 should be seen in this respect. The burgesses were caught up in a new environment in which the great regality and forest which bordered Peebles had been brought back into the hands of the crown. Whilst this changed the position of the local officials directly, it also marked a shift in the burgh's position. The burgesses seem to have recognised the potential advantages of this. Their creation of a written narrative of the events into which they inserted the king's letter confirming their liberties was skilfully done. The narrative created a clear image of the currour's servant as an intruder onto the ground and rights, both ancient and recently confirmed, of the burgh. Like John Gledstanes and Thomas Lowis, the currour, James Pringle, found it hard to compete with this corporate action and entrenched culture of legal action. Within the local context a community of burgesses represented a powerful judicial and political presence.

Notes

1 See in particular, C. Hawes, 'Community and public authority in later fifteenth-century Scotland', unpublished PhD thesis, University of St Andrews, 2015, pp. 49–75, and J. Kopaczyk, *The Legal Language of Scottish Burghs*, Oxford: Oxford University Press, 2013, pp. 114–36.
2 St Andrews University Library, B65/23/4c.
3 See, for example, H. Booton, 'Burgesses and landed men in North-East Scotland in the later middle ages: A study in social interaction', unpublished PhD thesis, University of Aberdeen, 1987; E.P. Dennison, D. Ditchburn and M. Lynch (eds) *Aberdeen before 1800: A New History*, East Linton: Tuckwell Press, 2002; M. Lynch, M. Spearman and G. Stell (eds) *The Scottish Medieval Town*, Edinburgh: John Donald, 1988; and E. Ewan, *Townlife in Fourteenth-Century Scotland*, Edinburgh: Edinburgh University Press, 1990.
4 See, for example, M. Verschuur, *Politics or Religion? The Reformation in Perth 1540–1570*, Edinburgh: Dunedin Academic Press, 2006 and M. Cowan, *Death, Life and Religious Change in Scottish Towns c.1350–1560*, Manchester: Manchester University Press, 2012.
5 For St Andrews, see M. Brown and K. Stevenson (eds) *Medieval St Andrews: Church, Cult, City*, Woodbridge: Boydell, 2017.
6 *Royal Commission of Ancient and Historic Monuments of Scotland: Peeblesshire*, 2 vols, Edinburgh, HM Stationary Office (hereafter HMSO), 1967, vol. 2, nos 481, 523, 539, and *Registrum Magni Sigilii Regum Scotorum* (hereafter *RMS*), 11 vols, eds J.M. Thomson et al., Edinburgh: HMSO, 1882–1914, vol. 2, no. 210.
7 This sum compares to Perth's rent of £80 and Edinburgh's rent of £34 13s 4d which indicate the lack of correlation between the level of rent required and the size of the burgh (*The Exchequer Rolls of Scotland* (hereafter *ER*), 23 vols, eds J. Stuart et al., Edinburgh: HM General Register House, 1878–1908, vol. 6, pp. 25, 32).
8 National Records of Scotland (hereafter NRS) B58/18/15.
9 *Charters and Documents Relating to the Burgh of Peebles 1165–1710* (hereafter *Peebles Charters*), Edinburgh: Scottish Burgh Records Society, 1872, pp. 157, 162, 165.
10 H. MacQueen, 'Pleadable brieves and jurisdiction in heritage in later medieval Scotland', unpublished PhD thesis, University of Edinburgh, 1985, pp. 86, 90.

11 *Peebles Charters*, no. 9.
12 *The Records of the Parliaments of Scotland to 1707*, ed. K. M. Brown et al., St Andrews, 2007–2020, <www.rps.ac.uk> (hereafter RPS) 1464/1/10 and *Liber Sancte Marie de Melros* (hereafter *Melrose Liber*), 2 vols, Edinburgh: Bannatyne Club, 1837, vol. 2, p. 390, no. 572.
13 NRS, B58/18/41.
14 Though Yellowlock cannot be identified further, his appearance with his book and his taking of the wax as a symbolic act may hint at his possession of some level of legal training or experience. The use of legal experts by officials and nobles in fifteenth-century Scotland requires further study.
15 Ewan, *Townlife in Fourteenth-Century Scotland*, pp. 45–8. Neither Haw nor Dixon appeared at the exchequer during the 1470s (*ER*, vol. 8, pp. 106, 200, 261, 321, 393, 470, 552, 632).
16 The notary who produced the instrument was named John Young.
17 NRS, B58/18/35 and *Peebles Charters*, no. 12.
18 *Accounts of the Lord High Treasurer of Scotland*, eds T. Dickson et al., 13 vols, Edinburgh: HM General Register House, 1877–, vol. 1, p. 44.
19 *ER*, vol. 8, pp. 478, 480.
20 *ER*, vol. 8, p. 587.
21 NRS, B58/18/43, and *Peebles Charters*, no. 13.
22 N. Macdougall, *James III*, Edinburgh: John Donald, 2009, pp. 100–67 and R. Tanner, *The Late Medieval Scottish Parliament: Politics and the Three Estates, 1424–1488*, East Linton: Tuckwell Press, 2001, pp. 191–218.
23 M. Brown, *The Black Douglases*, East Linton: Tuckwell Press, 1998, pp. 23–5.
24 *RMS*, vol. 1, appendix 1, no. 38.
25 W. Fraser (ed.) *The Douglas Book*, 4 vols, Edinburgh, 1885, vol. 3, no. 292. For the seminal discussion of the nature of Scottish regalities, see A. Grant, 'Franchises north of the border: Baronies and regalities in late Medieval Scotland', in M. Prestwich (ed.) *Liberties and Identities in the Medieval British Isles*, Woodbridge: Boydell and Brewer, 2008, pp. 155–99.
26 Brown, *The Black Douglases*, p. 242.
27 *Melrose Liber*, vol. 2, no. 564.
28 For what follows, see the analysis of Ettrick Forest and Scottish hunting reserves in general in J.M. Gilbert, *Hunting and Hunting Reserves in Medieval Scotland*, Edinburgh: John Donald, 1979, especially pp. 129–30, 147–50.
29 *ER*, vol. 11, pp. 393–4. 'It is plenyeit that the marchis and indwellars within the bondis about the said forrest distroyis the wod and der gretummlie'.
30 *ER*, vol. 11, p. 394.
31 Brown, *The Black Douglases*, pp. 166–70.
32 *Peebles Charters*, no. 9.
33 Fraser, *Douglas*, vol. 3, no. 428.
34 NRS, GD150/14 (f).
35 Brown, *The Black Douglases*, pp. 299–308 and Christine McGladdery, *James II*, Edinburgh: John Donald, 2015, pp. 147–58.
36 RPS 1455/8/2. Notwithstanding this act, 18 years later Ettrick Forest was granted by James III to Queen Margaret (*RMS*, vol. 2, no. 1143).
37 *ER*, vol. 6, pp. 225, 371, 443, and *ER*, vol. 8, pp. 43, 141.
38 Gilbert, *Hunting and Hunting Reserves*, p. 142.
39 *RMS*, vol. 2, nos 58–9.
40 For the Pringles' service to the earls of Douglas, see Brown, *The Black Douglases*, pp. 167, 217, 230, 290, 294, 300, 317.
41 Fraser, *Douglas*, vol. 3, nos 88, 97, 431.
42 *RMS*, vol. 2, nos 773–5. William also became guardian of the lands of his nephew, the young Archibald earl of Angus (*RMS*, vol. 2, no. 774).

43 NRS, GD8/6 and *RMS*, vol. 2, no. 1418. James earl of Buchan was the second son of James I's queen, Joan Beaufort, by her second husband. Buchan also received custody of Newark Castle which had been the principal Black Douglas residence in the Forest and in 1479 was charged with felling trees and killing deer by the currours (NRS, GD157/71, 73, and *ER*, vol. 8, pp. 208, 483, 585, 587).

44 *RMS*, vol. 2, no. 781; Fraser, *Douglas*, vol. 3, no. 101; David Crichton was sheriff of Edinburgh in 1469. During the 1470s, he was keeper of Threave and Edinburgh Castles and a royal envoy to Denmark and France (*ER*, vol. 8, pp. 28, 164, 253, 269, 353).

45 *ER*, vol. 7, p. 623, and vol. 8, pp. 46, 139, 210, 353, 478, 585.

46 Perth and Kinross Archives B59/24/13/1; A.A.M. Duncan, *James I King of Scots 1424–1437*, Glasgow: University of Glasgow, 1984, p. 23; M. Brown, *James I*, Edinburgh: Canongate, 1994, pp. 172–93; and M. Brown, '"That old serpent and ancient of evil days": Walter Earl of Atholl and the death of James I', *Scottish Historical Review* 71, 1992, pp. 23–45.

47 *Charters and Other Documents Relating to the Royal Burgh of Stirling*, Glasgow: Scottish Burgh Records Society, 1834, pp. 36–8.

48 *Extracts from the Council Register of Aberdeen*, ed. J. Stuart, Aberdeen: Spalding Club, 1844, pp. 8, 23–4; Perth and Kinross Archives B59/24/13/1; *Charters and Other Documents Relating to the City of Edinburgh*, ed. J.D. Marwick, Edinburgh: Scottish Burgh Records Society, 1871, nos 30 and 47.

49 'Aberdeen Burgh Registers', *Scotland's Places*, online, <www.scotlandsplaces.gov.uk/digital-volumes/burgh-records/aberdeen-burgh-registers>, vol. 5/1, p. 467 (accessed 21 June 2019).

50 *Aberdeen Council Extracts*, p. 6. See also below, pp. 212 and 221 note 49.

51 M.H. Brown, 'Prelates, citizens and landed folk: St Andrews as a centre of lordship in the late middle ages', in Brown and Stevenson, *Medieval St Andrews*, pp. 205–22.

52 *ER*, vol. 5, pp. 31, 36, 67, 233, 258–9, 305, and *Extracts from the Records of the Burgh of Edinburgh 1403–1528*, Edinburgh: Scottish Burgh Records Society, 1849, pp. 254–7.

53 Perth and Kinross Archives B59/23/4.

54 Perth and Kinross Archives B59/26/1/1.

55 Perth and Kinross Archives B59/26/1/2.

56 'Auchinleck Chronicle', in McGladdery, *James II*, p. 161. For further discussion of this event, see M.H. Brown, 'The downcasting of the house of Dupplin: Burghs and politics in fifteenth-century Scotland', in S. Boardman and D. Ditchburn (eds) *Kingship, Lordship and Sanctity in Medieval Britain*, forthcoming.

57 *Charters of the Royal Burgh of Ayr* (hereafter *Ayr Charters*), Edinburgh: Scottish Burgh Records Society, 1883, no. 19

58 Ibid., no. 20.

59 Ibid., no. 22.

60 Ibid., no. 48.

61 Ibid., no. 49.

62 Ibid., no. 21.

63 Ibid., no. 23. Our burgesses are

> daylie summond be oure letres and officiaris to compeir in Edinburcht and uther placis to pas upone assisis and ar compellit be oure shiref of Air and his deputis to pas upone inquestis and assisis in our shireff courtis of Air.

64 The easy availability of this document may indicate that the burgesses had anticipated the appearance of Yellowlock and his actions. I am grateful to Dr Amy Blakeway of the University of St Andrews for this suggestion.

65 NRS, B58/18/41.

66 Hawes, 'Community and public authority', pp. 49–75.

67 *Ayr Charters*, no. 23

68 NRS, B58/18/35, and B58/18/41. 'James be the grace of god king of scotis to all and sundry oure liegis and subditis quhais knaulage thir oure l[ett]res salcum gretings. Wit ȝe that … oure burgh of peblis is ane ald fre burgh of oure realme feft and foundit be oure progentouris of maist nobli mynde with liberties preuileges and fre burrowage like as utheris oure burowis as preuilegit in tyme bigane'.
69 *Peebles Charters*, no. 9 and NRS, B58/18/20.
70 *Peebles Charters*, no. 14.
71 Ibid., no. 15.
72 NRS, B58/18/47.
73 *Peebles Charters*, no. 24 and p. 279. In 1528, Cademuir was incorporated into a barony created for George Elphinstone of Henderstoun, whose family were also burgesses of Peebles (*Peebles Charters*, no. 27).

7

PAX URBANA. THE USE OF LAW FOR THE ACHIEVEMENT OF POLITICAL GOALS

Jörg Rogge

The maintenance of urban peace (*pax urbana*, or *fride*, *vrede* in low German) was an important goal for the inhabitants and citizens[1] of towns, and for the members of town councils during the later middle ages.[2] Peace keeping within the town walls was a necessity for the communal living of all town inhabitants. However, it was not always easy for the urban authorities to uphold the peace because the city space was divided into several quarters and parishes. Braunschweig for example had five independent districts ('Weichbilde'); the districts had their own rights and administration with separate councils.[3] There were special areas of peace in the towns, which did not belong to the *pax urbana* secured by the city council but were under the legal administration of different clerical institutions like churches, monasteries, chapels or even graveyards.[4] Furthermore, the citizens and inhabitants of German towns in the north-western parts of the Empire were members of different guilds, associations of craftsmen and/or fraternities.[5] All of these institutions had specific rights and claimed juridical authority over their members. Therefore, it was necessary to find a way to establish a sense of community to give citizens and inhabitants the idea of a shared purpose and mutual obligation. The goal for the town council and its members was to strengthen the unity of the people and the civic accord inside the city walls in order to defend it against encroachments.[6]

In the first part of the chapter I will discuss the means by which city councils created and maintained urban peace inside the city walls. It will be shown that in this respect, urban peace formed the basis for security in the city and the foundation for the most important vested interest of the citizens as well as of all inhabitants: the undisturbed and wide-ranging pursuit of their economic objectives. The second part of the chapter focuses on conflicts between largely autonomous towns and their town lords, who, in the last third of the fifteenth century, tried to regain control over the cities' administrations and courts of law. I aim to show that upholding the peace was a paramount feature of urban legal culture. By looking at the means and practices used by the towns' authorities to reach this goal, we can learn more about how law 'works' in a society.

Pax urbana as a foundation for communal living in the towns

The urban peace in late medieval German towns depended on the *universitas civium* (community), which was in legal terms a *coniuratio communis* or *coniuratio pax*.[7] Every citizen had to become a member of the *universitas* by a promissory oath, sworn on the gospel or a reliquary. Every member obliged himself to abide by the self-given standards and rules. With his oath, he agreed to accept due punishment in case he broke any rules. Furthermore, he had to assist the town's authorities to uphold the law and help to catch trespassers.[8] As a member of a confederation ('Eid- oder Schwurgemeinschaft'), the citizen had to pay taxes, perform guard duty by day and by night and defend the walls and gates of the town when the authorities told him to.[9] But the citizen also had some important advantages. He was a free person, he had the chance to choose a profession and he was allowed to bequest his property to whomsoever he wished. The citizen had the right to elect members of the city council and had – at least hypothetically – passive suffrage; he could be elected. Furthermore, he had the privilege to seek justice at the city court and in most cases nobody could take legal action against him outside the urban jurisdiction.[10]

Since the thirteenth century most German towns had developed a political and juridical administration – consisting of councils, courts, legal professionals and some kind of police force – which had the duty to secure the peace and the unity within the town for all citizens and other dwellers (servants, maidservants, journeymen and so on), who also had to swear an oath ('Beisassenheid') but who did not enjoy the same rights as free citizens.[11] In principle, every inhabitant of the town could enjoy the urban peace as well as protection against injustice of any kind. But the guarantee of justice by the city council did imply that vigilantism or violent revenge for an alleged or factual injustice was forbidden.

The town council also organised the defence of the town's freedom against external enemies. The paramount objective of urban councils and courts was to keep the peace within the city walls because legal peace was crucial to securing and promoting trade and craft. Without urban peace, it was challenging or even impossible for tradesmen to conduct their business successfully. But not just the urban economy was affected by the disturbance of the peace. The unity of the citizens and inhabitants as well as harmony (*unio*) and the common good (*bonum commune*) were at stake too. The inscription at the outer Holstentor in Lübeck (erected in the sixteenth century) summed this idea up nicely: *Concordia domi et foris pax sane res est omnium pulcherrima*.[12]

Let us now take a closer look at the different legal areas of the *pax urbana* which touched on matters from mundane daily communal living to more intense political crises. It was the main function of the urban peace to regulate the mutual prosperity of all urban dwellers. In the municipal laws, peace (*friden*) designated the manner in which citizens and inhabitants should interact. In the later middle ages, the form that the peace took depended on the legal system of each individual town. In the legal culture of especially German towns peace and law were identical.[13] Town laws, for example, specified where inhabitants could legally dump their manure or where they could keep their pigs and poultry. Problems often arose when dwellers tried to unload their excrement near the wells because this could contaminate the water. Perpetrators in these cases had to face a peace fine ('Friedensstrafe') because they had disturbed the urban peace by ignoring the rule concerning hygiene in the town. Another important issue was the mundane behaviour of inhabitants on streets and squares, in churches and taverns. One could become a breaker of the peace by shouting and/or swearing in public or by walking home from a tavern without holding a light.[14] Whereas the offences mentioned earlier were in most cases only punished with fines, those with a specific level of interpersonal violence, like verbal disputes (sometimes along with a fistfight) or the drawing of knives, were punished with shameful penalties like standing at the pillory – penalties that were meant to taint the honour of peace breakers.[15] Major offences like burglary, thievery and the infliction of serious or deadly injuries were punished with corporal punishments.[16]

Personal honour was political capital for men with ambitions. It was essential for members of the political elite to legitimise their social position and their role as political officers like councillor, mayor, city treasurer and the like. The towns were governed by members of the urban elite (the urban nobility, very wealthy tradesmen, people with independent means and, in the fifteenth century, guild masters as well) who acted as members of the council. On the one hand, these members of the elite tried to distance themselves from the main body of citizens; on the other hand, they tried to maintain a hierarchy of prestige and honour among themselves. Although these men were legally equal to other citizens, their social status and prestige were different. This fact led to tensions between families and individuals of the urban elite. The urban peace was at risk if a member of the council, for example the mayor, acted in a way that created the impression that he wanted to overcome the council, was pursuing his individual benefit instead of the common good and tried to erect an autocracy. Bertram Wulflam, mayor in the Hanseatic town of Stralsund in the second half of the fourteenth century, was such a man.[17] His opponents criticised him because he refused to draw up accounts and he stored tax revenues in his house. Thus, his fellow councillors had no way to check how he used the town's money. He was also accused of consulting his wife more than the members of the council. In 1391 an opposition led by Karsten Sarnow finally forced him to give public account for the budget. He refused to do this, and instead took his family and fled to Lübeck.

In 1487 an uprising against the government in Braunschweig was sustained in particular by well-off craftsmen and social climbers. This uprising occurred because the council was under the influence of an increasingly small group of patrician families.[18] These families were accused of using their influence to promote relatives and kin into offices, thus preventing suitable candidates from other patrician families being elected. Office holders – the customs clerk and the law clerk – were accused of misusing their position and influence in order to pursue their personal interests and of damaging the common good. Apart from that, members of the lower ranks joined the insurgents, because they wanted the council to take care of the common people by lowering the beer price and by building a storehouse or granary. So while the elite was struggling over the occupation of town and council offices, ordinary people demanded measures against the consequences of bad harvests and price increases. In both cases, but for different reasons, the insurgents claimed that the council had broken the urban peace and that the insurgents themselves had taken measures to restore it. In all cases similar to those mentioned here, there was an option to restore the urban peace if the troublemaker left the town either voluntary or involuntary because he wanted to avoid a court suit or had been sentenced to exile.[19]

Discontent with the handling of the towns' finances by the council or with specific members of the council stirred up the tensions between the citizens and often led to violent protest. In the eyes of ordinary citizens, such mishandling was a breach of the urban peace, because they as taxpayers had to compensate for the loss. Along with material reasons for upheaval in a city, the mentality of the citizens has to be considered. Most of them respected the councillors as long as they fulfilled their duties properly and in line with the fundamental understanding that they were in office for the common good of the town and its inhabitants and not for their private interests. In case the patricians in the council seemed to ignore the requirements of good government, they were accused of showing arrogance (*ubirmute*). Citizens in Lübeck protested against councillors in 1408 because they saw themselves governed by the council in the same way peasants were ruled by the lord of a manor. Other complaints were related to the financial management of the council, because only a few aldermen were running this important aspect of the government. The citizens regarded this as a breach of the urban peace as well as a breach of the aldermen's oaths of office.[20]

The conflicts among guilds and crafts were another perennial challenge to the peace. Such disputes often occurred because the council was seen to favour a particular craft guild. This led to mutual complaints about the unfair business practices of the opponent. In Braunschweig in the 1480s the blacksmiths complained about the hucksters who, like the blacksmiths, sold knives and nails. The hucksters, who had shops in the town, were, in turn, dissatisfied because peddlers were allowed to sell spices and other goods three times a week in the open air.[21] The craft guilds' members demanded of the council to act in their benefit and were displeased when the council refused to do so. As a consequence, there was a permanent tension in the town and it only needed a spark to provoke a conflict or even an uprising. For the ordinary craft and guild members the urban peace was the basis for their business activities. They saw this peace disrupted in every case in which their business was restricted by the aldermen's economic policy to their disadvantage.

The urban peace (*friden*) as the foundation for communal living in the towns fulfilled various functions. It was a means to secure the inviolability of life and limb, the protection of one's property and the preservation of the value of material goods. Furthermore, it helped the citizens and inhabitants to settle disputes and live together. However, councils and protesters alike used the norms and regulations in the municipal laws concerning the urban peace to legitimise their political goals. As we have seen, the practice to keep the peace and the best way to uphold it or to restore it after it had been disrupted was highly controversial for council and citizens, craftsmen and guilds. Nevertheless, the parties on either side of the conflict tried to find ways to solve their issues and to re-establish urban peace – and to restore peace meant to follow the regulations of the urban law. The drawing up of so-called letters or charters of peace ('Friedbriefe') is evidence for the efforts of all those involved in making the city space a peaceful place to live in.[22] The *Friedbriefe* were the product of negotiations between parties, who had for example fought over political participation and the constitution of a town (the right to vote) or over business concerns (the right to sell specific items) with each other. With the signing of charters, the parties bound themselves to an agreement, which sought to restore the peace in the town.

Pax urbana as a result of arbitration procedures between town councils and lords

The establishment and perpetuation of urban peace were integral components of the political and legal culture in the German towns in the later middle ages. The efforts to make the space within the city walls a safe haven for citizens and inhabitants alike involved, in the first place, legislation by the council and efforts to put it into effect. The power of the councils to govern a town derived from the lords of the towns. In the case of imperial cities, the lord was the Emperor, but most towns received their charters and privileges for self-government in the thirteenth and fourteenth centuries from noble lords. In many cases, the award of such privileges was the result of struggles between the citizens and the lord of the town, which were often decided in the town's favour.[23] Until the second half of the fifteenth century, many German towns had become more or less independent political units and the actual lords did not intervene intensively in the affairs of the citizens. This changed after the middle of the century, and it became apparent that the lords wanted to recover their authority over the towns within their territory.

What actually happened was that bishops, dukes and other town lords sought ways to regain control over the towns. This was an important aspect of the so-called 'state building' process, which took place on the territorial level in Germany.[24] The feudal lords referred to their old rights and tried to put them into effect again, sometimes by using force against the towns and their office holders. Therefore, councils and office holders had to defend their legal status against the attempts to curtail their legal and political power and scope. In this context, we find another notion of *pax urbana*. Here, urban peace was the result of the settling of conflicts between a town and its citizens on one side and the lord of the town on the other side. This is a second striking feature of the legal culture in German towns around 1500.

To conclude a *pax urbana* with the lord of the town was a means to secure important features of a town's self-government, because the citizens had not been able to resist encroachments in every case. I will explain this by comparing the fate of Halle/Saale and Magdeburg, which both came under attack by their lord, the archbishop of Magdeburg, in 1478/1479 and 1496/1497, respectively. Archbishop Ernst (1476–1513) was pursuing a policy of pressure and enforcement of his acquired rights against the towns in his lordship.[25] Being the superior lord of the towns in his archdiocese, he wanted to transform the largely independent municipalities into county towns ('Landstädte') under his direct rule. It is necessary to mention that Ernst became the administrator of Magdeburg in 1476 when he was 11 years old. Therefore, his father, Duke and elector Ernst of Saxony (1441–1486), and his councillors directed the policy and ruled in his name. Between 1485 and 1487, he gained personal independence and pursued his own territorial policy, which was more or less in line with his father's. Saxon troops conquered Halle in September 1478. This event marked the end of autonomy for Halle, because the citizens lost their right to legislation (*burkore*) within the town and the archbishop could reject newly elected members of the council if they displeased him. Furthermore, the town had to cancel its membership of the Hanseatic League, to which it had belonged since its inception. The symbol of the town's liberties – the statue of Roland by the market place – was encased in wood.[26] The Roland sculpture had symbolised the *libertas* (freedom) of the town; it expressed autonomy from the lord.[27] Its encasing sent a clear message: the autonomy of the town, which had consisted of self-government and legislation and had been based on the association of the citizens, was abolished.

The question arises as to why the councillors in Halle had not been able to negotiate a *pax urbana* like their fellows in Magdeburg had a few years later. Since the 1430s, there had been internal strife among the owners of the salt springs, the so-called 'Pfänner',[28] who represented the urban patricians on one side and members of the guilds and craft guilds on the other side. Members of the *Pfänner* had been accused only to pretend to foster the common good of the town, while in fact pursuing their private interests. Over the years, a deep mutual distrust had developed and the tension between the social groups reached a climax in 1476. The *Pfänner* wanted the support of their fellow citizens against Archbishop Ernst, who demanded (for the first time) payments before he was willing to approve their use of the salt springs, which he regarded as some kind of fief.[29] The *Pfänner* argued that all citizens, belonging to a *universitas civium* and all equal in legal respect, had to contribute to the confirmation of their springs by the archbishop. Alternatively, they were to fight together for the continuation of the privilege not to pay for the permission to use the salt springs. The craft members in the council, on the contrary, argued that a payment had to be made by the *Pfänner* alone because they gained most of the profit from the production of salt. They – together with the majority of the citizens – thought that the patricians only emphasised the legal equality of all citizens in order to rescue their own economic and social position at the expense of the community. Therefore, councillors of the craft guilds like Hans Seele (a blacksmith) or Jakob Weissack (a shoemaker) collaborated with the lord of the town to disempower the *Pfänner* economically and politically. Markus Spittendorf, who was a citizen of Halle and an attentive observer of the conflict, summarised the ubiquitous hostility during the last years of the 1470s as follows: 'wir von Halle hasseten und neideten uns, und einer verfolgte den anderen' ('we, citizens of Halle, hated and envied each other, and one quarreled with the other').[30] This constitutes the crucial point. It was reasonably easy for a lord to subdue a town under his rule if the citizens had not been able to find a common ground to defend their liberties and autonomy. The kind of urban peace that Halle 'enjoyed' after the conquest was one dictated by the lord of the town. The citizens were no longer associated with each other as members of a community; they had become subjects to feudal rule.

We do not know whether Archbishop Ernst thought using military force would help him subdue all towns in his dominion, because he and his father managed to conquer Quedlinburg in 1477 and Halberstadt in 1486 in this way. In both cases, the towns lost their liberties like Halle and were subjected to the archbishop's rule.[31] However, when Ernst approached Magdeburg in the 1490s, things turned out differently.

A council ruled Magdeburg. Ever since 1330, the five most important guilds (cloth merchants, grocers, furriers, shoemakers/tanners, tailors) annually elected one member each to the council; the other guilds (butchers, bakers, brewer, blacksmiths, sign makers, goldsmiths, sheet maker and 'Schröter' (transport workers)) chose another five aldermen.[32] These ten councillors co-opted two patricians. The members of council provided the civic officers like the mayor, the treasurer, the keeper of the account books and so on. The members of the council and the officers were responsible to and had to work for the *utilitas publica* or *Gemeinen Nutzen* (common good) of the community and town. In the final 30 years of the fifteenth century, two goals of the council's policy were of particular importance in respect to the political key category, the common good. The first goal of the political activities of the council was to guarantee peace, order and justice within the city walls. In this respect, the councillors and judges in Magdeburg acted in line with the practice in the towns described in the first part of this chapter. In the following, I will concentrate on their goal to defend and secure the freedom of the citizens against the attacks of regional princes; to that end, the councillors pursued the imperial freedom ('Reichsfreiheit'). Typical features of this freedom were military sovereignty over the walls and gates, the right to levy taxes, the control over all economic activities within the walls and freedom of action in all law affairs.

The troubles between Archbishop Ernst and the council of Magdeburg began in the 1480s when the lord questioned the legal status of Magdeburg. In 1482, he demanded the payment of approximately 9,000 *gulden* for the defense of the Empire against the Turks. The council, in turn, claimed to pay this money directly to the Emperor, which indicated that Magdeburg was only responsible to the Emperor without any middling overlord. The conflict dragged on for several years and was waged at the imperial court with arbitrators from both sides who exchanged arguments for and against the imperial status of Magdeburg. In the end, the aldermen agreed to an arbitration award in 1486: they paid the money and did homage to the archbishop. However, this conflict shows the political strategy of Magdeburg's council: act as a unity, avoid violence or using force, use all means for diplomacy and wait for the next chance to argue with the archbishop over the legal status of the town. The next chance became available in the middle of the 1490s.

Since the arbitration award in 1486, the council tried to show that Magdeburg was *de facto* still a free city. One possibility to demonstrate this was to practice the highest jurisdiction and administer capital punishment, like that of a man who had been convicted of being a cabbage thief and was duly hanged.[33] The archbishop, for his part, arrested citizens in the town, a power that the council claimed for itself. Ernst also accused the council that it had allowed attacks on clerics in the city. Like the administration of law, the suzerainty over the walls and gates was an indicator of the legal status of a town, and the council was determined to defend it. But Ernst, in his turn, also claimed these rights. Furthermore, the council asserted that the archbishop had disrupted the urban peace by attacking the market or sales monopoly of the town. He allowed the selling of wine and beer in taverns run by the chapter of the cathedral and had granted the staple right without the council's permission. Other contested points were toll and dues, property rights and rights of use, use of the water bodies and more generally the lordship over the town.[34]

As in Halle in 1476 and in Halberstadt 1486, the *iura et libertates* of Magdeburg were at stake. Both parties alleged that their opponent interfered with their fundamental rights; from the perspective of the council, the archbishop was a peace breaker. Ernst on the other hand saw another unruly government that refused to accept his supremacy. The situation was similar to the conflict with Halle 25 years ago. Yet there were significant differences. His father and brothers, who had used the sword to achieve their political objectives, had carried out the action against Halle and Halberstadt. Archbishop Ernst tried to gain power by different means: he sought the recourse of the law rather than that of military force. Another difference was that the council in Magdeburg was not divided during the period of this conflict. There is no evidence of unrest or discontent within the council or the city. Therefore both parties agreed to settle the disputes in a *fruntlich guttlich handel* ('freundlichen und gütlichen Ausgleich'; an amicable settlement), which in practice meant by way of an arbitration procedure.

Instead of preparing for a military conflict, both parties, citizens and archbishop, finally agreed to install a court of arbitration and each party was to nominate members. A court of arbitration ('Schiedsgericht') in contrast to a court of law was based on a contractual agreement and aimed to mediate in conflicts by compromise and not by judgement.[35] The archbishop appointed Nicolaus von Zinna and Woldemar, prince of Anhalt; the council of Magdeburg was represented by Heyne Alemann, a former mayor, Heise Rulffs, a juryman of the town's court, and Hans Kotze. The court was given the power to decide on the contentious points and the parties agreed to accept the arbitral decision. The arbitrators were to handle the legal dispute between the archbishop and the council as amicable negotiators (*gutliche hendeler*) and not as judges.[36] As a second step both parties appointed representatives who had to defend the respective claims and reject the mutual accusations before the board of arbitrators. The negotiators of the archbishop were Adolf, provost of the cathedral chapter, Ludwig, guardian of the Franciscan order, Andreas Proles, Heinrich Loser and Johannes Breitenbach, doctor of canon and civil law. Thomas Sulte and Heinrich Alemann, mayors, together with the legal adviser Thomas Mauricii, defended the arguments of the citizens.[37]

The results of the negotiations were drawn up in a charter in January 1497. With this charter, an urban peace (*pax urbana*) was set up and the relations between the archbishop – the factual lord of the town – and the citizens of Magdeburg were built on a new basis.[38] The accord was effective until 1666, the year in which Magdeburg was incorporated into the emerging state of Brandenburg. But this was not an urban peace between the citizens of a town (by swearing mutual oaths as we have seen earlier); this was a *pax urbana* between the town and its lord, which certainly had an impact within the city walls.

With regard to the administration of justice, it was decided that the jurisdiction of the city court did not include the areas of clerical immunity, which also comprised the new market on the 'Domfreiheit'. The clergy and members of the archbishop's court remained subject to canon law only. However, the officials of the council and the archbishop should prosecute disturbers of the peace.[39] In contrast, the council successfully defended its control over the walls and gates of the town. The archbishop and his servants, in turn, had the right to enter the town as they liked.[40] Concerning the sales monopoly, the citizens had to accept that the archbishop or the cathedral chapter could sell wine and beer in pubs and taverns, but the council was allowed to prohibit the citizens to buy in these taverns.[41] The council accepted the town rule of Archbishop Ernst, but simultaneously he acclaimed the *iura et liberates* of the city.[42] He conferred two annual fairs and received 6,666 florins in return.[43]

The regulations in the charter were a compromise. Archbishop Ernst was recognised as the lord of the town and this strengthened his position as a prince in the Empire and as a feudal lord. The council did not succeed in its attempts to expand or even defend the freedom of the town. However, it was very successful concerning the economic disputes, because as part of the treaty the merchants and craftsmen got numerous forms of relief which fostered their businesses, not least because now the urban peace was secured by the mutual obligations described in the charter.

It is important to stress that such arbitration proceedings were a feature of urban legal culture around 1500. The board of arbitrators was a court neither of the town nor of the archbishop. As a result, its decision was not a verdict. The arbitrators declared that they had decided on the lawsuit and the countersuit in terms of reconciliation, amicable agreement and friendship ('sune, guthe und fruntschafft'). They offered a compromise that would be acceptable for both sides. The use of this mode to address the conflict indicates that both parties recognised each other as equals. They tried to find a solution on the basis of a consensus or broad agreement. By using the process of arbitration, the parties showed their willingness to respect each other and to come to terms with the arbitral decision. The charter of January 1497 is evidence of this, because with it the decision was transformed into a legally attested treaty between the archbishop and the council of Magdeburg. It was valid for all persons within the urban space, not only for specific groups of inhabitants. This procedure enabled both parties to achieve some of their aims: the council of Magdeburg for its citizens regarding the economic prospects, and Archbishop Ernst, because he was recognised as the feudal lord of the town. Therefore both parties had achieved their most important political objectives for the time being.

Concluding remarks

Urban peace is not only an important feature of legal practice in the German towns, but a social term, which characterises a specific form of human cohabitation. We can gain more insight into the social, economic and political aspects of town life when we study the *pax urbana*. We can distinguish at least two types of urban peace: on the one hand, a municipal peace, which depended on the association of citizens and, on the other hand, a negotiated peace, which depended on the mutual agreement of a town council and the lord of the town. One could argue that there was also a third kind of urban peace which was settled as a solution in the struggle between a town and its feudal lord such as, for example, in Braunschweig in 1487 and 1503. In those years, the dukes of Braunschweig issued letters of favour ('Huldbriefe') in which they granted the council the right of legislation, military sovereignty and legal jurisdiction as well as confirming the urban privileges.[44] These different kinds of urban peace had in common that they were based on the idea of solving struggles by negotiation between two more or less equal partners. In all cases mentioned in this chapter, urban peace was the answer to a conflict. This indicates that the upholding of *pax urbana* was identical with the effective implementation of the norms of urban law in mundane practice. In this respect, the urban peace was at the core of urban legal culture.

The examples of Magdeburg and Braunschweig, who had been able to negotiate with their lord because the aldermen and the citizens were united, are not, however, typical for the overall situation in Germany around 1500. Halle is more typical in this respect. In the majority of towns, councils developed from an institution that represented, and acted in the name of, the association of citizens into a kind of authority that tried to turn the citizens into its subjects.[45] This was an intention that town councils shared with territorial lords. The *pax urbana* was thus no longer the product of mutual negotiation and respect, but a peace dictated from above. During the sixteenth century, this development had an effect on urban legal culture. Instead of informal arbitration proceedings to reconcile conflicts and restore peace, court proceedings became dominant. As a consequence, urban legal culture became increasingly constricted to the formal procedures contained in the laws. Trained lawyers in imperial and canon law gained the most important influence on legal culture in towns and elsewhere in Germany.

Notes

1 I would like to thank Edda Frankot for polishing my English and the editors of this volume for their helpful comments.

I use the term 'citizen', from the Latin *civis*, to indicate the members of the *universitas civium* who had citizenship. The *universitas* (community) was a corporative body and as such a fictional legal and immortal person. The corporation was represented by the council, which also carried out legal business and financial obligations. One has to distinguish this corporative body from the association of the inhabitants (society), whose members had the same rights and obligations. In the later middle ages, the transition from the association to the corporative body is reflected by the marginal inscriptions on the seals from *sigillum civium* to *sigillum civitatis*; E. Isenmann, *Die deutsche Stadt im Mittelalter 1150–1550*, Wien/Köln/Weimar: Böhlau, 2012, p. 214.

2 G. Wittek, '*fride* und *pax* als Bezeichnungen für spätmittelalterlichen städtischen Frieden', *Jahrbuch des Vereins für niederdeutsche Sprachforschung* 120, 1997, pp. 59–78.

3 F.J. Arlinghaus, 'The myth of urban unity: Religion and social performance in late medieval Braunschweig', in C. Goodson et al. (eds) *Cities, Texts and Social Networks, 400–1500: Experiences and Perceptions of Medieval Urban Space*, Farnham: Ashgate, 2010, pp. 215–32. In 1487 even the lord of Baunschweig, Duke William the younger, recognised the fact that it encompassed five towns: 'der viff stede vnser staid to Brunswig'; M. Garzmann (ed.) *Urkundenbuch der Stadt Braunschweig*, vol. 5, Hannover: Hahn, 1994, p. 248.

4 F. Schmieder, *Die mittelalterliche Stadt*, Darmstadt: Wissenschaftliche Buchgesellschaft, 2005, pp. 113–7. For the ecclesiastical precincts in English towns, see C.D. Liddy, *Contesting the City. The Politics of Citizenship in English Towns, 1250–1530*, Oxford: Oxford University Press, 2017, pp. 66–8.

5 Isenmann, *Die deutsche Stadt*, pp. 793–830.

6 An example is given in the second part of this article.

7 A. Black, 'The commune in political theory in the late middle ages', in P. Blickle (ed.) *Theorien kommunaler Ordnung in Europa*, München: Oldenbourg, 1996, pp. 99–112, and K.S. Bader and G. Dilcher, *Deutsche Rechtsgeschichte. Land und Stadt – Bürger und Bauer im Alten Europa*, Berlin/Heidelberg/New York: Springer, 1999, pp. 400–3.

8 E. Isenmann, 'The notion of the common good, the concept of politics, and practical policies in late medieval and early modern Germany cities', in E. Lecuppre-Desjardin and A.L. van Bruaene (eds) *De Bone Communi. The Discourse and Practice of the Common Good in the European City (13th–16th c.)*, Turnhout: Brepols, 2010, pp. 107–48, at pp. 114–5. These duties are very similar to the obligations in Scottish towns; C. Hawes, 'The urban community in fifteenth-century Scotland: Language, law and political practice', *Urban History* 44, 2017, pp. 365–80, at pp. 375–6

9 In Lübeck, a man was considered a citizen if he 'waket und shotet mit uns' ('when he watches and pays taxes with us'); A. Graßmann (ed.) *Lübeckische Geschichte*, Lübeck: Schmidt-Römhild, 1988, p. 232.

10 In this respect, the German towns are comparable to English towns; see Liddy, *Contesting the City*, p. 41: 'In cases within the city, citizens were to be tried only by their peers'.

11 Since the thirteenth century scholars used the terms *cives simpliciter* (citizen per se) and *cives secundum quid* (citizen with certain restrictions) to mark the difference; K. Schreiner, 'Teilhabe, Konsens und Autonomie. Leitbegriffe kommunalere Ordnung in der politischen Theorie des späten Mittelalters und der frühen Neuzeit', in P. Blickle (ed.) *Theorien kommunaler Ordnung in Europa*, München: Oldenbourg, 1996, pp. 35–61, at pp. 37–8.

12 Isenmann, *Die deutsche Stadt*, p. 448 (Translation: 'Internal unity and peace outside (the city walls) are good for all indeed'). The outer Holstentor was demolished in the nineteenth century.

13 W. Jansen, 'Friede', in *Geschichtliche Grundbegriffe*, vol. 2, Stuttgart: Klett-Cotta, 1975, pp. 543–91, at p. 546, and Isenmann, 'The notion of the common good', p. 120: peace is preserved by justice and legislation and therefore under the law.

14 G. Wittek, 'Stadtfrieden. Über das Zusammenleben in der hoch- und spätmittelalterlichen Stadt', *Die alte Stadt. Zeitschrift für Stadtgeschichte, Stadtsoziologie und Denkmalpflege* 21, 1994, pp. 165–81, at pp. 173–4.

15 Isenmann, *Die deutsche Stadt*, p. 513. In this respect, legal culture in the German towns was quite similar to the practice in Scottish towns. E.L. Ewan, 'The community of the burgh in the fourteenth century', in M. Lynch (ed.) *The Scottish Medieval Town*, Edinburgh: Donald, 1988, pp. 228–43, at p. 233, stated with regard to Aberdeen: 'Humiliation before the community was considered to be a powerful deterrent'.

16 Bader and Dilcher, *Deutsche Rechtsgeschichte*, p. 646.

17 J. Rogge, 'Ehrverletzungen und Entehrungen in politischen Konflikten in spätmittelalterlichen Städten', in K. Schreiner and G. Schwerhoff (eds) *Verletzte Ehre. Ehrkonflikte in Gesellschaften des Mittelalters und der Frühen Neuzeit*, Köln: Böhlau, 1995, pp. 110–43, at pp. 114–6.

18 H.L. Reimann, *Unruhe und Aufruhr im mittelalterlichen Braunschweig*, Braunschweig: Waisenhaus Buchdruckerei und Verlag, 1962, pp. 107–9.

19 In April 1374, members of the patrician families fled from Braunschweig after an uprising against the council; M. Puhle, 'Die Braunschweiger "Schichten" (Aufstände) des späten Mittelalters und ihre verfassungsrechtlichen Folgen', in M. Garzmann (ed.) *Rat und Verfassung im mittelalterlichen Braunschweig*, Braunschweig: Waisenhaus-Druckerei, 1986, pp. 253–1, at p. 240; in 1375, patricians and their families had to leave Nordhausen; B. Kannowski, *Bürgerkämpfe und Friedebriefe*, Köln/Weimar/Wien: Böhlau, 2002, p. 44; in Lübeck, most members of the patrician council were forced to leave the town in 1408; Isenmann, *Die deutsche Stadt*, p. 276.

20 Graßmann, *Lübeckische Geschichte*, pp. 249–53; Kannowski, *Bürgerkämpfe*, pp. 26–9; see R.A. Rotz, '"Social struggles" or price of power? German urban uprisings in the late middle ages', *Archiv für Reformationsgeschichte* 76, 1985, pp. 64–95, for an overview of conflicts between citizens and councils in Germany.

21 Reimann, *Unruhe und Aufruhr*, pp. 109–10.

22 Kannowski, *Bürgerkämpfe*, p. 4, gives examples from the Hanseatic town Rostock 1428: 'dorch nutticheit und eynes fredes willen' ('utility and the will for peace'), and from Braunschweig 1445: 'dorch eyndracht unde vrede samitheit willen' ('for unity and peace for all'). Again, in 1446, the council in Braunschweig called together struggling parties in order to 'desse sake endighen und to frede setten' ('to end the struggle and bring about peace'); *Chroniken der deutschen Städte*, volume 16 (= Braunschweig vol. 2), Leipzig: Vandenhoeck & Ruprecht, 1880, p. 515.

23 With a focus on north-western towns of the Empire: W. Ehbrecht, *Konsens und Konflikt. Skizzen und Überlegungen zur älteren Verfassungsgeschichte deutscher Städte*, Köln/Weimar/Wien: Böhlau, 2001, and see also B. Scheper, *Frühe bürgerliche Institutionen norddeutscher Hansestädte. Beiträge zu einer vergleichenden Verfassungsgeschichte Lübecks, Bremens, Lüneburgs und Hamburgs im Mittelalter*, Köln/Wien: Böhlau, 1975.

24 W. Reinhard (ed.) *Power Elites and State Building*, Oxford: Scientia Bonnensis, 1996; E. Schubert, *Fürstliche Herrschaft und Territorium im späten Mittelalter*, 2nd edn, München: Oldenbourg, 2006; and G.A. Loud and J. Schenk (eds) *The Origins of German Principalities, 1100–1350. Essays by German Historians*, London/New York: Routledge, 2017.

25 Ernst was the second son of Ernst, Duke and Elector of Saxony. He was born into the politically important dynasty of Wettin, which controlled most of Saxony, Meißen and Thuringia; J. Rogge, 'Ernst von Sachsen, Erzbischof von Magdeburg und Administrator von Halberstadt (1476–1513)', in W. Freitag (ed.) *Mitteldeutsche Lebensbilder. Menschen im späten Mittelalter*, Cologne: Böhlau, 2002, pp. 27–68.

26 J. Rogge, 'Reden, Streiten und Verhandeln. Innerstädtische Kommunikation und Stadtkonflikte in den 1470er Jahren in Halle', in W. Freitag and M. Ruprecht (eds) *Aufruhr, Zwietracht und Gewalt. Konfliktlagen in der halleschen Stadtgesellschaft vom Mittelalter bis zur Neuzeit*, Halle: Mitteldeutscher Verlag, 2006, pp. 28–41.

27 K. Schreiner, 'Iura et libertates. Wahrnehmungsformen und Ausprägungen "bürgerlicher Freyheiten" in den Städten des Hohen und Späten Mittelalters', in H.J. Puhle (ed.) *Bürger in der Gesellschaft der Neuzeit. Wirtschaft – Politik – Kultur*, Göttingen: Vandenhoeck & Ruprecht, 1991, pp. 59–106, at p. 81.

28 M. Hecht, *Patriziatsbildung als kommunikativer Prozess. Die Salzstädte Lüneburg, Halle und Werl im späten Mittelalter und Früher Neuzeit*, Köln/Weimar/Wien: Böhlau, 2010, p. 31.

29 Ibid., pp. 133–4.

30 J. Opel (ed.) *Denkwürdigkeiten des Hallischen Rathsmeisters Spittendorf*, Halle: Hendel, 1880, p. 218.

31 G. Wittek, 'Stadtfrieden – ausgewählte Beispiele aus Halle, Halberstadt, Quedlinburg und Stendal im Vergleich', in G. Wittek (ed.) *Concordia Magna. Der Magdeburger Stadtfrieden vom 21. Januar 1497*, Frankfurt am Main: Lang, 2006, pp. 171–82.

32 M. Puhle (ed.) *Magdeburg 1200. Mittelalterliche Metropole, Preußische Festung, Landeshauptstadt. Die Geschichte der Stadt von 805–2005*, Stuttgart: Theiss, 2005, pp. 103–5.

33 G. Wittek, 'Die Verteidigung der Magdeburger Stadtfreiheit gegen Erzbischof, König und Reich – fixiert im Stadtfriedensvertrag vom 21. Januar 1497', in Wittek (ed.) *Concordia Magna*, pp. 17–48, at p. 28.

34 Ibid., pp. 30–1.

35 J. Weitzel, 'Schiedsgericht', in *Lexikon des Mittelalters*, vol. VIII, Stuttgart: Metzler, 1995, pp. 1454–5.

36 See K. Kroeschell, *Deutsche Rechtsgeschichte*, vol. 2, Opladen: Westdeutscher Verlag, 1980, p. 33 on the difference between the *arbiter*, who was bound to the rules of law, and the *arbitrator*, who was free of such an obligation. He also mentions the influence of canon law on the development of the arbitration proceedings.

37 *Urkundenbuch der Stadt Magdeburg*, vol. 3, Halle: Scientia-Verlag, 1896, no. 1028, pp. 602–15, at pp. 602–3. Concerning the manner in which the arbitrators resolved the conflict: *alsz von ynen hirzu verordente gutliche hendeler der selbigen yrer gebrechen, spenne und irniszs[...] nach unserem besten vorstentniszs und gnugsamer vorgehabter betrachtunge aller ummestende und gelegenheit der selbigen parthien und irrigen sachen, so wir mit ankerunge unsers truwen vleisz, mughe und arbeit lange zceit derhalben gehabt und vorgewant, in der sune, guthe und fruntschaft gericht, beteidingt und entschieden in form, massze und weise, wie hir nachfolget und sunderlich.*

Translation (as verbatim as possible): 'Appointed by them as amicable negotiators to handle their legal disputes, friction and discords [...] according to our best understanding and close assessment of all circumstances and the interests of the parties and their disputes which, using our honest diligence, capacity and labour, we had expended for a long time, we have negotiated, evaluated and decided [the legal disputes] in a way of reconciliation, good understanding and friendship in the following manner'. All translations made by me. See also Wittek, *Verteidigung*, pp. 34–35.

38 *Urkundenbuch der Stadt Magdeburg*, pp. 602–15.

39 *Urkundenbuch Magdeburg*, p. 609 (concerning the jurisdiction of the archbishop in the town): *Anclage den bevehel und commission, so unser gnedigster here in sachen der burger der alden stadt zu thun pfleget, auch die appelacion, so an unsern gnedigsten hern von den schultisz und scheppfem der alden stadt gethan betreffende, sein also beteidinget, dass unser gnedigister here die sachen und gebrechen, der wegen ein burger der alden stadt vor sein gnaden verclaget, so die selbige sach ein geistlich sach, an den tumprobest aidr seinen officiall, so abir die selbige werntlich were, an schulttisz unnd schepfen egenanter alden stadt weisen und remitieren sall.*

Translation: 'Concerning the complaints against the power of disposition and sovereignty, which our merciful lord exercises in the affairs of the burgesses of the old town and the appellation, which the mayors ['Schultheiss'] and aldermen direct to our lord, it was agreed, that our merciful lord's litigations and breaches of law, because of them a burgess of the old town takes action at the archbishop's court, in case it is a clerical lawsuit, should assign the case to the provost of the cathedral chapter or his official; but if it is a secular issue, (he) should assign the case to the village mayor and the aldermen'.

40 *Urkundenbuch Magdeburg*, pp. 610–1 (concerning the defence fortification): *Unser gnedigster here und seiner gnaden nachkomen ertzbischove zu Magdburgk fur sich und seiner gnaden dyner und vorwanten den ingangk und uszgangk durch den mollnhof unnd den rotten thurm und bergkfride zu fusze, pferdt und mit wagen zu tage und nacht haben sall.*

Translation: 'Our gracious lord and his successors as archbishops of Magdeburg shall have for themselves as well as for their servants and subordinates the right to enter and leave the town through the mill yard, the red tower and the keep by foot, horse and carts by day and night'.

auch sal der rath alle ander thurme, thor, die graben, das gemewr, der wegen dan clagen und widerclagen durch unsern gnedigsten hern und den rath angestallt, usz gunst und gnedigen willen unsers gnedigisten hern und seiner gnaden capittels hinfurder zu ewigen gezeiten innehaben die zu bewaren, zu behuten, auch mit notturfftigem gebeude zu enthalten, doch eyme itzlichen andern an seinem rechten ane schaden und abbruch.

Translation: 'The council shall keep all the other towers, gates, ditches and masonry, which had been contested between our gracious lord and the council with lawsuits and counter-claims, by the favour and the will of our gracious lord and his grace's· (cathedral) chapter, henceforth and forever in order to preserve and protect them as well as to maintain them by necessary construction work, but without damage or disturbance of mutual rights'.

41 *Urkundenbuch Magdeburg*, p. 611 (concerning the serving of wine and beer): *Umb forderung den weinkeller, das anczapfen des weins und biers zu Gaterszleben betreffende sein in der gestalt geschieden, dasz desz capittels weinkeller und schencken ane alle irnisz und vorhinderunge desz raths bleiben sal, doch mag der rath iren burgern, dasz sie sich desselbigen kellers, weins und biers nicht gebrauchen, vorbite und die velligen buessen.*

Translation: 'In regard of the claims concerning the wine cellars and the tapping of wine and beer in Gaterleben, it is ruled that the wine cellars and taverns [of the cathedral chapter] should be without any disturbance and impairment by the council. Nevertheless, the council is entitled to prohibit its citizens to use the cellar, the wine and the beer. The council can impose a penalty on those who have committed such abuse'.

42 *Urkundenbuch Magdeburg*, p. 613: Obligation of council and citizens: *alsz gehulte, getruwe und gehorszame underthane und alsz unserm rechten hern zustehn und angehoren, dem wir auch redeliche dinsts thun wollen, alsz wir von rechte zu thun pflichtig sein.*

Translation: 'as favor receiving, faithful and obedient subjects, we are under the control of our legal lord, whom we will provide with honest service as we are obligated by the law'.

Obligation of Archbishop Ernst: *dasz wir sie lassen sullen und wullen bey irem rechte, bey yrer freiheit und bey yrer wonheit, die sie von alder gehabt haben.*

Translation: 'that we want them to maintain their right, their freedom and their customs, which they have had of old'.

43 *Urkundenbuch Magdeburg*, pp. 614–5.

44 *Urkundenbuch Braunschweig*, pp. 247–9 (charter from 1487) and pp. 268–70 (charter from 1503).

45 Bader and Dilcher, *Deutsche Rechtsgeschichte*, pp. 726–7.

8

RECALCITRANT BRIDES AND GROOMS

Jurisdiction, marriage and conflicts with parents in fifteenth-century Ghent

Chanelle Delameillieure and Jelle Haemers

On 1 July 1433 the *schepenen* or aldermen of Ghent (the main city in the county of Flanders) reached a verdict in a remarkable case. They declared that Simon van Formelis was not liable in the complaint of his eldest son Jan, who had asked his father to pay 50 pounds *groten* (the local currency). Jan was in urgent need of cash because of the debts he had contracted for his wedding party, and therefore he asked his father to fulfil an earlier promise. Shortly before, Jan had abducted Gertrude of Strépy, the daughter of Jan of Oostkerke (a nobleman from the duchy of Brabant), whom he had married without the consent of his father or the bride's parents. Simon recognised that he had promised to pay an annuity as a marriage gift shortly after he was informed about the abduction, because he felt 'with heartfelt grief' (*met herteleet*) that he had to compensate for the dishonour his son had inflicted upon his father-in-law when Jan married his daughter. However, Simon put forward that he had never *definitively* promised to pay the annual sum because his son did not appear after Simon had repeatedly asked Jan to discuss the precise conditions of the payment. While the aldermen of Ghent agreed with Simon on this line of reasoning, they also did justice to Jan. He was allowed to ask his father for a generous wedding gift, although Simon was not obliged to pay him 50 pounds *groten* immediately because Jan had been reluctant to make a definite agreement about it.[1] The makeshift decision solved the conflict, though in the end it would take father and son three months to discuss the marriage settlement. More than 18 years would pass before the aldermen pronounced a final verdict in the case. The documents from all this litigation form the evidence of this paper.

This chapter will explore urban cultures of law through the example of conflicts concerning marriage. We will show how children (like Jan) could enlarge their scopes of action by refusing the role of being only an object of familial marriage strategies, but also how they used the legal system in order to achieve personal goals. Historians rarely hear the voices of children when they are reconstructing the history of marriage. As the main method of settling conflicts between households, maintaining the family patrimony and extending the power of a lineage, marriage has long been approached by historians as a strategy of parents and extended families to overcome the uncertainties of life. The patrimonial concerns mattered especially to socio-economic elites, to which the families in our case belonged. In reality, therefore, weddings were more rational than they were emotional. Scholarship has tended to consider sons and especially daughters to be 'victims' of the family's marriage plans. For example, Claude Lévi-Strauss in his famous 'Elementary structures of kinship' argued that girls were an 'object of exchange' in the negotiations between parents over marriage, though others have contested his claim because of its universal nature.[2] In his essay 'Matrimonial strategies', sociologist Pierre Bourdieu also described the 'structural victims' (*victimes structurales*) of marriage policies: younger sons as chess pawns and daughters as toys without volition in the marriage market.[3] Martha Howell called this 'trade endogamy': families married within the same trade in order to secure business relationships and stabilise property.[4] Yet Howell and many others have nuanced the representation of medieval marriage practices studied by Lévi-Strauss, Bourdieu and their followers; future spouses did have a say, they were richly endowed and sometimes they were 'accomplices' in the negotiations preceding marriage. In Ghent, for instance, it was customary to take the wishes of the future couple into account when the marriage settlement was discussed, though certainly the bride could not take a leading role. Families, particularly the father of the household, decided upon the partner, the marriage gift and the future inheritance.[5] Parenthood, family relationships and matrimonial strategies were not solid structures, but could be negotiated.[6] Following this logic, the marriage of Jan van Formelis and his charge against his father would be brave assaults on the well-established norms and expectations of matrimonial arrangements.

Yet, was Jan's resistance successful? Recalcitrant children could try to prevent marriage to someone chosen by their parents through a clandestine marriage to a partner of their choice. As we will see, urban elites promulgated bylaws that punished such practices severely. There is some evidence of young men who resisted against forced marriages by refusing to go through with their parents' marital plans.[7] The Ghent case of 1433 demonstrates that the arsenal deployed by unwilling grooms and brides to resist their parents' will included not only refusal and clandestine marriage but also judicial strategies. As Daniel Smail has concluded, citizens were increasingly 'consuming' justice when they were angry rather than resorting to violence; in the later middle ages, citizens 'notarised' their enmities by legal process in court.[8] A detailed study of Jan and Gertrude's amorous adventures and juridical perils gives us access to such legal strategies used by 'structural victims' to negotiate the marriage conditions determined by their respective families. Using remarkable, little-known sources, the private contracts and dispute settlements of Jan and Gertrude, we will demonstrate that both brides and grooms took matters to court if they felt victimised by their families. Even though their lawsuits were not always successful, the main actors in our case did have the power to contest the marriage contracts arranged by their parents. The favourable legal position of women in the urban society of the Low Countries gave them opportunities to navigate social and legal structures, but at the same time the relative wealth and the prominent social position of the main actors determined their access to justice. The urban setting in itself is also an important factor, because the customs and bylaws of Ghent gave citizens the rights and judicial means to bring such cases to court. Thus, it will be argued that the legal culture of cities created an advantageous environment for citizens to solve marital and inheritance conflicts in a peaceful way.

Jan and Gertrude before the Ghent aldermen

The body of sources for this study consists of ten contracts and lawsuit adjudications recorded in the annual registers of the aldermen of the *Keure* and *Gedeele*.[9] The city of Ghent had two benches of aldermen (*schepenen*) who recorded the final verdicts they pronounced in cases brought before them. Although the boards acted together occasionally when important cases were under discussion (as we will see), in general each met separately in accordance with their distinct mandates. While the *Keure* issued urban ordinances, judged civil and criminal cases and punished offenders, the *Gedeele* focused on the cases that involved orphans, testaments, inheritance conflicts and the like. Chosen from the elite groups (powerful families and guild leaders), each board of 13 aldermen also registered private contracts for sales, loans and agreements of all kinds.[10] For extra insurance and an extra payment, the clerk recorded the legal act in the aldermen's annual register. Although the documents in these registers are predominantly from wealthy and middle-class citizens and therefore represent only a small fraction of all the economic acts of this large city, both sets of registers contain the ordinary acts of thousands of people. Each board recorded the documents separately in a series of registers, which survive from the second half of the fourteenth until the end of the eighteenth century. They are a rich resource for historians, but they are notoriously difficult to handle due to their quantity and the fact that no one has ever made an effort to index them systematically.[11]

Three aspects of these *schepenregisters* make them extremely valuable for research on marital conflicts. One strength is that they provide insight into the civil aspects of marriage. While the registers of the episcopal courts only concern matters that interested the Church, city aldermen regulated economic and social matrimonial issues.[12] The accounts of the episcopal court of Tournai (the bishopric to which Ghent belonged) record fines for adultery, clandestine marriage, divorces etc., evidence that allows historians to study moral attitudes, sexual deviancy and marital offences.[13] The registers of the aldermen, on the other hand, include contracts about marriage gifts, verdicts in disputes between spouses and the like. Second, historians have often used sources deriving from the repression of citizens who had broken marital law (such as remission letters, sentence books and bailiff or city accounts recording fines) to examine marital conflicts, which has turned unwilling brides and grooms into criminals because they were subject to punishment.[14] In contrast, as Monique Vleeschouwers-Van Melkebeek has shown, the Ghent registers reveal the social aspects of marriage, such as the relationship between the couple and their parents after an abduction.[15] A third advantage is that the registers feature women as well as men, and young people as well as authority figures. Many historians have already shown how fruitful research in the Ghent *schepenregisters* can be for understanding women and their legal capabilities, the history of orphans, domestic life and similar subjects.[16] Our case study of two people suing their parents(-in-law) will add an interesting, albeit modest, contribution to the social history of the parent-child relationship. Because of their focus on clerical evidence, studies of 'marital victims' have minimised the efforts of young brides and grooms to defy their parents. In contrast, the Ghent *schepenregisters* include evidence of the attempts of sons and daughters to contradict their parents and evade the unfavourable effects of marriage practices.

Where did the protagonists of our case study belong on the social scale? Simon came from a wealthy family that ranked among the high society of Ghent's political elite.[17] Some of his ancestors were part of a powerful broker family that had accumulated a rich patrimony within the town and its hinterland. He lived in the Sint-Michielsstraat, a main commercial street, and held the fief of Sint-Denijs-Boekel (south of Ghent). Born in the third quarter of the fourteenth century, he was an old man by the time his oldest son Jan sued him. He had established a notable reputation and had not yet finished his impressive career. A respected jurist and doctor of the law, Simon began his career in city administration in 1400 as a *pensionaris*, an official responsible for judicial affairs, one of the most important offices in the city. He was later appointed by the duke of Brabant to the Council of Brabant, the highest court in that neighbouring duchy. Simon's rapid rise in ducal office is illustrated by his appointment as president of the Council of Flanders by the Burgundian Duke John the Fearless in 1409. Simon's talents as a jurist took him to the upper circles at the court of the duke, who also asked him to undertake important diplomatic missions abroad. His tenure as president probably ended in 1437, and he died on 8 March 1447.

Simon's children also belonged to the Ghent establishment. His wife, Catherine Van Lovendegem, a noble woman from the Ghent hinterland, gave birth to a daughter (Catherine) and three sons: Jan, Gerard and Steven. While Jan was named (together with Steven) as a squire in a list of noblemen joining the Ghent army to participate in Duke Philip the Good's fight against the English at Calais in 1437,[18] Steven was the only brother who held political office in his home town. He was alderman in Ghent in 1441 and 1445, and three times treasurer of the town. The close connection of the Van Formelis family and the court would turn out badly for Steven. He was held responsible for the (alleged) financial mismanagement of the town in the 1440s and was executed in December 1451 by rebelling craftsmen. We will return to this episode, because it is probably not a coincidence that Jan's effort to undo his father's marriage settlement also resurfaced in that year. The Formelis family clearly took the duke's side, a position that resulted in the traumatic death of Simon's son in a perilous period for the duke's local sympathisers. Jan escaped the macabre dance because he had never held political office in his home town. However, his eldest son, also named Jan, followed his grandfather's path to serve the Burgundian court.[19]

Less is known about Gertrude van Oostkerke. Her father, Jean de Strépy, was lord of Oostkerke (today, Oisquercq in French or Oostkerk in Dutch), a fief in Brabant (near Tubize, southwest of Brussels),[20] which included a castle with the adjacent lands and buildings (Hof van Oostkerke), extensive lands (such as the Grootemeersch), woods (including the Bosch van Oostkerke) and annuities.[21] The castle was demolished and today the only building with medieval architecture in Oisquercq is the church, perhaps the same church that hosted our couple's official marriage ceremony. Gertrude's mother (Isabel of Voorde) also came from a noble family, based in the county of Flanders. In short, Gertrude belonged to an important noble lineage closely connected to the duke of Brabant. It was a respected family because it had jurisdiction over justice within the fief.[22] Gertrude was also an attractive prospective bride for a family with noble aspirations because she was the eldest daughter of Sir Jan, who only had two daughters (the youngest was called Yolente) to the best of our knowledge. Perhaps Jan of Strépy had a strategic plan for the marriage of his oldest daughter. But suddenly Jan van Formelis appeared on the scene. Table 8.1 lists the main events of our case.

TABLE 8.1 Chronology of events in the case of Gertrude van Oostkerke and Jan van Formelis

Chronology	
Spring 1433	Abduction and marriage of Gertrude and Jan
1 July 1433	Jan sues Simon over the marriage gift
17 July 1433	Gertrude receives a marriage gift from her father
7–9 October 1433	Jan receives a marriage gift from Simon
2 June 1441	Separation contract of Jan and Gertrude
30 September 1441	Gertrude sues her stepfather over the conditions of her marriage gift
13 August 1450	Gertrude sues her brother-in-law over the validity of Simon's marriage gift
12 November 1450	Gertrude proves that Simon had given a marriage gift before the wedding took place
16 March 1451	The aldermen nullify Simon's marriage gift

The abduction of Gertrude van Oostkerke

The documents under scrutiny state that Gertrude had been abducted (*ontscaect*) by Jan. Perpetrators used abduction in the middle ages to force the victim into a marriage advantageous to the perpetrator but unwanted by the victim's family. Sometimes a man took a (wealthy) woman by force and tried to get her to agree to marry, and sometimes a man and woman took off together to get married in secret, thereby circumventing parental interference. As the Church considered clandestine marriage valid, a marriage to which both partners agreed could not be broken by parents or anyone else.[23] However, to be legal, the clandestine marriage did need to be confirmed afterwards in a church. Late medieval law and justice emphasised the consent of both partners, making it an essential determinant of the legal outcome of an abduction case.[24] It is noteworthy therefore that in the case of Jan and Gertrude nothing is said about whether Gertrude followed and married her abductor willingly. The sources do tell us that neither Jan nor Gertrude's parents were pleased with the *scaec*. Not only had Jan taken Gertrude away without the consent of her father, but Jan's father stated that 'he was not aware of his son's plans and that neither he, nor his wife, gave Jan permission for his undertaking'.[25] It thus seems that the abduction came as a surprise to both sets of parents.

Abduction was considered a serious offence. Marriage was usually a process rather than a single event. There were consultations between families and spouses and discussions within each family, followed by a betrothal, the actual ceremony and a feast. Abduction precluded a 'processual marriage',[26] because the abductor often married his victim in a clandestine ceremony, or the families had to make rapid arrangements in order to limit the damage and shame caused by the abduction.[27] There were strict laws preventing young people from flouting social norms by abducting. Two major legal texts on the matter survive in Ghent. The earlier text, the *Groot Privilege* of 8 April 1297, granted by the count of Flanders, Guy of Dampierre, ordered the abductee to be disinherited.[28] Men often abducted rich women to gain wealth and position by forcibly connecting themselves to elite families. The *Groot Privilege* eliminated this motivation by taking away the property that made the abductee an attractive victim. The disinheritance was not required if her family involved itself and agreed to a reconciliation and her marriage to the abductor. However, in 1438, Duke Philip the Good promulgated a new ordinance after a petition by the city council.[29] From now on, cohabiting or marrying one's abductor was always punished with disinheritance, regardless of a possible reconciliation. The Ghent laws ordered banishment or execution of the abductor.

As many historians have noted, there was a significant difference between law and actual legal practice. In fact, in this case Jan was not punished and Gertrude did not lose her inheritance. In practice, Jan may have had to pay a 'composition', a sum paid to escape prosecution, although that is not mentioned in the sources. Given the strategic importance of marriage, choosing a proper spouse mattered greatly in late medieval Ghent, especially for families at the top of the social scale, such as the families of Jan and Gertrude. While normally a marriage took place only after careful consideration, Jan had decided to take his chance by abducting Gertrude and presenting Gertrude's family and his own with a *fait accompli*. The abduction likely happened during the spring of 1433 and was followed by an official wedding in a church and a party celebrating the marriage. Some documents state that Gertrude's father insisted on this official celebration. The proper solemnization by a priest inside or in front of a church in the presence of witnesses transformed the clandestine union between Jan and Gertrude into a legal marriage. While Simon may not have agreed to the marriage initially, the fact that the spouses were not prosecuted shows that he was at least determined to make the best of it. These events occurred before 1 July 1433, the date when the first verdict in favour of Simon against his son Jan was pronounced (noted earlier). As a consequence of the clandestine marriage, the families did not have time to follow the normal procedure, i.e. to begin discussing the practical aspects of the marriage and arrive at a marriage settlement agreeable to all parties. Typically the couple's parents or other relatives arranged and concluded marital agreements orally.[30] According to Ghent's customary law, the families had to discuss a marriage gift before the actual marriage in order for it to be valid. Written gift contracts listed all the marital gifts to the couple from parents and families, along with conditional provisions. These wedding gifts should not be confused with dowries. The dotal system did not exist in Flanders, where inheritance law stipulated that all children of the same marriage, regardless of age and sex, received an equal share of the inheritance. The wedding gifts served to enhance the child's appeal as a marriage partner (if one of the families was richer than the other, for example) and support the young couple at the beginning of their conjugal life.[31] Therefore this case offers excellent evidence to explore the tensions between marriage gifts and inheritance practices in late medieval Flanders.

In the case of Jan and Gertrude, the marital terms were discussed before they were officially married, as required by customary law. Immediately after the abduction, but before the official wedding in the church, the two fathers and other relatives hastily met in the house of a Christoffels Van Ydeghem in the village of Voorde, located approximately halfway between Oostkerke and Ghent. At this gathering, the couple's relatives tried to resolve the difficult situation that their children had created and normalise their relationship, as is nicely illustrated by the words Simon van Formelis spoke to Jan van Oostkerke: 'And I am happy and I thank God that it is settled and that we are good friends'.[32] We only know of this meeting because it was mentioned in a lawsuit brief registered by the aldermen 20 years later, when a conflict arose over the alleged promises made in Voorde. Although we do not know the precise agreement, according to the 1450 document Simon promised his son 25 pounds *groten* upon his marriage with Gertrude and another 25 pounds *groten* after Simon and his wife died. Promising a large sum of money was a typical way to settle a rape or abduction amicably, as is shown by Simon van Formelis' words to the abductee's father: 'I gave my son more than you gave your daughter [...] and I did this for my honour because of the rude act that my son did to you'. By offering money, the abductor's family might persuade the other family to agree upon marriage instead of going to court.[33] Both fathers thus sought to reach a compromise, precisely the type of reconciliation that would be prohibited only five years later in 1438 by the new ordinance of Philip the Good, as noted earlier. However, soon after the wedding a conflict arose between Jan and his father over the wedding gift. This conflict marked the first of the 20 years of disputes in which Jan and Gertrude argued with their parents and parents-in-law about alleged promises of money and sought to annul certain conditions placed on their marriage gifts.

The tumultuous history of a marriage settlement

After the meeting in Voorde and the official wedding, the aldermen registered two contracts listing the wedding gifts that Jan and Gertrude were receiving from their fathers. Gertrude's contract was registered shortly after the marriage, on 17 July 1433.[34] Gertrude's father gave his daughter and son-in-law the fief of Oostkerke along with other items. This contract does not mention the abduction, and the clerk drew up the contract in the normal manner for a wedding. Simon Van Formelis registered his contract three months later because of the conflict that had arisen between him and his son, that is to say the conflict mentioned at the beginning of this chapter. Jan summoned his father to the court of the aldermen of the *Keure* because Simon refused to pay the annuity of 50 pounds *groten*. As described in the introduction, Jan and Simon agreed to settle the conflict soon, in accordance with the aldermen's decision. Three months later, on 9 October 1433, Jan and Simon appeared again before the aldermen of the Keure, who then officially registered a contract listing all the gifts Simon gave to his son and his new wife because of their marriage. This contract also does not include a single word about the abduction which preceded the marriage.

There are two significant aspects to these contracts. The first is the requirement in both contracts that a portion of the wedding gift be returned to the estate upon the death of the parents. Wedding gifts could not contradict the principle of equal inheritance, since these gifts were really only an advance on the child's inheritance. When the parents died and their estates were divided, a part of all gifts had to be returned to the estate to comply with the law of equal inheritance and to avoid favouritism.[35] Jan and Gertrude's contracts include stipulations that they had to return portions of what they had received at their marriage when their parents died. The contract of Jan van Oostkerke sets the following condition: after his death, his daughter and son-in-law had to return 4,000 'nobles' (a local currency[36]) to Jan's estate. After Simon's death, Jan van Formelis had to put into the estate either 3,000 nobles or the fief of Sint-Denijs-Boekel, which he received after his marriage.[37] The conditions in both contracts became the subject of disputes in later lawsuits. Another significant aspect is that the discussions between Jan van Formelis and his father did not go smoothly, since the contract about the gifts was not registered until three months after the lawsuit between father and son. The probability of contention in the negotiations between Jan and his father is reinforced by the act recorded in the register right after the copy of the marital contract. On 7 October, two days before the sealing of Simon's marriage gift contract, Jan officially promised to demand nothing more from his parents in the future. He promised to 'release his father' from any future accusation concerning his matrimonial goods, 'while at the same time trusting his father and mother to reasonably compensate him'.[38] As it turned out, Jan found this promise difficult to keep.

Jan was not the only troublemaker. His wife also set herself up as a persistent litigant, bent on achieving her goals through legal actions against her family and in-laws. However, before going more deeply into her legal agency, we must consider another episode in Jan and Gertrude's tempestuous conjugal life. In June 1441, Jan and Gertrude separated 'in bed and board'. After eight years of living together, they agreed to divide their matrimonial property. Such a separation (called 'a mensa et thora') occurred regularly in the Low Countries. It meant that the marriage was still valid (because it could not be destroyed) but that husband and wife would live apart.[39] The episcopal court had the jurisdiction to approve and declare such separations, but secular authorities dealt with the socio-economic consequences. The ecclesiastical record of Jan and Gertrude's divorce does not survive, but we know that they applied afterwards to the aldermen to arrange apportionment of their property and care of their children. The aldermen's registers state that the couple came in accord (*eendrachtelic comen*) to the court to register the division of their goods, indicating that Gertrude and Jan had agreed to the practical arrangements for their separation.[40] Henceforth, each would own and manage his/her own property. Jan assumed the custody and support of their two sons, while Gertrude did the same for their daughter. Jan and Gertrude could now live in separate residences and were no longer obliged to fulfil their conjugal duties. Furthermore, they were no longer considered one legal entity.[41] The source reads that Gertrude became *haers sellefs wijf* ('her own woman'), meaning that she was no longer subject to her husband's guardianship. She could now initiate lawsuits on her own and did not need her husband's approval, nor did she have to inform him of her actions.

Although in July 1433 there was no sign of a conflict between Gertrude and her father about their arrangement, Gertrude did try to escape paying 4,000 *nobelen* to the estate after her father died. In September 1441, shortly after her separation, Gertrude sued her stepfather Jan Blanckaert, who was acting on behalf of his wife, Gertrude's mother. She requested to be released from the condition in her father's gift contract requiring her to pay her father's other heirs 4,000 *nobelen*. Gertrude wanted the aldermen to invalidate this stipulation because (1) she was not present at the time the marriage settlement was discussed and so had not given her consent; (2) the clause disadvantaged her by favouring her younger sister Yolente. Gertrude considered the aforementioned sum too high, because as a result her sister would receive more of their parents' estate, which she charged was 'unreasonable'.[42] Gertrude's reference to her absence is particularly important because the presence of the spouses was not obligatory in marriage gift negotiations. Due to their socio-political and economic importance, these events were usually reserved for male relatives. However, in Ghent, female relatives were often involved, and it was customary to hear the future wife's opinion.[43] Nevertheless, local custom considered her consent less important, and it was not a requirement for the validity of the gift.

It is thus not surprising that the aldermen sided with Jan Blanckaert and rejected Gertrude's argument. Jan argued that he had not been involved in the discussions over his stepdaughter's marriage. Moreover, Jan claimed that Gertrude's allegation about the inequality of the inheritance of the sisters was not a matter for the Ghent aldermen. Agreeing with him, the aldermen declared that Gertrude had sued the wrong man and directed her to pursue the matter with her father's heirs rather than with her stepfather. The case was left at that, and the aldermen did not pass final judgement. Though Gertrude did not win the issue, she may have taken legal action in another court, even though there is no surviving evidence. In any case, Gertrude had clearly presented herself as a bold legal agent for the first time. Her act shows that women had legal options, and that they were not afraid to use them. Gertrude's appearance before the aldermen might merely be explained by the fact that she could sue without the consent of her husband because she was now *haer sellefs wijf*. Historiography generally states that a wife's loss of legal personhood upon marriage was often accompanied by practical limits on female economic and legal engagement, whereby wives were prohibited from suing in the common law courts.[44] However, Gertrude soon took the lead as a married woman as well.

Gertrude as accuser in turbulent times

A decade later, Gertrude reappeared as a pursuer in court, no longer as *haer sellefs wijf*, but again as the legal wife of Jan Van Formelis, indicating that the couple had reunited. In 1450, the clerk of the aldermen listed the two as a married couple, with no explanation of why (or when) Gertrude and Jan had decided to live together again. However, it seems Gertrude appeared on her own before the aldermen, for the clerk named Jan only as her husband, not as a party in the case.[45] Historians have recently reassessed married women's legal capability, arguing that wives could initiate legal and economic actions as long as these actions served the household.[46] Even though Gertrude is described as the initiator of the case, Jan thus indubitably supported her plea. The verdict pronounced by the aldermen on 13 August 1450 was in favour of Gertrude's claim against her brother-in-law Gerard Van Formelis. In this suit, Gertrude claimed that Gerard should pay Simon's original marriage gift, the 50 pounds *groten* he had promised to pay his son. Since Simon had died three years before, the heirs were now dealing with his estate. Now, after Jan had possessed and reaped the benefits of the marriage gift Simon gave him in October 1433 (namely the fief of Sint-Denijs-Boekel given in lieu of a 50-pound *groten* annuity) for 17 years, Gertrude required that an annual sum of 50 pounds *groten* should be paid to Jan. What had happened?

Times had changed. The city of Ghent had been in revolt against Duke Philip the Good since 1449.[47] Tension grew in the city, leading to an open clash between different factions later in 1451. While some of the urban elite joined the Ghent artisans in their revolt against the duke, Steven van Formelis, Simon's youngest son, sided with the duke, as his father would have expected. As mentioned earlier, this led to Steven's imprisonment and execution in December 1451. Steven had slowly but surely become a *persona non grata* in town, but it seems that Jan, who had always avoided politics, and especially Gertrude were now taking advantage of the current *animus* towards the family to sue Jan's brother Gerard. As neither Gertrude nor Jan sided with the Ghent rebels, Gertrude may have been making the best out of changing fortunes. Perhaps she had thought it unwise to charge Gerard shortly after Simon's death because of Steven's political power at that time. Thus it seems that she now seized the chance to sue during a moment of political weakness for her brothers-in-law.

In court Gertrude argued that Simon had promised Jan the annuity *before* the marriage took place. Following Gertrude's abduction, in Voorde Simon had promised to pay Jan 25 pounds *groten* annually after his son's marriage and an additional 25 pounds *groten* annually after Simon's death. In acts dated 7 and 9 October of that year, Jan and Simon had agreed to commute this gift from an annual payment to property (such as the fief of Sint-Denijs-Boekel). Now, however, Gertrude claimed that these acts were invalid because they violated local custom. There are in fact several cases of the aldermen nullifying marriage gifts after they discovered that the *huwelicke voorwaerde* (the marriage conditions made up *before* the marriage) differed from the actual marriage gift.[48] However, Gerard countered that it was very strange that Gertrude, who had enjoyed the gift for more than 17 years, had suddenly changed her mind. Referring to the charters of 7 and 9 October 1433, he added that Jan himself had promised never to bring charges over his marriage against his father again and had received extensive gifts shortly after it had been celebrated. The self-confident Gertrude ignored the substance of his counterargument, using (again) the argument that these documents were illegal because she was absent when they were sealed.

What was the outcome of the suit? On 13 August, the aldermen asked Gertrude to prove that Simon had promised the annuity *before* the marriage had taken place. Shortly afterwards, Gertrude must have shown the aldermen a charter signed by Simon explaining the exact circumstances of the abduction, the charter quoted earlier as evidence of the details. The aldermen's verdict on 12 November concludes that the marriage 'was contracted between Jan and Gertrude afterwards, and the marriage vows had not yet been made in church when Simon made his promise'.[49] As a result, the aldermen allowed Gertrude to proceed with the case. Some weeks later, a heated discussion took place before the aldermen. Among other charges, Gertrude argued that a man was not allowed to nullify *huwelicke voorwaerde* without the consent of his wife (or vice versa) because of the potential for deceit implicit in such a unilateral decision. Gertrude claimed the wife's presence in such a case was enshrined in local rights and customs. Although she argued that Gerard should pay the annuity of 50 pounds *groten* immediately, Gerald did not acquiesce. He fought back against Gertrude's argument, countering that a husband could obligate the couple without the consent of his wife.[50] In their final verdict on 16 March 1451, the aldermen wisely did not accept any of these arguments because local custom was unclear on the topic. They limited the scope of their decision to the chronology of the marriage conditions. They nullified Simon's marriage gift because he had promised 50 pounds *groten* *before* Jan's marriage had taken place, which invalidated the recorded document of 9 October 1433. As a consequence, the property Jan received at that time was returned to Simon's estate, which was to be divided according to custom as soon as possible. In short, Gertrude won the case, but her husband lost his property.

Unfortunately, we have little information on the final division of the inheritance. The aldermen requested three times that all parties bring in evidence and documents to settle the estate, culminating in a last request on 9 March 1452. However, a final decision of the case has not survived.[51] If the two parties composed a document dividing Simon's estate, it would be among the thousands of acts registered after the Ghent revolt. Both parties may have fled the city after their last appearance in front of the aldermen in March 1452. Shortly afterwards a battle in Oudenaarde between ducal troops and the Ghent urban militias ended in defeat for the city. For more than a year there was war in the Ghent countryside, until the final victory of Philip the Good in July 1453. Presumably the family settled the conflict some years later. It is clear that Jan remained in possession of the fiefs of Oostkerke and Sint-Denijs-Boekel, because his son Jan junior inherited both fiefs after his father's death in 1475.[52] Ironically, the fief Jan senior had inherited from his own father Simon ended up in the hands of the Borluut family of Ghent after one of his own children was abducted. In 1457 Jan's eldest daughter Jooszijne was abducted by Lieven Borluut, whom she married 'with her consent but against the will of her parents'.[53] Perhaps mindful of their own parents' clemency, Jan and Gertrude did not disinherit their daughter. That is another episode of the turbulent matrimonial history of this remarkable family.

Conclusion

The relatively easy access to legal institutions in towns like Ghent gave citizens welcome opportunities to defend their rights. By mapping out the aftermath of a private abduction settlement, this chapter shows that age and gender were aspects of legal culture, especially concerning the question of who had access to courts, who used the law and local customs, by what means and to what ends. Not only do we endorse the views of several scholars who have argued that women in different stages of their life cycle were able to use the courts to their advantage, we also shed light on the use of judicial means in the course of conflicts between generations, as our case suggests that recalcitrant children resisted their parents through litigation.

The dispute about our couple's wedding gifts and inheritance reveals Ghent's sophisticated legal culture, in which litigious actions within competing kin groups could drag on for years. Indeed, this case shows multiple alternating litigants who regularly referred back to earlier promises and actions made by the counterparty. This reveals a remarkable degree of consciousness about such matters' legal validity and shows that young people were able to operate within the patriarchal structures of their time by using the law to their advantage. It is certain that wealthy citizens like Gertrude and Jan Van Formelis made full use of the opportunities that Ghent's legal system offered to them. Both Gertrude and Jan stubbornly sued their parents and their in-laws to rid themselves of stipulations that they considered to be unfavourable. Although neither one was rebelling against the existing marriage pattern that favoured mighty parents who prioritised their political and economic goals when they chose spouses for their children, both manoeuvred within the system to oppose their parents' will. The clandestine marriage of Jan and Gertrude may have been motivated by a desire to resist their parents' will, or even by love. In any case, Gertrude and Jan did not slavishly accept the plans their parents had determined for them. Running away and suing were the best options for recourse with the most chance of success.

The advantageous rights enjoyed by citizens in towns such as Ghent made them active participants in marriage negotiations, inheritance settlements and distributions of property within families. Our fifteenth-century Ghent heroine, Gertrude, appears to have been a relatively independent woman who negotiated tenaciously over marriage and property, sometimes for her own sake, sometimes on behalf of her husband. Clearly, she and her husband were well informed about local custom, which they actively applied in practice in order to make the best of a difficult situation. Studying the economic activities of married women in Ghent, Shennan Hutton has demonstrated that their legal capability in actual practice derived from the property they inherited from their families of origin, Ghent's property custom and widespread acceptance of women's public performance of property management, both with and without their husbands.[54] To that we may add that matrimonial policies and judicial actions in the afterlife of marriage arrangements also belonged to the woman's domain, at least for the woman in this study. Others must verify if this was a widespread pattern, or if it was truly an exception in what is generally considered to be a father's world.

Notes

1 Stadsarchief Gent (hereafter SAG), series 301, no. 32, fol. 152v.

2 C. Lévi-Strauss, *Les structures élémentaires de la parenté*, Paris: Presses Universitaires de France, 1949, p. 548: 'la relation d'échange n'est pas entre un homme et une femme mais entre deux groupes d'hommes et la femme y figure comme un des objets de l'échange'. A reaction can be found in J. Goody, 'Inheritance, property and marriage in Africa and Eurasia', *Sociology* 3, 1969, pp. 55–76. A good introduction to this discussion is D. Lett, *Famille et parenté dans l'Occident médiéval (Ve-XVe siècles)*, Paris: Hachette, 2000.

3 P. Bourdieu, 'Les stratégies matrimoniales dans le système de reproduction', *Annales. Économies, Sociétés, Civilisations* 27, 1972, pp. 1105–27.

4 M. Howell, 'The social logic of the marital household in cities of the late medieval Low Countries', in M. Carlier and T. Soens (eds) *The Household in Late Medieval Cities. Italy and North-Western Europe Compared*, Leuven: Garant, 2001, p. 194. See also her *The Marriage Exchange: Property, Social Place, and Gender in Cities of the Low Countries, 1300–1500*, Chicago/London: University of Chicago Press, 1998.

5 M. Danneel, *Weduwen en wezen in het laatmiddeleeuwse Gent*, Leuven: Garant, 1995, p. 180 and S. McSheffrey, *Marriage, Sex, and Civic Culture in Late Medieval London*, Philadelphia, PA: University Press, 2006, p. 138.

6 A. Guerreau-Jalabert, 'Observations sur la logique sociale des conflits dans la parenté au Moyen Age', in M. Aurell (ed.) *Les stratégies matrimoniales*, Turnhout: Brepols, 2013, p. 427. See also A. Fine, C. Klapisch-Zuber and D. Lett, 'Liens et affects familiaux', *Clio* 34, 2011, pp. 7–16.

7 C. Wieben, 'Unwilling grooms in fourteenth-century Lucca', *Journal of Family History* 40, 2015, pp. 263–76.

8 The practice of customary vengeance declined as citizens found law courts increasingly attractive as venues for the pursuit of their emotions like hatred and anger (D. Smail, *The Consumption of Justice. Emotions, Publicity, and Legal Culture in Marseille, 1264–1423*, Ithaca: Cornell, 2003, p. 243). Buylaert claimed that a similar tendency has diminished factional violence between families in medieval Ghent (F. Buylaert, 'Gestion de vengeances et conflits privés de l'élite de Gand à la fin du Moyen Age', *Revue du Nord* 94, 2012, pp. 805–25).

9 We have published these contracts in J. Haemers and C. Delameillieure, 'Het herteleet van Simon van Formelis. Familieruzies, erfeniskwesties en het huwelijk in laatmiddeleeuws Gent', *Handelingen van de Maatschappij voor Geschiedenis en Oudheidkunde te Gent* 71, 2017, pp. 73–88.

10 J. Decavele, 'Bestuursinstellingen van de stad Gent (einde 11de eeuw-1795)', in W. Prevenier and B. Augustyn (eds) *De gewestelijke en lokale overheidsinstellingen in Vlaanderen tot 1795*, Brussels: Algemeen Rijksarchief, 1997, pp. 277–320, and A. Nevejans, 'Aldus staet in scepenen bouc... De registers van de Gentse schepenen van de Keure in de 14de eeuw', *Handelingen van de Maatschappij voor Geschiedenis en Oudheidkunde* 56, 2002, pp. 53–64.

11 SAG, series 301 (*Keure*) and 330 (*Gedeele*). For instance, the register of the *Gedeele* of 1450–1451 (no. 25) contains 1,914 documents, the year 1451–1452 contains 1,566 and the year 1452–1453 contains 3,154 acts. The figure for 1452–1453 is considerably higher as a result of the wars and high mortality Ghent faced in these years; many acts record the guardianship of orphans (namely 1,352 vs. 200–300 in an average year). An 'aldermanic' year started on 15 August, when the city fathers were elected, and ended on 14 August the year thereafter.

12 P. Reynolds, *How Marriage Became One of the Sacraments: The Sacramental Theology of Marriage from Its Medieval Origins to the Council of Trent*, Cambridge: Cambridge University Press, 2016, p. 35.

13 M. Vleeschouwers-Van Melkebeek, *Compotus sigilliferi curie Tornacensis: Rekeningen van de officialiteit van Doornik (1429–1481)*, Brussels: Koninklijke Academie van België, 1995. A case-study for the bishopric of Cambrai: M. Vleeschouwers-Van Melkebeek, 'Aspects du lien matrimonial dans le Liber Sentenciarum de Bruxelles (1448–1459)', *The Legal History Review* 53, 1985, pp. 43–97.

14 See, for instance, F. Vanhemelryck, *De criminaliteit in de ammanie van Brussel van de late middeleeuwen tot het einde van het ancien régime (1404–1789)*, Brussels: Koninklijke Academie van België, 1981, and M. Greilsammer, *L'envers du tableau. Mariage et maternité en Flandre médiévale*, Paris: Colin, 1995.

15 M. Vleeschouwers-Van Melkebeek, 'Mortificata est. Het onterven of doodmaken van het geschaakte meisje in het laatmiddeleeuwse Gent', *Bulletin de la Commission*

Royale pour la publication des anciennes lois et ordonnances de Belgique 51–52, 2010–2011, pp. 357–435.

16 D. Nicholas, *The Domestic Life of a Medieval City: Women, Children, and the Family in Fourteenth-Century Ghent*, Lincoln: University of Nebraska Press, 1988; S. Hutton, *Women and Economic Activities in Late Medieval Ghent*, New York: Palgrave Macmillan, 2011; Danneel, *Weduwen en wezen*; and M. Carlier, *Kinderen van de minne. Bastaarden in het vijftiende-eeuwse Vlaanderen*, Brussels: Koninklijke Academie van België, 2001.

17 The following is based on M. Boone, 'Formelis (Simon van)', *Nationaal Biografisch Woordenboek* 13,1990, 286–92; J. Dumolyn, *Staatsvorming en vorstelijke ambtenaren in het graafschap Vlaanderen (1419–1477)*, Leuven: Garant, 2003, passim; and F. Buylaert, *Repertorium van de Vlaamse adel (ca. 1350–ca. 1500)*, Ghent: Academia Press, 2011, pp. 229–32.

18 F. Buylaert et al., 'De adel ingelijst: "adelslijsten" voor het graafschap Vlaanderen in de veertiende en vijftiende eeuw', *Bulletin de la Commission Royale d'Histoire* 173, 2007, p. 124.

19 J. Haemers, *De Gentse opstand (1449–1453). De strijd tussen rivaliserende netwerken om het stedelijke kapitaal*, Kortrijk: UGA, 2004, pp. 81–2. In 1479, Archduke Maximilian of Austria appointed Jan Jr. as bailiff of the *Oudburg*, the surrounding countryside of Ghent; see J. Haemers, *For the Common Good. State Power and Urban Revolts in the Reign of Mary of Burgundy, 1477–1482*, Turnhout: Brepols, 2009, p. 124.

20 C. Stroobant, 'Notice historique et généalogique sur les seigneurs d'Oisquercq et de Val', *Annales de l'Académie d'Archéologie de Belgique* 5, 1848, pp. 351–3. About the Brabantine nobility: P. De Win, 'De adel in het hertogdom Brabant in de vijftiende eeuw. Een terreinverkenning', *Tijdschrift voor Geschiedenis* 93, 1980, pp. 391–409, and M. Damen, 'Prelaten, edelen en steden. De samenstelling van de Staten van Brabant in de vijftiende eeuw', *Bulletin de la Commission Royale d'Histoire* 182, 2016, 5–274.

21 SAG, series 301, no. 32, fol. 151r.

22 This means that they had the right to punish criminals and even pronounce the death penalty.

23 On the difference between illegality and validity in late medieval canon law, see M. Vleeschouwers-Van Melkebeek, 'Classical canon law on marriage: The making and breaking of households', in Carlier and Soens (eds) *The Household in Late Medieval Cities*, p. 16.

24 C. Delameillieure, 'Partly with and partly against her will. Female consent, elopement, and abduction in late medieval Brabant', *Journal of Family History* 42, 2017, pp. 351–68.

25 SAG, series 301, no. 41, fol. 59r (12 November 1450): 'dat hij uwer dochter wechleede sonder uwen danc'; SAG, series 301, no. 32, fol. 152v (1 July 1433): 'naer dat tzijnre kennesse commen was dat Jan zijn zone buten den consente van hem ende den joncfrouwe zijnre moeder ontscaect hadde de dochter van Janne van Oestkerke'.

26 Reynolds, *How Marriage Became One of the Sacraments*, p. 160.

27 Marriages contracted in a domestic sphere through words of present consent were not considered clandestine or atypical in late medieval London; see S. McSheffrey, 'Place, space and situation: Public and private in the making of marriage in late medieval London', *Speculum* 79, 2004, pp. 961–71. However, Donahue has shown that in the Low Countries, 'but not in England, informal marriage without any aggravating factors was, in many places, punished by automatic excommunication'; C. Donahue, *Law, Marriage, and Society in the Later Middle Ages: Arguments about Marriage in Five Courts*, Cambridge: Cambridge University Press, 2008, p. 602.

28 A. Gheldolf, *Coutume de la ville de Gand*, Brussels: Gobbaerts, 1868, pp. 450–1.

29 Ibid., pp. 623–5.

30 P. Godding, *Le droit privé dans les Pays-Bas méridionaux du 12e au 18e siècle*, Brussels: Algemeen Rijksarchief, 1987, p. 281.

31 Danneel, *Weduwen en wezen*, pp. 171–2. On women in the Low Countries, see A. Bardyn, 'Women in the medieval society', in V. Lambert and P. Stabel (eds) *Golden Times. Wealth and Status in the Middle Ages in the Southern Low Countries*, Tielt: Lannoo, 2016, pp. 283–317.

32 SAG, series 301, no. 41, fol. 59r (12 November 1450).
33 Danneel, *Weduwen en wezen*, pp. 171–2.
34 SAG, series 301, no. 32, fol. 151r (15 July 1433).
35 Danneel, *Weduwen en wezen*, p. 171.
36 In the fifteenth century, a skilled labourer had to work seven days to earn 1 noble.
37 SAG, series 301, no. 32, fol. 151r (15 July 1433), and SAG, 32, fol. 24v (9 October 1433).
38 SAG, series 301, no. 32, fol. 24v (7 October 1433).
39 M. Vleeschouwers-Van Melkebeek, 'Marital breakdown in the consistory courts of Brussels, Cambrai and Tournai: Judicial separation a mensa et thoro', *The Legal History Review* 72, 2004, pp. 81–9.
40 M. Vleeschouwers-Van Melkebeek, 'Eendrachtelic commen ende vriendelic vereffent: boedelverdelingen voor de schepenen van de Keure van Gent tussen echtparen gescheiden van tafel en bed, 1439–1450', *Handelingen van de Koninklijke Commissie voor de Uitgave der Oude Wetten en Verordeningen Van België* 47, 2006, no. 11.
41 S. Butler, *Divorce in Medieval England: From One to Two Persons in Law*, London: Routledge, 2013.
42 'Eerst aenghesien dat se noyt present was daer de vorseide huwelike voorwaerde passeerde te wette noch daerinne consent drouch'... 'andersins zo waere joncvrouwe Yolente van Oostkerke haar jongste zustre meer ghescepen thebbene van vader ende van moeder dat zo de ouste was dat de juge nemmermeer redelic dincken zoude alzo hoopte int rechte' in A. Coenen, 'Haer sellefs wijf. Het zelfstandig optreden van de gescheiden vrouw in het laatmiddeleeuwse Gent, 1427–1471', *Handelingen van de Koninklijke Commissie voor de Uitgave der Oude Wetten en Verordeningen Van België* 51–52, 2010–2011, no. 40/2.
43 Danneel, *Weduwen en wezen*, pp. 178 and 180.
44 B. Kane and F. Williamson, 'Introduction', in B. Kane and F. Williamson (eds) *Women, Agency, and the Law, 1300–1700*, London: Pickering & Chatto, 2013, pp. 6–7. See also several case studies in C. Beattie and M. Stevens (eds) *Married Women and the Law in Premodern Northwest Europe*, Woodbridge: Boydell, 2013.
45 SAG, series 301, no. 40, fol. 89v (13 August 1450).
46 A. Bardyn, 'Women's fortunes. Gender differences, asset management and investment in late medieval Brabant', unpublished PhD thesis, KU Leuven, 2018, pp. 25–66, and T. Phipps, 'Female litigants and the borough court. Status and strategy in the case of Agnes Halum of Nottingham', in R. Goddard and T. Phipps (eds) *Town Courts and Urban Society in Late Medieval England, 1250–1500*, Woodbridge: Boydell, 2019, pp. 90–1.
47 Haemers, *De Gentse opstand*, pp. 163–75.
48 Danneel, *Weduwen en wezen*, p. 174. See also Godding, *Le droit privé*, p. 283, and R. Jacob, 'Mobilité sociale et coutumes familiales dans la France du nord et dans les Pays-Bas méridionaux', in W. Prevenier (ed.) *Marriage and Social Mobility in the Late Middle Ages*, Ghent: Rijksuniversiteit Gent, 1989, pp. 35–49. More general: J. Gilissen, *Le statut de la femme dans l'ancien droit belge*, Brussels: Librairie Encyclopédique, 1962, vol. 2, pp. 255–321.
49 'Ende dat thuwelic daerup sloot ende voortghinc tusschen denselven Janne ende joncfrouwe Gheertruut zinen wive ende de gheboden van hem beeden en waeren noch niet ghedaen ter kerken als de vorseide worden ghevielen' (SAG, series 301, no. 41, fol. 59r (12 November 1450)).
50 From a legal point of view, a wife lost the capacity to contract debts because Ghent's customs determined that a man was the head of the household (see Gilissen, *Le statut de la femme*, passim and Bardyn, 'Women in the medieval society').
51 SAG, series 301, no. 25, fol. 164r (28 July 1451), fol. 229r (26 January 1452) and fol. 356r (9 March 1452). Jan or Gertrude alternately appeared in court representing each other in these cases; in July 1451, for instance, it was Gertrude who was present 'with the consent of Jan, her husband'.

52 Buylaert, *Repertorium van de Vlaamse adel*, p. 230. See also Rijksarchief Gent, Fonds Borluut, no. 31.

53 SAG, series 301, no. 44, fol. 78v (31 March 1457).

54 S. Hutton, 'Property, family and partnership: Married women and legal capability in late medieval Ghent', in Beattie and Stevens, *Married Women*, p. 157. See also E. Kittell and K. Queller, 'Widows and wives in medieval Flanders', *Social History* 41, 2016, 436–54, and J. Haemers, A. Bardyn and C. Delameillieure (eds) *Wijvenwereld. Vrouwen in de middeleeuwse stad*, Antwerp: Vrijdag, 2019.

PART IV

Law in practice, in and out of court

9

LEGAL BUSINESS OUTSIDE THE COURTS

Private and public houses as spaces of law in the fifteenth century

Edda Frankot

The vast majority of legal sources record business that was dealt with in 'official' spaces such as town halls, court houses and the chambers of clerks and notaries. Courts could also be held in spaces where large groups of people could gather, such as squares or churches. But legal culture was not confined to the official forum of a law court or to official spaces. Many legal transactions were conducted in other places, such as houses, inns and taverns, but we know much less about them. This is because many of these transactions remained unrecorded. Those that were recorded, either because they took place in the presence of officials or because they subsequently became the subject of a conflict, provide us with vital information on how the law operated outwith the context of official legal fora like the courthouse. Why did court officials accept the legal validity of any business that was transacted without their interference or supervision? An important piece of the puzzle in this respect is the ritual associated with 'wijncoep' (German *Weinkauf*, translated by Tlusty as 'contract drink'[1]). This ritual was conducted in some regions of northern Europe in the later middle ages in both domestic dwellings and drinking houses to bind parties and their witnesses together in an obligation.

The study of taverns and inns as spaces of hospitality and sociability has been a popular topic in recent times.[2] The fact that public houses also played a significant role in local trade receives regular mention, but is rarely the subject of in-depth research.[3] The use of pubs as 'spaces of law', that is to say as locations where transactions were conducted which were legally valid and recognised, is noted regularly, but without going into any detail or offering any examples.[4] The role of private homes for the same purpose is even less known.[5] This chapter will focus on these 'alternative' legal spaces and how they were used to transact legal business. It will also determine how their owners facilitated these transactions.

Finally, it will analyse the role of the physical space and of any associated rituals in accepting these contracts by both legal officials and the general public.

As will become clear in what follows, there did not exist a strict division between public and private houses in the later middle ages in northern Europe.[6] Domestic dwellings could provide hospitality for part of the year or when required. This ambiguity is confirmed by contemporary terminology, which rarely provides a clear picture of the role or status of a specific space. In both the Low Countries and in Scotland, for example, places offering hospitality are often referred to simply as 'houses' and only rarely as taverns or inns ('herberg' in Dutch). This does not, however, mean that we cannot distinguish taverns from domestic dwellings at all, just that there existed many forms between fully public and fully private houses.[7] The question of the distinction between public and private in the middle ages and early modern period has been investigated by a number of scholars in recent years. They have mostly argued against the image painted by Georges Duby in the *History of Private Life* of a clearly distinct private sphere within the interior of a home in the middle ages.[8] It was the presence of people or, more specifically, people outside the family unit which made an occurrence public. As the examples studied here confirm, the distinction between public and private (and shades in between) is not so much spatial as situational.[9]

The main focus of this chapter is the town of Kampen. Kampen was one of the main trading towns in the eastern Netherlands from the thirteenth to sixteenth centuries. Situated near the mouth of the IJssel River, it had access to the North Sea via the Zuiderzee. The IJssel moreover provided an important waterway with the Rhineland and especially Cologne. The town was involved with the Hanse for much of the later middle ages. As a trading and transhipment point, Kampen played host to merchants and goods from all over northern Europe and public houses played an important role in providing spaces to conduct business. Kampen's *Liber Testium* records many transactions conducted in houses of varying kind in the last two decades of the fifteenth century.[10] But Kampen was by no means the only town in northern Europe where legal business was conducted in such spaces. In fact, such practices are noted in the Netherlands, Germany, Switzerland, Scandinavia and England.[11] In the context of this volume and its focus on Scotland and its neighbours, and for comparative purposes, it is perhaps useful to start with briefly setting out the circumstances in Aberdeen in the later fifteenth century.

There is very little evidence in the main series of Aberdeen registers of the fifteenth century of any legal business taking place outwith the courthouse. This is because these sources mainly record court proceedings, and generally very concisely at that. There is only one example of a conflict resolution by four men, one of whom was the provost and another a former provost, to take place in 'the tavern'.[12] Another source from the late fifteenth century does provide ample evidence. This is the oldest so-called Sasine Register, which is, in fact, a type of notarial protocol book. It includes a significant number of acts made in houses in the presence of a notary. In addition, it contains documents which were enacted on the soil of the land that was the subject of an agreement. In July 1491, for example, John Logan rescinded his property in the hands of Thomas Fife, one of the bailies. This was done 'super solum dicte terre'.[13]

There are only a few examples of documents recorded in the protocol book that were enacted specifically in taverns. Many more note that they were agreed in houses or town houses. It may well be that some or many of these were actually drinking houses. This is confirmed by the fact that three owners of 'houses' where transactions are said to have taken place appear as owners of a tavern elsewhere.[14] It is likely, then, that some of the other 'houses' functioned as taverns as well. In the seventeenth century, too, taverns or inns were referred to simply as the house of its owner.[15]

A majority of the legal business recorded in the Sasine Register was conducted in other locations, like the tolbooth, the council house, St Nicholas Church or one of the other religious buildings in the city, such as St Katherine's Chapel or Greyfriars' Church.[16] The bishop's palace in Old Aberdeen is also occasionally recorded, as is the cathedral and the brand new university there.[17] At other times, transactions took place outside: at the cemetery, by the mercat cross, on the 'common royal road' ('communi via regia') or at one of the fishings.[18] These spaces were either relevant to the case in hand, like those conducted on the property that was the object of the transaction, or they had a symbolic meaning. Bedos-Rezak noted that, in thirteenth-century France, court officials witnessed and wrote deeds in cemeteries, in front of churches and at crossroads, sites that were 'consecrated by layers of religious traditions – Celtic, Roman, Christian'.[19] This meaning was later appropriated by the city halls.[20] It is likely that these sites had a similar symbolic meaning in late medieval Aberdeen. The question remains, however, how spaces like taverns and residences can be considered within this context. Joachim Eibach has argued that a house was considered as a legal space ('Rechtsraum') of its own, with the man of the house ('Hausvater') wielding his authority. This was not an autonomous legal space unconnected to the outside world and with its own rules, but one in which the *Hausvater* should offer protection on behalf of the authorities.[21] As such, a house may have lacked the symbolic meaning of other sites, but it was a space that offered the peace and protection of its authority figure.

There is a variety of locations recorded in the Kampen register too, but there the majority of transactions appears to have taken place in houses of varying kind. The difference between the two is probably partly the result of the character of the source: the Aberdeen register records notarial acts, that is to say first-hand documentation regarding specific transactions, whereas the Kampen evidence is formed by witness statements set down in writing in the *Liber Testium*. These statements were most likely presented as evidence in court in a civil suit and concerned agreements that had been made orally at an earlier time. Neither of the two sources are a complete record of legal transactions conducted in each of the towns. The Aberdeen register probably mainly includes business from the town's elite who sought to have their dealings, especially property transactions, recorded. It may be that they preferred a specific type of (high-status) location, like the symbolic sites mentioned earlier, or elite town houses. In Kampen, on the other hand, the *Liber Testium* probably only documents deals that went awry. These deals include those between masters and journeymen or servants, sales of small amounts of goods and the reconciliation of disputes. As such, the parties were potentially from a greater range of social and economic backgrounds. Drinking houses played an important role in urban social networking and were natural places for many transactions to take place.[22] This was no doubt the case in both Kampen and Aberdeen. The difference noted in the extent of the use of houses is therefore unlikely to be one of legal culture.

Another point with regard to the type of evidence is the nature of the transaction and how it was concluded. In Kampen, many of the agreements were sealed with a drink – the *wijncoep*. This practice was common in high and late medieval Germanic lands to bind everyone present to the deal, that is to say the two parties in an agreement and the attracted witnesses, the *wijncoepsluden* (sg. *wijncoepsman*). The drinking of wine, beer or other alcoholic beverages can be considered a public confirmation of the legal transaction or arrangement. It also functioned as proof that the act had taken place.[23]

The transactions from Aberdeen were all conducted in the presence of a notary and recorded by him. There is no mention anywhere in the Sasine Register of *wijncoep*. Of course, this does not necessarily mean that there was no drinking involved in these transactions to seal the deal – it may be that it was considered too obvious or irrelevant to record. But judging by how regularly it was reported in the less formally formulated evidence from Kampen and considering how central the *wijncoep* was to settling any legal business there, it is more likely that drinking was not a fundamental part of the transaction ritual in Aberdeen. It is significant, perhaps, that no equivalent word in Scots or English for *wijncoep* is known. It may simply not have been part of legal culture in Scotland and England.[24] There is, however, mention of other performative acts in the Council Registers: the exchange of a God's penny, which will be discussed further below, and the ceremonial handing over of a clod of earth in property transfers.[25]. In addition, the recording of business in writing may in itself have been a performance that rendered other symbolic acts less important.

Of course, a ritual involving alcoholic drinks presupposed a location where such drinks were available. This is perhaps the most likely cause of the difference in location use between Aberdeen and Kampen. Drinks could be taken to any location, but it would have been more practical to conduct a transaction which required alcoholic beverages on premises where these were freely available, that is to say in a drinking house or domestic dwelling.

The *wijncoep*

In order to obtain a better appreciation of the use of houses of varying kind, we will now turn our attention to Kampen, its *Liber Testium* and the practice of *wijncoep*. The *Liber Testium* includes, among other things, testimonies from the years 1483–1493. It is not always clear why specific testimonies were recorded. Often, they are headed 'in den schelinge tusschen': 'in the dispute between', that is to say that they were given as part of civil proceedings before the town court. But other entries include no indication of an associated court case. Regularly there is a short note at the end which includes the name(s) of one or two men: the current burgomasters. They were the two aldermen in charge of the daily administration of justice in Kampen.[26] It appears, then, that all the testimonies were given before the lower court of burgomasters. Although not all entries specify that they functioned as evidence in a civil case, they all appear in the same format. All start with the names of the witnesses followed by 'tugen' (pl.) or 'tuget' (sg.): give witness. This suggests that they may all have been intended to have a similar role, that is, to serve as evidence in court.

Another possibility to consider is that the testimonies in the *Liber Testium* functioned as a confirmation in front of town officials of an oral transaction that had taken place in a house in front of witnesses, that is to say that the parties perhaps requested these witnesses to ratify the transaction in court. This is unlikely for a number of reasons. The first is that the *Liber Testium* includes both acknowledgements and testimonies which concern the sale of immoveable property. The acknowledgements were made by the sellers of the property themselves, and as such seem more suitable ratifications of a sale before the court than a testimony by witnesses. Also, contrary to these acknowledgements, the testimonies are rarely precisely dated. They tend to concern transactions which took place a while ago; sometimes cases go back two, three or even four years. Alijd Stevens and Stijne van Malsen in 1484 recalled, for example, that they had witnessed Hille Luttike giving a gilded ring to Greta, an English woman, four years before.[27] It is likely, then, that the majority of the testimonies that are being investigated were recorded as part of a civil case because a problem of some kind had arisen between the two parties involved in the legal transaction or agreement. The *Liber Testium* thus only recorded a small portion of the business that took place in the public and private houses of Kampen. The transactions as witnessed by the *wijncoepsluden* and others did not need to be recorded to be recognised by the court as legally valid. That the testimonies concerning them were accepted in the *Liber Testium* as evidence supports this interpretation.

There are three different types of formal witnesses which feature in the *Liber Testium*: the *wijncoeps-*, *dedinges-* and *moetsoensluden*. The first are associated mainly with sales and rentals and any references to *wijncoep* are included in entries concerning sales or conflicts after a sale. At times witnesses in such cases are named as 'wijncoeps- en dedingesluden'. The latter is a term meaning arbitrator or perhaps more generally negotiator. A 'moetsoen' is a reconciliation, and a 'moetsoensman' (pl. *moetsoensluden*) is therefore a negotiator in a reconciliation. The differences between the three types are not very clear-cut in the sources, and in many entries the terms are not used at all. Another word that is associated with these entries is 'gelage'. This can mean food and drink, but also the group of people sharing this food and drink, and the costs associated with it.

The *wijncoep* itself was either paid for by the buyer, or its costs were shared between buyer and seller.[28] Occasionally, it is stated that the costs of the *wijncoep* would be deducted from the price of the goods. As such, it functioned as a down payment, though the money was not received by the seller, but spent on the drink which would bind the two parties and their witnesses to the agreement. The acceptance of the drink by the seller meant that he would damage his reputation if he did not deliver the goods.[29]

Sometimes a sample of goods would be brought into the *gelage* to persuade the buyer. In 1492 two building stones of a batch of 8,000 to be sold were brought into the gathering. The buyer declared himself satisfied with their quality.[30] A similar arrangement was made when a horse was sold to a miller, who was allowed to try out first if the horse would pull.[31] At other times, the agreement allowed for a cooling off period, generally until the next day. For example, a seller of wool gave a buyer a day to examine the merchandise properly. If the latter did not like the goods well enough, the former would return the money as well as reimburse the costs of the *wijncoep*.[32] This practice may have prevented anyone regretting a sale made while under the influence of alcohol, though the evidence is too slight to assume that this was a general rule. There are also a few examples of property transactions in which the husband consulted his wife. It appears that houses and associated pieces of land belonged to both spouses together. In 1487, for example, a seller of a house left the *gelage* saying that he wanted to consult his wife on the discussed deal. After his return the transaction was sealed with a drink paid for by the buyer.[33] A couple of years earlier the five *wijncoepsluden* in a sale of half the 'verbeterschap'[34] of a house and yard confirmed that the seller's wife had already consented to the sale at the same venue the other day.[35]

All these details about the circumstances of a *wijncoep* come from legal practice. There are no regulations concerning this topic in the Kampen laws at all. The only mention of *wijncoep* is in the *Gulden Boeck*, in a by-law of 1385, which determines that the person who was confirmed in the rental of the town waters or other communal property should be held responsible for paying for the *wijncoep*.[36] But there is nothing confirming the amount of witnesses required, the exact ritual involved or the space where proceedings should be conducted. This lack of regulation suggests that the customs concerning *wijncoep* had existed unchanged since before the recording of the town's by-laws in the fourteenth century. It was a ritual so established that there was no need to put it in writing.

It was different in some other areas of northern Europe. Gustafsson has investigated the regulations in Scandinavia and northern Germany, and found symbolic acts associated with the sale of goods in various town laws from the thirteenth century onwards. In some places this was 'winkop' or 'litkop', which may or may not have been the same thing, in others a 'God's penny', 'Holy Ghost penny' (*hilegen geystes penninc*) or 'confirming penny' (*fästepäninge*), but also a handshake.[37] It may be that these practices were put in writing because they indicated a change with earlier rituals. Some authors have suggested that the God's penny replaced the *wijncoep* in the course of the middle ages.[38]

The God's penny was also used in Kampen and Aberdeen. In Kampen it certainly did not replace the *wijncoep*. The two symbolic acts were, in fact, used side by side. The God's penny is not referred to as regularly as the *wijncoep* and it was rarely utilised on its own. In 1482, for example, two ship's parts were transferred from two men to a buyer. God's pennies were exchanged and the cost of the *wijncoep* shared between them.[39] Elsewhere, the exchange of a God's penny is associated with an employment contract: in 1486 Loy Seylmaker hired a man and gave him a God's penny. Loy also provided the wine for the *wijncoep*.[40] In the same year another contract was ended by returning the penny, which suggests that it functioned as a symbol of the agreement which the other party held on to, rather than that it was paid to be given to charity or as a down payment.[41] Handshakes are mentioned on a few occasions too, and they too appear to have been used in addition to the *wijncoep*.[42]

Legal transactions in houses

When analysing the entries from the *Liber Testium* that specify that a legal transaction or agreement took place in a house, it has to be noted that there are similar entries in the same register which do not include a location and which may well have occurred, or likely also did occur, in a similar place. But the following quantification is more an indication of the type of business that took place than an attempt to calculate exact percentages. A total of 123 entries were analysed in which some legal business was conducted in a public or private house. Of these, 56, nearly half, concern sales. The majority of products only appear once, from tools, animals and a valuable purse with silver fittings to items of food such as fish, and merchant goods from abroad like raisins and ash. But there are some things that feature more regularly: ships or ship's parts, immovable goods, horses, various grains, stones and rope. Of the other entries, 14 relate to the settlement of conflicts which are not further specified, and between two and five each concern the arrangement of marriage, work or carriage contracts, the rental of property, the exchange of goods and the settlement of an inheritance.

About 70 different locations are named where this business took place, of which 20 are mentioned more than once (see Table 9.1). Six of these locations were established drinking locations: the wine cellar ('wijnkelder') and five named taverns (*In den Gulden Hoern, In de Lappe, In den Pellicaen, In den Vranckrijck* and *In den Witten Aern*). The wine cellar and named taverns were used relatively regularly for these transactions: 27 times altogether. There were two other houses which appear to have been commonly utilised for this type of business: that of Jacob van Zutphen and especially that of Gise Blankert.

Other evidence from within the *Liber Testium* confirms whether a house was used as a drinking venue on a more regular basis. The *Liber Testium* also includes

TABLE 9.1 Legal transactions in houses in Kampen: locations named more than once

Name of house/owner	*Number of times*
Gise Blankert	11
Wine cellar ('wijnkelder')	7
In den Witten Aern	6
Jacob van Zutphen	5
In den Gulden Hoern	4
In den Pellicaen	4
In de Lappe	3
In den Vranckrijk	3
Broesken	3
Lambert Berentsz.	3
Lubbert Jansz.	3
Merten Voirne	3
Berent Swartken	2
Geert ten Holten (*In den Moriaen*)	2
Jacob Schroer	2
Jan van Wilsem	2
Johan *In de Zwanen*	2
Wijnken Wesselsz.	2
Willem Tiel	2
Willem van Rossen	2

testimonies on a large amount of other business. Most useful for our purposes are statements about brawls, some of which resulted in wounding, and comments or insults made in houses and taverns. Information about the storage of grains, which suggests that a location may have served as a small hub for local trade, is also noteworthy. Adding this information adds 37 locations to a total of 107, and 11 with 2 or more entries to a total of 31. The wine cellar and named taverns already mentioned continue to play an important role, as does Gise Blankert's house.

It is clear that a few of the houses which are not referred to by a house name but by its owner did function as permanent drinking venues. The houses of Jacob van Zutphen and Gise Blankert are the most obvious examples of this. Like in Aberdeen, it was not uncommon to refer to taverns by their owner's names, as for example the *In den Witten Aern* is also known as 'Berents huys in den Witten Aern'.[43] Blankert's house is only ever referred to by his name, but it is called a 'herberge' on one occasion.[44] It also features as a location where legal business was transacted and where drinking occurred more regularly than at any other place in the late fifteenth century.[45] In order to gain a better insight into the workings of a late medieval public house and its keeper in Kampen and into how legal business was facilitated, we shall zoom in on this establishment and its landlord.

Case study: Gise Blankert's public house

Blankert himself first appears in the sources in 1458 using his full first name, Gijsbert, suggesting that he may not have been the well-known and established figure that he became in later years.[46] He became a burgher of Kampen at some point before 1483.[47] His son-in-law[48] was Frederik Rijnvis, who between 1481 and 1507 acted alternatively as alderman and councillor of Kampen.[49] This suggests that Blankert was a well-respected man. This is confirmed by some other pieces of evidence. In 1487 he was among four 'tuychwerdige gelovige mannen' – trustworthy and reliable men sworn in before the court to testify in a particular case.[50] Blankert was also able to use a seal: in 1484 he and the town's bell maker Geert van Wou co-sealed an 'oervede', an oath foreswearing violence, at the request of the oath swearer, a man from Nijmegen.[51] In 1485 he appeared as one of the deans of the Rhine skippers' guild and in 1488 he presided over a case as deputy sheriff ('onderschout').[52]

That publicans were generally respectable people fits in with the image described by Hermesdorf, who confirms that in the Low Countries, aldermen and even some members of the nobility were involved in running public houses.[53] Especially inns where merchants lodged who might rely on their hosts to act as middlemen would need to be run by men of good reputation. In Bruges, where the dependence of merchants on innkeepers was more institutionalised than in most places, the ability of a landlord to utilise his network effectively, and respectability and trustworthiness were key components in working this network to the Hanseatic merchants' advantage.[54]

There is some evidence suggesting that Blankert himself was involved in trade. His office of dean of the Rhine skippers' guild is an important clue, as is his part ownership of a ship with his son-in-law.[55] He may no longer have been steering any ships up the Rhine himself, but he likely had a network of skippers and merchants through the guild. In addition, through his place of business he came into contact with a wide range of people and was called upon to act as a witness in a great variety of cases or to stand surety for merchants from outside of town. The latter were most likely patrons of his tavern or his own business partners. Rye was also stored in his house on occasion, for example for Friesian merchants in 1482/1483.[56] All of this suggests that his was a larger establishment with storage facilities in which merchants could stay overnight. In the vast majority of cases, however, Blankert's house is not differentiated in any way from the other houses in which legal business was conducted in late medieval Kampen. It is simply referred to as his house.

The first time Blankert's house appears is in 1474, when Henric Olger of Groningen was banished for throwing a jug at Gise in Gise's own house and for failing to pay the fine of 80 pounds.[57] In the same year Blankert stood surety for Willem van Dort (of Dordrecht) who had to pay a large fine to the town.[58] These references are mostly from other sources, but Gise Blankert appears most regularly in the *Liber Testium*, both as a witness to transactions and/or as the owner of the house in which the legal business took place. The majority of these cases are from the period 1483–1487. After 1487 Blankert features much less regularly, though it is clear he was still running his business. It may be that his daughter Else took over around 1493. In that year we find the first reference to Else Blankert's house.[59] It is also the last year that Gise appears, though that may partly be because there is a gap in the evidence. The last time his house is named is in 1491.

Generally, when transactions were conducted at Blankert's house, a group of people sometimes said to be *in gelage* was present. There is usually no further indication of their exact location in the house. In 1483, for example, Gise Blankert and his fellow publican Berent Jansz testified and swore that they had mediated ('gededinget') in the reconciliation ('moetsoene') between skipper Lubbert Jacobsz and Claes Jansz of Monnickendam concerning the freight of one last of tar at Gisen's house.[60] In this case it may have been that both publicans mediated on behalf of one of the parties. Perhaps one was staying with Gise and the other in Jansz's *In den Witten Aern*. In 1487 Gise Blankert and two other men acted as *wijncoep-* and *dedingesluden* settling a dispute between Johan van Wilsem and Dirck van Millingen in his house.[61] Blankert played an active role in most of the cases which were transacted at his premises as witness or as mediator. A significant number concerned merchants and/or skippers from outside of Kampen or larger quantities of merchandise.

Other transactions were also conducted at his house and Gise was not always involved personally. In another case of 1487, for example, three men testified that they had been present when Herman the miller had bought a horse that he wanted to use to pull his cart from Geert Rotersz.[62] There are also a few cases in which Blankert was named as witness or mediator, but which do not name a location. It is likely that these also took place at his house.

The house of Gise Blankert was regularly used as a location for conducting various types of transactions, though many of them concerned larger quantities of merchandise and shipping. There is no evidence of sales of houses, for example, nor are there any marriage contracts or settlements of inheritances, or at least there are no recorded civil cases concerning such subjects. The house was frequented by merchants and skippers from outside Kampen, and during their stay they used it to conduct at least some of their business there. As the owner, Gise Blankert was an obvious person to act as witness and mediator in any transactions. That he was a well-respected burgher of Kampen, as well as a dean of the Rhine skippers' guild, will also have made him an attractive partner. He may have been able to advise on suitable and unsuitable business relations, available merchandise and legal procedures to follow.[63]

Public and private houses as spaces of law

There are several other locations named in the sources which were obviously places that functioned as drinking houses on a permanent basis. The houses which had actual names, presumably accompanying a sign outside, are the most recognizable of these, as is the wine cellar, which was run by the town council. Some of these places only figure once or twice and some taverns known from other sources do not figure in the *Liber Testium* at all.[64] But the question remains what the exact status was of the other locations used as legal spaces in the *Liber Testium*. Houses which also appear quite regularly in this register, like that of Jacob van Zutphen, were most likely also permanently in use as drinking establishments. In many cases, however, a house only appears once or twice, and it may be that it only occasionally opened its doors to guests or that the owners hosted a group of people for a specific legal transaction in which they may have been involved themselves.

In 1484 a few examples were recorded which took place in houses that do not appear elsewhere in the sources. Half a ship was sold in Herman Dyrcksz's house about two years before, according to the testimony of four men, one of whom was the landlord of the *In den Raven*.[65] In Evert Hermansz's house a sale had been agreed of 200 raisins between Willem Geertsz and Ysebrant Baers.[66] In this case the testimony was made by Evert Hermansz himself and two others. On 26 October five men testified that they had been present in Femme, Tielman van Hoorn's widow's house when she rendered account of certain amounts of money to her late husband's son.[67]

There is no evidence in any of these three cases that the houses were functioning as drinking establishments, nor do these houses appear elsewhere as such. The entries do not clarify the status of the witnesses in the legal transactions. In all three it just states that they had been present: 'dat sie dair over ende an gewest hebben' or a variation of that wording. There is no mention of a *gelage* or of *wijncoep*, both of which are associated with drinking, though the latter not necessarily in a tavern as we will see below. It may be, therefore, that in these cases a group of people had gathered in a private home for the specific purpose of witnessing a legal agreement. Or it may be that the record is imprecise. It does seem especially likely in the last of the three cases that the gathering took place in a domestic dwelling, as its owner was one of the parties in the agreement. Similarly, in 1491 a group of people was gathered in the house of a tradeswoman to witness the sale of 19 saddles.[68] The details of the *wijncoep* are phrased in such a way that it appears that beer was brought along or would be consumed elsewhere rather than that it was available at the woman's house. Hers was therefore probably rather a workshop than a tavern.

On 23 April 1487, on the other hand, three men who had sat 'in den gelage' at the house of one of the three, Jacob Lambersz Scroer, testified that a fourth had been there with them when another had come in.[69] In this case only a conversation was recorded. The house of Jacob Lambersz, whose name 'Scroer' probably indicates that he was a tailor, does not appear again, but it is clear that in this case the location did, at least temporarily, function as a drinking venue. In 1491, Wolter Jansz testified that he came into Jan Daemsz's house and was called to the 'gelach' of Daemsz and Berent Wolt who were negotiating a deal on a certain amount of oats. Warner Topken delivered a similar testimony.[70] In this case the two men appeared to have come to the premises for a drink and were subsequently called upon to witness the agreement. Whether Daemsz's house usually functioned as a tavern is unclear, but it appears to have done on this occasion. Similarly, in London, Mc Sheffrey also notes examples of people being pulled in to witness a marriage contract when they happened to walk by.[71]

A year later Stijne Alberts and Johan Berentsz testified that they had been present in Lubbert Steenmesler's house about a month before, when Geert Westerwolt had sold Hendrik Evertsz a horse which would be paid off in terms. The sale was 'bewijncoepet'. The entry does not specify whether the two witnesses were the *wijncoepsluden* or not. So how should we interpret this transaction? How are these five people, one of them a woman, connected? Are they in a private house for the sole purpose of witnessing a sale, in a house which is temporarily used as a drinking venue, or in a permanent tavern? Did Alberts and Berentsz just happen to witness the sale or did they have a more formal role? It is difficult to answer these questions if we do not know the meaning of any omissions in the record. Of course, another question that can be asked is whether it matters just where the transaction was conducted as long as it was formally witnessed and confirmed with a drink. The protection and peace offered by the house as a legal space was also a factor.

Like in other towns and localities in the Low Countries and northern Germany, there did not exist a strict division between public and private houses in Kampen in the fifteenth century when it came to hospitality. Anyone might be allowed to tap beer or wine in their own house, though regulations differed from town to town and region to region. So a person might buy up a small amount of beer, open up their house to customers for a short space of time for some additional income and until the beer was finished, and otherwise ply whatever trade they normally plied.[72] In Kampen there were regulations in place that allowed for only one type of beer or wine to be sold at premises at any one time and for anyone to run only a single establishment.[73] The serving of wine was also restricted, in that the license belonged to the town ('onse stat') for part of the time and to the community ('de ghemeente') for the rest of the year.[74] When the town had it, wine was tapped in the wine cellar and no one else was allowed to serve it on pain of a fine. When the community took over, any offences occurring in the houses where wine was being served would be penalised as if they had happened in the wine cellar. As the town's drinking house, higher fines were handed out for any misdeeds conducted in the cellar. These by-laws confirm that anyone could serve beer or wine from their house in Kampen and that some houses would not have functioned as drinking venues throughout the year.

Peyer argues that there may have been a difference in status of houses between public and private. A public home had to be open to everyone, whereas in a private dwelling the owner could refuse entry to a person. A guest would also enjoy more protection in a private house, for example, against punishment or debt collection. But as there could be many forms between private and public houses in this period, it is sometimes difficult to make an exact distinction.[75] The surest sign of a drinking establishment, according to Peyer, is just that: a physical sign and a name to go with it. The only evidence in Kampen as to any potential official opinion on public versus private is that in 1483, it was laid down in a by-law that no one could be refused beer by any tappers before 10 o'clock at night.[76] This suggests that a house was considered public when beer was being tapped there. Tlusty agrees that a tavern stopped being public after curfew.[77] As such, it was not so much the space that was inherently public, but the activity that was conducted somewhere and the people it involved.

The same can be said about the transaction of business or making of an agreement. These activities, conducted in the presence of gathered witnesses or mediators, were public ceremonies, irrespective of the space where they occurred. The performative ritual that accompanied the transaction not only bound the parties and their witnesses, but it also functioned as a public confirmation. If it was performed in accordance with a social script, the contract was considered legal and binding and accepted by the court.[78] The *wijncoep* was also conducted with the expectation by the participants that it would be considered valid. As Reyerson has concluded, a business deal required a belief that the process in which it came about was legitimate and that its execution could be enforced.[79] In Aberdeen, agreements were perhaps not necessarily accompanied by a drink, but there the ritual of writing performed by a notary functioned as the public act. The presence of an official in the guise of the notary and the act of writing differentiate this ritual from that in Kampen, but it would be anachronistic to consider the resulting contract to be comparable to modern notarial instruments. As Hepburn and Small confirm elsewhere in this volume, documents could subsequently be utilised in court rituals which underlined their ceremonial power.[80] As legal instruments, the contracts had the same authority in their respective jurisdictions. Indeed, in both towns oral and written contracts existed, though the evidence considered here may suggest differently. There is no evidence that Kampen officials preferred written to oral contracts. In fact, a sampling reveals that the practice of *wijncoep* was just as strong in the 1520s as it was in the 1480s and 1490s despite the fact that many other aspects of the town's administration started to be recorded in writing in the second half of the fifteenth century. In Aberdeen written contracts may have been more common in the last decades of the fifteenth century, but there, too, symbolic acts like a transfer of the God's penny continued to exist.[81]

With regard to whether the status of the location mattered for the legality of the transactions that were conducted there, the answer is probably no. There is no evidence in the sources from Kampen that a named public house was considered a legal space of higher or lower status than a private house. In none of the cases is a transaction claimed to be invalid because of the unsuitability of the location. Neither is there any indication that business conducted in a residence was seen as insufficiently public and therefore suspect.[82] Of course, the protection of the *Hausvater* as a figure of authority was the same in all houses. A permanent drinking house was a more logical place to conduct these transactions because that is where witnesses were naturally available, as were the ingredients for the contract drink. But witnesses could also be gathered in a private house and drinks could be acquired. As it is not always possible to establish whether a transaction took place in a tavern or a private home, it is difficult to say whether overall more business was conducted in drinking houses or not. In Aberdeen, too, there is no indication that the sites which may have had a historical or religious meaning were considered more suitable locations for legal transactions than taverns or domestic spaces. McSheffrey has noted that, with regard to marriage contracts in late medieval London, certain rooms in a house appeared to be preferred to others.[83] There is no sign of this in Kampen and Aberdeen, though in the latter there are one or two references to chambers within a house. It is likely, then, that this further aspect of space was not considered to be relevant.

With regard to houses, it is true that a transaction in a tavern could get more publicity than that in a private home, as there could be additional onlookers who did not act as formal witnesses. In 1484, for example, four men testified about a case of reconciliation which had taken place in the village of Zalk two years earlier. Two of them had been 'moetsoenslude', while the other two had been bystanders ('ommestanders').[84] But for the legal validity of the transaction, this does not appear to have made any difference. One does wonder whether the testimony of the formal witnesses was considered more valuable in court or not. In the majority of entries, it is not specified what the status of the witnesses was. It is likely that most of them had engaged in the contract drink and that the record is simply imprecise, but we cannot be certain.

Conclusion

The use of taverns, inns and houses to conduct a great variety of transactions is a prime example of how legal culture was not confined to the official forum of a law court. The ways in which these transactions were performed, moreover, give us insight into the legal behaviour of fifteenth-century urban citizens. There are four points which the discussed examples serve to illustrate. First, instrumental in making the *wijncoep* and other ceremonies part of legal culture was their recognition not only by the parties involved, but also by the authorities. Administrative recognition allowed for a practice of conducting legally binding transactions outside the courthouse and without any involvement of court officials. That is, of course, until something went wrong, and parties actively sought resolution in court as is evidenced in the *Liber Testium*. That is the second point. The third is that, until parties appeared in court and witnesses were asked to give testimony, the practice in Kampen was still wholly oral in the late fifteenth century. The witnesses to the contract could testify as to its content and their testimony was accepted as proof in court. This is worthy of note in a period which saw legal practice increasingly being documented in writing. Of course, in Aberdeen similar transactions appear to have been conducted in the presence of a notary and were recorded by him already, though these transactions too were conducted, at least partially, in houses. Finally, a transaction conducted in a house appears to have had an equal status in law to that confirmed in a courthouse. The legal space in which it was conducted was not so much physical as situational and ceremonial. It was inhabited by the *gelage*, the small community temporarily joined through the act of the *wijncoep*.

Notes

1 B.A. Tlusty, *Bacchus and Civic Order. The Culture of Drink in Early Modern Germany*, Charlottesville/London: University of Virginia Press, 2001, pp. 103–14.

2 For example, Ibid.; B. Kümin and B.A. Tlusty (eds) *The World of the Tavern: Public Houses in Early Modern Europe*, Aldershot: Routledge, 2002; O.R. Constable, *Housing the Stranger in the Mediterranean World. Lodging, Trade and Travel in Late Antiquity and the Middle Ages*, Cambridge/New York: Cambridge University Press, 2003; B. Kümin, *Drinking Matters. Public Houses and Social Exchange in Early Modern Central Europe*, Basingstoke/New York: Palgrave Macmillan, 2007; J.R. Brown, 'The landscape of drink: Inns, Taverns and Alehouses in early modern Southampton', unpublished PhD Thesis, University of Warwick, 2007; and M. Hell, *De Amsterdamse herberg 1450–1800. Geestrijk centrum van het openbare leven*, Nijmegen: Vantilt Uitgeverij, 2017.

3 A notable exception is A. Greve, *Hansische Kaufleute, Hosteliers und Herbergen im Brügge des 14. und 15. Jahrhunderts*, Frankfurt am Main: Peter Lang, 2011.

4 A few examples are given in Hell, *Amsterdamse herberg*, for example, pp. 10, 53–4. It is noted in: B.H.D. Hermesdorf, *De herberg in de Nederlanden*, Arnhem: Gysbers & Van Loon, 1977 (unchanged from 1957 edition), pp. 89–90; H.C. Peyer, *Von der Gastfreundschaft zum Gasthaus. Studien zur Gastlichkeit im Mittelalter*, Hannover: Hansche Buchhandlung, 1987, pp. 224–7; B.A. Hanawalt, 'The host, the law, and the ambiguous space of medieval London taverns', in B.A. Hanawalt, *'Of Good and Ill Repute'. Gender and Social Control in Medieval England*, New York/Oxford: Oxford University Press, 1998, pp. 204–23, at p. 113; Tlusty, *Bacchus and Civic Order*, Ch. 6; B.A. Tlusty, '"Privat" oder "öffentlich"? Das Wirtshaus in der deutschen Stadt des 16. und 17. Jahrhunderts', in S. Rau and G. Schwerhoff (eds) *Zwischen Gotteshaus und Taverne. Öffentliche Räume in Spätmittelalter und Früher Neuzeit*, Cologne: Böhlau Verlag, 2004, pp. 53–73, at pp. 54–5; Y. Kawana, 'Trade, sociability and governance in an English incorporated borough: 'formal' and 'informal' worlds in Leicester, *c.* 1570–1640', *Urban History* 33, 2006, pp. 324–49; Kümin, *Drinking Matters*, pp. 97–8; S. Gustafsson, 'Sale of goods around the Baltic Sea in the middle ages', in J. Wubs-Mrozewicz and S. Jenks (eds) *The Hanse in Medieval and Early Modern Europe*, Leiden/Boston: Brill, 2013, pp. 129–48. For the nineteenth century, see L. Magnusson, 'Markets in context: Artisans, putting out and social drinking in Eskilstuna, Sweden 1800–50', in M. Berg (ed.) *Markets and Manufacture in Early Industrial Europe*, London/New York: Routledge, 1991, pp. 292–317, specifically pp. 312–7. For drinking houses as 'political spaces', see J.R. Brown, 'Drinking houses and the politics of surveillance in pre-industrial Southampton', in B. Kümin (ed.) *Political Space in Pre-industrial Europe*, Farnham: Ashgate, 2009, pp. 61–80, at p. 62.

5 For the use of houses in contracting marriage in late medieval London, see S. McSheffrey, 'Place, space and situation: Public and private in the making of marriage in late-medieval London', *Speculum* 79, 2004, pp. 960–90.

6 A development of 'deprivatisation' of venues providing hospitality appears to have taken place in the transition from medieval to early modern. Tlusty, 'Das Wirtshaus in der deutschen Stadt', p. 64. The Reformation moreover sometimes resulted in increased government interference in tavern business. Brown, 'Drinking houses and the politics of surveillance', p. 65. This means that the medieval and early modern public houses are not always comparable.

7 A public house is a general term for any place of hospitality. Inns and taverns are normally distinguished by their size and facilities, the former being larger and having rooms for guests to stay overnight, but in the middle ages the terminology was not as clear-cut. In Aberdeen, for example, the word 'tavern' appears to be used for houses where foreign merchants were staying. 'Tavern' and 'drinking house' are here used as synonyms for public house. The general term 'house' is here used as a blanket term when speaking about public and private houses at the same time. Concerning the problem of terminology, see also Hell, *Amsterdamse herberg*, p. 11.

8 G. Duby (ed.) *A History of Private Life, Volume II: Revelations of the Medieval World*, Cambridge, MA: Harvard University Press, 1993.

9 McSheffrey, 'Place, space and situation', pp. 972–3, 986; F. Riddy, 'Looking closely: Authority and intimacy in the late medieval urban home', in M. Erler and M. Kowaleski (eds) *Gendering the Master Narrative: Women and Power in the Middle Ages*, Ithaca, NY: Cornell University Press, 2003, pp. 212–28, at p. 215; G. Schneider, 'The Public, the Private and the Shaming of the Shrew', *Studies in English Literature 1500–1900* 42, 2002, pp. 235–58, at p. 236; S. Weddle, 'Woman's place in the family and the convent: A reconsideration of public and private in Renaissance Florence', *Journal of Architectural Education* 55, 2001, pp. 64–72, at p. 66; and B. King-Richter, 'Das Privathaus als Wirthaus', in Rau and Schwerhoff (eds) *Zwischen Gotteshaus und Taverne*, pp. 99–117.

10 Gemeentearchief Kampen (hereafter GAK), Rechterlijk Archief (hereafter RA), no. 6 (hereafter LT). This oldest *Liber Testium* is part of a series. The second oldest starts in 1505 and there is an almost continuous run from then until 1811.

11 See note 7.

12 E. Frankot, A. Havinga, C. Hawes, W. Hepburn, W. Peters, J. Armstrong, P. Astley, A. Mackillop, A.R.C. Simpson and A. Wyner (eds) *Aberdeen Registers Online*, Aberdeen: University of Aberdeen, 2019, <www.abdn.ac.uk/aro> (accessed 1 March 2019) (hereafter ARO entry ID), ARO-8-0603-06 (25 September 1506).

13 Aberdeen City and Aberdeenshire Archives (hereafter ACAA), CA2/1/1 (hereafter SR), p. 228 (15 July 1491).

14 Robert Blindsele (tavern: SR, p. 790; house: SR, pp. 127, 258); James Kintor (tavern: SR, p. 23; house: SR, p. 112); and David Menzies (tavern: SR, pp. 770, 843; house: SR, pp. 283, 632).

15 See, for example, the kirk session records from St Nicholas and Old Machar, respectively: ACAA, CH2/448/6, St Nicholas kirk session minutes 1651–1661, pp. 224, 230, 233; ACAA, CH2/1020/2, Old Machar kirk session minutes 1639–1655, pp. 132, 141. I am grateful to Dr Barry Robertson for providing these examples.

16 SR, pp. 625, 636 (*domo consulum*); pp. 694, 1011 (St Nicholas Church); p. 617 (St Katherine's Chapel).

17 SR, pp. 271, 708, 912 (bishop's palace); pp. 773, 830 (cathedral); p. 910 ('apud novum edificium universite Abirdonensis'). The university was founded in 1495.

18 SR, pp. 635, 644, 1016 (mercat cross); pp. 325, 550, 659, 664 (cemetery); pp. 669, 677, 798 (*communi via regia*); pp. 567, 993 (fishings).

19 B. Bedos-Rezak, 'Civic liturgies and urban records in northern France, 1100–1400', in B.A. Hanawalt and K.L. Reyerson (eds) *City and Spectacle in Medieval Europe*, Minneapolis/London: University of Minnesota Press, 1994, pp. 34–55, at p. 44 and K. Reyerson, 'Rituals in medieval business', in J. Rollo-Koster (ed.) *Medieval and Early Modern Ritual: Formalized Behaviour in Europe, China and Japan*, Leiden: Brill, 2002, pp. 81–103, at pp. 95–6, also notes the use of public streets for the transaction of business deals and recording in thirteenth-century Montpellier.

20 Bedos-Rezak, 'Civic liturgies', p. 45.

21 J. Eibach, 'Das Haus: zwischen öffentlicher Zuganglichkeit und geschützter Privatheit (16.–18. Jahrhundert)', in Rau and Schwerhoff (eds) *Zwischen Gotteshaus und Taverne*, pp. 183–203, at pp. 184, 190–1.

22 Magnusson, 'Markets in context', p. 314.

23 M.G. Fischer, 'Weinkauf', in *Handwörterbuch zur deutschen Rechtsgeschichte*, vol. V, Berlin: Erich Schmidt Verlag, 1998, cols 1234–5.

24 There are a few examples from sixteenth-century St Andrews in which one party drinks to another as part of a reconciliation; *St Andrews Kirk Session Register*, part I, ed. D.H. Fleming, Edinburgh: Scottish History Society, 1889, pp. 168–9 (August–December 1563) and note (1580; 1593). Fleming calls the drinking a 'sign of concord and forgiveness'. I am grateful to Professor Elizabeth Ewan for providing these examples. There are also entries in the gild court book of Dunfermline in which there is mention of 'wyn silvir' in the context of the admission of guild brothers and 'neighbours' (for example on fol. 5v, 23 May 1444; fol. 6r, 27 February 1445). In Dunfermline's gild court, too, reconciliations occasionally involved wine, as did the associated amercement (fine) (for example on fol. 7r, 3 February 1448). *The Gild Court Book of Dunfermline, 1433–1597*, ed. E.P.D. Torrie, Edinburgh: Scottish Record Society, 1986, pp. 10, 12. I am grateful to Dr Claire Hawes for pointing me to this source. In England, there is evidence of drinking when contracting marriages in fifteenth-century London. McSheffrey interpretes this as celebratory drinking, though it is not specifically presented as such in the sources; McSheffrey, 'Place, space and situation', pp. 982–3 and S. McSheffrey, *Love and Marriage in Late Medieval London*, Kalamazoo: Western Michigan University, 1995, pp. 45–6.

25 This symbolic act continued to exist into the twentieth century; see the photo of a twentieth-century transfer of land ceremony in *Registers of Scotland and the General Register of Sasines 1617–2017*, Registers of Scotland [2017], p. 24.

26 The full body of aldermen or aldermen and council would administer higher justice; *Kamper Schepenacten 1316–1354*, ed. J.A. Kossmann-Putto, Zwolle: J.J. Tijl, 1955, pp. 4, 7–8.

27 LT, fol. 38v (30 June 1484).

28 Kampen conformed to the practice elsewhere. See Fischer, 'Weinkauf', cols 1234–5.

29 Tlusty, *Bacchus and Civic Order*, pp. 107–8.

30 LT, fol. 171v (1492).

31 LT, fol. 98r (1487).

32 LT, fol. 35r (1483 or 1484).

33 LT, fol. 88v (1487).

34 This is the amount with which the property had increased in value during the rental period.

35 LT, fol. 68v (17 October 1485).

36 GAK, OA, no. 6, fol. 58v (1385). Published in *Overijsselsche Stad-, Dijk- en Markeregten. Vol. I, Stadregten, eerste stuk: Boeck van Rechten der Stad Kampen, Dat Gulden Boeck*, Zwolle: Vereeniging tot Beoefening van Overijsselsch Regt en Geschiedenis, 1875.

37 Gustafsson, 'Sale of goods', pp. 133–9. Handshakes were also used in thirteenth-century Montpellier; Reyerson, 'Rituals in medieval business', pp. 88–9.

38 S. Ulrich, *Untersuchungen zum Einfluss des lübischen Rechts auf die Rechte von Bergen, Stockholm und Visby*, Frankfurt am Main: Peter Lang, 2008, p. 153, as cited in Gustafsson, 'Sale of goods', p. 138, n. 44.

39 LT, fol. 13r (1482).

40 LT, fol. 108v (1486).

41 Gustafsson, 'Sale of goods', pp. 137–8 and n. 39–41.

42 For example, LT, fol. 93r (1487); fol. 98r (1487).

43 Concerning the practice to refer to public houses by the name of the owner, see also Hermesdorf, *De herberg*, pp. 70–2.

44 Blankert is forbidden by the court to buy any more foreign beer than he is able serve in his 'herberge ende huse'; GAK, RA, no. 2, fol. 30r (26 October 1490).

45 Blankert's business may have been taken on by his daughter Else after his death or retirement (see below). Her house is referred to as 'In de Sleutel' in GAK, RA, no. 10, fol. 139r (4 February 1523).

46 GAK, RA, no. 1, p. 95 (1458).
47 Blankert's name cannot be found in the *Burgerboek* (GAK, Oud Archief (hereafter OA), no. 232), in which new burghers were recorded. This may be because he was registered under a different name, that is to say as the son of his father rather than under his uncommon last name, or because he did not become a burgher until after 1469 when the extant register finishes. He is specifically referred to as a burgher on a number of occasions, for example, LT, fol. 31r (1483), fol. 40r (1484). In Amsterdam, publicans had to be 'poorters'; Hell, *Amsterdamse herberg*, p. 29.
48 Rijnvis may also have been his brother-in-law, but this would mean that Gise's sister was also called Else, like his wife and his daughter. His daughter appears to have been widowed in 1483 and could have remarried in 1484. Rijnvis as Blankert's 'swager': LT, fol. 36r (1484); Rijnvis as Else Blanckert's husband: GAK, RA, no. 75, fol. 245v (16 April 1488); inheritance of Else Blankert's [late] husband: GAK, RA, no. 76, fol. 75r (19 June 1483).
49 GAK, OA, no. 275.
50 LT, fol. 94r (1487).
51 GAK, RA, no. 2, fol. 15v (24 July 1484).
52 GAK, RA, no. 75, fol. 198v (27 April 1485); LT, fol. 124v (6 January 1488).
53 Hermesdorf, *De herberg*, pp. 30–6. See also Tlusty, *Bacchus and Civic Order*, pp. 41–3 and Kümin, *Drinking Matters*, pp. 58–62. For literature suggesting that publicans were not respectable, see Tlusty, *Bacchus and Civic Order*, pp. 8–9. Nonetheless, establishments with bad reputations existed in most places; see for example the houses being accused of holding a 'bad inn' ('kwade herberg') in Kampen; for example, GAK, RA, no. 1, p. 79 (1448), and in Amsterdam: Hell, *Amsterdamse herberg*, pp. 39–49. See also the government's sense of anxiety concerning drinking houses as potential spaces of lewd business, political discord and sexual deviance in Protestant Southampton in the seventeenth century. Brown, 'Drinking houses and the politics of surveillance', p. 65.
54 Greve, *Hansische Kaufleute*, p. 73.
55 LT, fol. 20v (1482).
56 LT, fol. 4v (*c.* 1482/3); fol. 21r (1483).
57 GAK, RA, no. 1, p. 121 (1474).
58 GAK, RA, no. 1, p. 378 (1 June 1474); SR, fol. 21v (1474), fol. 29r (1475), fol. 38v (1476).
59 GAK, RA, no, 2, fol. 37r (1493). She also appears in a list of fines in 1490 and as landlady in 1493 and 1497; GAK, OA, no. 402, fol. 183r (1490); GAK, RA, no. 2, fol. 37r (1493); GAK, RA, no. 1, p. 150 (1497).
60 LT, fol. 31r (1483).
61 LT, fol. 95v (1487).
62 LT, fol. 98r (1487).
63 Cf. the role of publicans in Bruges, Greve, *Hansische Kaufleute*, pp. 70–8.
64 I have come across 18 different names so far in the various fifteenth-century registers of Kampen.
65 LT, fol. 41v (1484).
66 LT, fol. 41v (1484).
67 LT, fol. 42r (26 October 1484).
68 LT, fol. 190v (1491).
69 LT, fol. 89v (23 April 1487).
70 LT, fol. 188v (1491).
71 McSheffrey, 'Place, space and situation', pp. 963, 983.
72 Peyer, *Gastfreundschaft*, pp. 221–2.
73 GAK, OA, no. 242, fols 17r-17v (1470).
74 GAK, OA, no. 5, no. LXIIII, fol. 27r (1446?); LXXIX, fol. 30r (1360?). Published in *Overijsselsche Stad-, Dijk- en Markeregten*.
75 Peyer, *Gastfreundschaft*, pp. 222–3; Hell, *Amsterdamse herberg*, p. 36.

76 GAK, OA, no. 242, fol. 34v (1483).
77 Tlusty, 'Das Wirtshaus in der deutschen Stadt', p. 67.
78 C. Burroughs, 'Spaces of arbitration and the organization of space in late medieval Italian cities', in B.A. Hanawalt and M. Kobialka (eds) *Medieval Practices of Space*, Minneapolis: University of Minnesota Press, 2000, pp. 64–100, at p. 65.
79 Reyerson, 'Rituals in medieval business', p. 102.
80 W. Hepburn and G. Small, 'Common books in Aberdeen, c. 1398–c. 1511', pp. 48–50. For notarial documents and ritual, see also Reyerson, 'Ritual in medieval business', pp. 81–103.
81 The God's penny is mentioned six times in the Aberdeen council registers: ARO-4-0116-01 (1437); ARO-4-0498-03 (1447); ARO-6-0889-04 (1484); ARO-6-0890-02 (1484); ARO-7-0204-06 (1490); and ARO-8-0930-01 (1509).
82 Cf. Political and religious meetings in private houses in the early modern period which were considered suspect; Tlusty, 'Das Wirtshaus in der deutschen Stadt', p. 60.
83 McSheffrey, 'Place, space and situation', p. 975.
84 LT, fol. 42v (1484).

10

CONFLICTS ABOUT PROPERTY

Ships and inheritances in Danzig and in the Hanse area (fifteenth to sixteenth centuries)

Justyna Wubs-Mrozewicz

If there is one subject that people quarrel about extensively and heatedly, it is property rights. It starts in the sandpit at a very young age with tugs of war over a toy, and ends when kith and kin are informed of a surprising last will. Especially the moment and context of a transfer of property rights, i.e. a sale, exchange, gift, compensation or inheritance, can be contentious. There are no universal rules which apply. Instead, there is a myriad of laws which have evolved from local customs or which have been adapted from other legal systems. These laws vary depending on whether they concern movable or immovable property, where the transfer takes place, which conditions had been agreed upon and often also on who is involved in the transfer. Making the transfer of property rights legal in a specific place has accordingly been an important task for institutions. In addition to attempting to create order in this specific place, these institutions also have to deal with the fact that elsewhere, other rules and laws apply.

In the middle ages and early modern period this resulted in the creation of vast amounts of parchment and paper for recording the activities of institutions and communication with rulers, city governments and other institutions. In southern and (from the sixteenth century onwards) western Europe, notaries played an important role as custodians of documents concerning property rights. In the north and especially in the Hanse area, the parties turned to urban councils for making transfers of property rights official. In the event of contesting such rights, urban administrative bodies and, to an increasing extent, higher-level institutions like courts established by rulers became arenas to untangle conflicting interests. Additional documentation like testimonies or letters, certified by notaries or urban governments, became crucial. For historians, the practice of recording at least part of the proceedings of court and administration and keeping these records in the urban or state archives resulted in a sharp increase in the amount of sources surviving from this period. It has also directed the focus of historians on to how property rights laws evolved in such a specific urban and regional setting, or on the level of the emerging states. However, once we take the often quite complex content of the cases into account and place them in the context of legal culture, the supralocal, supra-regional and even supra-state perspectives appear. Many legal cases were not restricted to one locality or jurisdiction, so addressing them meant crossing not only geographical boundaries, but also boundaries created by the use of laws and customs. Both pre-modern institutions and pre-modern actors involved in property right transfers, such as for instance heirs or sellers, had to deal with the existing diversity of approaches of different localities.

This chapter argues that when we take several cases connected with Danzig (modern Gdańsk) and the Hanse area (i.e. the Baltic and North Sea regions) as an example, variation appears as the norm. There was an understanding that there existed different variants of law and legal practice which could apply to an individual's case: in various cities, on various levels (i.e. including appeals) and even in various courts within a city. Besides proceedings in courts, arbitration and mediation took place. Moreover, there was an implicit understanding that when cases became intricate, there were also other means at hand, for instance urban or state diplomacy. My point is that establishing and contesting property rights in northern Europe was a matter of a composite legal culture and a culture of pragmatic diplomacy. Danzig is illustrative because of a number of reasons. It was a vibrant commercial centre which connected Baltic and North Sea trade, it was a member of the Hanse, it was an important political and juridical entity in the autonomous region of Royal Prussia, and it was the main harbour of the Polish Crown. Various layers of law, politics and economy shaped the city, which then translated into various practices and perspectives. Moreover, the very position of the city was conditioned by its overseas connections and its hinterland.[1]

I would like to discuss two areas of contesting property rights in the Baltic and North Sea regions, which involved crossing multiple boundaries. The first one concerns conflicts about ships and three short case studies involving Danzig, La Rochelle, the Low Countries, Italy, Scotland, Norway and Portugal as either places of origin, places of described conflicts or places where a resolution was attempted. For two of the cases studies, sources have been analysed in detail elsewhere, but they will be addressed here from a different angle. Ships provide an excellent example of how movable property was framed by law and handled by legal practice.[2] Second, I will delve into the issue of inheritances through three further case studies exploring the intricate web of family and business ties in and between cities and regions, including Danzig and Prussia, Lübeck, Groningen and Antwerp. Inheritances offer distinct insights into such relations, especially when they were contested.[3] In both areas of analysis, the underlying problem was that the mobility of skippers, merchants and their families made the question of property rights complex. The ensuing conflicts created a need to discuss such complexities in detail. The case studies have therefore been chosen not only on the basis of their transboundary content – and for two of them, their link to Scotland – but also on the basis of their ability to convey various perspectives.

The discussions of the complexities of the cases unveil two important aspects of legal culture. On the one hand, they show what was considered normal and usual in specific cases and localities. And on the other hand, they show that dealing with property rights conflicts involved a range of strategies: preventing clashes, de-escalating them or, of course, making attempts to resolve them. As such, this topic also contributes to the overall dynamic of conflict management in the Baltic and North Sea areas, which is the subject of my present research project.[4] There, one of the main premises is that in order to grasp the place and the role of conflict in pre-modern society, different dynamics than only conflict resolution have to be considered. The project connects, complements and partly challenges insights from the legal, social, economic, political and diplomatic history of pre-modern northern Europe. It is constructed as a bottom-up analysis of sources anchored in nine mercantile cities in northern Europe, from London to Reval (modern Tallinn).[5] The case studies discussed in this chapter stem from research which has preceded the project, and are drawn primarily from the State Archives in Gdańsk and the Archives of the Realm in Brussels.

Ships

Perhaps not surprisingly, ships have always been property of fairly high value. Therefore they were often co-owned, and in the early modern period the shares could be held by tens if not hundreds of people, as a way to spread risks.[6] Also cities and states owned or chartered ships if it served their purpose, prominent examples being the galleys of Venice used for trade or the *Friedeschiffe* of Hanseatic cities which were to keep privateers at bay.[7] The high value of ships came on the one hand from the pragmatic side of ship ownership, enabling owners to conduct trade, transport people, explore new coastlines or wage war. The price of ships, much like that of cars nowadays, was determined by their size, type and function, their age and overall state as well as the place and circumstances of the purchase.[8]

On the other hand, ships as property were also status markers. This is apparent from the Anglo-Saxon and Viking ship burials: chieftains ventured on their last voyage in a fashion which was to demonstrate the scale of their activities and power.[9] Both the imprint of the seventh-century Sutton Hoo ship and the well-preserved ninth-century Gokstad ship show that a ship in the context of royal death can be seen as the equivalent of a throne in the context of royal life.[10] Medieval and renaissance ships were depicted as images of power.[11] Also, the growing size of ships and fleets of late medieval and early modern rulers, often lavishly adorned, was a clear demonstration of status and might. The shipbuilding activity could turn into a missile race of sorts. The examples of the Spanish Armada and the English fleet at the time of Elizabeth I are well known.[12] Another good example is the competition between two cousins, the Danish Fredrick II and the Swedish Erick IV, in the dominance of the Baltic in the 1560s.

It resulted in Fredrick's appropriation of Dutch and Danzig ships to build up the navy on the one hand, and Erick's building of the gigantic *Mars* (1,800 tons) on the other hand.[13]

Ships were thus valuable for a number of reasons, and could be very much sought after by merchants, cities and rulers. Approaching ships as property means that we can focus on what kind of property right transfers were possible: sale and purchase of (parts of) the ship, stealing (including privateering), swapping, loans, inheritances or even income from insurance if the ship perished in storms or battles. All such transfers, obviously, had a legal side. There exists a large body of literature on each of these aspects, which in turn creates a context for the case studies.[14] Of course, the property approach also applies to the cargo they carried, but this topic can only be broached very briefly here as the prime focus is on the vessels. Instead, it is important to point out that the value of ships, and the fact that they could be subject to property transfer in various ways, was also intrinsically connected to the fact that they were tokens of connections. They were means of transport and of putting people into contact with each other, like they still are today. Their very purpose was to move from A to B and so on, meaning that they moved from one political, juridical and social context to another. The core of their activity was thus embedded in having to function in different contexts, and the shipowners, skippers and crew must have been aware of it. Calling in each port reminded them of it, time and again.[15] If needed, they referred to these differences in courts to defend their actions. For instance in a recently investigated 1565 case, Dutch seamen pointed out in the court in Danzig that it was not the custom in Amsterdam to certify in writing where they were intending to go, so the lack of such a document should not be held against them. The municipal court apparently accepted this argument. The fact that there had been very frequent trade and hence ship connections between the Low Countries and Danzig, and that there was a desire to maintain them despite an ongoing war, must have played a role here.[16]

This means that – following the research of Edda Frankot – matters of ships and shipping were approached in the legal (and diplomatic) practice of plurality and diversity.[17] The lack of one uniform system of maritime law in northern Europe entailed a need for adaptability, and allowed explanation of the legal, social and even political context of a case. Furthermore, even within one city, there was no guarantee that similar cases would be tried in the same way as the context could still differ. When property rights of ships became very complex from an international point of view, diplomacy was called in at an urban or state level. In the aforementioned 'fleet growth' contest between the Danish and Swedish kings in the 1560s, rulers like the Polish king or the regent of the Netherlands were repeatedly called on to intervene and regain ships which had been confiscated or, in the words of the Danish Fredrick, 'borrowed'.[18]

We will now examine three cases in more depth. The first case study, to illustrate how challenging but also flexible the approach to ships as property was, concerns the story of a caravel which caused several political crises. Beata

Możejko reconstructed a social history of this ship, and her original and meticulous analysis is the point of departure for the discussion here.[19] The caravel was a new type of ship which appeared in the Baltic in the second half of the fifteenth century: a three-masted ship with flush (edge to edge) planking and about 800 tons of carrying capacity used for trade and warfare. The vessel in question went on her first voyage in the 1460s, under the name *Pierre de La Rochelle*, as property of a French salt merchant. On arrival in Danzig in 1462, it suffered a serious accident in the harbour, and had to undergo extensive repair. As a result, the skipper took out a high-interest bottomry loan with Danzig councillors and returned to France.[20] The caravel was left as security in Danzig. After the death of the owner in 1464, and possibly on the basis of investments for the construction of the ship in La Rochelle in the first place or other debts, the French King Louis XI considered himself its owner. He declared the loan and thus security agreement with the Danzig councillors null and void, since it was against French law. The councillors thought otherwise, and wanted to retrieve not only the loan, but also the due interest. A lengthy dispute ensued, in which the city council itself mediated and later appointed arbiters. At the same time, the council sent letters to the French king to establish the course of events and the magistrates also asked the Polish king to support its citizens though diplomatic means. Fellow Hansards became involved, specifically the officials of the Kontor in Bruges, who feared reprisals from the French king.[21] A significant added value of the Hanse was that it could function as an institution of conflict management for its members.[22] In the meantime, the condition of the ship in the harbour was deteriorating fast, and there were even plans to deconstruct it. Eventually though, in the context of the Anglo-Hanseatic war (1469–1474), the caravel was repaired by the city with some investment of the Kontor in Bruges. The Danzig council assumed collective ownership of the ship and renamed it *Peter of Danzig* in 1471 (as it is generally referred to in the historiography). In 1473, when it was under the command of the privateer Paul Beneke, the vessel then became entangled in a large-scale political conflict. It captured a Florentine galley under the Burgundian flag and was captured in the context of the ongoing war between England and the Hanse when it was on its way from Bruges to Italy. Juridical and diplomatic conflicts over the very valuable cargo of the Peter of Danzig, among which was Memling's *Last Judgement*, went on for decades.[23]

What is most striking about this case from the point of view of the present chapter is how intertwined the legal and diplomatic means were and how intricate the question of the ownership of the vessel (and later also of the captured cargo) proved to be. One of the main points was whether the bottomry loan was legal, as the French skipper was formally not allowed to take out such a loan. This shows that both the place of a possible transfer of rights to a property and the groups involved played a role. The matter of the ship was resolved in a natural way when it was destroyed after lightning struck it in La Rochelle in 1475 (some would probably call it fate), but the issue of the cargo was resolved in a painfully political way. In an attempt to keep Hansards (and among them Danzigers) from moving to Antwerp and have their Kontor there, the city of Bruges took over the payment of the damages to the heirs of the Florentines. This was to no avail, as it turned out – the Kontor was *de facto* moved to Antwerp.[24]

The second case under examination here involves sixteenth-century Scotland, as documented in the archive in Gdańsk.[25] At some point in the 1510s a Portuguese ship had been captured by a Danzig citizen, Hinrick Berner. He later came with it to Scotland, which proved to be a poor choice for a safe haven. The Scottish king seized the ship and had Hinrick Berner imprisoned. Hinrick managed to escape twice, and apparently also saw an opportunity to spread news of the events to his hometown. Subsequently, the Scottish king declared the ship and its cargo (salt) his own property, and put the ship under the command of a Peter Jerner. This skipper then sailed with it to Danzig in the 1520s, which was again an unfortunate destination. The ship was arrested in the harbour by city officials, and what followed was a case before the bench of aldermen, one of the juridical bodies in Danzig.[26] The bone of contention was who was to be considered the owner of the ship: the Danzig skipper (Hinrick Berner) or the Scottish king. A wealthy Danzig burgher, Jakob Kempe, who had connections in the Portuguese trade, became guarantor for Hinrick Berner and apparently wanted to help him to retrieve the ship. The court ruled that the vessel could not be handed over to Berner (yet), but that more information had to be obtained from Scotland. This can be seen as part of the legal culture where testimonials and documentation were increasingly used in court proceedings in the sixteenth century.[27] However, it could also have been a tactical move, because this was an effective way to maintain the *status quo* and prevent possible political escalation. It is a pity that the surviving sources do not disclose how the affair ended. However, for the purpose of the argument here, they do show that this type of 'long-distance' conflict about the ownership of a vessel was not considered out of the ordinary, and that there were legal and diplomatic mechanisms and expectations in place to manage the situation.

The final case involving a ship also has a link to Scotland.[28] In 1544, while the Low Countries were at war with Scotland,[29] a Deventer-owned ship sailing from Danzig was captured by Scottish privateers.[30] At that time, Scottish sailors were building up their reputation as a danger at sea.[31] The incident happened close to the Norwegian coast. The descriptions which were recorded in the later legal proceedings contain salacious elements such as the story that a money treasure was hidden in the ship while the Scots were boarding, or the fact that the Dutch were left in Norway in their underwear and with hardly any money to make their way home ('geheel naect ghepilieert'). The real issue, once again, was the question of the ownership of the vessel. It was resold twice, and after the second sale it got into the hands of an Antwerp merchant. Apparently, the Deventer owners caught wind of this when the new ship owner approached the coast of Holland, heading towards Amsterdam. The Deventer merchants, some of whom were members of the city council, decided to put up a juridical fight. They had the ship arrested and the goods confiscated, apparently including several pairs of shoes which had allegedly been stolen – a creative sartorial revenge, one might say. But the arrest was temporary, and had to be resolved properly. The merchants from Deventer contested the property rights before a sequence of courts: the municipal court in Amsterdam, the regional Court of Holland and eventually the appellate court called the Great Council of Malines. It is in this court that the proceedings investigated here have been found (a serendipitous discovery since the documentation of the lower courts has only survived in a very fragmented way). The point made by the Deventer traders was that they had been unaware of the ongoing war between the Low Countries and Scotland, which had influenced their decision regarding the ship. They had thought it was safe to sail and trade. Therefore, they argued the case should not be seen in the context of privateering and prize law. Instead, they sought to frame it as a matter of piracy and unlawful appropriation. In other words, both sides considered the ship to be their own property and were willing to contest their claim in three consecutive court cases. Once again, the eventual outcome is unknown, but this case shows that property rights were subject to an ongoing interpretation of the law (by various courts) and political influence.

Inheritances

At first sight, inheritance may appear to be a straightforward matter, as long as the will of the deceased has been written down properly or custom makes it clear who the beneficiaries are to be. Actual practice can be much more complicated, and high fees of lawyers are indicative of the stakes in the interpretation of rights. Inheritances concern property rights related to immovable and movable property, including money. For the purposes of this chapter, it is not the 'content' of the inheritance that is of interest, but rather the manner of handling it. Inheritances were contested and the proceedings were carefully documented. This documentation forms a large part of conflict management sources which have survived in urban archives in northern Europe. Also, the richness of the sources has resulted in a large body of literature on inheritances, with recent rising focus on the position of women and minors. The relevant scholarship is concerned with both the system and institutions pertaining to inheritances, that is to say the (local) law and customs, as well as the agency of various groups pursuing their rights to an inheritance or challenging testaments and family members.[32] It must be highlighted that the analysis of sources on inheritances is not always straightforward, and can even be frustrating if one wants to learn more about how a conflict proceeded. Sometimes, the references are quite brief: agreements could be reached before legal proceedings were needed, and it often sufficed simply to register the outcome in municipal books. Using an abstract example: Peter and John came to the court and testified that they had resolved the issues concerning the inheritance from their uncle. All persons were burghers in Danzig, and the property was located there, as well.[33] By contrast, more complex cases involving heirs from various cities can show that more communication was necessary and therefore more written explanation was produced. In addition, diplomatic intervention was sometimes necessary, which sheds further light on the matter.

What is quite striking when studying such cases is that there was apparently a well-developed understanding that inheritance laws varied in northern Europe – or in Europe in general, for that matter. There were at least two main policy lines, which took the form of laws and customs: on the one hand there existed the idea that (a part of) property should not be divided, that is to say that patrimony should remain secure. Property could be gendered, which resulted not only in favouring sons in inheriting land, but also connecting specific possessions to women.[34] On the other hand, ideas were developed that movable and immovable property, for instance jewellery and land, respectively, should be divided among family members, including women. For instance, according to the Scandinavian tradition, which was transmitted in part to England, daughters got half of the value of the land that sons received – though this was not the case in all the English counties.[35] To make it more complicated, the definitions of movable and immovable could vary and develop over time, as Martha Howell has shown by the example of Ghent. Also, the two general policy lines could be translated into a myriad of specific forms of legal and social practice. This could mean that in concrete cases, land could for instance be seen as legally movable, that is alienable, while a jewel had to remain in the family. Both inheritance policy and inheritance practice could thus be flexible notions in Europe in the late middle ages and the early modern period, at a time when commercial connections and migration increased.[36]

The case of Danzig, which was at the same time part of Royal Prussia (an autonomous region within the Polish Crown) and a member of the Hanse, is interesting from the point of view of inheritance policy and practice. Both policy lines come to the fore in Royal Prussia.[37] The notion that the most substantial part of a property, especially land, should be passed on to one main heir was present among the nobility. It pertained mostly to male family and kin, as women had limited rights to inherit.[38] In contrast, laws in a commercial city like Danzig did allow the division of both movable and immovable property. Within the city borders, houses and their location were the most valuable possession. Daughters, widows and other surviving female kin were entitled to a share of an inheritance as well as to the protection of courts and custodians. Scholars have repeatedly underlined that this was an influence of Flemish law.[39] Tracing the roots and transfer of laws has long been a domain of legal history. What is more interesting in this context is the fact that apparently the urban setting prompted the adaptation, and above all the use of law which created space for women. Clearly, Hanseatic magistrates regularly heard women or their guardians in court. Such adaptation seems to have been quite a logical step in an area of high mobility of merchants and skippers: a legal practice which protected not only men, but also their spouses and children probably instilled a greater sense of stability. One of the cases presented below will illustrate this dynamic. In other words, it could be seen as one of the measures to decrease risk in the Hanse.[40] A question which cannot be addressed here, but which could be explored further, is to what extent the continuation of businesses after a husband died, depended on women. This would shed further light on how inheritance – and private property – mattered in the context of trade networks.

Differences in legal practice ran not only along lines of social status. When looking at the area in which Hanseatic merchants operated, it is clear that there were differences between cities, for instance between Lübeck and Antwerp. Inhabitants of these cities were well aware that the precise division of inherited property between kin could vary depending on the location and its legal jurisdiction, as it still does now. This division could take into account the dowry brought in to a marriage, children from various marriages, the status of new spouses, the handling of debts incurred and so on and so forth. When an inheritance case crossed over different jurisdictions between cities, knowledge of the local law as well as practices was key. In the Hanse area, the high mobility of merchants, skippers and craftsmen, for shorter periods and also for longer periods of settlement abroad, led to complications. Family ties extended across the Baltic Sea and North Sea, and so could the property which was to be inherited. Thorough documentation of ownership was therefore essential, often supplemented by additional proof. This was one of the factors behind the culture of extensive written communication in the Hanse.[41] When inheritance matters could not be resolved at the level of individuals and their families, the possibility of intervention by the home cities of potential heirs and even by rulers and their governments loomed in the background.

Once again, specific examples serve to illustrate these more general points. In a first example from 1551, a lengthy inventory was made of the possessions of Jacob Kempe in Danzig. We made a brief acquaintance with him in the case mentioned earlier, when he stood surety for Hinrick Berner in the Portuguese-Scottish ship drama.[42] During his lifetime, Jakob Kempe was a commercial agent for King Gustav I of Sweden, and he traded with Portugal, Lübeck and Amsterdam, among other places. Already during his lifetime, he was called 'the very rich Jacob Kempe'.[43] The inventory shows that he had indeed amassed great wealth: the long list contains several houses in prime locations in the city as well as storage rooms on the granary island which was the commercial heart of Danzig. On top of this, there was extensive movable property. It was all a marker of the economic and social position of Kempe as merchant, for traders like him, channelling the grain from the hinterland through Danzig to Western Europe, were among the most wealthy and influential inhabitants of the city. Moreover, his connections become apparent when we see among his heirs the members of the Ferber family, one of the leading families in the urban council, which also provided several consecutive burgomasters.[44] There were also many heirs residing in places outside of Danzig. The file is very large and still awaits a proper analysis, an exercise which goes beyond the scope of this chapter. What may be said, however, is that the untangling of this inheritance took several years. Moreover, it is striking that the Polish king intervened twice with letters on behalf of some of the heirs. Other cases have indicated that securing the intervention of a ruler in this way was a possible route to try to speed up the process, especially when foreigners were involved.[45] In one of such letters the king once expressed bewilderment that the city was so slow in handling matters of non-denizens, as this could be detrimental for trade.[46]

A second case, also from Danzig, shows how family ties could suddenly become more important once inheritance was in play, and what role city councils could have in handling such a situation.[47] In 1562, a woman from Groningen called Grete van Essen filed a request to choose new custodians for her daughter. The girl had moved from Groningen to Danzig to live with a great aunt, and after several years became her sole heir. The type and size of inheritance is not specified in the sources, but it must have been substantial enough to raise the issue with Danzig's magistrate. Considering the ensuing request of the mother to have it brought to Groningen, it was probably movable property. In this new situation, the mother wrote that her heart could not bear to be separated from her child any longer, nor to let her live in a foreign country surrounded by foreign people (in Low German: 'ys myn moederlycke herte tot mynen kynde beweghen gheworden dat myn kynt aldaer in vremde landen onder vremde luyden solde verkeren'). Consequently, she wanted her daughter (and the inherited property) to come to Groningen with a new custodian. She added that it was more natural for a child to be with her mother than in a foreign country, especially because it was a girl ('de nature eschet dat kynt nutter en beter by syn moeder dan yn vremde landen tho syn besunderlynghe soe het eyn dochter en gheen soen ys'). Of course, until then neither the distance between Danzig and Groningen nor the fact that her child was a daughter appears to have hindered the arrangement. But she may have feared that the inheritance would be contested, especially because the heir was a girl. The letter shows that Grete sought the support of the magistrates of her home city, Groningen, for her claim. It also shows that she received this support. The document is as much an example of urban diplomacy as of legal proceedings, illustrating that the boundary between them was fluid. City magistrates were, as this example shows, willing to serve as intermediaries in inheritances matters, including when it was a case involving women only.

Finally, the case of Hinrick van Resen may be considered.[48] This Danzig citizen had been an administrator in the Bruges Kontor, which means that he was an experienced and respected member of the Hanseatic community. In the 1520s, during a conflict between Hansards, Hollanders and Danes, a ship was seized by Danzig privateers.[49] Reprisals followed. Among other issues, the goods of Hinrick were arrested and he himself was imprisoned and put to trial before the Great Council of Malines. Danzig and other Hanseatic cities made great diplomatic efforts to free him (and silence him, as he continued to flood authorities with letters, which in this case were counterproductive). The Polish king, the regent of the Netherlands and the emperor all became involved. It was a lengthy case, which was never properly resolved, but in the context of this chapter it is important to point out that it also resulted in a very messy inheritance case, which again continued for a couple of decades. How should one approach the matter of property rights of goods which had been arrested and never returned? And how should debts be treated which had been incurred by Hinrick while in prison, not because of his own actions but because of the political moves of other Hansards? Ownership of Hinrick's goods had already been contested, but that of his heirs was even more tricky. In 1535, legal proceedings were conducted before the Danzig council between heirs of Hinrick van Resen (and his brother Willem) on the one hand, and a burgher from Antwerp called Hinrick Wolf on the other hand. The proceedings proper were destroyed or lost during WWII, but correspondence surrounding the case has survived and there is also a summary of the perished sources. Some of Hinrick Resen's property was apparently kept in the Bruges Kontor, while another part was in the hands of the council in Antwerp. Eventually, it was the emperor who again intervened in the matter, which by then had evolved into an altogether new conflict.[50]

Conclusions

The property rights cases presented here, relating to ships and inheritances, have been chosen because of the transregional connections which lay at their heart. An important consideration is that such cases were usually better documented than more internal affairs. The main conclusion which can be drawn here is that a pluriform transregional context was apparently no hindrance in conducting trade, dispatching ships or living in various towns and trying to retrieve inheritances. The connections certainly made the affairs more complex, but the complications seem to have been approached as part and parcel of the intended commercial activities. There was knowledge of the diversity of rules, of legal practices and of the legal fora which had jurisdiction, as well as of the possibility to navigate between them. The presented cases show that the use of urban, state and also organizational (Hanse) diplomacy was very much intertwined with legal actions.

One might pose the question of what these complex, transregional cases meant for the more ordinary, internal cases which undoubtedly made up the majority of legal business entertained by urban courts. On the basis of the contents of the particular cases noted here, the transregional cases could be treated as an entirely different category. By extension it might be argued that they were exceptional and even misleading in helping us to understand urban legal culture in its usual forms in these northern European cities. However, we must keep in mind that the same contestants of property rights, such as for instance Jacob Kempe, were involved in both 'internal' and 'external' conflicts, that is, in matters pertaining both to Danzig only, and to those reaching beyond its boundaries and framed by the context of the Hanse, the Polish Crown, or contacts with Scotland or Portugal. Also, the very same councillors and judges were adjudicating such internal and external conflicts, drawing from the same pool of knowhow of laws and legal practice in northern Europe. They did not need to apply an entirely different logic in handling these affairs. The same people were also involved in diplomacy and – something which has not been discussed in this chapter but applies as well – in arbitration and mediation in internal and external conflicts. There were no fixed boundaries between diplomatic, judicial and extrajudicial conflict management on the one hand, and internal and external conflicts on the other hand.

In other words, the six short cases presented here illustrate not only the possibilities of dealing with property rights in a transregional context, but also offer a glimpse of how internal affairs were approached, and why there was no presumption that any one law or regulation would always lead to the same solution. If there was a shared urban legal culture in northern Europe, it was a culture of accepting local variation and making flexibility a virtue.

Notes

1 On Danzig, see J. Wubs-Mrozewicz, 'Danzig (Gdańsk): Seeking stability and autonomy', in W. Blockmans, M. Krom, and J. Wubs-Mrozewicz (eds) *The Routledge Handbook of Maritime Trade Around Europe*, London: Routledge, 2017, pp. 247–72; B. Możejko (ed.) *New Studies in Medieval and Renaissance Gdańsk, Poland and Prussia*, London: Routledge, 2017, and M. Bogucka, *Baltic Commerce and Urban Society, 1500–1700: Gdańsk/Danzig and Its Polish Context*, Aldershot: Routledge, 2003. On the Baltic and North Sea from a maritime regional perspective, see D. Kirby and M.-L. Hinkkanen, *The Baltic and the North Seas*, London: Routledge, 2013.

2 T. Johnson, 'Medieval law and materiality: Shipwrecks, finders, and property on the Suffolk coast, ca. 1380–1410', *The American Historical Review* 120(2), 2012, 407–32.

3 M.G. di Renzo Villata (ed.) *Succession Law, Practice and Society in Europe across the Centuries*, Berlin: Springer, 2018, and P. Heady and H. Grandits (eds) *Distinct Inheritances: Property, Family and Community in a Changing Europe*, Münster: LIT Verlag, 2003.

4 VIDI grant 2018–2023, Netherlands Organization for Scientific Research (NWO).

5 For a description of the project, see J. Wubs-Mrozewicz, 'Conflict management and interdisciplinary history. Presentation of a new project and an analytical model', *The Low Countries Review of Social and Economic History/TSEG* 15(1), 2018, pp. 89–107.

6 R.W. Unger, *The Ship in the Medieval Economy, 600–1600*, London: Croom Helm, 1980, and R.W. Unger, 'Ships and sailing routes in maritime trade around Europe 1300–1600', in Blockmans, Krom, and Wubs-Mrozewicz, *Maritime Trade*, pp. 17–35.

7 K. Fritze and G. Krause, *Seekriege der Hanse*, Berlin: Brandenburgisches Verlaghaus, 1997, p. 44.

8 There is no comprehensive study of this aspect of shipbuilding and the sale of ships. Some indications in S. Jenks, *Das Danziger Pfundzollbuch von 1409 und 1411*, Cologne: Böhlau, 2012, pp. XXXVI–XLVI, and B. Możejko, 'Shipping and maritime trade in Gdańsk at the turn of the 14th century: The maritime and commercial background of the sinking of the copper ship in 1408', in W. Ossowski (ed.) *The Copper Ship: A Medieval Shipwreck and Its Cargo*, Gdańsk: Naradowe Muzeum, 2014, pp. 57–74, at p. 59.

9 J. Bill, 'Viking ships and the sea', in S. Brink and N. Price (eds) *The Viking World*, London: Routledge, 2008, pp. 170–80 and G. Larsson, 'Ship and society: Maritime ideology in Late Iron Age Sweden', unpublished PhD thesis, University of Uppsala, 2007.

10 M.O.H. Carver and A.C. Evans, *Sutton Hoo: A Seventh-Century Princely Burial Ground and Its Context*, London: British Museum Press, 2005 and Bill, 'Viking ships'.

11 J.C. Flatman, *Ships and Shipping in Medieval Manuscripts*, London: British Library, 2009; R.W. Unger, *Ships on Maps: Pictures of Power in Renaissance Europe*, London: Palgrave, 2010; and S. Rose, *Medieval Naval Warfare, 1000–1500*, London: Routledge, 2002.

12 J. McDermott, *England and the Spanish Armada: The Necessary Quarrel*, New Haven, CT: Yale University Press, 2005.

13 J. Glete, *Swedish Naval Administration, 1521–1721: Resource Flows and Organisational Capabilities*, Leiden: Brill, 2010; J. Wubs-Mrozewicz, 'Neutrality before Grotius: A City, a State and Seven Salt Ships in the Baltic (1564–1567)', *Journal of Early Modern History* 22(6), 2018, pp. 446–74; and J. Wubs-Mrozewicz, 'Witnessing the sea: Testimonials of seamen in the 'Seven Salt Ships' case (1564–1567) as sources for maritime, social, and legal history', *International Journal of Maritime History* 30(4), 2018, pp. 701–23.

14 Unger, *The Ship*; E. Frankot, *Of Laws of Ships and Shipmen: Medieval Maritime Law and Its Practice in Urban Northern Europe*, Edinburgh: Edinburgh University Press, 2012. On war, piracy and privateering in northern Europe, see, for instance, K. Friedland, 'Maritime law and piracy: Advantages and inconveniences of shipping in the Baltic', in A.I. Macinnes, T. Riis, and F.G. Pedersen (eds) *Ships, Guns, and Bibles in the North Sea and Baltic States, c.1350–c.1700*, East Linton: Tuckwell, 2000, pp. 30–8; T.K. Heebøll-Holm, *Piracy in the English Channel and the Atlantic c. 1280–c.1330*, Leiden: Brill, 2013; and L. Sicking, 'Naval warfare in Europe, c. 1330–c. 1680', in F. Tallett and D.J.B. Trim (eds) *European Warfare, 1350–1750*, Cambridge: Cambridge University Press, 2010, pp. 236–63. An exciting new approach is Maria Fusaro's ERC project on general average.

15 R. Ward, *The World of the Medieval Shipmaster: Law, Business and the Sea, c.1350–c.1450*, Woodbridge: Boydell, 2009; C. Deggim, 'Zur Seemannsarbeit in der Handelsschiffahrt Norddeutschlands und Skandinaviens vom 13. bis zum 17. Jahrhundert', *Hansische Geschichtsblätter* 119, 1999, pp. 10–15; M. Kowaleski, 'The shipmaster as entrepreneur in medieval England', in B. Dodds and C. Liddy (eds) *Commercial Activity, Markets and Entrepreneurs in the Middle Ages*, Woodbridge: Boydell, 2011, pp. 165–82; R. Lee, 'The seafarers' urban world: A critical review', *International Journal of Maritime History* 25(1), 2013, pp. 23–64; and K. Friedland, *Mensch und Seefahrt zur Hansezeit*, Cologne: Böhlau, 1995.

16 Wubs-Mrozewicz, 'Witnessing the sea', 716.

17 Frankot, *Of Laws of Ships*. See also G. Landwehr, *Das Seerecht der Hanse (1365–1614). Vom Schiffordnungsrecht zum Seehandelsrecht*, Hamburg: Vandenhoeck & Ruprecht, 2003 and A. Cordes, 'Lex maritima? Local, regional and universal maritime law in the middle ages', in Blockmans, Krom, and Wubs-Mrozewicz, *Maritime Trade*, pp. 69–85.

18 R. Häpke (ed.) *Niederländische Akten und Urkunden* (hereafter NAU), Lübeck: 1913–1923, vol. 2, nos 224, 228, 233, 340, 501 and Rijksarchief Brussels, 1074 no. 209 I 074, no. 149 fols 9–10.

19 B. Możejko, *Peter von Danzig: The Story of a Great Caravel, 1462–1475*, Leiden: Brill, 2019 (translation of a book in Polish of 2011) and B. Możejko, 'The seven voyages of the great caravel Peter von Danzig – A new type of ship in the southern Baltic in the late medieval period', in G. Huber-Rebenich, Ch. Rohr, and M. Stolz (eds) *Wasser in der mittelalterlichen Kultur/Water in Medieval Culture: Gebrauch – Wahrnehmung – Symbolik*, Berlin: De Gruyter, 2017, pp. 229–41. As Możejko notes, there is a scientific debate whether it was a caravel or a carrack. The contemporary sources consistently refer to the ship as a caravel.

20 Bottomry loans refer to the keel or bottom of the ship; when they are not repaid, the ship is forfeited.

21 On the role of the Hanse in the Baltic and North Sea regions, see R. Hammel-Kiesow, *Die Hanse*, Munich: C.H. Beck, 2014; S. Selzer, *Die mittelalterliche Hanse*, Darmstadt: WBG, 2010; and J. Wubs-Mrozewicz, 'The Hanse in medieval Europe: An introduction', in J. Wubs-Mrozewicz and S. Jenks (eds) *The Hanse and Late Medieval Europe*, Leiden: Brill, 2013, pp. 1–35.

22 J. Wubs-Mrozewicz, 'The late medieval and early modern Hanse as an institution of conflict management', *Continuity and Change* 32(1), 2017, pp. 59–84.

23 B.G. Lane, 'The patron and the pirate: The mystery of Memling's Gdańsk last judgement', *The Art Bulletin* 73(4), 1991, pp. 623–40; R. De Roover, *The Rise and Decline of the Medici Bank 1397–1494*, Cambridge: Harvard University Press, 1963; and M. Walicki, *Hans Memling Sąd Ostateczny* [*Hans Memling. Last Judgement*], Warszawa: Wydawnictwa Artystyczne i Filmowe, 1990.

24 J. Wubs-Mrozewicz, 'Mercantile conflict resolution in practice: Connecting legal and diplomatic sources from Danzig c. 1460–1580', in H. Pihlajamäki, S. Dauchy, A. Cordes and D. De Ruysscher (eds) *Understanding the Sources of Early Modern and Modern Commercial Law*, Leiden: Brill, 2018, pp. 7–31; O. Gelderblom, *Cities of Commerce: The Institutional Foundations of International Trade in the Low Countries, 1250–1650*, Princeton: Princeton University Press, 2013; and O. Meltzing, 'Tommaso Portinari und sein Konflikt mit der Hanse', *Hansische Geschichtsblätter* 33, 1906, pp. 101–23.

25 Archiwum Państwowe w Gdańsku (State Archives in Gdańsk), hereafter APG, 300,43/5B fols 283–6.

26 Wubs-Mrozewicz, 'Danzig', p. 260.

27 As suggested by research results from several northern European archives, consulted in the context of my current research project on conflict management. Both quantitative and qualitative changes took place.

28 I have discussed the communicative aspects of this case, including how the declaration of war was conducted, in 'Die Städte an der Zuiderzee und IJssel in der Hanse: Informationsaustausch, Konflikte und Konfliktlösung', *Hansische Geschichstblätter* 134, 2016, pp. 19–38.

29 J.D. Tracy, 'Herring wars: The Habsburg Netherlands and the struggle for control of the North Sea, ca. 1520–1560', *Sixteenth Century Journal* 24(2), 1993, pp. 249–72; J.D. Tracy, *Holland under Habsburg Rule, 1506–1566: The Formation of a Body Politic*, Berkeley: University of California Press, 1990; and M. 't Hart, *The Dutch Wars of Independence. Warfare and Commerce in the Netherlands, 1570–1680*, New York: Routledge, 2014.

30 Rijksarchief Brussels, Grote Raad van Mechelen, Beroepen uit Holland doss. no. 461. The dossier pages are numbered in a not entirely consistent way, and it is obvious that it is incomplete.

31 D. Ditchburn, 'Piracy and war at sea in late medieval Scotland', in T.C. Smout (ed.) *Scotland and the Sea*, Edinburgh: Rowman & Littlefield, 1992, pp. 35–58; S. Murdoch, *The Terror of the Seas? Scottish Maritime Warfare, 1513–1713*, Leiden: Brill, 2010; compare E. Frankot, 'Aberdeen and the east coast of Scotland: Autonomy on the periphery', in Blockmans, Krom and Wubs-Mrozewicz, *Maritime Trade*, pp. 411–27. On the relations between the Low Countries and Scotland in this period, see L. Sicking, *Neptune and the Netherlands: State, Economy, and War at Sea in the Renaissance*, Leiden: Brill, 2004.

32 M. Howell, *Commerce Before Capitalism in Europe, 1300–1600*, Cambridge: Cambridge University Press, 2010; M. Danneel, *Weduwen en wezen in het laat-middeleeuwse Gent*, Gent: Garant, 1995; L.I. Hansen, 'Inheritance, property and marriage in medieval Norway', in C. Beattie and M.F. Steven (eds) *Married Women and the Law in Premodern Northwest Europe*, Woodbridge: Boydell, 2013, 11–30; B. Hanawalt, *The Wealth of Wives: Women, Law, and Economy in Late Medieval London*, Oxford: Oxford University Press, 2007; S. Cavallo and L. Warner (eds) *Widowhood in Medieval and Early Modern Europe*, London: Routledge, 2014; and M. Korpiola, 'Testamentary freedom in law and practice in medieval Sweden: Conflicts and coexistence', in di Renzo Villata, *Succession Law*, pp. 149–65.

33 On the role of chanceries and the various municipal books, see, for instance, for the Low Countries, J.F. Benders, 'Urban administrative literacy in the northeastern low countries: A comparison of Groningen, Kampen, Deventer, and Zutphen, twelfth-fifteenth centuries', in M. Mostert and A. Adamska (eds) *Writing and the Administration of Medieval Towns*, Turnhout: Brepols, 2014, 97–121.

34 K. Gottschalk, 'Does property have a gender? Household goods and conceptions of law and justice in late medieval and early modern saxony', *The Medieval History Journal* 8(1), 2005, pp. 7–24.

35 A.L. Erickson, *Women and Property: In Early Modern England*, London: Routledge, 2002, p. 62.
36 Howell, *Commerce Before Capitalism*. For the intensification of trade and migration in Europe in the period 1300–1600, see the contributions in Blockmans, Krom and Wubs-Mrozewicz (eds) *Maritime Trade*.
37 On Royal Prussia, see K. Friedrich, *Brandenburg-Prussia, 1466–1806: The Rise of a Composite State*, London: Palgrave, 2011, p. 201; K. Friedrich, *The Other Prussia: Royal Prussia, Poland and Liberty, 1569–1772*, Cambridge: Cambridge University Press, 2000; E. Kizik (ed.) *Prusy Królewskie: Społeczeństwo, kultura, gospodarka 1454–1772* [*Royal Prussia: Society, Culture, Economy 1454–1772*] Gdańsk: Muzeum Naradowe, 2012, as well as B. Dybaś and D. Makilla (eds) *Prusy i Inflanty między średniowieczem a nowożytnością. Państwo – społeczeństwo – kultura* [*Prussia and Livonia between the Middle Ages and the Early Modern Period. State, Society, Culture*] Toruń: Wydawn. Uniwersytetu Mikołaja Kopernika, 2003.
38 Usually, among nobility the *primogenitus* was favoured. This was the main way to protect lineage among nobility in Europe, though this does not mean that there was no divergence from this policy line; see, for instance, the case of Zeeland nobility in A. van Steensel, 'Noblemen in an urbanised society: Zeeland and its nobility in the late middle ages', *Journal of Medieval History* 38(1), 2012, pp. 76–99.
39 E. Kizik, 'Prawo w Prusach Królewskich [Law in Royal Prussia]', in Kizik, *Prusy*, pp. 96–109, esp. 97.
40 S. Jenks, 'Capturing opportunity, financing trade', in Blockmans, Krom and Wubs-Mrozewicz (eds) *Maritime Trade*, pp. 56–76.
41 J. Wubs-Mrozewicz, 'Kopieergedrag', *Tijdschrift voor Geschiedenis* 127(4), 2014, pp. 603–24.
42 APG, Vv, 225.
43 P. Simson (ed.) *Danziger Inventar 1531–1591: mit einem Akten-Anhang*, Munich: Duncker & Humblot, 1913, no. 73 and note 5 p. 5, nos 221, 891, 1065, 1495.
44 E. Bojaruniec, 'Social advancement among patrician families in Gdańsk in the Late middle ages and the Early Modern Period as exemplified by the Ferber family', *Acta Historica Universitatis Klaipedensis* 29, 2015, pp. 150–70, and H. Zins, *Ród Ferberów i jego rola w dziejach Gdańska w XV i XVI w* [*The Ferber Clan and Their Role in the History of Gdańsk in the Fifteenth and Sixteenth centuries*], Lublin: Towarzystwo Naukowe Katolickiego Uniwersytetu Lubelskiego, 1951.
45 Z. Rymaszewski, *Sprawy gdańskie przed sądami zadwornymi oraz ingerencja królów w gdański wymiar sprawiedliwości XVI-XVIII w* [*Danzig Cases Before Royal Courts and the Intervention of Kings in Danzig's Legal Proceedings in the Sixteenth–Eighteenth Centuries*], Warsaw: Zakład Narodowy im. Ossolińskich, 1985, and J. Wubs-Mrozewicz and A. Wijffels, 'Diplomacy and advocacy. The case of the King of Denmark v. Dutch Skippers before the Danzig City Council (1564–1567)', *The Legal History Review* 84(1–2), 2016, pp. 1–53.
46 APG, 300,27/35 fols 136r-–137v.
47 APG, 300,53/795, fols 17r–17v.
48 From a different angle, examined in J. Wubs-Mrozewicz, 'Mercantile conflict resolution in practice: Connecting legal and diplomatic sources from Danzig c. 1460–1580', in Pihlajamäki, Dauchy, Cordes and De Ruysscher (eds) *Commercial Law*, pp. 7–31.
49 APG, 300,27/11, fols 268r–268v; APG, 300,27/35 fols 136r–137v; APG, 300 D 20/401, 403, 405; APG, 300, 27/10 fols 129–30; APG, 300,27/11 fols 18r–19v; APG, 300,27/11 fols 321v–322r; *Hanserecesse/Hanserezesse*, Leipzig: Duncker & Humblot 1870–1970 (hereafter HR) series 3: volume 8, 794 note 1; HR 3:9 no. 133 § 5; HR 3:9 no. 598; HR 3:9 no. 598 § 39; NAU, vol. 1 no. 58.
50 APG, 300,53/795 fol. 1.

11

'MALICE' AND MOTIVATION FOR HOSTILITY IN THE BURGH COURTS OF LATE MEDIEVAL ABERDEEN

*Jackson W. Armstrong**

One of the ways in which legal culture may be understood is through investigation of the language and idiom of law, in the use of certain terminology and its wider array of meanings. This chapter explores the use of particular terms of art in court cases heard in the burgh of Aberdeen in the fifteenth century. In doing so it suggests that the written registration of a certain multilingual terminology of malice captured a record of social relations among the inhabitants of the town. The significance of this terminology in its legal context is weighed up, and its importance is identified for understanding what it can reveal about motivation for hostility and about how the mechanisms of the law might serve to capture and record social relations of enmity.

'Malice' is a term detectable in Aberdeen's medieval council registers, as are some of its variants. In one case before the court of the bailies in 1450 a man accused of 'communi brigacione' was ordered to abstain from his misdeeds or 'malificijs'.[1] In 1456 another man testified that he had come into the Gallowgate not out of any 'provocation of malice' but to conduct business. The burgh council in 1484 ordained that George Browne would lose his liberty if he were to do any offence or 'provocation of malice' against a family group he had been found guilty of assailing.[2] There are also several references to offences done 'maliciouslie in worde'[3] or, in Latin, 'in verbis maliciosis'.[4] 'Malice' of course is a term current in Middle Scots and Middle English derived from French and Latin, denoting wickedness, ill will or rancour.[5] Other terms broadly synonymous with malice may also be identified, such as in the stipulation that those chosen by the council in 1467 to lease the burgh's property were to act without 'favour or hattrende [hatred]'.[6] About 1411, an attempt was made to debar a man from inclusion in a jury (in Scots called an 'assize') because he was the 'mortalis inimicus' of the principal party, and similarly in 1467 the council ordained that the 'strublans and inimite [enmity]' between two men was to be 'forborn in tym to cum'.[7] When a fugitive fled from an accusation of wrongs in 1484 which amounted to 'public offens',[8] and he was noted to persevere 'in his malice', it was laid down that 'the hale toune has takin and takis the querelle [on him]'. All were required to act to detain the 'trespassour' if he showed his face.[9] Finally, in three separate instances, parties involved in matters before the bailie court were to seek the forgiveness of their erstwhile victim, including one David Adamson in 1489, asked to 'Remitt the Rancour of his hert for the saide offence done to him' by James Cheyschame and John Halt.[10]

Malice is perhaps most closely associated with matters criminal and, in the Anglo-American legal tradition, with the term 'malice aforethought' and the classification of homicide.[11] Much of the history of the late medieval English law of homicide has turned on a parliamentary statute of 1390 which set out that no pardons should be allowed 'pur murdre mort de homme occys par agait assaut ou malice purpense treson ou rape de femme'.[12] Scholarly discussion has focused upon how many categories of culpable homicide were recognised in 1390 and how many operated in practice in its aftermath, and upon the extent to which the phrasing 'ex malicia precogitata' in indictments denoted deliberateness or actual premeditation.[13] Some have argued that it could refer to true premeditation, but that 'everything depended upon context',[14] and even the holder of the strictest view in favour of 'deliberateness' also acknowledges that 'malicia precogitata' was relevant to motive.[15] More recent work on felony and anger in the thirteenth and fourteenth centuries has demonstrated the layered meanings of these terms in their legal and 'nonlegal cultural contexts', a point to which we shall return later.[16] It has been shown that the actual specification of malice aforethought was rare in the early decades of the fifteenth century, and that it was only in the sixteenth century that the two categories of culpable homicide, murder (defined by malice aforethought) and manslaughter, would solidify in English law.[17]

With regard to the Scottish jurisdiction there is a small body of work that has explored the legal history of the parallel subject north of the border.[18] The focus of attention there, given 'the absence of recorded cases'[19] and relatively sparse source survival from the later middle ages, has been on the legal treatise *Regiam Majestatem*,[20] and on national legislation concerning the availability of remissions and sanctuary (and particularly the statutes enacted in 1370, 1372, 1469 and 1504).[21] Sellar has argued that while the actual legal terms of art changed over time, the development of homicide and its terminology 'points to the consistent and uninterrupted use of the term malice aforethought to describe a premeditated, rather than a merely deliberate homicide, from at least the later fourteenth until the eighteenth century'. In the fourteenth century the term of art was the Latin 'precogitata malicia' which was translated into Middle Scots as 'forthocht felony'.[22] In an earlier study I showed that in the 1490s the justice ayre considered two main types of homicide, recorded in Latin as 'interfectio' and 'precogitata felonia' (with 'murder' only very rarely mentioned),[23] and the case has been made by Grant that the term murder in Scotland denoted a specifically secret killing at least up to the end of the fifteenth century.[24] Recent work undertaken by Dropuljic on homicide in the justiciary court in the seventeenth century suggests that murder in fact long remained a concept 'in flux'.[25] Dropuljic identifies a tree of homicide classifications starting with a division between murder and slaughter; then subdividing the latter into slaughter with '*precogitat* malice' and slaughter without '*precogitat* malice'; and finally subdividing the latter into 'slaughter *chaudmella*' and 'accidental slaughter'.[26] The term 'chaudmella' is first attested in a statute of 1372 to describe excusable homicides committed in sudden heat of the moment, and appears in 1469 rendered into Scots as 'suddante'.[27]

The copious legal cases recorded in Aberdeen's municipal registers are ripe ground for interrogation of the terminology of malice in Scotland, and in fact they demand to be put to use, given the general dearth of surviving court records from the period. Of course the cases recorded in the registers are not concerned with homicide – that fell within the jurisdiction of the sheriff and his records[28] – but with non-lethal offences which the burgh courts were competent to hear. This presents another opportunity. Given that the Aberdeen case material turns the focus of attention away from homicide and its classification, the occurrences which are recorded show 'malice' at work more clearly than has previously been possible, freeing us from the need to evaluate the term in relation to types of killing.

National legislation

Before proceeding with the local evidence we must first consider its national context. In the late fourteenth and early fifteenth centuries the Scottish parliament enacted legislation concerning the definition and procedure to be applied to non-lethal violent offences. The first came in 1384 and in Latin it specified that accusations of mutilation, wounding or beating done 'ex precogitata malicia' should be brought before a judge according to a procedure similar to that set out for homicide, and that these cases should end in redemption of a convicted defender and payment of satisfaction to the complaining party.[29] The matter of intent could be expressed in other language in this period too, but more generally one writer has argued for an extension of 'precogitata malicia' to cover non-lethal violent wounding.[30]

Then in 1426 an act (given in Scots, the language used generally for legislation in the personal reign of James I from 1424) concerned with 'kepin of the kyngis pece' set out procedures to be followed by officers of law, including bailies of burghs, when receiving complaints of peace breaking. They were to 'inquer diligently' whether the deed was 'done apon forthocht fellony or throu suddande chaudemellay'. In the former case the officers of the law were to charge the persons accused ('trespassouris') with breaking the king's peace, then see the victim compensated according to the degree of their injury ('assythit eftir the quantyte of the skaythe that he has sustenyt') and finally place the life and goods of the 'trespassouris' in the king's will, which meant that satisfaction was also to be made to the crown. In the latter case, also described as 'sudane chaucemelle', the injured party was to pursue their claim against their opponents according to the 'ald lawis of the realme'.[31] In 1432, more specific provision addressed fighting in burghs and elsewhere, regardless of whether a complaint was made by the victim. The king's officers (aldermen, bailies or sergeands in burghs) were to arrest both parties involved and before the sun set convene an assize to determine whether 'it be forthocht felony or suddand don'. In the latter case, the 'auld law' was to be followed, and in the former case the offender was to be put in prison until amends were made to the victim.[32] This was followed by a statute specifically for fights in towns. That addressed pursuit of anyone accused of 'forthocht felony' who escaped arrest in town. The urban officials were immediately to alert the sheriff or the officers of the jurisdiction to which the fugitive had fled of his presence and his 'mysdeid'.[33] It is clear from this legislation that the terminology best known in terms of homicide was relevant to a wider field of violent offences. It is also noteworthy that by 1432 a fight ('bargane') itself could be described in shorthand fashion as 'forthocht felony', even if this simply denoted the circumstance of the offence. A similar usage can be seen in pardons (known as remissions in Scots law) which are recorded in the register of the royal privy seal.[34]

The local evidence: typology and chronology of cases

The extent to which any of this national legislation was received or implemented in local practice may now be considered. In the cases heard before Aberdeen's various courts in the fifteenth century (1398–1501) there are 47 case entries which include an accusation of 'precogitata malicia' or 'forthocht felony'. There are none which appear in the register volume which covers 1501–1511.[35] This tally excludes entries which mention such terms indirectly, as in the example of Henry of Kyngorn in 1459. Following his condemnation for 'perturbacione' of several men, including the alderman (the town's leading official, also known as the provost), Henry was to submit before the alderman and bailies at high mass to ask forgiveness and to be admonished not to commit again 'sic like trespass na bargane noght of forthocht felowny or of his provocacion' on pain of banishment, and he was to be confined in the tolbooth until this act of submission was completed.[36] These 47 entries, which do include an accusation of acting out of aforethought malice or felony, are set out chronologically in Table 11.2. A typical selection may be found among cases heard in the bailie court on 9 January 1448, when John Fichet was accused of 'iniusta perturbacione ex precogitata malicia' against William Chene and Simon Mad his servant. Fichet denied this and an assize acquitted him. In the next entry, John Voket the son was also accused of 'perturbacione ex precogitata malicia' of the same William and Simon; he too denied this and was acquitted. Then, William and Simon themselves were accused of the 'dicta perturbacione ex precogitata malicia' and were convicted by the assize. This was followed by a fourth entry recording that the convicted men gave sureties (in lawburrows, a procedure for making pledges to keep the peace) that John Fichet, John Voket and all other neighbours within and without the burgh would be kept from harm, and that they were to make emendation to the injured parties.[37]

These inter-related entries for *Fichet & Voket* v. *Chene & Mad* are illustrative of the wider group of cases, in that they occurred in the bailie court (the *curia ballivorum*). All entries occurred in this jurisdiction except for four which are to be found before the 'curia legalis tenta per ballivos' (1450, 1450, 1465, 1469),[38] two in a court held 'before the aldirman and ballies' (1479, 1482)[39] and one in which the court is unspecified (1467).[40] All this suggests that a range of burgh courts, not just those associated with a greater degree of formality in regularity or officials, were competent to treat these cases.[41] The selection of entries just mentioned is also illustrative in other ways. The parties involved were all men, and this is always so among the 47 cases (bar a single exception).[42] This exceptional case also presents 'precogitata malicia' in association with the offence of 'perturbacio'. As can be seen in Table 11.1, of the 47 offences relevant here, 36 included 'iniusta perturbacione' (some 76.6 per cent). The Scots translation of this offence is 'wrangwise strublance',[43] and the registers are replete with cases alleging this transgression (by men and women), particularly in the Latin form up to the 1480s, and in the vernacular from the 1460s onwards. The fullest comment to date on 'strublance' comes from a recent study on later sixteenth-century Scotland by Falconer. The analysis presented there identifies *strublance* as a broad category of offence in Aberdeen which encompassed a general sense of causing a disturbance, either to an individual person, or to a town official, or to a court or the town itself, and normally carried out in a public place. *Strublance* could be conducted in word or in deed, and it amounted to 'the disturbance of the community through breach of peace involving verbal or physical violence'.[44] Falconer's analysis is relevant to the cases of *perturbacio* and *strublance* observed in the fifteenth century, particularly in emphasising the sense of peace-breaking involved, either the personal peace of an individual or the corporate peace of the town. What is more, it may be tentatively suggested that *strublance* was never strictly defined, and so it enabled the burgh courts to exercise a flexible jurisdiction over a range of violent affairs that might otherwise be competent only to the sheriff court. All that said, only a small minority of the total number of *strublance* offences in the registers

TABLE 11.1 Offences associated with *precogitata malicia/forthocht felony*

Offence	*No.*
Perturbacione/strublance (only, or with other offences)	36
Felonia precogitata/forthocht felony (only, or 'action' of)	3
Breaking of surety (only)	2
Forthocht felony and breaking of surety (together)	1
Violenta vulneracione (only)	1
Percussione (only)	1
Iniusta lesione (only)	1
Inobedencia (against burgh officers)	1
Forthocht malice (done to a servant '*in the fisching of his wattir*')	1
Total	**47**

were in fact associated with 'precogitata malicia'. Several other associated offences are set out in Table 11.1, including disobedience to a town officer, the breaking of a surety and certain acts of personal violence (*vulneracione, percussione, lesione*).

There are two occasions when an 'action of forthocht felony' was brought in court, one simply to note that the action was to be delayed until the alderman's return (1461) and the other that the action was continued to a future date (1469).[45] The 'actiones' between the parties involved in the latter case some weeks later were assigned to be put before the abbot of Arbroath 'ad finiendum' when he next came to town, and the following month an ordinance by the alderman and council appears to have made a final pronouncement on the 'distrublans' between the parties.[46] In a third case (1462), a party found a legal surety to promise he would respond to the bailies for a 'felonia precogitata' of which he was accused, suggesting this described the offence itself.[47] There is frustratingly little to be said about these 'actions' of 'forthocht felony', although it should be clear that the sense of the term action as used here appears to refer to a general sense of a legal matter moved by one party against another, rather than the more specific sense of the various actions which came into use before the superior courts of the lords auditors and lords of council (described as the 'conciliar session' by present-day historians) in the later fifteenth century.[48] As with the remissions for 'forthocht felony' in the privy seal register already noted, there is a lack of information recorded about the precise nature of the wrong in these cases.

The years in which each case entry occurs are set out in Table 11.2. The year of the first entry's appearance is 1444. Given the national legislation reviewed earlier, which was of legal relevance since the 1380s, why cases involving 'precogitata malicia' should only begin to be recorded in a local jurisdiction like that of Aberdeen in the mid-1440s – more than ten years after the legislation of 1432 which made specific provision for burghs – is an obvious question. The bailies' broadening of the scope of their attention to include 'precogitata malicia' may well be related to unrecorded discussions about the range of local authority during the turbulent minority of James II (which lasted from 1437 through to 1449). In 1440 and again in 1441, the council had appointed a baron influential in the town's hinterland, Sir Alexander Irvine of Drum, to the office of 'captain and governor' of the burgh. This position was not renewed in 1442, and in 1445, the council resolved that they would not do so again, agreeing that no lord should be made a captain of the burgh in future.[49] In the same year, on 30 April 1445, the council declared its intention to petition for a grant of the 'fredome to be schirrefis' within the burgh, and made provision for the costs of this endeavour to be estimated. There is no evidence that Aberdeen was successful in securing this shrieval jurisdiction, but in later decades other burghs were granted such powers, for instance Edinburgh in 1482 and Stirling in 1501.[50] It is perhaps probable that the appearance of cases involving 'precogitata malicia' in the mid-1440s was related to the interest of the burgh elite in seeing the various urban jurisdictions for which they were responsible exercised more fully than in the past.

It is even more difficult to venture a satisfying explanation for why the run of cases comes to an end in the 1490s. The last entry to be found is from 1496, one of only three that decade and following upon just two in the 1480s. These decades were generally a time of experiment and accelerated change in the law and in legal procedure at the national level.[51] Similar patterns may be detected locally in Aberdeen, too. In this period the number and length of entries in the registers expands, coincident with greater use of the vernacular. The revival of procedure for doom falsing was an innovation to be found at this time, as was discussed in the introduction to this volume.[52] It was also in 1496 that the last reference to the 'curia legalis' occurs in the registers.[53] So it may be that in a time of general dynamism and fluidity the local jurisdictional experiment begun in the 1440s with 'precogitata malicia' and 'forthocht felony' drew to its end. In these decades perhaps it was another jurisdiction, like that of the sheriff or of the justice ayre, which took over or re-absorbed cases of non-lethal 'precogitata malicia' from the burgh courts. Yet if this were so, the records of the Aberdeen sheriff court from 1503 to 1600 as calendared by Littlejohn give no indication of the use of these terms, and the justiciary records relating to Aberdeen do not survive until later in the sixteenth century.[54] Evidence may be found, however, of a similar jurisdiction exercised in another burgh about this time. In 1500 an action was brought before the superior court of the lords of council against a bailie of Haddington and other men of that town. The lords presiding found that the bailie had proceeded disorderly 'in defraud of justice' having led to the acquittal of those accused in an 'accione of blude and as is presumyt of forthocht felony'.[55] Thus, Aberdeen appears not to have been alone in exercising such a jurisdiction even if it ceased to do so in the 1490s. Further investigation of the fragmentary records of other burghs from the fifteenth century, and those which survive in much greater quantity from the following century (including those of Aberdeen after 1511), may yet help to build up the wider legal context of this type of offence more fully.[56]

The meanings of malice and felony

We have already seen in the preceding discussion of homicide and national legislation that the Latin terms 'precogitata malicia' and 'precogitata felonia' appear to have been interchangeable in the later middle ages. This point is perhaps made most explicit in an entry in the so-called Aberdeen 'sasine register', a volume with diverse contents covering the period 1484–1502. An entry in that register dated 30 June 1487 records the remission secured by the accused killers of Andrew Suither: 'pro morte … per ipsos ex precogitata ~~malissi~~ malici[a] seu ~~phelo~~ felonia'.[57] Here the clerk seems to have struggled with the correct spelling of 'malicia' and 'felonia' (perhaps as he listened to a document read out loud), and the phrasing appears to be taken from the royal letter of remission which nevertheless made explicit that 'malicia' and 'felonia' were to be understood as carrying an equivalent meaning. Further linguistic complexity comes in the translation between Latin and the Middle Scots vernacular. In the Aberdeen council register volumes used in the present survey and set out in Table 11.2, there are ten occurrences of 'forthocht felony' (including one duplicate entry)

TABLE 11.2 Entries including accusation of *precogitata malicia/forthocht felony*

Term of art	*Year*	*Reference*
precogitata malicia	1444	ARO-4-0384-03
precogitata malicia	1447	ARO-4-0470-07
precogitata malicia	1447	ARO-4-0470-08
precogitata malicia	1447	ARO-4-0480-06
precogitata malicia	1447	ARO-4-0498-05
precogitata malicia	1448	ARO-4-0510-04
precogitata malicia	1448	ARO-4-0510-05
precogitata malicia	1448	ARO-4-0510-06
precogitata malicia	1448	ARO-5-0024-03
precogitata malicia	1448	ARO-5-0024-04
precogitata malicia	1449	ARO-5-0028-04
precogitata malicia	1450	ARO-5-0096-06
precogitata malicia	1450	ARO-5-0096-07
precogitata malicia	1456	ARO-5-0286-06
precogitata malicia	1456	ARO-5-0286-07
precogitata malicia	1457	ARO-5-0321-03
precogitata malicia	1459	ARO-5-0363-08
precogitata malicia	1460	ARO-5-0393-04
precogitata malicia	1460	ARO-5-0393-05
forsocht felony	1461	ARO-5-0424-09
precogitata felonia	1462	ARO-5-0508-03
felonia precogitate	1462	ARO-5-0508-04
precogitata felonia	1464	ARO-5-0518-02
precogitata malicia	1465	ARO-5-0527-08
precogitata malicia	1467	ARO-5-0599-02
precogitata malicia	1467	ARO-5-0607-02
precogitata malicia	1467	ARO-5-0610-02
precogitata malicia	1467	ARO-5-0612-07
forthoucht felny	1469	ARO-5-0732-02[a]
precogitata malicia	1470	ARO-6-00110-06
forthoucht felony	1469	ARO-6-0084-04
forthoucht felny	1471	ARO-6-0138-08
precogitata malicia	1471	ARO-6-0166-06
for thocht fellon'	1472	ARO-6-0178-01
forsocht felloune	1472	ARO-6-0184-03
precogitata malicia	1472	ARO-6-0184-04
precogitatam maliciam	1474	ARO-6-0318-04
precogitata malicia	1474	ARO-6-0318-08
forthocht felony	1474	ARO-6-0327-03
precogitata malicia	1475	ARO-6-0390-05
precogitata malicia	1476	ARO-6-0425-05
felonia precogitate	1477	ARO-6-0494-07
precogitata malicia	1479	ARO-6-0589-08
forthocht malice	1482	ARO-6-0721-04
precogitata malicia	1489	ARO-7-0152-08

Term of art	*Year*	*Reference*
forthocht fellone	1492	ARO-7-0337-03
forthocht fellone	1493	ARO-7-0462-04
forsoicht fellone	1496	ARO-7-0746-04
Total		**47 (48[a])**

a Duplicate of ARO-6-0084-04.

and one instance of 'forthocht malice'. This suggests a clear equivalence between 'felony' and 'malice' in Middle Scots, as well as in Latin.[58]

In Latin, in fourteenth- and fifteenth-century Scotland, there are very few references to be found to 'felonia' used in any context other than 'precogitata felonia'.[59] There is one parliamentary item which mentions the offences of 'felonia et proditione' in 1344, but this appears to be an exception.[60] Historians familiar with English legal history will be well aware that in the later middle ages 'felony' came to acquire a particular technical meaning in England. Wrongs were divided into felony and trespass. The class of offences that were of the most heinous nature (i.e. concerning the 'pleas of the crown') came to be known as felonies, and that technical terminology has survived in the Anglo-American tradition.[61] Work by Kamali on the 'layered' meanings of felony in medieval England has also helped to nuance how the historical term 'felony' is to be understood: a legal wrong but also a choice of action that was wicked and closely linked to ideas of premeditation, deliberation and malice.[62] By contrast to England, despite some gestures in this direction in the 1240s, the law in Scotland did not use 'felony' to describe a particular class of serious offences. Instead, if we look at examples in the vernacular, we can see a different path taken by this word in Scotland.[63] In the parliamentary records only a very few occurrences of the term appear apart from the context of 'forthocht felony'.[64] If we turn to the wider contextual meanings of 'felony', taking examples from Middle Scots writing, the range of associations carried by this term in the later middle ages is instructive. Whereas Scotland differed from England in not adopting felony as a class of offence, it remained in step with the English cultural context explored by Kamali. What is more, it arguably had a further specific connotation in Scotland. William Dunbar wrote in his *Dance of the Seven Deadly Sins*: 'Nixt in the dance followit Invy/fild full of feid and felony/hid malyce and dispyte/for pryvie hatrent that tratour trymlit'.[65] A similar pairing of 'fellony or feid' occurs in *The Buke of the Howlat*, and in another text felony is closely linked with the identification of a 'mortale inimy'.[66] John Barbour's *Brus* offers numerous further examples, including the line 'Na felloune betwixt thaim was'.[67] Thus the range of meanings of 'felony' conveyed in these indicative examples encompassed fierceness, cruelty and wickedness – a very similar semantic field to that of 'malice', and indeed there appears to have been fluidity between the two words.[68] The usage of 'felony' in the illustrations just given also points to a sense in which the term more precisely connoted a state of feud and mortal enmity.

Case outcomes

The entries presented earlier for *Fichet & Voket* v. *Chene & Mad* show a typical outcome for cases involving offences done 'ex precogitata malicia' – typically a fine, arrangements for compensation and possibly a pledge to keep the peace in the form of lawburrows. We have seen that the thrust of national legislation in this area was to limit the scope for pardons, or to introduce a rigorous procedure for offences done out of malice (as opposed to *chaudmella*) such as seeking to confine an offender to prison until emendation was paid to the injured party, or arresting both parties involved in the case of a fight and instantly convening an assize to determine the matter. By contrast, the non-lethal cases recorded in the Aberdeen registers do not suggest that this process was closely adhered to, or at least that if it was followed, it was not recorded in detail (however, the case noted earlier of Henry of Kyngorn involved his confinement in the tolbooth). In fact, parties were accused of acting out of malice (and an assize convicted or acquitted on the matter) in a small proportion of cases. Only 47 are found across the whole century, in the context of thousands of recorded cases (and of a total number involving *perturbacio* or *strublance* numbering more than 1,500). There is only one occurrence in the entire corpus of a case which seems to be an equivalent to *chaudmella*. In 1465, the bailies sitting 'pro tribunali' themselves accused David de Hill of the 'iniuste perturbacione' of Andrew Williamson, the mair of Buchan, in the exercise of his office. Presumably the mair of Buchan had been accosted while present within the jurisdiction of the burgh, although this goes unstated in the entry. Hill took advice from his forespeaker and denied the charge. An assize of nine was elected (their names are given in the entry) to determine the matter, and declared that Hill had not acted against the mair in exercise of his office but 'ex subitanea Ira' – out of sudden anger. He was thus acquitted by the assize, although he then confessed to the offence and was to make amends according to law.[69]

When offences were found to have been done with 'precogitata malicia' or 'forthocht felony', there seems to have been no specific consequences to follow from such a verdict that differed from a conviction for *perturbacio* or *strublance* alone. In the vast majority of cases with malice, the guilty party was fined (amerced) by the court and instructed to make emendation to the victim. If particular consequences had flowed from a conviction of acting out of malice, it might suggest that the finding was relevant in terms of indicating a degree of deliberateness or premeditation of the wrong. It should be said that the level of fine imposed was not recorded, so it remains possible that these offences were amerced at a heavier rate of penalty. However, in practice, malice brought no special consequences, and these records suggest that all that mattered was that the question of malice was considered by the court as to whether it existed as a motivation for the offence and that the finding was placed on record. The question that seems to have been under examination was whether an injury had arisen from a prior enmity – a 'malice' or 'felony' – existing mutually between the parties or harboured by one party against another. The formal consideration of this question in court thus made that prior hostility a fact openly acknowledged.[70] Placing it on a shared, communal record seems to have been what mattered most. In one case the victim of *perturbacio* done out of aforethought malice went further and asked for a notarial instrument to record the court's finding against his adversary.[71] In another, one man asked for a 'testimonial' of the court to record how his counterparty had challenged him in court to 'fecht in the said querel' by casting down his hat, to which he responded by asking for the matter to be 'determyt be the law and the assise'.[72]

It is possible to test the point by looking for evidence in the wider *ARO* corpus to suggest that pre-existing enmities did, in fact, colour some of the cases under consideration. One such example explains the motivation for hostility between two townsmen. This concerns the entry for *Alexander de Strathachyne* v. *Thomas Blyndsele* in 1449. Some four years earlier, Strathachyne had been fined in the bailie court for 'bustwiss spekyn to Tom Blindzell the ballye in his office doyng', and the assize enjoined him that in future he must be 'nothir barganour [quareller] na twlyour [trouble-maker] bot at his powar to let sic thing to be done'. He failed to adhere to this requirement. In 1449 both men were convicted of *perturbacio* against each other, but it was recorded separately that the assize found Strathachyne to have acted 'ex precogitata malicia'.[73] Another example relates to the confrontation of *Thomas Quelp* v. *David Dun* in 1456, where both parties broke their sureties out of aforethought malice, and the entry convicting Quelp recorded that this was done 'ex precogitata malicia inter ipsum et Dauid Dun'. A search reveals that in the preceding year Quelp had been fined for the *perturbacione* of Dun, and seven years earlier Dun had been accused of the *perturbacione* of Quelp.[74] This evidence suggests that prior hostility could leave its traces in the legal record giving weight to how a 'malice' or 'felony' was understood when it came to be alleged in court.

Conclusions

As to findings more strictly concerned with Scottish legal history, it was noted earlier that Dropuljic's study of homicide in the seventeenth century found a category of 'slaughter' with *precogitat* malice, 'in the sense of prior discord between the panel and the defunct, as opposed to forethought or planning of the actual killing'.[75] That point would tend to support the view I have taken here that 'precogitata malicia' or 'forthocht felony' in non-lethal affairs in the fifteenth century was used in practice to record a prior hostility between the party injured and the party complaining. In turn, reflecting on Dropuljic's later evidence, an implication of the present study would be to suggest in fact that 'forthocht felony' and '*precogitat* malice' shared an interchangeable meaning that may have mattered in the seventeenth century as much as in the earlier period.[76]

More generally, an examination of malice in the urban courts of Aberdeen offers a new vantage point into the language of enmity in late medieval Scotland. Sellar argued that in terms of homicide, the emergence of the categories of 'forthocht felony' or 'precogitata malicia' and *chaudmella* in the later fourteenth century (alongside the older categories of murder as secret killing and simple homicide, given in *Regiam*) marked a move 'away from the world of the blood feud towards a public criminal law' where 'all killing becomes technically criminal'.[77] For Sellar, actual premeditation was the significant point.[78] Yet the evidence considered here does not suggest that, in non-lethal affairs, determining a 'malice' or 'felony' was significant because it measured deliberateness or premeditation in an offence. What it does suggest, if anything, is that simply recording a 'malice' or 'felony' was most important in those cases which came before the burgh's judicial officers. National legislation in the form of parliamentary statutes was not translated swiftly into local operation and practice. Even when in 1444 the Aberdeen courts first recorded a case involving 'precogitata malicia', they do not appear to have followed the legislated procedure in any strict manner. The determination of malice was appended to a pre-existing process for cases of *perturbacio* or *strublance* which had a wide jurisdictional utility. In this regard, it would seem that the 'world of the blood feud' – or, at least, a world with a vocabulary of enmity describing hostile social relationships – was not left behind with the emergence of 'forthocht felony'. Rather, the courts were used as a means to register these hostile relations in writing. What is more, this was not the world of rural landowners and the nobility, but the urban *milieu* of merchants, artisans, shipmen and those who served as important civic officials themselves. Here we can see an aspect of a late medieval enmity culture operating among townspeople and recorded in their use of the law. Noting the observations on gender made earlier, we can go further to say that this was a culture that operated almost exclusively among townsmen.

It was noted earlier that three mentions of 'forthocht felony' alone identify the legal action. As with remissions for 'forthocht felony' in the privy seal register counted by Grant or those cases of 'precogitata felonia' found in the justice ayre records of the 1490s,[79] we have no information about the precise offences involved. Are we to assume that such a case if heard before the ayre (or a sheriff court for that matter) was likely to involve homicide, whereas such a case if heard before a burgh court rather involved a non-lethal assault? What follows from the discussion presented here is the suggestion that what was most important for the parties who appeared in court – the assizes elected to reach a decision and the presiding officials – was simply the determination of a prior hostility. This would help to explain the ambiguity encompassed in actions and offences identified as 'forthocht felony' alone. The actual underlying offence was of secondary significance. Of primary importance when this occurred was putting to work the mechanisms of the law and its terms of art to record the relevant social relations. If the evidence bears the weight of this suggestion, the Aberdeen records point to a similarity with late medieval Marseille in that the burgh courts and their records were used as a means to determine the existence of malice and register it with the authority of publicity in 'the written archive of knowledge'.[80] For urban cultures of law, there is the wider problem, yet to be fully understood, of how the legal terminology of malice related to the language of social emotion and conflict more generally, in the sense of hatred and enmity. That problem is one to be pursued in a European context.[81]

Notes

* I am grateful to the anonymous reviewer, and my co-editor, for their comments, to audiences at the North American Conference on British Studies (2018) and at Aberdeen (2017, 2018, 2019), and to Stephanie Dropuljic and Elizabeth Ewan for their input. All errors remain my own.

1 E. Frankot, A. Havinga, C. Hawes, W. Hepburn, W. Peters, J. Armstrong, P. Astley, A. Mackillop, A.R.C. Simpson and A. Wyner (eds) *Aberdeen Registers Online*, Aberdeen: University of Aberdeen, 2019, <https://www.abdn.ac.uk/aro> (accessed 1 July 2019) (hereafter ARO entry ID), ARO-5-0098-08. On 'malefices' in a later period, see Sir George Mackenzie, *The Laws and Customs of Scotland in Matters Criminal*, ed. O.F. Robinson, Edinburgh: Stair Society, 2012, tit. 1, c. 1, pp. 5–6; tit. 1, c. 4, pp. 11–2.

2 ARO-5-0282-09 (1456) '... non veniebat in vico furcarum ex aliqua prouocacione malicie sed pro negociis ex pediendis'. ARO-6-0882-02 (1484) '... ordinatur quod si dictus georgeus talem imposterum fecerit offensam et prouocacionem malicie contra prefatas personas ...'.

3 ARO-7-0090-03 (1488).

4 ARO-5-0486-14 (1463); ARO-5-0566-02 (1465); ARO-5-0635-01 (1468); ARO-6-0144-02 (1471); ARO-6-0158-09 (1471); ARO-6-0742-08 (1482); and ARO-6-0765-07 (1482).

5 'Malice *n.*', *Dictionary of the Scots Language*, Scottish Language Dictionaries Ltd, 2004, <http://www.dsl.ac.uk/entry/dost/malice_n> (accessed 1 May 2018).

6 ARO-6-0034-03.

7 ARO-2-0175-09, ARO-2-0175-13 (1411); he was elected anyway: ARO-2-0176-01. In ARO-6-0441-03 (1467), both parties were to 'kepe hartlie kyndnes and tendirnes as accordis amangis nychtbouris of the ton'.

8 ARO-6-0825-01.

9 ARO-6-0836-08.

10 ARO-7-0128-07. See also ARO-7-0254-04 (1491) and ARO-7-0417-03 (1493).

11 J.M. Kaye, 'The early history of murder and manslaughter' (parts 1 and 2), *Law Quarterly Review* 83, 1967, pp. 365–95, 569–601; T.A. Green, 'Societal concepts of criminal liability for homicide in medieval England', *Speculum* 47, 1972, pp. 669–95; and T.A. Green, 'The jury and the English law of homicide, 1200–1600', *Michigan Law Review* 74, 1976, pp. 413–99.

12 Quoted in T.A. Green, *Verdict According to Conscience: Perspectives on the English Criminal Trial Jury, 1200–1800*, Chicago: University of Chicago Press, 1985, p. 75, n. 29.

13 Kaye, 'The early history of murder', pp. 386–7, 388–9, 389–90, 394–5, and Green, 'Societal concepts of criminal liability for homicide', pp. 691–4.

14 Green, 'Societal concepts of criminal liability for homicide', p. 691 (quote), and Green, 'The jury and the English law of homicide', p. 463, n. 182.

15 Kaye, 'The early history of murder', p. 376 (see also pp. 372, 374).

16 E.P. Kamali, '*Felonia Felonice Facta:* Felony and intentionality in medieval England', *Criminal Law and Philosophy* 9, 2015, pp. 397–421, esp. pp. 400–1, 418–9, and E.P.

Kamali, 'The devil's daughter of hell fire: Anger's role in medieval English felony cases', *Law and History Review* 35, 2017, pp. 155–200, esp. pp. 164 (quote), 185, 196–7.

17 Kaye, 'The early history of murder', pp. 389–90, 394–5; Green, 'The jury and the English law of homicide', p. 472, and J.H. Baker, *An Introduction to English Legal History,* 3rd edn, London: Butterworths, 1990, pp. 601–2. Further on malice in an English context, see the chapter on 'Discord' in my book, *England's Northern Frontier: Conflict and Local Society in the Fifteenth-Century Scottish Marches,* Cambridge, Cambridge University Press, 2020, pp. 270–307.

18 W.D.H. Sellar, 'Forethocht felony, malice aforethought and the classification of homicide', in W.M. Gordon and T.D. Fergus (eds) *Legal History in the Making: Proceedings of the Ninth British Legal History Conference Glasgow 1989,* London: Hambledon Press, 1991, pp. 43–59; W.D.H. Sellar, 'Was it murder? John Comyn of Badenoch and William, earl of Douglas', in C.J. Kay and M.A. MacKay (eds) *Perspectives on the Older Scottish Tongue: A Celebration of DOST,* Edinburgh: Edinburgh University Press, 2005, pp.132–8; and A. Grant, 'Murder will out: Kingship, kinship and killing in medieval Scotland', in S. Boardman and J. Goodare (eds) *Kings, Lords and Men in Scotland and Britain, 1300–1625: Essays in Honour of Jenny Wormald,* Edinburgh: Edinburgh University Press, 2014, pp. 193–226.

19 Kaye, 'The early history of murder', p. 376. See also Sellar, 'Forethocht felony', pp. 46, 56 on sources.

20 Sellar, 'Forethocht felony', p. 48, quotes from *Regiam* the passage distinguishing between 'murdrum' and 'simplex homicidium'. On remissions for killing in earlier sources, see Grant, 'Murder will out', p. 215.

21 *The Records of the Parliaments of Scotland to 1707,* ed. K.M. Brown et al., St Andrews, 2007–2020, <www.rps.ac.uk> (accessed 1 June 2018) (hereafter RPS), RPS 1370/2/26; RPS 1372/3/6; RPS 1469/25; RPS A1504/3/107; and RPS 1504/3/25. There was evidently other legislation passed in 1384, but the relevant MS folio is wanting (see note † at RPS 1384/11/6 and RPS 1384/11/9 which refers back to the lost ordinances on homicide). See also 1432/3/2–6 (on procedure 'quhare ony man beis slane', mentioning also forthocht felony). On remissions: RPS 1484/2/34; RPS 1487/10/5; and RPS 1491/4/12. See also A.A.M. Duncan (ed.) *Scottish Formularies,* Edinburgh: Stair Society, 2011 (*sub* styles B68, E14).

22 Sellar, 'Forethocht felony', p. 56, see also pp. 50, 53.

23 J.W. Armstrong, 'The justice ayre in the border sheriffdoms, 1493–1498', *Scottish Historical Review* 92, 2013, pp. 1–37, at p. 27.

24 Grant, 'Murder will out', p. 224.

25 S.A. Dropuljic, 'The classification of murder and slaughter in the justiciary court from 1625–1650: Malice, intent and premeditation – food "forethought"?', *Aberdeen Student Law Review* 7, 2016, pp. 121–47.

26 Dropuljic, 'The classification of murder and slaughter', pp. 145–7.

27 On *chaudmellee* and 'suddante', see Sellar, 'Forethocht felony', p. 49; Sellar, 'Was it murder?', pp. 133–5, 138; and Baker, *Introduction to English Legal History,* p. 601.

28 The 'diet books' of the Aberdeen sheriff court survive from 1503 onwards. See D. Littlejohn (ed.) *Records of the Sheriff Court of Aberdeenshire,* 3 vols, Aberdeen: New Spalding Club, 1904–1907, vol. 1, pp. 89–100.

29 RPS 1384/11/9 (and see note † at RPS 1384/11/6).

30 Grant, 'Murder will out', pp. 216, 218. Simpson, examining RPS 1392/3/1, identifies 'intentis affectibus' in the act's preamble as a way to express aforethought intent; A.R.C. Simpson, 'Procedures for dealing with robbery in Scotland before 1400', in A.R.C. Simpson, S. Styles, E. West and A.L.M. Wilson (eds) *Continuity, Change and Pragmatism in the Law: Essays in Memory of Professor Angelo Forte,* Aberdeen: Aberdeen University Press, 2016, pp. 95–149, at pp. 134, 136.

31 RPS 1426/10. On 'coming in will', see Armstrong, 'The justice ayre in the border sheriffdoms', p. 11. On James I's legislation and its relationship to enactments from 1370–1399, see Grant, 'Murder will out', p. 217.

32 RPS 1432/3/8. On the 'Auld Lawes', see A. Taylor, *The Shape of the State in Medieval Scotland 1124–1290*, Oxford: Oxford University Press, 2016, pp. 16, 272n. and 457–64, and A.R.C. Simpson and A.L.M. Wilson, *Scottish Legal History: Volume One 1000–1707*, Edinburgh: Edinburgh University Press, 2017, pp. 59–64.

33 RPS 1432/3/9. This and RPS 1432/3/8 follow 1432/3/2 and 1432/3/4, which are about pursuit of homicides, the latter specifically about homicides in burghs.

34 Again, see RPS 1432/3/9. On remissions found in M. Livingstone et al. (eds) *Registrum Secreti Sigilii Regum Scotorum*, 8 vols, Edinburgh, 1908–1982 (hereafter *RSS*), vol. 1, pp. 1–386, which are for 'forthocht felony', not specifying the nature of the underlying offence; see Grant, 'Murder will out', pp. 218–9.

35 The total is strictly 48 if ARO-5-0732-02, a duplicate entry of ARO-6-0084-04, is counted separately.

36 ARO-5-0364-04.

37 ARO-4-0510-04, ARO-4-0510-05, ARO-4-0510-06 and ARO-4-0510-07.

38 ARO-5-0096-06, ARO-5-0096-07, ARO-5-0527-08 and ARO-5-0732-02/ARO-6-0084-04 (duplicates).

39 ARO-6-0589-08 and ARO-6-0721-04.

40 ARO-5-0607-02.

41 For comment on the various courts of the burgh, see W.C. Dickinson (ed.) *Early Records of the Burgh of Aberdeen, 1317. 1398–1407,* Edinburgh: Scottish History Society, 1957, pp. cxvii–cxxv. A preliminary assessment by Edda Frankot of 'The records of the medieval burgh courts of Aberdeen' across the fifteenth century was given at the Scottish Records Association annual conference in Edinburgh, November 2017.

42 ARO-7-0152-08. In this case, the victims were Patrick Oge and his (unnamed) wife.

43 As in ARO-6-0327-03.

44 J.R.D. Falconer, *Crime and Community in Reformation Scotland: Negotiating Power in a Burgh Society*, London: Pickering & Chatto, 2013, pp. 101–4, quote from p. 102. For 'strublance in word', see, for instance, ARO-6-0898-08 (1485).

45 ARO-5-0424-09 (1461): 'The action of forsocht felony folouit be Thomas of Chamour and Cristy Litstar on Alexander Scrogis is resplatit to the hame cumyng of the aldirman'. The other is ARO-6-0084-04 (1469).

46 ARO-6-0086-02 and ARO-6-0088-05.

47 ARO-5-0508-04.

48 As in ARO-1-0050-09 ('Actio mota inter Johannem Spryng et Patricium Crane...', 1398). For the actions before the session, see Simpson and Wilson, *Scottish Legal History*, pp. 118–25 and M. Godfrey, *Civil Justice in Renaissance Scotland: The Origins of a Central Court*, Leiden: Brill Academic Publishers, 2009, pp. 268–354.

49 ARO-4-0211-02, ARO-4-0253-02, and ARO-5-0706-01. S. Boardman, 'The burgh and the realm: Medieval politics c.1100–1500', in E.P. Dennison, D. Ditchburn, and M. Lynch (eds) *Aberdeen before 1800: A New History,* East Linton, 2002, pp. 203–23, at 216.

50 ARO-5-0701-04: 'Item it is sene speidful to the Counsaile to trete give thai may get the fredome to be schirrefis within the ton' and to mak a coste tharapon'. For other burghs, see Dickinson, *Early Records,* p. cxl. I am grateful to Edda Frankot for bringing this to my attention and discussion on the point.

51 See the summary in Simpson and Wilson, *Scottish Legal History*, pp. 118–23.

52 On vernacularisation, see the contribution by Anna Havinga in this volume. Doom falsing is addressed in the introduction to this volume.

53 ARO-7-0761-03, noted by Frankot, 'The records of the medieval burgh courts of Aberdeen'.

54 Littlejohn (ed.) *Sheriff Court of Aberdeenshire*, vol. 1 (Records prior to 1600). In some instances, the need for a case heard in the burgh court to be superseded by the sheriff court or a higher court was considered explicitly: ARO-5-0393-04 (1460) and ARO-6-0138-08 (1471).

55 G. Neilson and H. Paton (eds) *The Acts of the Lords of Council in Civil Causes, 1496–1501,* Edinburgh: s.n., 1918, p. 419. I am grateful to William Hepburn for bringing this reference to my attention.
56 For example, J. Stuart (ed.) *Extracts from the Council Register of the Burgh of Aberdeen, 1398–1570,* Aberdeen: Spalding Club, 1844, p. 135 (from 1530), and W. Chambers (ed.) *Charters and Documents Relating to the Burgh of Peebles,* Edinburgh: Scottish Burgh Records Society, 1872, p. 232 (from 1556); R. Renwick (ed.) *Extracts from the Records of the Royal Burgh of Lanark,* Glasgow: Carson & Nicol, 1893, p. 46 (from 1569). Neither is mention to be found in the first 100 pages of Aberdeen's council register thirteen; J. Armstrong, S. Convery, E. Frankot, A. Macdonald, A. Mackillop, A. Simpson and A. Wilson (with others), *The Aberdeen Burgh Records Database,* Aberdeen, 2014, <www.abdn.ac.uk/aberdeen-burgh-records-database> (accessed 1 December 2019).
57 Aberdeen City and Aberdeenshire Archives (ACAA), Sasine Registers (CA/2/1), CA/2/1/1, p. 81 (30 June 1487), and a similar entry appears at p. 85. I am grateful to Edda Frankot for bringing this reference to my attention.
58 In ARO-6-0184-03 (1472), the vernacular 'le forsocht felloune' is interjected within the Latin entry (i.e. instead of *precogitata malicia* used in the following entry). See also Sir John Skene, *De Verborum Significatione,* Edinburgh, 1597, *sub* 'Forthocht-fellony, *praecogitata malitia*'.
59 For the latter, see the Latin charters recording grants of regality at RPS 1452/6/3 and RPS A1476/7/2.
60 RPS 1344/2.
61 Baker, *Introduction to English Legal History,* pp. 572–3.
62 Kamali, '*Felonia Felonice Facta*', pp. 400–1, 418–9 (quotes).
63 For the 1240s, see Taylor, *Shape of the State,* p. 139. For the division of crimes in the later seventeenth century, see Mackenzie, *Matters Criminal,* ed. Robinson, tit. 2, pp. 21–3. I am grateful for discussion on this point with Andrew Simpson.
64 RPS 1432/3/2 'sik men that has done sik felonny agayn the king and fugitive fra the law'; RPS 1432/3/3 'sic a felone trespass agayn the kingis majeste'; and RPS 1483/3/147 'to vnderly the law for the felone refe made apone our souerane lordis liegis'.
65 William Dunbar, *Dance of the Seven Deadly Sins,* in J. MacQueen and W. MacQueen (eds) *A Choice of Scottish Verse 1470–1570,* London: Faber and Faber, 1972, p. 124.
66 J. Rawson Lumby (ed.) *Bernardus de cura rei famuliaris: With some Early Scottish Prophecies, etc.,* London: Early English Text Society, 1870, p. 6: 'Gef that thi mortale inimy … may nocht schaw furtht his felony' (from a late fifteenth-century vernacular paraphrase of a letter of St Bernard of Clairvaux); and Richard Holland, *The Buke of the Howlat,* ed. R. Hanna, Edinburgh: Scottish Text Society, 2014, p. 165: 'Thir ar fowlis of effect, but fellony or feid'.
67 John Barbour, *The Bruce,* ed. A.A.M. Duncan, Edinburgh: Canongate, 1997, pp. 747 (quote), 55, 57, 61, 67, 117, 119, 151, 163, 167, 177, 181, 197, 199, 729, 731, 765, 769. This is not an exhaustive list.
68 The Dunbar, Bernard and Howlat quotations just noted are given in 'Felony *n.*', *Dictionary of the Scots Language,* <http://www.dsl.ac.uk/entry/dost/felony_n> (accessed 1 May 2018).
69 ARO-5-0541-07. See also Baker, *Introduction to English Legal History,* p. 601n, on English indictments '*ex subito casu*', or by sudden chance.
70 It is worth noting RPS 1318/14 on the repledging of animals. This act provides that anyone interfering in this process, should *their malice become known* and attainted, they will be fined, viz. '…Et qui aliter fecerit et malicia sua cognita fuerit et attainta sit in amerciamento decem librarum'.
71 Both parties entered pledges for lawburrows: ARO-5-0599-02, ARO-5-0599-03, ARO-5-0599-04 (1467).
72 ARO-6-0327-03 (1474).

73 ARO-5-0028-03, ARO-5-0028-04, ARO-5-0028-05 (1449) and ARO-4-0408-04 (1445).

74 ARO-5-0286-06, ARO-5-0286-07 (1456); ARO-5-0237-04 (1455); and ARO-5-0036-04 (1449, this being among the cases recorded for the chamberlain ayre).

75 Dropuljic, 'The classification of murder and slaughter', pp. 126–9, quote at p. 129.

76 Ibid., pp. 145–6. It may follow that in Dropuljic's case material, 'forthocht felony' need not be associated with the offence of murder at all.

77 Sellar, 'Forethocht felony', p. 50.

78 Ibid., p. 56. Sellar's related argument (as at p. 50) is that murder came to be incorporated within 'forthocht felony'. This is challenged by Grant, 'Murder will out', p. 223.

79 Grant, 'Murder will out', pp. 218–19, and Armstrong, 'The justice ayre in the border sheriffdoms', pp. 23, 26.

80 D.L. Smail, *The Consumption of Justice: Emotions, Publicity, and Legal Culture in Marseille, 1264–1423*, Ithaca, NY: Cornell University Press, 2003, p. 213.

81 D.L. Smail, 'Hatred as a social institution in medieval society', *Speculum* 76, 2001, pp. 90–126 and R.J. Bartlett, '"Mortal enmities": The legal aspect of hostility in the middle ages', in. B.S. Tuten and T.L. Billado (eds), *Feud, Violence and Practice: Essays in medieval studies in Honor of Stephen D. White*, Farnham: Ashgate, 2010, pp. 197–212.

PART V

Men of law in Scotland

12

BELLS, CLOCKS AND THE BEGINNINGS OF 'LAWYER TIME' IN LATE MEDIEVAL SCOTLAND

David Ditchburn

On 22 May 1548 Robert Hoveson, a walker by trade, was convicted by the burgh court of Aberdeen of insurrection. The details of his misdemeanours, which involved other craftsmen too, remain largely obscure, and it is not clear what prompted Hoveson and his accomplices to hurl intemperate abuse at the ruling elite of Aberdeen. We do know, however, that another target of Hoveson's wrath was the town clock, which was located in the tolbooth, the municipal building in which the financial dues owed to the town were collected and from which the civic officeholders in Scottish towns (the provost and bailies) governed the wider urban community. Hoveson was ordered to repair the clock which he seems to have damaged during his altercation with the town's civic dignitaries. His assault had, however, been launched on one of the most visible symbols of communal identity and his actions, the burgh court decided, required further punishment. Hoveson and an accomplice were, therefore, ordered to appear barefoot and barelegged on the Sunday which followed eight days later. Attired only in their shirts and each carrying a candle, the two men were then told to ask the provost and bailies publicly for forgiveness. Should they, or others, repeat the offence they were to be branded on the cheek and banished from the town.[1]

The violence which scarred Aberdeen in 1548, and its recriminations, begs questions about how time was measured; who measured time; why time was measured; and the ways in which time was understood by late medieval and early modern societies. These are not, of course, inherently new questions of historical research, any more than the events which disturbed Aberdeen in 1548 were (seemingly at least) unparalleled elsewhere. In the Flemish textile-manufacturing town of Commines, penalties had been decreed in 1361 for workers who seized the bell which marked the start of the working day and rang it to encourage insurrection, and a few years later, in 1378, the Ciompi too had sought control of the bells across Florence in order to proclaim their revolt.[2] There is maybe a difference to be drawn between bells which heralded a popular rising and bells (or clocks) which were deliberately targeted for seizure or attack because they symbolised authority. Hoveson's actions in Aberdeen could – perhaps – be interpreted as evidence of social tension between craftsmen and the merchant elite which dominated government of the towns. If so, the Aberdeen episode of 1548 might seem to offer support for the controversial role which, according to Jacques Le Goff, bells, clocks and time came to play in late medieval and early modern society. Le Goff drew a distinction between, on the one hand, what might be called 'church time' and what, on the other hand, might be dubbed 'merchant time'. Towns were pivotal to this differentiation and their commercial and industrial instincts challenged ecclesiastical notions of time. Time, for Le Goff, became something which could be bought and sold much like other commodities. Time was, to quote Le Goff, 'no longer associated with cataclysms or festivals, but rather with daily life', and it followed that the clocks which were erected in towns across the Latin West from the fourteenth century were 'instrument[s] of social, economic and political domination'.[3] Hoveson's actions could, however, be interpreted in many other ways too. Moreover, Le Goff's hypothesis has been widely critiqued, though, as yet, neither his theories nor those of his critics have greatly impinged upon historical analysis of medieval and early modern Scotland.[4] Part of the purpose of this chapter is, therefore, to examine the Scottish evidence, such as it is, in the light of scholarship pertaining to the understanding of time in other countries of the Latin West during the later middle ages. Since, moreover, the theme of this volume is legal culture, particular attention will be given to the innovative role, in Scotland at least, which men of law played in structuring contemporary perceptions about time.

Long before the invention of mechanical clocks towards the end of the middle ages, medieval societies had devised means by which to tell the time.[5] These skills and conventions were not suddenly abandoned when clocks appeared. In port towns such as Aberdeen and Dundee it was not uncommon even in the sixteenth century to mark time by the 'three tides' of the sea or elsewhere to measure the day as extending from sunrise to sunset.[6] Especially perhaps in rural communities, more precise timing might be determined by routine agricultural chores and the quotidian needs of animals. These were clearly understood by those who tended livestock and without necessary recourse to mechanical instruments. Even in rural areas, however, instinct and experience in determining when particular chores had to be undertaken were to some extent supplemented by the timely sound of bells emanating from churches and monasteries. Although the Cistercian order of monks supposedly had little interest in the construction of 'lofty bell towers', from an early stage in their existence most monasteries (whatever their brand of monasticism) possessed bells encased in timber or stone-made belfries.[7] The marking of the regular canonical services was central to monastic purpose and function, in Scotland as it was elsewhere, and monks needed some means by which to identify when they should be at prayer.[8] During the day beams of light perhaps helped, on particular days at least: it has been persuasively argued, for example, that the architectural design of Crossraguel Abbey deliberately directed light onto the high altar of the monastic church on the church's patronal feast days.[9] Even, however, if we accept this, natural light offered little assistance in marking the daily, and especially the nocturnal, hours of monastic prayer. Sundials too were unreliable and in winter water clocks were susceptible to freezing. For clergymen, then, sounds which marked time were an important accoutrement to other mechanisms of telling time. Notwithstanding their supposed earlier prissiness, by the end of the middle ages even Cistercian abbeys such as Culross and Kinloss were investing in new bell towers,[10] and while monastic prayers themselves were a largely private matter, the acoustic reach of the monastic bells which proclaimed prayer stretched well beyond the cloister. Nevertheless, given the monastic geography of the country, much of Scotland remained well outwith the earshot of monastic bells.

The sonic impact of the parish church penetrated the countryside more extensively. While the number of rural parish churches which possessed bells is difficult to determine exactly, many clearly did and had done so for some time. Early medieval hand bells are known of in several places, such as Fortingall and Little Dunkeld (diocese of Dunkeld), and larger bells and/or belfries dating from the early sixteenth century or before survive at several rural locations, including Abercorn (d. St Andrews), Comrie (d. Dunblane), Crimond/Rattray (d. Aberdeen), Dalgety (d. Dunkeld), Dunning (d. Dunblane), Dyce (d. Aberdeen), Errol (d. St Andrews), Fowlis Easter (d. St Andrews), Kinneil (d. St Andrews), Kirkmaiden (d. Galloway), Rayne (d. Aberdeen), Tibbermore (d. Dunkeld) and Strathbrock/Uphall (d. St Andrews).[11] The list is far from exhaustive, but the point to be taken from it is clear. Assuming that the bells of these parish churches marked time at least occasionally, time was not an exclusively urban concept, even though the most explicit evidence of time consciousness in medieval Scotland derives from towns.

Scotland's urban sonic landscape was, nevertheless, probably less cacophonous than that of many continental towns. At Tournai, for example, aside from the city's cathedral, which by the mid-fifteenth century possessed 20 bells, bells are also attested with certainty in all but 2 of the 11 other parish churches in the town by the fifteenth century, with several more located in the monasteries, friaries, chapels and hospitals which dotted the urban landscape. By the early sixteenth century there were at least 70 (and probably more) bells hung in a variety of religious establishments in Tournai. To these must be added the secular bells of the town, of which there were two by the thirteenth century and at least four (including a bell which marked the start of work) by the fourteenth century, located in the town's belfry. These were supplemented by yet other bells positioned at the town's gates and by hand bells.[12] By contrast, Aberdeen's sonic landscape was comparatively quiet. In the royal burgh, the parish church of St Nicholas possessed at least two bells, named Lawrence and Mary, by the mid-fourteenth century.[13] There appears to have been another bell (probably a hand bell) at St Katherine's chapel, but we do not know if bells adorned the town's other religious buildings – which by the mid-sixteenth century included four mendicant establishments and five hospitals – nor for certain if the bells of the parish church were supplemented by civic bells other than another hand bell.[14] The ecclesiastical burgh of Old Aberdeen – about one and half miles or approximately a 30-minute walk from the royal burgh, but on most days probably within its earshot – was seemingly better provisioned with bells, at least after the foundation of the university at King's College in 1495. There, around 12 bells – including five larger bells named Trinity, Mary, Michael, Gabriel and Raphael, five smaller bells 'for marking the middles of the hours' and two additional bells 'for daily use' – were located in the bell tower, while three others (presumably hand bells) were placed on altars in the College chapel.[15] Meanwhile, more bells were to be found at the other end of the ecclesiastical burgh's main highway in St Machar's Cathedral. An early sixteenth-century writer noted that building work in the mid-fourteenth century had seen the erection there of new bell towers, though we do not know how many bells were hung in them.[16] By the early sixteenth century, two of the cathedral's bells had been dissembled and gifted to the Snow Kirk, the new parish church of Old Aberdeen, carved out of adjacent parishes in the early sixteenth century: the second-hand cathedral bells (named Schochtmadony and Skellat) had perhaps become superfluous after the construction of a new central tower to the cathedral, which was designed to hold three bells.[17] There seems little doubt, however, that the two burghs of Aberdeen boasted significantly fewer bells than Tournai – especially before the foundation of Aberdeen's university in 1495 – and that Tournai was better provisioned with bells at an earlier date than Aberdeen.

In part, of course, this was a matter of size. Tournai was a medium-sized Netherlandish town, but still with a population of possibly ten times that of Aberdeen. Aberdeen housed perhaps slightly more than 5,000 inhabitants in c. 1290, maybe only 3,000 in 1408 and around 5,500 in the 1570s.[18] Of course, given the paucity of sources, evidence for Scotland is much thinner than that for many of the great continental towns and it perhaps, therefore, underestimates the sonic landscape of Scottish towns. Nevertheless, there were significant structural differences between Scottish towns and those in many other countries, notably in relation to parish size, which perhaps also partly explain the more modest number of bells recorded in Scottish towns. Aside from the dual town of Edinburgh/Canongate and the belated parochial creation of Old Aberdeen at the end of the fifteenth century, all other towns in Scotland were situated within a single parish unit and this obviously had an impact on the number of bells in Scottish towns. The sonic competition which multi-parish towns encouraged was largely absent from Scotland.

The provision of bells, meanwhile, was probably also curtailed by their expense: several were imported from the Low Countries. The cost of bells probably encouraged the sharing of sonic space by the ecclesiastical and secular authorities. In Aberdeen, for example, the care and maintenance of the ecclesiastical bells and of the campanile in the parish church of St Nicholas were at least in part the responsibility of the burgh authorities.[19] Such interaction was not unusual, even in very large towns such as Bruges, where the secular authorities paid for the bells of the church of St Donatian to be rung during the annual Holy Blood procession and ensuing fair.[20]

Of course, in both large and small towns, bells served many different purposes. They might mark specific times; in the later fifteenth century Aberdeen's bells were rung daily at noon and at six o'clock.[21] But, as Claire Hawes has pointed out, hand bells in particular were also 'closely tied to the decision-making processes of the burgesses and to their public assertion of authority'.[22] Bells alerted the urban population to meetings of one kind or another, including commercial activities and public roups.[23] They warned the community of attack or pestilence or fire;[24] and on a more joyous occasion, the bells of all the churches [*sic*] of St Andrews were rung to mark the inauguration of the town's university in 1414, while those in Ayr heralded the safe return of the king from France in 1537.[25] The acoustic reach of a town's bells, it has been suggested, defined a town's territorial extent, as much as did land and law.[26] But that many bells were bestowed with saintly names points to their role as devotional accoutrements too.[27] Following Old Testament scripture, bells were believed to ward off death.[28] When rung for liturgical purposes their peel was prolonged.[29] They summoned the faithful to prayer (often for the dead) and they were rung to mark religious festivities, in Ayr, for instance, on Halloween (31 October) and All Souls' Day (2 November).[30] Bells thus became fitting objects of conspicuous devotional display, gifted by wealthy burgess families such as the Leiths of Aberdeen and the Spaldings of Dundee.[31] Marking specific time, then, was only part of a bell's function. Bells announced events as much as time; and the multi-purpose nature of bells meant that they continued to have purpose, and to be installed long after clocks had begun to usurp their function in marking hourly time. The merchant gild, for example, paid for a new bell to be erected in early sixteenth-century Dunfermline, while in the 1510s and 1520s Perth boasted several new bells and in 1556 Dundee sought to exchange a bell recently purchased in Flanders for a larger model.[32] This, moreover, was not an indication of Scottish backwardness. In 1528, new bells were installed in the belfry of the great commercial emporium of Bruges, as they were in several other Netherlandish towns of this period.[33] Everywhere, bells still served an important function.

Still, 'bell time' was not as exact as clock time was subsequently to become: bell hours were often of unequal length, measuring one-twelfth of the day and of the night and therefore seasonably variable.[34] Mechanical clocks, by contrast, ultimately offered more accurate and equal measurement of the hour, even though they generally did not as yet subdivide the hour into minutes. Still, during the course of the fourteenth century they became common in many of the greater towns and churches of Christendom and by the end of the following century they could even be found in small Alpine settlements such as Münster and Ernen in the upper Valais.[35] Even in the largest medieval towns, however, public clocks were far from numerous. Aside from those in ecclesiastical and private space,

Venice boasted only three public clocks – one on the façade of San Giacometto di Rialto, another in the clock tower at St Mark's Square (these two close to the city's commercial districts) and a third at its great industrial complex of the Arsenal – while until the seventeenth century Bruges had only two (one in the town house and another in the belfry).[36] While the arrival of clocks in Scotland was almost certainly later than in the major towns of Christendom – the paucity of the Scottish sources is again unhelpful in this respect – they can certainly be identified in Scotland by at least the mid-fifteenth century. There was already a clock at Ayr, for instance, by 1429 and another in Aberdeen by 1454, and even the much smaller town of Peebles possessed one by 1462.[37] Elsewhere, clocks almost certainly predated their first recorded mention but by at least the mid-sixteenth century their presence was noted in several towns, including Dundee, Dumbarton, Edinburgh, Haddington, Lanark, Selkirk and Stirling, as well as in the new university town of Old Aberdeen.[38] Beyond the major conurbations we can be much less sure about the extent to which clocks had penetrated the rural landscape but it seems unlikely that the small settlement of Abernethy (Perthshire) or the barony of Alloway (Ayrshire) were alone in possessing a clock by the mid-sixteenth century.[39] To those clocks publicly displayed, we may add at least some which were in the private possession of the royal and ecclesiastical elite and very probably some in monasteries too: given that the remote English house of Farne, off the Northumberland coast, possessed a clock of some sort by 1394 it seems highly likely that wealthier establishments on the Scottish side of the border did too.[40]

Although we can assume that many of the clocks recorded in Scotland by the sixteenth century were weight-driven, we know little about their appearance or (aside from that in Dundee) their technological specification. It seems unlikely that they were multi-dialled or as ornate as those still evident in Bern, Lund and Prague, though those in Dundee and Edinburgh did strike half-hourly by the mid-sixteenth century at least, and that erected in Dundee in 1543 also delivered more prolonged chimes at 4 am, 12 noon and 9 pm. We know too that in Scotland, as elsewhere, clocks appeared in both secular and ecclesiastical settings, both in tolbooths (as at Aberdeen and Edinburgh) and in churches (as at Abernethy and Stirling), though this did not necessarily reflect competition between 'church time' and 'merchant time' any more than the bells which clocks supplemented had been of exclusively religious purpose and controlled solely by the ecclesiastical authorities.[41] Indeed, it is significant in this respect that in 1453, when entering office, Aberdeen's clock keeper performed the religious ritual of swearing an oath 'to do his diligent business' to maintain the town's clock; and that, as indicated at the start of this article, when Robert Hoveson broke the clock in Aberdeen's tolbooth his misdemeanour required a punishment framed in religious ritual.[42] Still, while bells might constitute devotional gifts, the clocks erected in Dundee at least, in 1543 and 1554, were secular and community enterprises, the first requiring a contract between the clockmaker and the town's representatives and the second paid for by a levy imposed by the council on taxpayers.[43]

Similar to bells, the diffusion of clocks was, however, limited at least to some extent by cost. The new clock erected in Dundee in 1543 and its replacement in 1554 each cost around £200, to which further expenditure could be expected. Clocks were not just practical instruments. They were often *objet d'art*, sometimes painted (as in Aberdeen, Dundee and Stirling), and they constituted fitting diplomatic gifts, presented, for example, to James IV (1488–1513) by French ambassadors in 1511–1512.[44] The maintenance of clocks required chords and copious supplies of olive oil, which had, of course, to be imported: in that sense clock time was, indeed, 'merchant time'. Clocks also required bells to strike the hours – a new bell for Haddington's clock cost £30 in 1557–1558[45] – and they bagged manpower too, for they rarely functioned for more than 24 hours (indeed, they often worked for only about 8 hours) before manual rewinding was required.[46] Clock maintenance was not a full-time occupation – in Dumbarton care of the town's clock was the responsibility of the schoolmaster, while in Aberdeen its maintenance was often entrusted to a goldsmith – but the responsibilities associated with maintenance, nonetheless, added, even if quite modestly, to total costs. In Haddington the keeper of the clock received an annual fee of £3 in the early 1550s, much less than the £10 set aside for the town's provost, the £13 6s 8d received by the town's schoolmaster or the daily wage of around 1s 6d which contemporary labourers might earn.[47] Of course, bells too had been oiled, ideally with olive oil too, and they too had been the responsibility of paid officials – those in churches usually coming under the care of a sacrist or the parish clerk. But once raised and ringing, bells generally required less outlay than clocks because the latter broke down more frequently. In 1535–1536, the town council of Ayr forked out 12s 2d for oiling, ringing and mending the bells; in the same year, materials and repairs to the town's clock cost £2 13s 8d.[48] Although blacksmiths, locksmiths and goldsmiths might all be able to undertake modest repairs – and in Aberdeen these craftsmen were augmented by a local friar, though significantly he was the brother of an Edinburgh goldsmith[49] – specialist clockmakers and menders were rare even in larger continental towns. Geneva, for example, had a single clock mender in 1449, but none by 1513 when its clock broke down.[50] Although there was a 'knokmaker' in Edinburgh by the 1540s, it is hardly surprising that when clocks stopped in Scotland it was sometimes necessary either, as at Selkirk, to wait for an itinerant clock mender or to send them abroad for repair.[51] In 1498, Bishop Elphinstone of Aberdeen entrusted his clock to Andrew Halyburton, the conservator of Scottish staple in the Low Countries, who presumably found it easier to find a specialist there than at home; and in 1535 Andrew Cullan, the provost of Aberdeen, was charged by his colleagues on the council with sending the town's clock to Flanders for repair.[52]

So for whom, then, were these costly instruments intended? In a predominantly rural society awareness of time was important at a seasonal and a daily level. The reminders of what needed doing and when were common themes of medieval calendars.[53] But unpredictable weather patterns made the allocation of agricultural chores to smaller units of time a largely pointless exercise.[54] Not everyone, then, needed to tell the time to the precise hour. Nevertheless, an ability to tell the time was probably not uncommon in urban Scotland (and perhaps further afield too) by at least the early sixteenth century. Indeed, we may differentiate between the ability to appreciate the duration of an activity and a particular moment. The audience which attended Sir David Lyndsay's *Ane Satyre of the Thrie Estaitis*, its female component in particular, was, for example, warned 'faill nocht to teme [empty] your bleddir' in anticipation of a lengthy performance.[55] By contrast, a more precise time awareness was demonstrated by the Frenchmen who quarrelled in the house of an Edinburgh burgess on 5 August 1548 who not only knew that their altercation had taken place between nine and ten in the morning, but that their compatriot, John Barron, had died at 'about the eleventh hour at the dead of night', following injuries sustained while interceding in the dispute.[56] Perhaps more impressively still, in 1502 Margaret Gibson, who had been assaulted by a female colleague while working in Dunfermline abbey's bakehouse, was able to time the altercation to between three and four in the morning, thanks to her own basic numeracy and to the chimes of the abbey's bells.[57] Margaret's accusations did not rely on the timing of the assault, but her ability to tell the time – a skill which she perhaps had learnt from the routines of work – was a convenient and persuasive embellishment to her allegations. Indeed, if we were to accept Jacques Le Goff's arguments, it was employers and employees who first developed a particularly new time consciousness in the later middle ages. Hours and minutes meant money, whether in the form of payments made by employers or wages earned by employees.

There are significant problems with this hypothesis with regard to Scotland. The comparatively large industrial enterprises of the sort which characterised textile production in the towns of northern France and the Low Countries (where Le Goff detected hour consciousness) were absent from Scotland, where industrial production (except perhaps in the new naval dockyard at Newhaven, developed by King James IV in the early sixteenth century) remained limited, both in terms of overall production and in the unit size of production. Absent too – so far as we know – were the work bells which marked the start and end of the working day in many continental towns. The striking of Aberdeen's bells at 12 noon and 6 pm and of Dundee's clock at 4 am, 12 noon and 9 pm were less probably related to work times than to other routines such as the beginning and end of curfews and church services. In addition, it is difficult to find evidence from Scotland that wages were normally determined by the hour and the minute rather than by the day. Admittedly, once again, our evidence is not substantial, and largely reliant on the payments made by the crown for labour. But, as was common throughout Europe until the eighteenth century, the crown, at least, almost always paid by the week or the day, not the hour.[58] That pay was normally rendered in late medieval Scotland by the week or the day is perhaps also suggested by the parliamentary legislation of 1469 which decreed that masons, wrights and other craftsmen should work on Saturdays until 4 pm.[59] The implication is that some workmen of this sort were finishing earlier on Saturdays, and that employers of such labour wanted more hours from their labourers in return for the weekly rate of pay which they paid. This, implicitly too, is suggested by the fine which was imposed on workers who contravened the new decree: they were to lose not a sum calculated by the number of hours missed at work, but rather by the equivalent of a week's work.

Of course, irrespective of how their pay was calculated, some workers did increasingly rely on their ability to tell the time accurately and in small units. Perhaps foremost among this group were mariners. Sandglasses are known to have been used on ships by the later thirteenth century, though the first Scottish evidence of their use, on royal ships, dates only from the early sixteenth century.[60] The precise purpose of the sandglass remains uncertain, though its use was probably not related to pay or to navigation, but rather simply to the regulation of seamen's watches, the passing sand proving a reliable measure in the wet and undulating conditions encountered on board ship.[61] Some sandglasses were used on land too – perhaps, for instance, that which is sometimes said to have belonged to Queen Mary (1542–1567)[62] – but there is little evidence that their usage was frequent before this or that they influenced wider public awareness of small units of time. Nevertheless, the need to identify hours was not restricted to mariners.

It was certainly assumed that the burgh authorities would be cognisant of hourly time. Parliamentary legislation took it for granted that such an awareness existed when it decreed, for example, in 1428 that lepers might only be admitted to burghs on three days in the week (Monday, Wednesday and Friday) from 10 am until 12 noon.[63] Similarly, it was decreed in 1436 that urban taverns should be closed 'after the strike of nine hours', and in 1504 that malt should not be sold before 9 o'clock in the morning.[64] National legislation of this sort was supplemented by many hour-specific local regulations too. Hucksters were not permitted to sell their goods in Aberdeen before 11 o'clock, while the Perth guild recorded in 1453 that 'no wheat be bought before xi hours … and that no meal be bought before xii hours', and in 1515 Edinburgh's council decreed that 'no stranger or outdwellar bringing meal to the market to sell make any merchandise thereof until the hour of xi before noon'.[65] Yet, while merchants (broadly defined) clearly required some hour awareness, if only to comply with commercial regulations, it is far from clear that the hour was central to all of their business considerations. The uncertain duration of sea voyages, for example, made it impossible to regulate international deliveries or dispatches by the hour, or even by the day or week. Debt repayments were normally timed to the day, but not the hour; and there was often considerable latitude over several days for rent payments too.[66] Hour awareness, it may be inferred, was more likely a matter of legal regulation than of business practice.

It follows that time was important to the law and to lawyers. Paul Brand has outlined the rhythms of the legal year in England, and Scotland adhered to its own annual norms.[67] Beyond this, as we have seen, the law sometimes stipulated specific times at which commercial activities, in particular, should begin or end. Courts, meanwhile, constituted public gatherings which convened, of organisational necessity, at preordained times which were, presumably, historic and well known to a local community and which it was not, therefore, necessary to record routinely.[68] Certainly the written records of neither burgh courts nor sheriff courts specify when exactly courts convened, nor when decisions were reached. The hour of cause (*hora causarum*) in ecclesiastical courts is also uncertain, though here too it seems likely that business began at a set hour in the morning.[69] More specific information survives for the highest secular courts. The details of specific cases, where they survive, often indicate a specific hour at which proceedings were to begin.[70] In the earlier sixteenth century the lords of council convened routinely in the morning and sometimes in the afternoon. Afternoon sittings were more common in summer than winter, but generally unusual, occurring, for instance, on only just over 10 per cent of days on which the court sat in 1524–1525.[71] When the college of justice, Scotland's highest judicial court, was established in 1532, its judges were required to 'enter the tolbooth and council house at viii hours in the morning daily and shall sit until xi hours is struck'.[72] It seems possible, perhaps even likely, that such a schedule had been inherited from the body which it succeeded, the lords of council. Nevertheless, the specific time at which the lords of council began their proceedings, when the court reassembled after its break for lunch and when it concluded its business for the day went largely unrecorded in the official record.[73] Although hour consciousness was important for the routine organisation of judicial business, it was not sufficiently important to be recorded in the court's official records.

Hour consciousness was, however, evident in another quasi-legal environment – that of the notary. Notaries, though not necessarily trained in law at a university, were both literate and in possession of some legal knowledge. Their work took them into churches, where they might formally record the election of a parish clerk or the repayment of debts at the altar, but they also performed their duties in secular habitats and in the open air, where they certified agreements relating to property, trade, marriage and other matters.[74] The documents which they drafted and authenticated were characterised by detail and linguistic precision and became a point of legal reference. Increasingly frequently, the detail which was recorded included reference to the hour at which the notary's business had been conducted. As early as 12 August 1371 a Moray notary had recorded an instrument at the 'hora tertiarum'.[75] Although edited out of most of the published protocol books, such exactness – though not uniform and usually approximate, as indicated by the frequent use in the records of the word 'quasi' – was common in notarial instruments drawn up around the country in the later fifteenth and sixteenth centuries.[76] Since we know that there was a public clock in the vicinity, it is perhaps not surprising that an Edinburgh/Canongate notary such as John Robson almost always recorded his protocols by the hour.[77] Some notaries were even more precise than Robson. William Gray, who spent much of his working life in St Andrews, almost always recorded a specific time on the protocols which he drafted between 1553 and 1559; unusually, some of his records were timed to the half-hour, and one, indeed, to between noon and 12.15 pm.[78]

Such precision (at least to the hour) was not confined to notaries who worked in busy urban areas. Alexander Gow, who was active between 1540 and 1558 in Edinburgh, but also in Fife, Kinross-shire and Perthshire, often included a specific hour of the day in his protocols.[79] Many of these protocols were drafted at Abernethy, where another notary, Thomas Dalrymple, also recorded an hour-specific protocol, with specific reference to the local clock, in 1555.[80] Dalrymple, who in 1555 was mainly active in the small settlements and countryside around Markinch in Fife, almost always hour-dated his protocols whether they recorded business in churches or cemeteries, houses or hostelries, in his office or even on a public road.[81] Meanwhile, a third of the deeds recorded between 1511 and 1547 by the Selkirk notary John Chepman included an hour-specific element to the dating clause.[82] While some of these documents were witnessed in urban locations, such as the courthouse of Lauder or the mercat cross of Selkirk – where Chepman no doubt was able to see or hear the town's clock – other business was transacted in rural locations, including around a dozen protocols attested, usually in the afternoon, at Farnylee in Selkirkshire.[83] That Chepman almost always noted the time when at Farnlylee indicates that he had a reliable means of telling the time even in a remote location, perhaps drawing on his own clock, or alternatively a clock which had been installed by the rising and affluent Kerr family which owned an estate there.[84]

The notary's working day was lengthy. As indicated in Figure 12.1, a few protocols were recorded as early as six o'clock in the morning and some as late as eight and nine o'clock in the evening, though there was a clear tailing off in the middle of the day, presumably to allow for a midday meal. None of Thomas Dalrymple's protocols, for example, were timed between 12 noon and 1 pm. Why, however, did notaries bother recording the hour? One possibility is that hour consciousness was simply a product of training and tradition, and indicative, therefore, of an international legal culture in which the earliest Scottish notaries learnt their craft. Notaries were originally authorised either by imperial or by papal authority; only in 1469 did parliament quash imperial authorisation, replacing it by that of the king.[85] This suggests that, initially at least, notaries

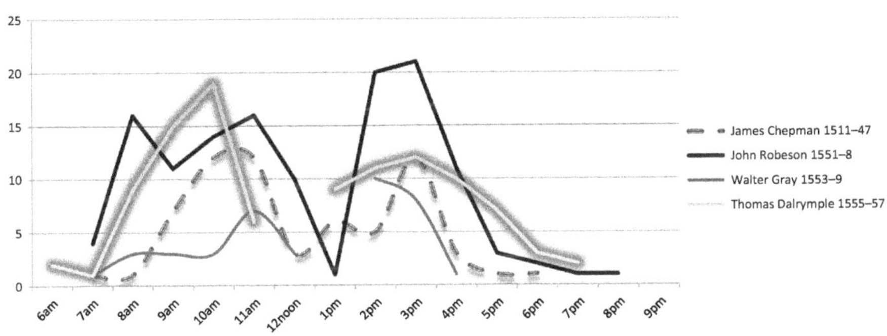

FIGURE 12.1 Hour-dating of protocols in selected notaries' protocol books.

were trained according to international norms and given that notaries could be approved by papal authority, Italy is one possible source of influence for Scottish practice. Certainly, even in the thirteenth century, protocols drafted in Genoa were usually dated by the canonical hour. It was not, however, customary, even in later centuries, to follow this practice in many other Italian towns, including Florence, Lucca and Pisa, in spite of the increasing precision which was often taken to describe the location at which notarial acts were witnessed in these towns.[86] More study needs to be undertaken of practice in the papal centres of Rome and Avignon,[87] but as things stand it is difficult to see why or how Genoese practices might have influenced those in Scotland, since this was not a town which maintained significant Scottish links.[88] Besides, papal authorization to create notaries was at least sometimes delegated to bishops in Scotland; even papal notaries need not, therefore, have had any close connections with Italy.[89]

If Genoese (and Roman) influence remains unproven in Scottish notarial practice, we might look elsewhere for precedents, especially to Scotland's immediate neighbours in England and the Low Countries. Exact times were occasionally noted in English notarial records, and more usually still in Flemish notarial documents, which (as in Genoa) might intimate the canonical hour, some other liturgical occasion or even a mealtime.[90] Notaries in both areas were, however – as in Scotland before c. 1370 but less exclusively thereafter – mostly of clerical standing and largely concerned with ecclesiastical business. While Flemish notaries did handle more commercial business by the fifteenth century, they (and the protocol books in which they recorded their transactions) seem never to have developed the significance which both attained in Italy and Scotland.[91] Notaries were, indeed, relatively rare in both England and the Low Countries. Even in the great emporia of Bruges, Ghent and Ypres only 52 have been identified between 1280 and 1440 compared with at least 75 known to have been active in Scotland between 1370 and 1420 alone.[92] Influence from abroad in Scottish notarial practice – including hour consciousness – is, then, possible. Against this, however, it should be remembered that just as it became more common for Scottish notaries to add mention of the hour to their documents, so they were less and less likely to have been trained abroad. Many, though far from all, Scottish notaries were graduates, but those that were, were increasingly able to study at one of the three Scottish universities founded in the fifteenth century. Their apprenticeship was more likely to have been undertaken in the diocesan courts of Scotland than abroad.[93] Of course, we cannot rule out significant foreign influences in both Scottish universities and episcopal courts, but it seems just as likely that seemingly idiosyncratic notarial practices in Scotland coincided with a revolutionary expansion in notarial activity in Scotland from the later fourteenth century.[94] It should perhaps be added that Bill Scott, the scholar who identified this 'revolution', was not someone prone to unwarranted exaggeration.

Whatever drove the inclusion of hour timing in Scottish protocols – whether it was foreign influence or an indigenous development – Scottish notaries could only record the time on their documents if they had a means by which to tell the time and if they were personally able to tell the time. They were clearly not alone in this skill, as clocks had been erected even in some rural areas and even women of relatively humble status, such as Margaret Gibson in her Dunfermline bakehouse, could count the hours. Hour consciousness was not, then, exclusive to towns, to men or to legal professionals. But the exclusively male and predominantly urban-based notarial branch of the legal profession was the first to deem it important to record the specific hour at which business was transacted. This is not necessarily to refute the deterministic and oft-quoted assertion by David Landes that 'the clock did not create an interest in time measurement; the interest in time measurement led to the invention of the clock'.[95] Still, clocks had appeared in late medieval and early modern Scotland for reasons other than an intellectual curiosity in time. They were fashionable and prestigious items as well as functional instruments, which required significant technological and financial investment. As demonstrated by the incident in Aberdeen with which this article commenced, they were not just machines which enabled individuals to mark moments in their daily lives. They symbolised communal identity and they constituted an ostentatious display of status and authority.

That, moreover, notaries could tell the time is an insufficient explanation for them demonstrating that skill in their notarial practice. So why did they? It is difficult to link their awareness of the hour to Le Goff's arguments about the secularisation of time. It is not clear that notarial practice was related to monetary considerations. Notaries set down a marker, not an account of the extent of their labour for which they might be billed. Only rarely did notaries record more than one instrument per day, so it seems unlikely that noting the hour was an organisational matter, to distinguish quickly between one protocol and another. Indeed, noting the hour may not have been primarily for the advantage of the notary at all. In most (though not all) protocols, the hour clause appeared not at the beginning of the record, along with the other markers of time (the day, the month, the year, the papal year and the indication), but rather towards the end of the document, immediately before the naming of witnesses.[96] This perhaps suggests that noting the hour was as much for the benefit of witnesses as it was for that of the notary. We may speculate that the hour and the location acted as a reminder to otherwise busy witnesses of what they had witnessed, should their memory be called upon at a later date. This is not, of course, to argue that late medieval and early modern people had suddenly become busier than those who lived in the pre-clock centuries. Rather, it is to suggest that hour timing – especially perhaps in towns where curfews, market regulations, work and church services were all, to some extent, framed by reference to the hour – had now become a social and cultural tool, designed to assist both the secular and clerical population in the ordering of their lives and memories.[97] Indeed, it is significant that in 1554–1555 the authorities of Edinburgh deemed it necessary to spend £39 5s 6d on the installation of a temporary bell and a borrowed clock while repairs were undertaken on the town's principal clock. In Edinburgh at least, the burgh council was acknowledging that even the temporary absence of a clock constituted a significant inconvenience. Reference to the hour had become an important element in how many people, notaries and their witnesses included, now framed their daily life.[98] And if so, it might be concluded that, in the myriad of private agreements which they recorded, notaries had become the guardians of private memory.

Notes

1 Aberdeen City and Aberdeenshire Archives (hereafter ACAA), Aberdeen Council, Baillie and Guild Court Registers (hereafter ACR), vol. 20, pp. 32–3. Public humiliation of the sort imposed in this instance was often imposed on others too who were deemed to have transgressed social convention. See, for example, ACR, vol. 15, pp. 570, 714, 734.

2 J. Le Goff, *Time, Work and Culture in the Middle Ages*, ed. A. Goldhammer, Chicago: Chicago University Press, 1980, pp. 46–7, and N. Atkinson, *The Noisy Renaissance: Sound, Architecture and Florentine Urban Life*, University Park, PA: Penn State University Press, 2006, pp. 184–92.

3 Le Goff, *Time, Work and Culture*, pp. 48, 35. See too the similarly influential article focused on a later period, but which makes some similar points; E.P. Thompson, 'Time, work-discipline, and industrial capitalism', *Past and Present* 38, 1967, pp. 56–97.

4 See, however, A.R. MacDonald, 'Urban archives: Endless possibilities', *Journal of Irish Scottish Studies* 9(2), 2019, pp. 29–49, at pp. 45–8, where the author has independently of me identified the example of Robert Hoveson, offering too some interpretations of his actions.

5 It is not known for certain when mechanical clocks were invented, but see L. Thorndike, 'Invention of the mechanical clock, about 1271 A.D.', *Speculum* 16(2), 1941, pp. 242–3, and J.D. North, *God's Clockmaker: Richard of Wallingford and the Invention of Time*, London: Hambledon, 2005.

6 ACR, vol. 15, pp. 16, 734; Dundee City Archives (hereafter DCA), Burgh and Head Court Books (hereafter BHCB), vol. 2 ('The Book of the Church, 1454-1525'), fol. 112v; *Protocol Books of Thomas Johnsoun, 1528–1578*, ed. J. Beveridge and J. Russell, Edinburgh: Scottish Record Society, 1920, no. 82; *Registrum de Panmure*, ed. J. Stuart, 2 vols, Edinburgh: s. n., 1874, vol. 2, p. 242.

7 Sometimes, however, belfries collapsed on account of lightning. See, for example, *Registrum Monasterii S. Marie de Cambuskenneth, A. D. 1147–1535*, ed. W. Fraser, Edinburgh: Grampian Club, 1872, no. 62; *The Charters of the Priory of Beauly*, ed. E.C. Batten, London: Grampian Club, 1877, p. 219.

8 On the Cistercians and bell towers, see T. Coomans, 'Cistercian architecture or architecture of the Cistercians?', in M.B. Bruun (ed.) *The Cambridge Companion to the Cistercian Order*, Cambridge: Cambridge University Press, 2012, pp. 151–69, at pp. 153, 159, and J. Burton and J. Kerr, *The Cistercians in the Middle Ages*, Woodbridge: Boydell, 2011, p. 76. For the canonical day, see Ibid., pp. 104–6, and E. Jamroziak, *The Cistercian Order in Medieval Europe, 1090–1500*, Abingdon: Routledge, 2013, p. 62.

9 I am very grateful to James Brown for sharing with me his research on this matter.

10 R. Fawcett, 'Culross abbey', in T.N. Kinder (ed.) *Perspectives for an Architecture of Solitude: Essays on Cistercians, Art and Architecture in Honour of Peter Fergusson*, Citeaux: Brepols, 2004, pp. 81–99, at pp. 95–7; R. Fawcett, *Scottish Architecture from the Accession of the Stewarts to the Reformation, 1371–1560*, Edinburgh: Edinburgh University Press, 1994, pp. 91–3; and *Records of the Monastery of Kinloss*, ed. J. Stuart, Edinburgh: Society of Antiquaries of Scotland, 1872, p. 33.

11 R.W.M. Clouston, 'The bells of Perthshire', *Proceedings of the Society of Antiquaries of Scotland* (hereafter *PSAS*) 122, 1992, pp. 453–508, at pp. 469–70, 479–83, 492, 505; F.C. Eeles, 'The church bells of Linlithgowshire', *PSAS* 47, 1912, pp. 61–94, at

pp. 63–9, 78–81, 93–4; F.C. Eeles and R.W.M. Clouston, 'The church and other bells of Wigtownshire', *PSAS* 107, 1975–1976, pp. 261–74, at pp. 265–7; and F.C. Eeles and R.W.M. Clouston, 'The church and other bells of Aberdeenshire [Part I]', *PSAS* 90, 1956–1957, pp. 130–60, at pp. 143, 147. On early medieval ecclesiastical hand bells, see F.C. Eeles, 'The Guthrie bell and its shrine', *PSAS* 60, 1926, pp. 409–20.

12 L. Leroux, *Cloches et société médiévale: Les sonneries de Tournai au Moyen Âge*, Louvain-la-Neuve: Tournai-Art et histoire, 2001, pp. 26–43.

13 *Cartularium Ecclesiae S. Nicholai Aberdonensis*, ed. J. Cooper, 2 vols, Aberdeen: New Spalding Club, 1888–1892, vol. 1, p. 15; vol. 2, p. 13.

14 ACR, vol. 19, p. 258. The best studied of the religious houses in Aberdeen is that of the Carmelites (R.M. Spearman, 'Aberdeen Carmelite friary: The documentary evidence', in J.A. Stones (ed.) *Three Scottish Carmelite Friaries: Excavations at Aberdeen, Linlithgow and Perth, 1980–86*, Edinburgh: Society of Antiquaries of Scotland, 1989, pp. 28–34), but there is no hint that the White Friars possessed bells or clocks. For the town's hand bell, see, for example, ACR, vol. 7, pp. 3, 27, 34, 186, 193, 238, 245, 260, 357, 522, 533, 550–1, 579, 633, 752, 811, 814, 963, 966.

15 H. Boece, *Murthlacensium et aberdonensium episcoporum vitae*, ed. J. Moir, Aberdeen: New Spalding Club, 1894, p. 95, and *King's College Chapel, Aberdeen: Its Fittings, Ornaments and Ceremonial in the Sixteenth Century*, ed. F.C. Eeles, Edinburgh: Oliver & Boyd, 1956, p. 22. See too J. Geddes, 'The bells', in J. Geddes (ed.) *King's College Chapel, Aberdeen, 1500–2000*, Aberdeen: Northern Universities Press, 2000, pp. 109–14.

16 Boece, *Murthlacensium et aberdonensium episcoporum vitae*, p. 24. See too P.J. Shipton, 'Bells restored to St Machar's', in J.H. Alexander et al., *The Restoration of St Machar's Cathedral*, Aberdeen: Friends of St Machar's Cathedral, 1991, pp. 26–32.

17 L.J. Macfarlane, *William Elphinstone and the Kingdom of Scotland, 1431–1514: The Struggle for Order*, Aberdeen: Aberdeen University Press, 1985, pp. 275, 314–6. Skellat was a generic name given to small bells which might be hung or hand rung. The meaning of the other bell's name is less obvious, though 'schocht' means 'to seek'.

18 B.S.M. Campbell, 'Benchmarking medieval economic development: England, Wales, Scotland and Ireland, *c.* 1290', *Economic History Review*, new series 61, 2008, pp. 896–945, at p. 910; R.E. Tyson, 'People in the two towns', in E.P.D. Dennison, D. Ditchburn and M. Lynch (eds) *Aberdeen before 1800: A new history*, East Linton: Tuckwell Press, 2002, pp. 111–28, at pp. 111–12. Estimates of Tournai's population are more difficult to come by, though see J.C. Russell, 'Late ancient and medieval population', *Transactions of the American Philosophical Society*, new series 48(3), 1958, pp. 1–152, at p. 84; N.J.G. Pounds, 'Population and settlement in the low countries and northern France in the later middle ages', *Revue belge de philologie et d'histoire* 49(2), 1971, pp. 369–402, at p. 402; W. Blockmans and W. Prevenier, *The Promised Lands: The Low Countries under Burgundian Rule, 1369–1530*, Philadelphia: University of Pennsylvania Press, 1988, pp. 153–4; and J. Roosen and D.R. Curtis, 'The "light touch" of the black death in the southern Netherlands: An urban trick', *Economic History Review*, new series 72(1), 2019, pp. 32–56, at p. 39. I have not been able to track down P. Lourens and J. Lucassen, *Inwoneraantallen van Nederlandse steden, ca. 1300–1800*, Amsterdam: University of Amsterdam Press, 1997.

19 ACR, vol. 5/2, pp. 767, 779; vol. 6, p. 978; vol. 7, p. 61; *Extracts from the Council Register of the Burgh of Aberdeen, 1398–1570*, ed. J. Stuart, Aberdeen: Spalding Club, 1844 (hereafter *Aberdeen Council Register*), pp. 112–4. See too D. McKay, 'The duties of the medieval parish clerk', *Innes Review* 19(1), 1968, pp. 32–9.

20 Brugge, Stadsarchief 206: Stadsrekeningen, 1390–1391, fol. 111r; 1391–1392, fols 95r–95v; 1392–1393, fols 96r–97v; 1393–1394, pt 2, fol. 66v; 1394–1395, fol. 81v; 1395–1396, fol. 83v; 1396–1397, fol. 92v; 1397–1398, fol. 95v; 1398–1399, fol. 92v; Stadsarchief 277: Presentwijnen, 1487–1488, fol. 9r. On the bells in Bruges more generally, see A. Janssens, *Middeleeuws Brugge door de ogen van Hans Memling (1465–1494)*, Leuven: Davidsfonds, 2015, pp. 43–5.

21 ACR, vol. 6, p. 978; vol. 7, p. 61.

22 C. Hawes, 'The urban community in fifteenth-century Scotland: Language, law and political practice', *Urban History* 44(3), 2017, pp. 365–80, at pp. 373–4.

23 *Extracts from the Records of the Burgh of Edinburgh, 1403–1589*, ed. J.D. Marwick, 5 vols, Edinburgh: Scottish Burgh Record Society, 1869–1892 (hereafter *Edin. Recs*), vol. 1, p. 37, and BHCB, vol. 3, 18 July 1554 (unpaginated).

24 *Edin. Recs*, vol. 1, pp. 50, 291, and *Aberdeen Council Register*, p. 92.

25 *Scotichronicon*, ed. D.E.R. Watt et al., 9 vols, Aberdeen/Edinburgh: Aberdeen University Press, 1987–1998, vol. 8, pp. 78–9, and *Ayr Burgh Accounts, 1534–1624*, ed. G.S. Pryde, Edinburgh: Scottish History Society, 1937, p. 20.

26 N. Atkinson, 'Seeing sound: Mapping the Florentine soundscape', in N. Terpstra and C. Rose (eds) *Mapping Space, Sense, and Movement in Florence: Historical GIS and the Early Modern City*, Abingdon: Routledge, 2016, pp. 149–68.

27 For 'Columba', 'George' and 'Mary' at Dunkeld, see *Rentale Dunkeldense*, ed. R.K. Hannay, Edinburgh: Scottish Historical Society, 1915, p. 314, and for 'Mary', 'Anne' and 'Jerome' at Kinloss, see *Records of Kinloss*, p. 33. The bells of St John's parish church in Perth were, by contrast, named *Ave Maria* and *Agnus dei*; Clouston, 'Bells of Perthshire', pp. 525–41.

28 Exodus 28: 33–4; 39: 25–6.

29 *King's College Chapel*, ed. F.C. Eeles, pp. 90–2.

30 On bells and remembering the dead, see, for example, BHCB, vol. 3, 8 January 1553–1554 (unpaginated); St Andrew University Library and Special Collections, B65/23/16; B65/23/63; B65/23/119; B65/23/187; B65/23/218; B65/23/225; B65/23/272; B65/23/297; *Registrum Episcopatus Glasguensis*, ed. C.N. Innes, 2 vols, Edinburgh: Maitland Club, 1843, vol. 2, pp. 312–4; 537–40. On Halloween and All Souls, see *Ayr Burgh Accounts*, pp. 25, 75, 78, 83; *Edin. Recs*, vol. 2, pp. 338, 351, 354, 363. See too M. Cowan, *Death, Life, and Religious Change in Scottish Towns, c. 1350–1560*, Manchester: Manchester University Press, 2012, p. 29.

31 For the Aberdeen example, see note 13; for the Dundee instance, see DCA, TC/CC1/43.

32 *The Gild Court Book of Dunfermline, 1433–1597*, ed. E.P.D. Torrie, Edinburgh: Scottish Record Society, 1986, p. 53; R.W.M. Clouston, 'The bells of Perthshire: St John's Kirk', *PSAS* 124, 1994, pp. 525–41; and BHCB, vol. 4, 16 September 1556 (unpaginated).

33 M.P.J. Martens et al., 'Texts, images and sounds in the urban environment', in A. Brown and J. Dumolyn (eds) *Medieval Bruges, c. 850–1550*, Cambridge: Cambridge University Press, 2018, p. 401.

34 See G. Dohrn-van Rossum, *Die Geschichte der Stunde. Uhren und moderne Zeitordnungen*, Munich: Deutscher Taschenbuch Verlag, 1995, pp. 110–14.

35 P. Dubuis, 'Des horloges dans les montagnes. Premières explorations en Valais XVe–XIXe siècles', *Vallesia. Bulletin annuel de la Bibliothèque et des Archives cantonales du Valais*, 1993, pp. 91–108, at p. 93. On the spread of mechanical clocks elsewhere, see C.H. Cipolla, *Clocks and Culture, 1300–1700*, New York: Norton, 1977, pp. 40–1; Dohrn-van Rossum, *Geschichte der Stunde*, ch. 5, and P. Glennie and N. Thrift, *Shaping the Day: A History of Timekeeping in England and Wales, 1300–1800*, Oxford: Oxford University Press, 2009, pp. 75–7.

36 V. Avery, *Vulcan's Forge in Venus' City: The Story of Bronze in Venice, 1350–1650*, Oxford: Oxford University Press, 2011, p. 84 and L. Gilliodts van Severen, *Le Carillon de Bruges*, Bruges: De Plancke, 1912, pp. 19–22.

37 Ayr, Ayrshire Archives (hereafter AAA), B6/12/1 (Ayr Burgh Court Book, 1428–1478), fol. 120v; ACR, vol. 5/2, p. 778; *Charters and Documents Relating to the Burgh of Peebles*, ed. W. Chambers, Edinburgh: Scottish Burgh Record Society, 1872, pp. 147, 195, 197, 200.

38 For Dumbarton, see Dumbarton Heritage Centre, West Dunbartonshire Archives (hereafter WDA), 1/10/5/2; for Dundee, Edinburgh, National Records of Scotland (hereafter NRS), CS6 (Acta Dominorum Consilii et Sessionis), vol. 20, fols

111r–112v; BHCB, vol. 3, 8 January 1553–1554; 3 September 1554; 11 September 1554 (unpaginated); *Acts of the Lords of Council in Public Affairs, 1501–1554: Selections from Acta Dominorum Concilii*, ed. R.K. Hannay, Edinburgh: H.M. General Register House, 1932, p. 547; for Edinburgh: *Registrum Domus de Soltre necnon Ecclesie Collegiate S Trinitatis proper Edinburgh*, ed. D. Laing, Edinburgh: Bannatyne Club, 1861, p. 158; *Edin. Recs*, vol. 2, p. 301; *Edinburgh Burgh Records: The Burgh Accounts*, ed. R. Adam, 2 vols, Edinburgh: Scottish Burgh Record Society, 1899, vol. 1, pp. 71, 103, 139–40, 171, 195, 233, 276; for Haddington: 'Haddington records: Books of the common good', ed. H.M. Paton, *Transactions of the East Lothian Antiquarian and Field Naturalists Society* 7, 1958, 46–80, at pp. 48–57, passim; for Lanark: *Extracts from the Records of the Royal Burgh of Lanark, A.D. 1150–1722*, ed. R. Renwick, Glasgow: Carson & Nicol, 1893, pp. 12, 16, 17; for Selkirk: P.S.M. Symms, 'Social control in a sixteenth-century burgh: A study of the burgh court book of Selkirk, 1503–45', unpublished PhD thesis, University of Edinburgh, 1986, pp. 64, 243–4; and for Stirling: *Extracts from the Records of the Royal Burgh of Stirling A.D. 1519–1666*, ed. R. Renwick, Glasgow: Scottish Burgh Records Society, 1887 (hereafter *Stirling Recs*), pp. 2, 8, 11, 45–6, 53; *Accounts of the Lord High Treasurer of Scotland*, ed. T. Dickson et al., 13 vols, Edinburgh: H.M. General Register House, 1877–1978 (hereafter *TA*), vol. 2, p. 159. For Old Aberdeen, see Eeles (ed.) *King's College Chapel*, p. 22. Less certain is Perth, though one of the town's bells was attached to some sort of timing device; Clouston, 'Bells of Perthshire: St John's Kirk, Perth', p. 527, but see too p. 537.

39 NRS, NP1/19 (Protocol Book of Thomas Dalrymple), no. 15; AAA, B6/28/1, p. 44. Abernethy was erected as a burgh of barony in 1458/1459 (G.S. Pryde, *The Burghs of Scotland: A Critical List*, ed. A.A.M. Duncan, Oxford: Oxford University Press, 1965, no. 146), though it is unlikely to have housed a significant number of inhabitants.

40 *TA*, vol. 4, p. 324; vol. 7, pp. 280, 459; vol. 8, pp. 109–10; J.G. Dunbar, *Scottish Royal Palaces: The Architecture of the Royal Residences during the Late Medieval and Early Renaissance Periods*, Edinburgh: Tuckwell Press, 1999, pp. 126, 175; *Ledger of Andrew Halyburton, Conservator of the Privileges of the Scotch Nation in the Netherlands, 1492–1503*, ed. C. Innes, Edinburgh: H.M. General Register House, 1867, p. 184; *Edinburgh Burgh Accounts*, vol. 1, p. 139; and J. Raine, *The History and Antiquities of North Durham*, London: J.B. Nichols & Son, 1852, p. 348. See too Ibid., p. 125 for bells and a clock at near-by Holy Island in 1533.

41 Glennie and Thrift, *Shaping the Day*, p. 128.

42 ACR, vol. 5/2, p. 778.

43 NRS, CS6, vol. 20, fols 111r–112r, and BHCB, vol. 3, 8 January 1553–1554 (unpaginated).

44 *Aberdeen Council Register*, p. 165; BHCB, vol. 3, 3 September 1554 (unpaginated) and *Stirling Recs*, p. 45. It should be noted however that in Edinburgh painting was simply functional, designed to protect against rust and weather damage: *Edinburgh Burgh Accounts*, 140. On clocks as diplomatic gifts, see *TA*, vol. 4, p. 324; and for elsewhere in Europe, V. Pérez Álvarez, 'The role of the mechanical clock in medieval science', *Endeavour* 39(1), 2015, pp. 63–68, at p. 65.

45 J. Muendel, 'Friction and lubrication in medieval Europe: the emergence of olive oil as a superior agent', *Isis* 86(3), 1995, pp. 373–93. For chords, see e.g. AAA, B6/12/1, fol. 120v; WDA, 1/10/5/2; for olive oil used to lubricate the clock at Peebles, see *Charters and Documents Relating to the Burgh of Peebles*, pp. 197, 200; for that applied to the bells in Ayr, see *Ayr Burgh Accounts*, pp. 21, 75, 94, 96; and for the cost of bells, 'Haddington records', p. 54.

46 Glennie and Thrift, *Shaping the Day*, pp. 33, 36. On the mathematical and technological aspects of early clocks, see Ibid., pp. 31–6.

47 'Haddington records', pp. 48, 51, 55 and A.J.S. Gibson and T.C. Smout, *Prices, Food and Wages in Scotland, 1550–1780*, Cambridge: Cambridge University Press, 1995, p. 313.

48 *Ayr Burgh Accounts*, p. 75.

49 ACR, vol. 7, p. 478; vol. 15, pp. 305, 384, 433, 567. See too J.P. Foggie, *Renaissance Religion in Urban Scotland: The Dominican Order, 1450–1560*, Leiden: Brill, 2003, p. 294.
50 Cipolla, *Clocks and Culture,* p. 64. On clockmakers generally, see Dohrn-van Rossum, *Geschichte der Stunde*, ch. 6.
51 NRS, CS6, vol. 20, fol. 111, and Symms, 'Social control in a sixteenth-century burgh', pp. 64, 244 n. 83.
52 *Ledger of Andrew Halyburton*, p. 184; ACR, vol. 15, p. 74. For clockmakers and menders in Bruges, see Severen, *Le Carillon*, pp. 27–33.
53 See, e.g., R.S. Wieck, *The Medieval Calendar: Locating Time in the Middle Ages*, New York: The Morgan Library, 2017, pp. 13–28.
54 This remained until very recently the case and perhaps still applies: 'We didn't have clocks at home. No one wore a watch in case it was lost up a cow's innards! In farming you live by daylight and nature, so clocks aren't important, even in the 1970s and 1980s. It is time to get up, to milk the cows, to feed the pigs, to eat, to sleep. No one says that it's five o'clock or twenty-five to eight. When I finally got a watch my parents spent time speaking in a very stilted manner saying, "it is time to feed the calves which is four o'clock"'. I am very grateful to Morag Evans for her memories relating to clocks and time when growing up in rural Moray.
55 D. Lindsay of the Mount, *Ane Satyre of the Thrie Estaitis*, ed. R. Lyall, Edinburgh: Canongate, 1989, p. 175 and G. Walker, '"Faill nocht to teme your bleddir": Passing time in Sir David Lindsay's *Ane Satyre of the Thrie Estaitis*', *Medieval English Theatre* 22, 2000, pp. 52–8. I am grateful to Eila Williamson for drawing this article to my attention.
56 *Edin. Recs*, vol. 2, pp. 138–9.
57 *The Burgh Records of Dunfermline*, ed. E. Beveridge, Edinburgh: William Brown, 1917, p. 126.
58 For example, *TA*, vol. 1, pp. 245–50, 296–7, 300–1, 346–7, 349–50, 379–80; vol. 2, pp. 25, 106, 272, 278, 382–3, 390, 396, 405, 442. (Pay was very occasionally made for half days of work: Ibid., vol. 1, p. 245; vol. 2, p. 382.) See too M. Armoux, 'Relations salariale et temps du travail dans l'industrie médiévale', *Le Moyen Age* 115(3), 2009, pp. 557–81 and Gibson and Smout, *Prices, Food and Wages*, chs 8 and 9, esp. pp. 277–85.
59 *The Records of the Parliaments of Scotland to 1707*, ed. K.M. Brown et al., St Andrews, 2007–2020, <www.rps.ac.uk> (accessed 10 February 2019) (hereafter *RPS*), 1469/29.
60 *TA*, vol. 3, pp. 180, 196, 337; vol. 4, pp. 298, 302, 454, 531.
61 R.T. Balmer, 'The operation of sand clocks and their medieval development', *Technology and Culture* 19, 1978, pp. 615–32, at p. 622.
62 London, Victoria and Albert Museum, F.48 ('Oil painting: Mary Stuart, Queen of Scots, with an Open Watch in Her Hand').
63 *RPS*, 1428/3/9.
64 *RPS*, 1436/10/9; 1504/3/52.
65 ACR, vol. 4, p. 33; *The Perth Guildry Book, 1452–1601*, ed. M.L. Stavert, Edinburgh: Scottish Record Society, no. 9; and *Edin. Recs*, vol. 1, p. 157.
66 For example, *RPS*, 1467/1/4; *Protocol Books of Thomas Johnsoun,* no. 82; ACR, vol. 5/2, pp. 714, 784; vol. 15, pp. 54, 719; St Andrews University Library, B65/2365c; B65/23/72c.
67 P. Brand, 'Lawyers' time in England in the later middle ages', in C. Humphrey and W.M. Ormrod (eds) *Time in the Medieval World*, York: York Medieval Press, 2001, pp. 73–104. No similar study has been undertaken for Scotland, though see S. Ollivant, *The Court of the Official in Pre-reformation Scotland*, Edinburgh: Stair Society, 1982, pp. 46–9, and occasional comment on the matter in D. Ditchburn, 'Religion, ritual and the rhythm of the year in later medieval St Andrews', in M. Brown and K. Stevenson (eds) *Medieval St Andrews: Church, Cult, City*, Woodbridge: Boydell, 2017, pp. 99–116, at pp. 108–9, 112–5.

68 *The Sheriff Court Book of Fife, 1515–1522*, ed. W.C. Dickinson, Edinburgh: Scottish History Society, 1928, pp. xxiv, n. 7, 406–7. See too *The Court Book of the Barony of Carnwath, 1523–1543*, ed. W.C. Dickinson, Edinburgh: Scottish History Society, 1937, pp. lxxiv–lxxviii.
69 Ollivant, *Court of the Official*, p. 49.
70 See, for example, *RPS*, 1430/54; 1488/10/4; 1493/5/30; 1493/5/58; 1494/11/105; 1504/3/6; 1504/3/7.
71 NRS, CS5, vol. 35, fols 1r–219r.
72 *Facsimiles of the National Manuscripts of Scotland*, 3 vols, Southampton: Ordnance Survey, 1867–1871, vol. 3, no. 20. By the seventeenth century, and perhaps earlier, the time of the court's sittings varied according to season. See J. Finlay, *Men of Law in Pre-Reformation Scotland*, East Linton: Tuckwell Press, 2000, p. 102, n. 104.
73 See, however, *RPS*, 1493/5/30; 1493/5/58; 1494/11/105.
74 See also the contribution by Frankot in this volume.
75 *Registrum Episcopatus Moraviensis*, ed. C. Innes, Edinburgh: Bannatyne Club, 1837, p. 172.
76 For published volumes in which the hour has been largely omitted, see, e.g., *Protocol Book of Gavin Ros NP, 1512–1532*, ed. J. Anderson and F.J. Grant, Edinburgh: Scottish Record Society, 1908; *Protocol Book of Sir William Corbet, 1529–1555*, ed. J. Anderson and W. Angus, Edinburgh: Scottish Record Society, 1911, though see no. 39; *Protocol Book of Sir Alexander Gaw, 1540–1558*, ed. J. Anderson and W. Angus, Edinburgh: Scottish Record Society, 1910, though see nos 12, 40, 51, 102. The editorial practice is especially clear in *The Calendar of Fearn: Text and Additions, 1471–1667*, ed. R.J. Adam, Edinburgh: Scottish History Society, 1991, Appendix A ('Ross entries in the protocol book of William Gray'), pp. 225–38, which includes the hour dating where protocols have been transcribed in full, but not in calendared entries. For examples of hour-timed instruments dating from the fifteenth century, see *RPS*, A1440/2/1 (drafted at Edinburgh in 1440); A1463/10/1 (Edinburgh, 1463); StAUL, UYSL110/PW/40 (St Andrews, 1460); UYSL110/PW/46 (St Andrews, 1468); B65/23/106 (St Andrews, 1487); B65/23/148 (St Andrews, 1497); NRS, B58/18/41 (Peebles, 1478); and for ACAA, Sasine Register, vol. 1, pp. 300–50, passim. That this was not uniform practice is, however, evident from three fifteenth-century Dumbarton instruments: WDA, 1/3/71 (1448); 1/3/3 (1469); 1/3/73 (1496).
77 NRS, NP1/14.
78 *The St Andrews Portion of the Protocol Book of William Gray, 1553–1559*, ed. R. Smart, Edinburgh: Scottish Record Society, 2015, *passim*, esp. nos 2, 12, 15, 17, 29, 35, 37. Even though most of his protocols were timed by the hour, occasionally (ibid., nos 6, 19, 25) Gray omitted the hour clause. He continued to date by the hour after he left St Andrews to work in Sutherland and Caithness (Edinburgh, National Library of Scotland, Dep. 314/25, fols 16r–43v, 45r–125v).
79 NRS, NP 1/7, fols 2v, 4r, 6r, 6v, 7v, 8r, 15r, 27r, 28r, 29v, 31r, 32r, 32v.
80 NRS, NP 1/19, no. 15.
81 NRS, NP1/19.
82 *Selkirk Protocol Books, 1511–1547*, ed. T. Maley and W. Elliot, Edinburgh: Stair Society, 1993, nos. A73, B31, B35.
83 *Selkirk Protocol Books*, nos A31, A36, A51–3; A55, A61–2, A78, A81, B13, B16–18, B21, B39, B41, B50.
84 *Registrum Magni Sigilli Regum Scotorum*, ed. J.M. Thomson, 11 vols, new edn, Edinburgh: Scottish Record Society and Clark Constable, 1984, vol. 2, no. 3443; vol. 3, no. 852.
85 *RPS*, 1469/20.
86 S.A. Epstein, 'Business cycles and the sense of time in medieval Genoa', *Business History Review* 62, 1988, pp. 238–60, esp. pp. 251–9. I am very grateful to my colleagues Catherine Lawless and Christine Meek, and to Frances Andrews, for advice regarding practice elsewhere in Italy.

87 See, however, *Il protocollo notarile di Lorenzo Staglia (1372)*, ed. I.L. Sanfilippo, Rome: Società romana di storia patria, 1986; *I protocolli di Johannes Nicolai Pauli. Un notaio romano del '300 (1348–1379)*, ed. R. Mosti, [Rome]: École française de Rome, 1982; and *Il notaio romano tra sovranita' pontificia e autonomia comunale (secoli XIV–XVI)*, ed. M.L. Lombardo, Milan: Giuffrè editore, 2012.

88 See, however, *Exchequer Rolls of Scotland*, ed. J. Stuart et al., 23 vols, Edinburgh: H.M. General Register House, 1878–1908, vol. 6, pp. 125, 202, 303, 395–6, 494, 594; vol. 7, p. 378, for the Genoese merchant who settled in mid-fifteenth-century Kirkcudbright, where he became the town's custumar. See too E. Frankot, 'A Genoese merchant in medieval Aberdeen – A case from the lost "volume three"', *Aberdeen Registers*, Aberdeen, 2016, <https://aberdeenregisters.org/2016/11/22/a-genoese-merchant-in-medieval-aberdeen-a-case-from-the-lost-volume-three/> (accessed 4 December 2019).

89 For example, *Calendar of Papal Registers: Petitions, 1342–1419*, ed. W.H. Bliss, London: H.M. Stationary Office, 1896, p. 401; *Calendar of Scottish Supplications to Rome. Volume VI, 1471–1492*, ed. A. Macquarrie, R.J. Tanner, and A.I. Dunlop, Edinburgh: Scottish Record Society, 2017, no. 1804.

90 C.R. Cheney, *Notaries Public in England in the Thirteenth and Fourteenth Centuries*, Oxford: Clarendon Press, 1972, pp. 117–18; M.T. Clanchy, *From Memory to Written Record: England, 1066–1307*, 2nd edn, Oxford: Blackwell 1993, p. 299; and J.M. Murray, *Notarial Instruments in Flanders between 1280 and 1452*, Brussels: Académie royale de Belgique, 1995, p. 115.

91 No notarial protocol books are known to survive from medieval England; N. Ramsey, 'Scriveners and notaries as legal intermediaries in later medieval England', in J. Kermode (ed.) *Enterprise and Individuals in Fifteenth-century England*, Stroud: Alan Sutton, 1991, pp. 118–31, at p. 125. In England, scriveners dealt with matters similar to those handled by notaries in Scotland, though very few of their records survive too. There is no indication of hour consciousness in that discussed in A.E.B. Owen, 'A scrivener's notebook from Bury St Edmunds', *Archives* 14, 1979, pp. 16–22.

92 J.M. Murray, 'Failure of corporation: Notaries public in medieval Bruges', *Journal of Medieval History* 12(2), 1986, pp. 155–66, at esp. p. 157 and W.W. Scott, 'William Cranston, notary public *c.* 1395–1425, and some contemporaries', in H.L. Macqueen (ed.) *Miscellany Seven*, Edinburgh: Stair Society, 2015, pp. 125–32, at p. 130.

93 J. Durkan, 'The early Scottish notary', in I.B. Cowan and D. Shaw (eds) *The Renaissance and Reformation in Scotland: Essays in Honour of Gordon Donaldson*, Edinburgh: Scottish Academic Press, 1983, pp. 22–3, 29–31. On notaries in Scotland more generally, see too W. Angus, 'Notarial protocol books, 1469–1700', in J.C. Brown (ed.) *An Introductory Survey of the Sources and Literature of Scots Law*, Edinburgh: Stair Society, 1936, pp. 289–300, and E. Ewan, 'Protocol books and towns in medieval Scotland', in W. Prevenier and T. de Hemptinne (eds) *La diplomatique urbaine en Europe au Moyen Âge. Actes du congrès de la Commission internationale de diplomatique, Gand 25-29 août 1998*, Louvain/Apeldoorn: Garrant, 2000, pp. 143–55.

94 Scott, 'William Cranston', p. 125.

95 D.S. Landes, *Revolution in Time: Clocks and the Making of the Modern World*, 2nd edn, London: Viking, 1999, p. 53.

96 For a slight variation, with the hour and witnesses appearing at the beginning of the protocol, see DCA, Burgh Protocol Book, vol. 1 (1518–1534), passim.

97 I have been influenced here by arguments formulated in B.H. Snyder, 'From vigilance to busyness: A neo-Weberian approach to clock time', *Sociological Theory* 31(3), 2013, pp. 243–66, esp. p. 258.

98 *Edinburgh Burgh Accounts*, vol. 1, pp. 139–40.

13

ANDREW ALANSON

Man of law in the Aberdeen Council Register, c. 1440–c. 1475?

*Andrew R.C. Simpson**

Revisiting trusted representatives in medieval Aberdeen

This chapter revisits one aspect of an earlier study, which considered the extent to which one can identify 'men of law' in medieval Aberdeen.[1] As was explained there, the meaning of the term 'men of law', sometimes given in Latin as *juris periti*, is difficult to reconstruct, and this may be because it was understood rather loosely in the period in question.[2] It could sometimes be used to refer to a range of individuals who acted in representative and clerical capacities for others. These included procurators, forespeakers and notaries public. Briefly, procurators were representatives who, once properly appointed, had the power to bind their clients by what they 'said and did' on their behalf.[3] Forespeakers were representatives who were engaged to speak in court on behalf of others present there. They probably lacked the powers of procurators to bind their clients, with whom, it is thought, forespeakers were present in court, but who could 'contradict or disavow' what was said on their behalf.[4] Notaries public discharged a range of functions, including the drafting of formal documents or 'instruments' on behalf of their clients, which would record legal transactions or the resolution of disputes and provide authoritative evidence of what had happened in any subsequent litigation.

Of these individuals, only notaries required any formal legal training or education. This took the form of an apprenticeship to an existing notary, which would be followed by a formal constitution of authority to act in this way, usually granted on ecclesiastical or imperial authority, or, after 1469, on Scottish royal authority, which was thereafter in principle exercised to the exclusion of that of the emperor.[5] By contrast, fifteenth-century procurators and forespeakers could – and probably most frequently did – act without any legal training, and from time to time with little or no experience of the courts in which they acted as representatives. As one Scottish legal historian has put it, such individuals might have accepted the label 'men of law', but they would not necessarily have allowed it to 'define' them.[6] First and foremost, their identity was shaped by other types of status, including those they enjoyed as clergymen, noblemen and merchant traders.

Looking at the evidence of fifteenth-century Aberdeen, the earlier study mentioned above used – admittedly rather arbitrary – criteria to identify the most active procurators, forespeakers and notaries public during the period from 1 January 1450 to 31 December 1460. There emerged five individuals who appeared more frequently than any others as trusted representatives for a series of clients in the burgh courts of Aberdeen during this period. In addition, the activities of two notaries public were traced in the council registers at this time, giving a list of seven men in total. They were Andrew Alanson, Alexander Blyndseil, Richard Kintore, John Kymedi, William Scherar, Master John Cadiou and Robert Leis, chaplain (Cadiou and Leis were the notaries).

Having identified these individuals – who might, or might not, have accepted the label 'man of law' – the study then proceeded to attempt to explain why they were chosen to act so frequently. The notaries' legal training obviously recommended them, but what about the other five men? Drawing on the evidence of the Aberdeen council registers from the period, it was argued that they were trusted to act so frequently neither because they were the richest and most powerful members of Aberdonian society nor because they had any particular legal training, but rather because they had extensive experience of holding offices within the burgh administration and so of operating the burgh courts. They had learned how to operate those courts by following the practice of others – perhaps in a rather mechanical fashion. For example, they knew the forms required to transfer property, at least according to the variant of the laws of the Scottish realm applied in Aberdeen.[7]

As has been explained elsewhere,[8] it has since transpired that one of these individuals, Andrew Alanson, would not have met the somewhat arbitrary criteria used to decide who should and should not have been included in the small group of trusted representatives mentioned above. Put briefly, those who acted as trusted representatives on five occasions or more for five clients or more during the period between 1 January 1450 and 31 December 1460 were included in the study. In the preliminary version of the *Aberdeen Registers Online* (*ARO*) which was used, a dispute in which Andrew Alanson acted as a representative was correctly transcribed, but mislabelled as having taken place in 1457; it in fact took place in 1467.[9] Once this error was detected, it became clear that Alanson appeared on fewer than five occasions between 1450 and 1460, and consequently did not meet the criteria for inclusion in the study.[10] Nonetheless, it remains true that Alanson had more experience than most when acting as a representative for others in the burgh courts of Aberdeen at this time. Furthermore, the conclusions drawn in the study are essentially unaffected if the evidence of his career is ignored.

While regrettable, the error just mentioned had what turned out to be the fortunate effect of drawing the attention of the present writer to consider Alanson's career in more detail. The results are presented below. First, the choice to focus on Alanson will be explained in some detail. In brief terms, Alanson's career enables one to see how the evidence of the Aberdeen council registers allows scholars to test, and also enrich, existing historical accounts of the development of Scottish legal history during the fifteenth century. Arguably, this is slightly truer of Alanson's life and work than it is of the others – although, as will be explained, in this regard Richard Kintore and Master John Cadiou could also be studied to great profit. Second, Alanson's work and career will be reconstructed.[11] Third, some concluding remarks will be offered.

Representation before the burgh courts, representation before parliament

Two episodes in Andrew Alanson's long career can be used to illustrate how studying his life and work can be used to enrich our understanding of fifteenth-century Scottish legal culture. The first comes from an inheritance dispute before one of the Aberdeen burgh courts in 1467, in the course of which Alanson acted as a procurator. The second relates to Alanson's work as a burgh commissioner, a representative of Aberdeen in Scottish parliaments – and probably also in a parliamentary commission – between 1470 and 1471. These episodes will be discussed here, and then their potential significance will be explained.

Andrew Alanson in the burgh courts and in parliament

In 1467, there arose a dispute over an inheritance following the death of one Angus Lilburn. The dispute, which was heard before one of the burgh courts of Aberdeen, was concerned with whether or not a particular royal writ, known as a brieve of inquest, should be implemented to give the disputed property to one claimant – Agnes Lilburn – or to her half-brother, John Lilburn.[12] The problem was that Agnes was a child of the first marriage of the deceased, and she was claiming that the lands were hers by right in preference to her half-brother, the son of the deceased's second marriage. The parties were represented by procurators; as has been explained they were formally constituted representatives who bound their clients by what they did on their behalf. One of Agnes Lilburn's procurators was Andrew Alanson.[13]

After the procurators had made various representations – which are, regrettably, unrecorded – the burgh officers presiding over the court, that is to say in this case the provost and the bailies, appointed an assize (in historical Scottish usage this was the name for a jury) to determine the outcome of the matter. The assize's function was to work out how to apply the royal brieve, and to this end the parties' procurators presented them with arguments in support of their clients' positions. Nonetheless, the assize remained uncertain as to the relevant law to be followed in this case. Put another way, it had difficulty in interpreting the instructions in the brieve. Therefore, it asked the provost and the bailies to postpone the matter until the next meeting of the head court of the burgh. In the interim, the assize asked the provost to write to seek advice from *iuris periti* (i.e. 'men of law', also referred to as *legis periti*) of 'other burghs, that is to say of Edinburgh, of Perth and of Dundee' as to how the case should be disposed.[14] The reply from the *iuris periti* of Edinburgh is intriguing; they stated that the daughter, Agnes, ought to succeed, 'vt patet in legibus burgorum In capitulo vbi dicit de homine habente duas vxores et cetera' ('as appears in the Laws of the Burghs, in the chapter where it discusses a man having two wives etc'). In other words, the view of the *iuris periti* of Edinburgh was that the brieve was to be implemented in accordance with a text known as the *Leges Burgorum*, the original version of which was in existence by the third quarter of the thirteenth century.[15]

As stated, Andrew Alanson was one of Agnes Lilburn's procurators. Arguably, Alanson can be identified with an individual who was called upon a few years later to consider the texts of medieval laws of the realm – probably including the *Leges Burgorum* – in more detail. This commission came in November 1469, when a meeting of the Scottish parliament in Edinburgh instructed several individuals to 'avise, commone and refer again to the next parliament or generale consail' concerning various matters. The commissioners were drawn from the three Scottish 'estates' of the clergy, the nobility and the burgesses. One of the proposals they were asked to consider was in favour of 'the reductione of the kingis lawis, *Regiam Majestatem*, actis, statutis and uthir bukis to be put in a volum and tobe autoriyit, and the laif to be distroyit'.[16] To explain, a major problem with the medieval laws of the realm was that they had been transmitted in a 'relatively uncritical and private system of manuscript collections'.[17] This meant that many different versions of the laws were in circulation, causing confusion when attempts were made to apply them in practice. The commissioners were instructed to meet to discuss the subject in Edinburgh on 12 March 1470, and amongst the four individuals appointed to represent the burghs was one Andrew Alanson.[18] At the next two parliaments, which began on 6 May 1471 and on 2 August 1471 (both in Edinburgh), Aberdeen was represented by its provost, Andrew Alanson, undoubtedly the same individual who had represented Agnes Lilburn in the dispute mentioned above.[19] It therefore seems plausible to suggest that this Andrew Alanson can be identified with the Andrew Alanson who was amongst those tasked with reviewing *Regiam Majestatem* and other medieval laws of the Scottish realm in November 1469. Regardless, in his role as a burgh commissioner, Provost Alanson was also involved in the parliamentary administration of justice; in that capacity, he sat as one of the lords auditors of causes and complaints in May 1471 and again in August 1471.[20]

Alanson's career in context

Why is any of this significant for Scottish legal historians or historians more generally? The earlier study of 'men of law' in medieval Aberdeen mentioned above made it clear that Alanson had extensive experience of the administration of the law as it was collectively understood in Aberdeen – albeit that constraints of space meant that a great deal more could still be said about this.[21] Presumably, he brought that experience to his representative work in the burgh courts on behalf of Agnes Lilburn, and also to his activities as a burgh commissioner in the administration of justice and law reform in meetings of Scottish parliaments in Edinburgh. In a very loose but real sense, it follows that his career exemplified one type of link that could exist between the resolution of disputes in the old courts of the medieval common law, on the one hand, and, on the other hand, the fora for the administration of justice that were being developed by parliament in the second half of the fifteenth century.

This is intriguing because contemporary sources indicate that the relationship between these two different groups of courts was complex. For example, it has been shown in the past that some litigants complained about the poor quality of the justice administered in the old courts of the medieval common law, often called their 'ordinary' courts. Consequently, they petitioned parliament and other 'central' bodies such as the royal council directly for remedies. One reason the litigants gave for their dissatisfaction was that the older courts were staffed by officials who lacked the sort of legal expertise and training that could be used to resolve the increasingly complex disputes that were arising in Scottish society during the late fifteenth and early sixteenth centuries. By contrast, many of the ecclesiastical judges who sat in the royal council, for example, did have that sort of training. Another problem was that the procedures of the medieval courts of the common law were frequently presented as being fraught with delay. Such delays can only have been made worse by the sorts of uncertainty that arose over the application of the brieve of inquest in the Lilburn dispute, which apparently arose from confusion and indeed ignorance concerning the substance and texts of the laws of the realm. During the late 1480s, 1490s and early 1500s, the resulting pressure from litigants seems to have led to the growing regularisation of the work of one of those central fora – the conciliar session; and the session, in turn, would be reconstituted as the College of Justice in 1532.[22]

Arguably, further light can be shed on these developments by studying the careers of individuals like Alanson in more detail. As has been explained, Alanson was extensively involved in the administration of justice in the burgh courts of Aberdeen, which were amongst the old courts of the common law. On at least two occasions, he was also involved in the administration of justice by parliament. In addition, he may have been involved – however passively – in an attempt to create an authoritative version of the texts of the medieval Scottish common law. The accounts of the work of the burgh courts in the recently transcribed Aberdeen council registers allow researchers to reconstruct a great deal of the experience that a man like Andrew Alanson brought to the roles just mentioned. Perhaps more usefully, the exercise of reconstructing his work also allows one to consider the extent to which the sorts of general legal historical trends discussed above were in operation, and to do so at a level of great detail.

Therefore, this chapter will attempt to reconstruct Alanson's career, with a particular focus on his work in the burgh courts and in the parliament. Such work will, it is hoped, lay a foundation for exploring the relationship between the work of the burgh courts of Aberdeen on the one hand, and that of more central fora for the administration of justice on the other. This, in turn, may ultimately help scholars to understand the extent to which litigants' dissatisfaction with the ordinary courts of the common law – at least in Aberdeen – facilitated the development of more 'centralised' courts in late medieval Scotland.[23] It should be mentioned briefly that the careers of Richard Kintore and Master John Cadiou might also be usefully discussed to advance this sort of research; like Alanson, both men were heavily involved in the administration of burgh affairs – and in particular in the work of the burgh courts[24] – and they were also burgh commissioners to parliament.[25]

Andrew Alanson

Origins and family background

Andrew Alanson first appears in the Aberdeen council registers on 5 October 1439. He had just witnessed an inspection of some lands behind the old tolbooth on the Castlegate, where it had been found that there was nothing moveable on the lands that could be used to satisfy an 'annualrent', a payment which was owed to a specific creditor *from the lands themselves* (i.e. from the individual who had tenure of those lands for the time being). If the payment was not forthcoming, the lands would ultimately be transferred to the creditor, so that they could be sold on by him to satisfy his debt.[26]

The family background of Andrew Alanson is unclear. There had been Alansons in Aberdeen for decades,[27] but it has not been possible to establish who Andrew's parents were. He had a brother, Thomas,[28] and at least one sister, whose son, Alexander Trail, would later engage in litigation with him.[29] At some point in his life, Andrew Alanson married a woman called Christian Cadiou.[30] She may have been a sister of Master John Cadiou, notary public.[31] The Alansons are not known to have had any children, and if they did they do not seem to have survived their father.[32] A record dating from 1445 describes Andrew Alanson as a 'mercator', i.e. a merchant trading in salmon, and the same record makes it clear that he was at the time of writing absent on business.[33] He must have been a burgess of Aberdeen and a member of the merchant guild, i.e. one with the highest trading privileges within the burgh community, because by 1447 he had been elected as one of the burgh councillors in a meeting of the guild court on 6 October that year.[34] Nonetheless, it should not be thought that Alanson's only connections were in Aberdeen; he had at least one powerful friend outwith the burgh. On 21 October 1446, he was described as a member of the earl of Crawford's household, and as a mark of favour to the earl the council resolved to grant Alanson a lease of the next fishing that would fall vacant – a promise that was honoured on 17 May 1448.[35] In the same year, Alanson was listed on a tax roll as living in the Even Quarter of Aberdeen, which lay roughly between modern-day Broad Street and St Nicholas Kirk.[36] As a result of the tax, he was required to pay ten shillings. Assuming that the amount of tax paid was linked with the level of one's wealth, this reveals that Alanson was not amongst the richest men in Aberdeen, but wealthier than the vast majority.[37]

The picture that emerges of Alanson in 1448 is that of a well-connected and reasonably well-to-do merchant burgess and guild brother of medieval Aberdeen who had begun to hold office in the administration of the burgh. By then, he had already appeared quite frequently in the Aberdeen council registers, primarily suing and being sued by others.[38] His litigation was not limited to the burgh courts; on one occasion, he sued Robert Blyndseil, a representative of one of the oligarchic families that dominated burgh affairs, for certain unspecified 'iniuris' before the court of the bishop of Aberdeen – presumably meaning the consistorial court. Exactly why the burgh court noted the decision to submit the dispute to arbiters chosen by both parties is unclear.[39] There is little reason here to rehearse the many claims that Alanson brought before the burgh courts during his life, but it is worth mentioning that he was already experienced in representing himself before the bailies before he started to represent others frequently.

Bailie, councillor and deputy chamberlain

On 30 September 1448, Alanson was elected to the office of bailie himself, along with three others;[40] this was a role he would hold again later in his career.[41] In that capacity, he would have been expected to preside over several of the burgh courts and to participate in the legal administration of the burgh. It may be worth emphasising that that now meant that Alanson was a royal officer presiding over royal courts. There he would have been required to administer the implementation of royal writs and brieves such as the brieve of inquest, already mentioned above; there is also extensive evidence of the use of brieves to compel the payment of debts in the burgh courts of Aberdeen at this time.[42] For example, on 23 June 1449, Bailie Andrew Alanson was presented with a brieve of distress to compel one Thomas Kintore to honour an obligation; this brieve could be used to seize property in satisfaction for debt.[43] Furthermore, the bailie did not only represent the king in the courts; for example, he also represented him in presiding over the formal delivery of rights in burgh lands. The ceremony in question was known as the ceremony of 'sasine'. It would take place on the lands that were to be transferred; there the bailie, acting on behalf of the feudal superior of the lands, the king, would symbolically hand over to the grantee earth and stone, or some other symbols.[44]

Alanson's first period in office as bailie was not without its difficulties. On 15 February 1449, Malcolm Forbes, David Dun and David Hervy were 'accusit of the disobeying of Androw Alaneson the balyhe'. Alanson seems to have demanded that the men put up security or 'lawburrows' for their peaceful behaviour.[45]

They had refused, maintaining that those who 'doutit' their good behaviour first had to swear an oath to that effect. They claimed that only then should they be required to give 'borowes of pes', as Alanson had demanded. The question was put to an assize, which indicated its wish to be 'forthir avisit with men of law' on the matter.[46] This was not the only occasion on which Alanson found it difficult to enforce his will as bailie. On 23 June 1449, John Barde was convicted by an assize for 'disobedience of Andrew Alanson, one of the bailies of the said burgh [of Aberdeen] in the exercise of his office, concerning which matter the said bailie sought instruments'.[47] In other words, he asked for formal documentary evidence of the dispute to be prepared, probably by a notary public and perhaps by Master John Cadiou.

Whatever difficulties he faced during his tenure as bailie, Alanson continued to participate in burgh administration. He was frequently elected to the burgh council during the 1450s.[48] He held other official roles too in the course of that decade; for example, on 6 February 1458 he served as one of four deputies of the chamberlain in the chamberlain's ayre when it visited Aberdeen that year.[49] The chamberlain was another royal officer who had responsibility for overseeing good governance in the burghs, and in particular the administration of justice and the receipt of revenues due to the crown.[50]

Trusted representative and procurator

While gaining this experience as an official in the administration of justice, Alanson was also active in representing a range of clients before the same burgh courts. He acted for four separate clients during the 1450s. First, on 14 October 1454, Thomas Scot in Bourtie parish, near Inverurie, made Andrew Alanson, John Scroggs the son and William Alanson his procurators 'in order to pursue Hugh Flesher for a cow'.[51] As was standard in such constitutions of procuratory, Scot promised to ratify whatever his procurators did in his name.[52] The dispute continued on 9 December 1454, when Hugh Flesher appeared and entered a defence, asking for 15 days to summon his 'warrantor'.[53] The warrantor would have been the individual who had transferred the cow to him in the first place, and the warrantor's obligation of warrandice would have obliged him to answer Scot's claim for the cow in place of Flesher.[54]

Second, a few weeks later, on 14 January 1455, and this time in the head court of the burgh, Andrew Alanson was back, acting for Walter Ewynson to have his case transferred or 'repledged' to the court of his lord, which was to be held at nearby Scotston on 3 February 1455. This could happen where a party alleged that his dispute should be heard before a different court; in this case, the point was that the lord had jurisdiction to hear disputes involving his man, and so the dispute was to be heard in the lord's court, and not in one of the burgh courts.[55]

Third, on 10 December 1455, Alanson appeared on behalf of one Sandris Harwar in the bailie court of the burgh, acting as Harwar's forespeaker.[56] Harwar was pursuing the master of a ship to account for some cargo. The shipmaster's forespeaker, Duncan of Clatt, responded that the master was under the king's arrest and so was not obliged to answer until freed from arrest. Andrew Alanson, acting for Harwar, 'strekat a borch', put up personal security that the shipmaster ought to answer.[57] Duncan of Clatt responded by putting up a borch himself that the shipmaster should not have to answer. Duncan of Clatt was found by the court to be in the wrong; he was found to be 'in an unlaw', i.e. he owed a penalty to be paid to the court, and the shipmaster was compelled to answer. At the same time, Harwar made Alanson and others his procurators in dealing with the matter going forward.

Fourth, on 9 April 1459 Alanson appeared for one James Williamson in the bailies' court of the burgh. Williamson was being sued by a shipmaster named Hans Snel, who alleged that Williamson owed him ten pounds Scots for the transportation of 200 barrels of onions. Alanson alleged that Snel had to deliver or at least produce and offer the onions to Williamson before the payment was to be made[58]; the ultimate resolution of the matter is unclear.

A man of law?

None of this should be taken to imply that Andrew Alanson was, or would have thought of himself, exclusively or primarily, as what contemporaries described as a 'man of law' or a *iuris peritus*. Indeed, on two occasions when *iuris periti* were mentioned in the records – which have already been discussed – it was in response to a perceived need to seek their advice in relation to disputes in which Alanson was either adjudicating or acting as a procurator. Of course, it does not follow that Alanson was not and could not have been seen as a 'man of law' himself. Nonetheless, even if he would have accepted or entertained that label, it is doubtful that he would have allowed it to define him.[59] Fundamentally, he was a reasonably wealthy and well-connected merchant burgess and guild brother of Aberdeen who was trusted by his peers in the administration of justice – as they understood it – and in the representation of others within the burgh courts. His trading activities continue to feature in the council registers too; on 11 March 1460, he was sued by Thomas Spens, Bishop of Aberdeen, for payment of debt relating to freight transported.[60]

In passing, it is worth noting that, in addition to his trading and administrative activities, Alanson was also a significant patron of the burgh kirk of St Nicholas and the church more generally. To name examples, he and his wife, Christian Cadiou, founded and endowed an altar to St Mary Magdalane within the kirk of St Nicholas.[61] Alanson also gifted an annualrent to the chancellor of Aberdeen Cathedral, and he presided over the endowment of the Franciscan Friary established in Broadgate in 1471.[62] In addition, he had his own chaplain, who in 1452 was Patrick Williamson.[63] Alanson's endowments of ecclesiastical institutions were sufficiently extensive to cause the nineteenth-century biographer of Aberdonian provosts to comment that he 'is best remembered by his various and generous grants for religious purposes'.[64] He also secured a guarantee that at least some such endowments could continue to be guarded and controlled by their patrons; in July 1470, the council provided that 'quhat that Androw alanson bringis or giffis in the inhourment [adornment] to the sayde altar [of Mary Magdalene] sall ramayn at the keping of the saide Androw and his airis and thair chaplaynnis'; it added 'euery man that giffis inhourment or feftment to the saide altar sal be maystiris and patrownis of thair awin gift'.[65]

Provost Alanson in the burgh council and in parliament

On 1 October 1470, Andrew Alanson was elected as provost of Aberdeen, to hold office for a year.[66] There seems to be no reason to doubt that he should be identified with the man of the same name who represented Aberdeen as burgh commissioner in a meeting of parliament in the old tolbooth of Edinburgh a few months later, on 6 May 1471.[67] On that day, three parliamentary committees were elected. The first was the committee of the lords of the articles, which was responsible for drafting legislation to be considered by the whole assembly sitting together.[68] Alanson was chosen to join this committee. The other two committees were those of the lords auditors of causes and complaints and of the lords for the falsing of dooms; they were elected to discharge parliament's significant judicial functions.[69] The first was able to deal with first instance complaints to parliament; the latter dealt with dooms already pronounced by inferior judges and had power to revoke them.[70] It is worth noting that Alanson served as one of the lords auditors of causes and complaints in the parliament of August 1471, giving him first-hand experience of judicial business transacted there.[71]

The legislation ultimately promulgated by parliament in May 1471 addressed a wide range of matters, from arrangements for the marriage of the sister of the king, James III (r.1460–1488),[72] to a prohibition on wearing new silk clothes for those whose income fell below a certain level.[73] It also enacted laws to deal with the value of money in Scotland and with perjury.[74] These last points may be significant for the purposes of this chapter, because the value of money and the problem of perjury were two of three matters which one 'Andrew Alanson' and others had been asked to 'avise uppoun' as part of a commission appointed in the preceding parliament in November 1469. The commission had instructed those appointed to meet in Edinburgh on 20 March 1470 to discuss the matters in question; it was in the following terms:

> Item, the hail thre estatis has committit ful powere to thir persounis underwrittin of the hail parliament to avise, commone and refer again to the next parliament or generale consail of thir materis underwrittin etc. In the first to avise uppone the inbringing of bullione in the realme and of the kepin of the mone in the realme, and to avise upone the course that the mone sal hafe etc. Item, of the reductione of the kingis lawis, *Regiam Majestatem*, actis, statutis and uthir bukis to be put in a volum and tobe autoriyit, and the laif to be distroyit. Item, to avise for reformationes for

> mane sworne athis and to set punytione thairupon. Item, to avise uppone all uthir articulis that salbe thocht spedful for the honour of oure soverane lorde and the commone gude of the realme.[75]

As already stated earlier, it is likely that the 'Andrew Alanson' appointed to this commission was indeed the Andrew Alanson who is under consideration in this chapter, and who attended the next parliament after 1469 which considered two of these three matters. If so, it is quite plausible to speculate that he already had views on the issue of the coinage, and in particular its debasement, which was a perennial problem in the reign of James III.[76] The matter had attracted interest from Aberdeen before. On 12 October 1467, Richard Kintore, burgess of Aberdeen – who had demitted office as provost a week earlier[77] – had presented a petition to parliament with Archibald Whitelaw, dean of Dunbar and the royal secretary, expressing concerns about this matter on behalf of the clergy and the burgh commissioners.[78] As regards the third matter addressed to the commissioners – the creation of an authoritative version of the laws of the realm – it is, of course, interesting that Andrew Alanson of Aberdeen may have been involved. A subsequent parliament of 1473 did legislate for the reduction of the laws of the realm to order, and it did so in terms that indicate a clear debt to the proposal of November 1469.[79] Nonetheless, Andrew Alanson is not known to have been present at that parliament; indeed, it is not certain that any representative from Aberdeen's burgh council actually attended.[80] Therefore, it is difficult to consider what contribution – if any – Alanson may or may not have made to the commission appointed in 1469. What is perhaps more interesting is that the original proposal of November 1469 may have been inspired in part by the sort of problem that Alanson and others in Aberdeen had come across in the burgh courts in the Lilburn dispute in January 1467. They seem to have been genuinely uncertain as to the correct law to be applied; and when the *juris periti* who advised the burgh council in Edinburgh – whoever they were – were consulted as to how best to resolve the inheritance dispute in question, they not only gave advice, but cited as authority for their opinion a passage in the *Leges Burgorum*. While further research is evidently required on the point, it may transpire that there was some link between, on the one hand, the promotion of the authority of the text of the *Leges Burgorum* by the *juris periti* of Edinburgh in 1467, and, on the other hand, the proposal to create an authoritative, accessible version of those laws in 1469. Studies such as the present one concerning Alanson's work in the burgh courts, then, may serve to help contextualise and make greater sense of the problem considered in November 1469.

Burgh statutes and acts of the king's parliaments

Alanson is not known to have attended any subsequent parliaments. Nonetheless, during his second term in office as provost, which began on 2 October 1473,[81] he took the interesting step of promulgating a burgh statute which sought effectively to re-enact parliamentary legislation of James II (r. 1437–1460) concerning the implementation of a small claims court. Alanson's statute, promulgated on 29 November that year, was in the following terms:

> The said day it is ordand and statute be the Aldirman and consel that all burges and nychtbour' dwelland within this burgh clamand ony sowmes within ane hundreth schillingis tobe wrangwisly haldin fra thame salbe servit within viij daies and salhafe na langar' dilatouris eftir the Act of the kingis parliament et cetera[82]

Why did Alanson and the council choose to do this? A little context may shed light on the matter. First, the 'Act of the kingis parliament' in question had been promulgated on 4 August 1455 during the reign of James II (r. 1437–1460). This provided that in each burgh within the realm there should be appointed 'viij or [xij] personis eftir the quantite of the towne chosin of secret consale and suorne tharto', who were to have the task of determining 'all matiris of wrang and unlawe within the burghe to waill of v li' or within apone viij dais warnyng'. James II's statute went on to explain its purpose, which was 'sua that in prejudice of the innocentis the delayar haif nocht the priwalege of the process of lawe, bot apon viij dais warnyng to be decidyt be the said personis'.[83]

Exactly why Provost Alanson felt the need to make fresh provision along these lines is unclear. As has already been stated, delay in the administration of justice was certainly a recurring concern amongst fifteenth-century Scottish legislators,[84] and Provost Alanson's express repetition of the rationale for the 1455 act in his own statute confirms that he and the burgh council were thinking in the same terms. It is possible that the provisions of the 1455 act were in desuetude, and that Alanson thought it appropriate to revive them due to specific concerns about the use of exceptions or defences to drag out disputes over small claims. Nonetheless, it does not seem to have been common practice for the burgh council to implement acts of Scottish parliaments through their own statutes or ordinances. The fact that the 1455 act was singled out for such attention in 1473 becomes even more intriguing when it is realised that the burgh council had *already* promulgated an ordinance implementing the act almost 20 years earlier. On 8 October 1456, about a year after the 1455 act was passed, the council, led by Provost John Fife,[85] had promulgated an ordinance in the following terms:

> Item it is ordanit and concludit be the hale counsaile that ilke monoundai thar' sal sit vj persounes of Counsaile to end al smal complayntis betuex nyghtboris of al soumes that ar within v lib' eftir the act' of the kingis parliament / and the persounes that sittis sal rais' of the wrangar' of ilke punde xij d' / and give the soume be les' than a punde xij d' And give monoundai beis hali / thai sal sit on the tvisdai[86]

This 'implementing' ordinance – if it may be called that – ignored the requirement that a minimum of eight members of the burgh council should sit on the new weekly court. Only six members of the council of Aberdeen were to be required to act in this way. The 'implementing' act also inserted a provision that the 'wrangar' should be fined 12 pence – this particular idea seems to have been dreamt up in Aberdeen (what was to become of the money collected is unclear). It is possible that the decision to implement the act through this ordinance was connected with other business dealt with by the council on 8 October 1456; on that day, the council appointed its commissioners to represent the burgh at the next general council of the realm, which was to be held less than two weeks later on 19 October. To explain, the general council was a 'sister institution' of parliament 'with almost identical powers, but lacking the ability to forfeit for treason'.[87] The representatives of Aberdeen at the general council were to be Provost John Fife, John Marr and Master John Cadiou.[88] Perhaps there was some sense that delay in the administration of justice was to be on the agenda at this general council, and perhaps it was felt prudent for the Aberdonian commissioners to be able to say that something had been done to implement the 1455 act. The general council of October 1456 did indeed develop 'sessions', judicial fora which could supplement the work of the ordinary courts;[89] and one effect of that would have been to address delay in the resolution of disputes.

Nonetheless, Provost Alanson decided to pass a new statute to 'implement' the provisions of the 1455 act afresh in 1473. It is intriguing to note that Alanson's statute, unlike the Aberdonian ordinance of 1456, made no reference to the idea of a court that would usually sit on every Monday. What Alanson's statute said was that if someone initiated proceedings to recover a debt worth 100 shillings or less then he was to receive justice within eight days, and no further delay was to be permitted. It is intriguing to note that this seems to have been how the 1455 act was actually handled in practice in several – apparently unrelated – disputes decided in the Aberdeen burgh courts in 1461.[90] In each case, one party came into court and alleged that he had initiated proceedings to advance a claim worth less than five pounds. In addition, on each occasion the pursuer alleged that he had initiated proceedings eight days earlier in accordance with the king's act in relation to such small claims. If the court accepted this – and on one occasion it required the pursuer to swear that the claim was for less than 5 pounds, in response to which the pursuer swore it was worth 4 pounds and 19 shillings[91] – then immediate judgement would be given in favour of the claimant.

Seen in light of these points, Provost Alanson's burgh statute of 1473 may provide an intriguing glimpse of the latitude which at least one burgh felt it had in implementing an act of the Scottish parliament. Perhaps the reason that the 1455 act received some attention in the first place was that the burgh did have to make its own provisions to implement it; after all, the act was silent as to *when* the court was to sit, and it did give each burgh discretion as to how many councillors were to sit on it. Nonetheless, even Provost Fife's ordinance of 1456 showed a willingness to exercise more 'discretion' than this. It had departed a little from the terms of the 1455 act itself, by only requiring six councillors to attend the weekly court rather than the minimum of eight councillors required by parliament. In addition, there is limited evidence to suggest that this weekly court actually sat. Nonetheless, the broad purpose of the 1455 act – to prevent delays in the administration of justice by refusing to countenance more than eight days of delay in the face of claims worth less than five pounds – was being honoured in the practice of the court in 1461. Arguably, Provost Alanson's statute of 1473 to the effect that those 'clamand ony sowmes within ane hundreth schillingis tobe wrangwisly haldin fra thame salbe servit within viij daies and salhafe na langar' dilatouris eftir the Act of the kingis parliament' was more indebted to the ways in which the Aberdonian burgh courts had sought to realise the *purposes* of the 1455 act than it was to the strict *provisions* of the 1455 act themselves. It does not seem to have revived a special weekly court of six councillors – assuming it had ever sat. Rather, it appears to have perpetuated the *Aberdonian* way of honouring parliament's perceived intention in 1455.

Final years

What turned out to be Alanson's final term in office as provost ended on 3 October 1474.[92] The last known reference to Andrew Alanson in the council registers is dated to 13 March 1475, when one Andrew Branche, son and heir of Thomas Branche, approached the council and asked for a fishing right that had pertained to his father. This right the elder Branche had assigned to Andrew Alanson; none-theless, in an apparent act of generosity, Alanson renounced the right he had in the fishings in favour of the younger Branche.[93]

Alanson himself was dead by 19 January 1476, when James III (r. 1460–1488) ordered the council of Aberdeen to uphold a gift he had made of a fishing that had pertained to 'vmquhile [the late] our louit Androw alanson burgess [of Ab-erdeen]'.[94] The anniversary of his death was still being marked in 1491 by the chaplains of St Nicholas with a sung mass on the Sunday immediately following the feast of St Bartholomew (24 August).[95] His widow, Christian Cadiou, sur-vived him for some time. Soon after his death, she was caught up in protracted litigation over leases of fishings that her husband had held when he died.[96] She, in her turn, gifted to the altar of Mary Magdalene 'one complete vestment of silk', including blue 'velvets' for a priest, a deacon and a sub-deacon, 'with a cope of the same colour, ornamented with gold'. She also gave 'a chalice of silver gilt, three ounces in weight'.[97]

Conclusion

Andrew Alanson might, or might not, have accepted the label of 'man of law'. Regardless, studying his career enriches our understanding of fifteenth-century Scottish legal history, and Scottish history more generally. It illustrates many of the trends in the development of the law identified by legal historians in re-markable detail. Some of the difficulties that litigants are thought to have faced in the administration of justice, such as delay, a lack of legal expertise amongst those responsible for making decisions and indeed uncertainty concerning the provisions of the supposedly authoritative texts of the law emerge clearly in the Aberdeen council registers. As regards delay, a statute of 1455 attempting to limit its effects in resolving disputes over small claims was implemented in various different ways by burgh councils between 1456 and 1473, latterly during Alanson's time as provost. While the express provisions of the statute were never fully applied, the council did attempt to uphold its overall purpose.

In addition, the Lilburn litigation, explored earlier in this chapter, provided an example of the difficulties that could arise due to the lack of legal expertise in the Aberdeen burgh courts. It will be recalled that Alanson represented Lilburn in court in a succession dispute; and in the course of that dispute, the question of Agnes Lilburn's right to inherit was referred to the provosts and 'men of law' of Dundee, Perth and Edinburgh. Perhaps significantly, only the provost of Edinburgh said he had been able to consult 'men of law'. In addition, the same response drew attention to a text of the medieval common law of Scotland – the *Leges Burgorum* – as an authority to be used in resolving the dispute. The difficulties in using such a text were well known; as already stated, part of the problem was that they were transmitted in a 'relatively uncritical and private system of manuscript collections'.[98] Parliament attempted to deal with this in 1469, and again in 1473, as discussed earlier.

The effects of all of these difficulties were felt and illustrated in the career of Andrew Alanson. So too were the various attempts to address these issues. As one must assume was the case with many of his predecessors as councillors, bailies and provosts of Aberdeen, Alanson had gained significant experience of the operation of the procedures of the Scottish common law, *at least as they were understood in contemporary Aberdeen.*[99] Arguably, he brought that experience to bear on his work as a judge in the burgh courts and as a trusted representative for his peers in the courts, both as a procurator and a forespeaker. He also presumably brought it to bear on his work as a lord auditor of causes and complaints in parliament, where he participated in attempts to address the perceived shortcomings of the ordinary courts through the provision of a supplementary first-instance parliamentary forum for the resolution of disputes. If that might have helped to address delays in the administration of justice, Alanson's statute of 1473 might have had the same effect; it certainly had the same intent. Furthermore, there is the tantalising possibility that Alanson participated directly in the commission that was tasked with advising parliament about the merits of reducing the medieval laws of the Scottish realm to a single, authoritative volume, with the 'laif' (the rest) to be 'distroyit'. Regrettably, it seems one can only wonder what he made of this proposal – if anything.

Nonetheless, however much experience he had of the operation of the law as applied in Aberdeen, it remained the case that he lacked formal legal training and expertise. Fundamentally, he was, and remained, a highly respected and trusted merchant burgess and guild brother of Aberdeen who knew a great deal about the operation of the Aberdonian burgh courts. In the decades following

Alanson's death, the legal world in which he had operated was gradually transformed. The so-called 'Education Act' of 1496 probably reveals a sense that leaving legal administration to experienced laymen with no formal training in the law was no longer satisfactory.[100] The statute provided that all 'baronis and frehaldaris' that were of 'substance' should educate their eldest sons, ensuring that they would spend 'thre yeris at the sculis of art and jure, sua that thai may have knawlege and understanding of the lawis'; the express aim of the act was that justice might 'reigne universalie throw all the realme, sua that thai that ar schireffis or jugeis ordinaris under the kingis hienes may have knawlege to do justice, that the pure pepill sulde have na need to seik oure soverane lordis principale auditouris for ilk small injure'. It has been suggested that Bishop William Elphinstone sought to go some way towards satisfying this apparent demand for greater legal learning and expertise through the foundation of a new university in Alanson's native Aberdeen in 1495.[101] Demands for such learning amongst those holding judicial office would only grow as time passed; and it came to be expected of the lords of the conciliar session, which had acquired de facto supreme jurisdiction in Scottish civil matters prior to its reconstitution as the College of Justice in 1532.[102]

It is a curious twist of history, and perhaps a fitting one with which to end the present chapter, that Alanson's legacy made a small but direct contribution to facilitate the growing demands for legal expertise, at least in his native Aberdeen. It will be recalled that Andrew Alanson and his wife, Christian Cadiou, had endowed an altar in honour of Mary Magadalene in the burgh kirk of St Nicholas. At some point before 1506, Bishop William Elphinstone acquired the right of patronage of the altar, and he used this as a basis for funding a bursary in Roman civil law at his new university.[103] Consequently, if one can discern the influence of major trends in contemporary legal development in Alanson's career, one can also see how such trends ultimately came to shape his legacy. In exploring these points, it is hoped that the present chapter has shown how much light the study of the newly transcribed Aberdeen council registers can shed on both the late medieval Scottish common law and also on the trusted administrators and 'men of law' who helped to shape it.

Notes

* I am grateful to Professor John Ford and the anonymous peer reviewer for comments on this chapter. Any errors remain my own.

1 A. Simpson, 'Men of law in the Aberdeen Council Register? A preliminary study, ca.1450–ca.1460', *Juridical Review* 2019, pp. 136–59. See also the *erratum* published in connection with this article at the end of the third issue of *Juridical Review* 2019 (no page reference present).

2 See H.L. MacQueen, *Common Law and Feudal Society in Medieval Scotland*, Edinburgh: Edinburgh University Press, Classic edition, 2016, p. 74.

3 J. Finlay, *Men of Law in Pre-Reformation Scotland*, East Linton: Tuckwell Press, 2000, p. 11.

4 Ibid.; for the points made here, see generally Ibid., pp. 10–11.

5 See, for example, J. Durkan, 'The early Scottish notary', in I.B. Cowan and D. Shaw (eds) *The Renaissance and Reformation in Scotland. Essays in Honour of Gordon Donaldson*,

Edinburgh: Scottish Academic Press, 1983, pp. 22–40. See also W.W. Scott, 'William Cranston, notary public c. 1395 to 1425, and some contemporaries', in H.L. MacQueen (ed.) *Miscellany Seven*, Edinburgh: Stair Society, 2015, pp. 125–32, and J. Finlay, 'The history of the notary in Scotland', in M. Schmoeckel and W. Schuber (eds) *Handbuch zur Geschichte des Notariats der Europäischen Traditionen*, Baden-Baden: Nomos, 2009, pp. 393–428, and Adelyn Wilson's contribution to the present volume.

6 Finlay, *Men of Law*, p. 7. See also Simpson, 'Men of law'.

7 Simpson, 'Men of law'.

8 See the *erratum* published in connection with Simpson, 'Men of law', at the end of the third issue of *Juridical Review* 2019 (no page reference present).

9 This edition is now published as E. Frankot, A. Havinga, C. Hawes, W. Hepburn, W. Peters, J. Armstrong, P. Astley, A. Mackillop, A. Simpson and A. Wyner (eds) *Aberdeen Registers Online: 1398–1511*, Aberdeen: University of Aberdeen, 2019, <https://www.abdn.ac.uk/aro> (last accessed 18 January 2020) (hereafter *ARO*). At the time of writing, a list of such corrigenda is being drawn up by J. Armstrong, to be addressed in any future published revised versions.

10 I am very grateful to Dr Edda Frankot for drawing my attention to this point.

11 This chapter relies upon the methodological assumptions outlined in Simpson, 'Men of law', pp. 149–50, when attempting to identify multiple references to a particular name in the Aberdeen council registers as being references to the same individual. Those assumptions will not be discussed further here.

12 On the brieves of inquest in an earlier period, see, above all, A. Taylor, *The Shape of the State in Medieval Scotland, 1124–1290*, Oxford: Oxford University Press, 2016, pp. 323–43.

13 ARO-5-0592-01 (12 January 1467); ARO-5-0593-08 (28 January 1467).

14 ARO-5-0592-01 (12 January 1467); ARO-5-0593-08 (26 January 1467); ARO-5-0620-08 (24 November 1467).

15 ARO-5-0602-01 (20 March 1467) (my translation); on the *Leges Burgorum*, see, for example, H.L. MacQueen and W.J. Windram, 'Laws and courts in the burghs', in M. Lynch, M. Spearman, and G. Stell (eds) *The Scottish Medieval Town*, Edinburgh: John Donald, 1988, p. 208.

16 *The Records of the Parliaments of Scotland to 1707*, ed. K.M. Brown et al., St Andrews, 2007–2020, <https://www.rps.ac.uk> (last accessed 18 January 2020) (hereafter RPS) 1469/34.

17 H.L. MacQueen, 'Regiam Majestatem, Scots law and national identity', *Scottish Historical Review* 74, 1995, pp. 1–25, at p. 15.

18 RPS 1469/35.

19 RPS 1471/5/12 (it is only in the transcript of the manuscript record that Alanson is referred to as being from Aberdeen, and there seems to be an error in the translation in this regard, perhaps as a result of a haplographical error); RPS 1471/5/14; RPS 1471/8/1; RPS 1471/8/22.

20 RPS 1471/5/12; RPS 1471/8/22.

21 Simpson, 'Men of law'.

22 For a much more sophisticated account of these changes, see, above all, A.M. Godfrey, *Civil Justice in Renaissance Scotland*, Leiden: Brill, 2009, pp. 1–160; see also MacQueen, *Common Law*, pp. 215–46, 256–63. These passages, originally written in 1993, should now be read alongside Godfrey's work, as explained in A. Simpson, 'Foreword: Common law and feudal society in scholarship since 1993', in MacQueen, *Common Law*, pp. xxix–lxi, at pp. xlvi–li.

23 In this, the Lilburn dispute may prove to be an instructive example; in spite of the clear opinion given in 1467, the dispute continued for some time, and indeed the lords of council became involved; see, for example, ARO-5-0640-01 (11 June 1468); ARO-6-0079-10 (10 October 1469).

24 For their involvement in burgh affairs, see Simpson, 'Men of law'; for Cadiou, see also H.W. Booton, 'John and Andrew Cadiou: Aberdeen notaries of the fifteenth

and early sixteenth centuries', *Northern Scotland* 9, 1989, pp. 17–20, and E. Gemmill (ed.) *Aberdeen Guild Court Records 1437–1468*, Edinburgh: Scottish History Society, 2003, p. 3; for Kintore, see A.M. Munro, *Memorials of the Aldermen, Provosts and Lord Provosts of Aberdeen 1272–1893*, Aberdeen: Printed for the Subscribers, 1897, pp. 49–51, 53.

25 See RPS 1467/10/7; RPS A1467/10/13; RPS 1471/5/14 (Kintore); RPS 1440/8/5; ARO-5-0796-01 (8 October 1456) (Cadiou).

26 ARO-4-0177-02; on annual rents in Aberdeen at this time, see the discussion in Simpson, 'Men of law', and G.L. Gretton, 'Feudal system', in K.G.C. Reid, *The Law of Property in Scotland*, Edinburgh: Lexis Nexis, para. 112; MacQueen, *Common Law*, pp. 226–7; and W. Croft Dickinson (ed.) *Early Burgh Records of Aberdeen 1317; 1398–1407*, Edinburgh: Scottish History Society, 1957, pp. lix–lxi.

27 See, e.g., ARO-1-0012-04 (5 December 1398); ARO-1-0259-11 (1 January 1405); ARO-2-0026-01 (1 January 1409); ARO-2-0080-01 (1409); ARO-2-0217-01 (11 November 1413).

28 See Munro, *Memorials*, p. 53 and J. Cooper (ed.) *Cartularium Ecclesiae Sancti Nicholai Aberdonensis*, Aberdeen: New Spalding Club, 2 vols, 1888–1892, vol. 2, p. 302.

29 ARO-6-0208-01 (23 October 1472); ARO-6-0219-01 (9 January 1473); ARO-6-0220-03 (11 January 1473).

30 See, for example, Munro, *Memorials*, p. 53; Cooper, *Cartularium*, pp. 188, 196; ARO-6-0460-05 (22 November 1476).

31 Her nephew was Master Andrew Cadiou, notary public; see, for example, ARO-6-0609-09 (18 January 1480), where reference can be found to a claim by Master Andrew that he 'suld be assignay til his awnt christiane of cadiou the spous of vmquhile Androw alanson quhom god assoilye'; see also ARO-6-0633-05 (20 May 1480) and ARO-6-0650-01 (2 October 1480)). Booton is incorrect to assert that Christian Cadiou was Master Andrew's *wife* in Booton, 'John and Andrew Cadiou', p. 18. If his claim at p. 17 that Master Andrew Alanson was the son of Master John Cadiou were substantiated by the evidence he cites at footnote 13, then one could firmly conclude that Master John Cadiou and Christian Cadiou were brother and sister. Regrettably, that is not the case; the evidence cited merely confirms that Master John Cadiou was dead by 1473. It may be that Booton was aware of other evidence establishing the link between Master John and Master Andrew firmly, but this has not been traced here. However, there must remain a strong possibility that Master John Cadiou, notary public, who died in or before 1473 (ARO-6-0260-10 (28 June 1473)), was indeed the father of Master Andrew Cadiou, notary public, who was active in Aberdeen in subsequent decades. I intend to explore the matter further elsewhere.

32 Munro, *Memorials*, p. 53.

33 ARO-4-0400-11 (19 April 1445); on his involvement in the salmon trade, see also ARO-4-0457-09 (14 November 1446).

34 ARO-5-0721-02 (6 October 1447).

35 ARO-5-0715-03 (21 October 1446); ARO-5-0730-02 (17 May 1448).

36 E.P. Dennison, A.T. Simpson, and G.G. Simpson, 'The growth of two towns', in E.P. Dennison, D. Ditchburn, and M. Lynch (eds) *Aberdeen Before 1800: A New History*, East Linton: Tuckwell Press, 2002, pp. 13–43, at pp. 31, 35.

37 ARO-4-0514-01 (1448); see Simpson, 'Men of law', which is indebted to the discussion in H.W. Booton, 'Burgesses and landed men in North-East Scotland in the later middle ages: A study in social interaction', unpublished PhD thesis, University of Aberdeen, 1987, pp. 63, 67, 69, 74, 80.

38 See, for example, ARO-4-0187-05 (14 December 1439); ARO-4-0297-010 (4 February 1443); ARO-4-0316-08 (8 July 1443).

39 ARO-5-0711-01 (13 October 1445).

40 ARO-5-0017-02 (30 September 1449). Regrettably, this date is given inaccurately in Simpson, 'Men of law'.

41 See ARO-5-0409-03 (16 October 1460).
42 See the discussion in Simpson, 'Men of law', citing, for example, ARO-5-0053-03 (23 June 1449); ARO-5-0138-09 (3 February 1452).
43 ARO-5-0053-03 (23 June 1449); on distress and the brieve of distress, see MacQueen, *Common Law*, pp. 40, 124.
44 Again, see the discussion in Simpson, 'Men of law'; MacQueen, *Common Law*, 140; Gretton, 'Feudal system', paras 89–90; ARO-5-0692-01 (16 December 1444); ARO-5-0237-02 (17 June 1455). For the handing over of earth and stone, see also the contributions by Hepburn and Small, and by Frankot, in the present volume.
45 For the statute making provision for 'lawburrows', see RPS 1430/24.
46 ARO-5-0036-05 (15 February 1450). It should be noted that this decision to seek further advice from men of law has only been traced twice in the corpus of records transcribed in ARO.
47 My translation from ARO-5-0053-02 (23 June 1449).
48 See, for example, ARO-5-0754-01 (13 July 1450); ARO-5-0781-03 (4 October 1454); ARO-5-0081-02 (7 October 1457).
49 ARO-5-0329-01 (6 February 1458).
50 Taylor, *Shape of the State*, pp. 259–62.
51 ARO-5-0214-07.
52 ARO-4-0149-08 (15 December 1438); ARO-4-0150-02 (15 December 1438).
53 ARO-5-0219-08.
54 The functions of the warrantor are discussed in A.R.C. Simpson, 'Procedures for dealing with robbery in Scotland before 1400', in A.R.C. Simpson, S.C. Styles, E. West and A.L.M. Wilson (eds) *Continuity, Change and Pragmatism in the Law: Essays in Memory of Professor Angelo Forte*, Aberdeen: Aberdeen University Press, 2016, pp. 95–149, at pp. 101–9 in particular.
55 On repledging, see, for example, Taylor, *Shape of the State*, pp. 274–7.
56 ARO-5-0249-09.
57 On the many functions of 'borchs' or 'borghs' or 'borrows', see, for example, RPS 1430/6, RPS 1430/7 and RPS 1430/9.
58 ARO-5-0362-02; ARO-5-0362-03.
59 Here I paraphrase Finlay, *Men of Law*, p. 7.
60 ARO-5-0394-01 (11 March 1460). On Spens, bishop of Aberdeen from 1459–1480, see, for example, L.J. Macfarlane, *William Elphinstone and the Kingdom of Scotland 1431–1514: The Struggle for Order*, Aberdeen: Aberdeen University Press, 1985, pp. 99, 116, 124, 128, 203, 217, 219.
61 Munro, *Memorials*, p. 52; Cooper, *Cartularium*, vol. 2, pp. 298–302.
62 Munro, *Memorials*, p. 52.
63 ARO-5-0156-05 (28 July 1452).
64 Munro, *Memorials*, p. 52.
65 ARO-6-0030-01 (July 1470).
66 ARO-6-0121-02 (1 October 1470).
67 RPS 1471/5/12. On the representation of the burghs in parliament, see, for example, A.R. MacDonald, 'The third estate: Parliament and the burghs', in K.M. Brown and A.R. MacDonald, *The History of the Scottish Parliament Volume 3: Parliament in Context 1235–1707*, Edinburgh: Edinburgh University Press, 2010, pp. 95–121.
68 On the lords, see, for example, R.J. Tanner, 'The lords of the articles before 1540: A reassessment', *Scottish Historical Review* 79, 2000, pp. 189–212.
69 On parliament's various judicial functions, see, for example, A.M. Godfrey, 'Parliament and the law', in Brown and MacDonald, *History of the Scottish Parliament Volume 3*, pp. 157–85, at pp. 161–8.
70 Godfrey, *Civil Justice*, pp. 21–6 and Godfrey, 'Parliament and the law', at pp. 163–4 in particular.
71 RPS 1471/8/22.
72 RPS 1471/5/2.

73 RPS 1471/5/7.
74 RPS 1471/5/8–9.
75 RPS 1469/34.
76 See, for example, R. Tanner, *The Late Medieval Scottish Parliament: Politics and the Three Estates, 1424–1488*, East Linton: Tuckwell Press, 2001, pp. 187–8, 191, 254.
77 ARO-5-0588-02 (6 October 1466); ARO-5-0614-04 (5 October 1467).
78 RPS A1467/10/13.
79 RPS 1473/7/17.
80 RPS 1473/7/2; RPS 1473/7/19; RPS 1473/7/49; RPS 1473/7/51; RPS 1473/7/62. Bishop Thomas Spens of Aberdeen was present, as these sederunt rolls make clear.
81 ARO-5-0272-02 (2 October 1473).
82 ARO-6-0280-01.
83 RPS 1455/8/10.
84 See the discussion in MacQueen, *Common Law*, pp. 258–9, for the problem more generally. For a few examples of fifteenth-century statutes that expressly exhorted judges and others involved in legal process to avoid delay in the administration of justice, see RPS 1401/2/9; RPS 1404/7–8; RPS 1430/20; RPS 1450/1/18; RPS 1455/8/10.
85 ARO-5-0795-01.
86 ARO-5-0795-03.
87 Tanner, *Late Medieval Scottish Parliament*, p. 1.
88 ARO-5-0796-01 (8 October 1456).
89 RPS 1456/9, which also shows that Provost John Fife was one of those appointed to sit on the first session. For this session, see Godfrey, *Civil Justice*, pp. 50–2.
90 ARO-5-412-04 (23 February 1461); ARO-5-0418-06 (20 April 1461); ARO-5-0424-01 (22 June 1461).
91 ARO-5-0418-06 (20 April 1461).
92 ARO-6-0311-02 (3 October 1474).
93 ARO-6-0353-01 (13 March 1475).
94 ARO-6-0417-01 (19 January 1476).
95 Cooper, *Cartularium*, vol. 2, p. 188.
96 See, for example, ARO-6-0437-04 (1 July 1476).
97 Cooper, *Cartularium*, vol. 2, p. 184.
98 See MacQueen, 'Regiam Majestatem, Scots law and national identity', p. 15. On some of the texts of medieval law, see now, above all, A. Taylor, *The Laws of Medieval Scotland: Legal Compilations from the Thirteenth and Fourteenth Centuries*, Edinburgh: Stair Society, 2019.
99 I am grateful to John Ford for helping me to appreciate the point that historians cannot yet be sure how much the Aberdonian application of the common law of the realm resembled that found elsewhere. Ford's contribution to the present volume is also instructive in relation to this point.
100 RPS A1496/6/4. Again, I am grateful to John Ford and to Graeme Small for comments that helped me think about the relationship between the experience of men like Alanson and the expertise that came to be expected of those administering justice in the last decades of the fifteenth century and the first decades of the sixteenth century.
101 Macfarlane, *Elphinstone*, pp. 312–3.
102 J.W. Cairns, 'Revisiting the foundation of the college of justice', in H.L. MacQueen (ed.) *Miscellany Five*, Edinburgh: Stair Society, 2006, pp. 27–50 and Godfrey, *Civil Justice*, pp. 79–160.
103 See I. Fraser, 'The later medieval burgh kirk of St Nicholas, Aberdeen', unpublished PhD thesis, University of Edinburgh, 1989, p. 134.

14

NOTARIES AND ADVOCATES IN EARLY MODERN ABERDEEN

Adelyn L.M. Wilson

The importance of understanding legal culture and its influences has been much stressed in recent years. Various attempts have been made by scholars to more clearly conceptualise the notion of 'legal culture'.[1] A significant factor in legal culture is the education received by members of the legal community.[2] Legal education affects how a community of lawyers thinks about the law, its rules and practices, which sources they should use in constructing their arguments and ultimately the nature of the legal system in which they operate.[3] Much work has therefore been done in recent years on legal education in Scotland.[4] At the same time, there remains much work still to do, particularly with regard to the legal communities based in towns beyond the capital city of Edinburgh.

The purpose of this chapter is to provide context to this volume on legal culture, by equipping readers with an understanding of the men of law in one such town during the early modern period.[5] Aberdeen was at this time both the urban hub for the north-east of Scotland and home to the second-largest legal community after that of Edinburgh.[6] This chapter will focus on two branches of the legal profession within Aberdeen's wider legal community, namely notaries and advocates. In doing so, it will build on existing scholarship and address gaps in the current understanding of local legal history, while also providing some context for the history of the local profession through comparison with the legal community based in Edinburgh.[7]

Notaries

The notarial profession

The term 'notary' has long applied to the category of men of law who are able to perform certain legal duties, most particularly the drafting of legal documents.

There are records of Scottish notaries from the thirteenth century, but the importance of the profession increased over the following centuries.[8] This increasing prominence was caused by several factors, including their role in evidencing land transactions and the professionalization of legal work.[9] By the early modern period, several acts of the Scottish parliament evidence the respect for notaries and the requirement for notaries to be present at certain ceremonies or transactions,[10] and registration either judicially or by notaries was necessary for the validity of certain documents or transactions.[11] This trend of increasing prominence of notaries evident in Scotland was not universal: W.W. Scott has suggested that it was not similarly present in England, largely owing to the different nature of legal practice and regulation of the profession by royal decree.[12]

Scottish notaries were the professional draftsmen of legal business, familial documents and land transactions.[13] They would keep copies of all the legal documents which they drafted in their personal protocol book.[14] This book was granted to them by the Court of Session when they were admitted to the profession, and when they died it was returned to that Court or, if the notary lived in a royal burgh, to the provost and bailies of the burgh.[15] This was, of course, in theory: John Durkan has previously observed that occasionally protocol books were destroyed, stolen or otherwise lost.[16]

Notaries might also hold one of several offices, including clerkships of towns, bishoprics and like institutions. Harold Booton has shown that there was an increasing tendency in Aberdeen to appoint a notary as the official town clerk.[17] For example, the position of town clerk (or alternatively 'common scribe of the burgh') was held in the burgh of New Aberdeen by the notaries John Kennedy, Thomas Mollisone and Walter Robertson consecutively from the decoupling of the office from the provostship in 1588 to at least 1640,[18] and by the sheriff clerk, Patrick Chalmer, from 1643 until he died three years later.[19] The neighbouring burgh of Old Aberdeen also hired notaries as the burgh clerk, which office was held from at least 1636 to 1643 by the notary William Wat.[20]

The authority granted to clerks appears to have been considerable. On 22 May 1609, it was declared that the Old Aberdeen bishopric's clerk, Mr Andrew Wat (very likely a relation to the aforementioned William Wat), 'shall be clerk in times coming to the whole sasines [i.e., land transactions] within the bishopric of Aberdeen and such as is not given by him to be null and of no force, strent nor effect'.[21] Neither that authority nor the office itself were irrevocably granted. The burgh clerk Alexander Sanderson was deprived of his office in 1654 'for some miscarriage of his office of clerkship being entrusted to him'.[22]

Likewise, there had been a continued tradition of notaries being appointed as clerks for local courts.[23] In early modern Aberdeen, the clerkship of the highest court in the area, namely the sheriff court, was held by the notaries and brothers Patrick and John Chalmer in the 1630s and 1640s,[24] and before them by Patrick's father-in-law, the notary, advocate and latterly master of canon law ('canonist') William Anderson.[25] Meanwhile, the notaries John Mackie, Alexander Sanderson and John Davidson were appointed as clerks to the lands and barony court of

Grandoun (now Grandhome).[26] The notary William Elmslie was the clerk to the local barony court of Little Finersie in 1633,[27] and the notary James Thomson was the clerk to the barony court of Leys in the early 1620s.[28]

Aberdeen's notarial community

Booton has concluded that '[l]ater medieval Aberdeen possessed a small group of vigorous and ambitious notaries'.[29] He identified that David Nicolson had risen to become 'the premier Aberdeen notary' by the 1520s.[30] This man was the patriarch of the Nicolson legal dynasty, which rose to prominence in the seventeenth century with his grandsons, the Edinburgh commissary John Nicolson of Lasswade and the Aberdonian commissary and master of civil law ('civilist') Thomas Nicolson of Cockburnspath, and his great-grandsons, the king's advocate Sir Thomas Nicolson and the collector of practicks Thomas Nicolson of Carnock.[31]

The notarial community in seventeenth-century Aberdeenshire can be partially reconstructed from the records. Around 110 men are mentioned as notaries in the sheriff court records between 1600 and 1660,[32] but of course this does not capture information about the notaries whose documents were not cited in such a court action. This would include, for example, the commissary clerks Thomas and Robert Garden of Blairton and the notary, advocate and clerk depute Alexander Spalding.[33]

The majority of these men are mentioned in relation to the production of legal documents involving local lands or transactions or their appearance in the sheriff court personally. They therefore appear to have had at least some involvement with legal practice within the region. Several are mentioned with sufficient frequency to suggest that they did a large quantity of work within the city and its immediate environs. During this sample period, 25 notaries were mentioned four times, 15 were mentioned five times, 8 were mentioned six times, 7 were mentioned seven times and 3 were mentioned more often. The three who were mentioned most frequently were, somewhat inevitably, the sheriff clerk Mr Patrick Chalmer and the substitute sheriff clerks John Hunter and Patrick Milne.[34] It is therefore possible to speculate that around 20–30 notaries were working in the immediate environs of Aberdeen at any time.

Aberdeen's notarial community thus appears to have been larger in the early modern period than it had been in the medieval period.[35] It also appears to have been larger than, if nonetheless broadly consistent with, the contemporary notarial community in Elgin, which was (like Aberdeen) a north-east Scottish town which formed a regional centre as well as the seat of a diocese. Jane Thomas has suggested that by the mid-seventeenth century 'there may have been between ten and twenty notaries active in the burgh at any one time' although 'they must frequently have acted for people from outwith the burgh as well as from within'.[36] The size of these notarial communities also appears to have been broadly consistent with, if somewhat larger than, the 14 or more notaries which Elizabeth Ewan has suggested worked in sixteenth-century Edinburgh.[37]

The education of notaries

The importance of the work of notaries resulted in tight control of admission to that profession from an early period. In 1469, an act of the Scottish parliament confirmed that the king could competently admit notaries through examination by the bishops of their 'faith, good fame, science and loyalty according for the said office', and ordained that the Holy Roman Emperor could no longer create Scottish notaries.[38] Thereby

> the Scottish crown moved to take control of the admission of all secular notaries ... This action can be seen in the context both of the strengthening of royal authority in Scotland and as part of increasing royal interference in town affairs.[39]

There were further attempts to improve the learning of notaries. In 1504, parliament required bishops to re-examine the capability, reputation and previous conduct of notaries within their diocese. Those who were found wanting and those found using 'false instruments' were to be punished, while those notaries who were found capable were 'to be sent with their writings to the king's highness, who will depute certain persons to examine them, and if they are suitable they are to be made regal, if they were not made regal before'.[40] The task of testing the capability of notaries fell to the lords of session (the judges in the Court of Session), with the support of the clerk to the admission of notaries.[41] Further attempts to regulate the qualification and capability of notaries were made by parliament in 1555 and 1563.[42]

In 1587, it was confirmed that the aspiring notary had to demonstrate their capability to the satisfaction of the lords of session. The aspiring notary had to show the standard of 'his writing and congruity by forming of some evidence', specifically one of several types of legal instrument. He also had to prove his 'reasonable understanding in the Latin tongue'.[43] Finally, he had to have spent seven years in service or apprenticeship to 'one of the lords of session, commissaries, writers to the signet or some of the sheriff, stewart or bailie clerks of the shire or common clerks of the head burghs of this realm'.[44] This was a much longer period in apprenticeship than had been spent by some notaries in the previous two decades,[45] and is as long as Durkan found any notary had spent on his apprenticeship during the medieval period.[46] However, this requirement of seven years' service with one of the various professionals listed appears to have been reduced in 1595 to five years but spent specifically in service to a notary.[47] John Finlay has observed, however, that even this shorter period 'was no longer being insisted upon' by the late seventeenth century.[48]

More will be said about the benefits of a period of apprenticeship below, but it is clear that, during those years, the aspiring notary would have practised drafting various kinds of documents and styles.[49] An example of work by an aspiring notary in Aberdeen is found in a copy of the practick books of the notary, advocate and commissary clerk depute, Alexander Spalding. The title page of the manuscript records that copying began on 19 November 1673 and was 'wreiten with the hand off Patrick Whyt'. The same scribe records on a subsequent page (also styled as a title page) that he entered as a notary public on 16 December 1673.[50]

It is noteworthy that some notaries would also have undertaken formal study of the arts at a university prior to their apprenticeship and admission to the notarial profession. W.W. Scott identified some Scottish examples of such men from the later fourteenth century,[51] while John Durkan has found that in the fifteenth century:

> [n]otaries in this period varied in status and qualifications... some describe themselves as bachelors of licentiates in degrees, one as a licentiate in civil or Caesarean law, while many claim to be masters of arts... One arts master added proudly that he was a graduate of Paris[.][52]

Likewise, regarding Aberdeen specifically, Booton found that four of a sample of nine local notaries of the fifteenth and early sixteenth centuries had graduated at a university, including the aforementioned David Nicolson and the father and son John and Andrew Cadiou.[53] This also appears to have been a pattern of education sustained into the later sixteenth and seventeenth centuries, including in the cases of the notaries and sheriff clerks William Anderson and John Chalmer.[54]

Advocates

The profession of advocacy in Aberdeen

The highest branch of the legal profession in Scotland was that of the advocates in Edinburgh. There the term 'advocate' applied to a particular group of men: professional pleaders who had been granted a right of audience in the Court of Session as the highest civil court in Scotland.[55] These men could be distinguished from the separate legal profession of writers, who would undertake other work on behalf of clients, most obviously providing advice on legal transactions.[56]

However, in Aberdeen as well as most other towns in Scotland, there was sufficient work to support a community of lawyers but not enough to allow for the same degree of specialisation seen in the capital.[57] The local men of law would both plead in the local courts and undertake tasks more typically associated with writers in Edinburgh. These men were known locally in Aberdeen as 'advocates', although in a different sense to how the term was applied in Edinburgh.[58]

A previous reconstruction of the community of advocates in Aberdeen has found that approximately 50 men entered as advocates during the sixteenth century, and almost 70 were admitted during the seventeenth century.[59] They would have worked alongside additional men who practised in the Aberdeenshire area but who had been admitted to the Court of Session in Edinburgh, so did not require separate admission to the inferior courts.[60] This included the seventeenth-century commissary court judges Thomas Nicolson of Cockburnspath and James Sandilands of Craibstone.[61] Overall, there were probably around 10–20 men practicing as advocates in Aberdeen at the same time for most of the early modern period, with most residing in New Aberdeen.[62] As with the notarial profession, this represents a considerable expansion of the local profession since the medieval period.[63]

Admission as an advocate or writer in Edinburgh

The combined scholarship of several legal historians has provided considerable insight into how aspirants were admitted into the profession and the right of audience in the Court of Session in Edinburgh. R.K. Hannay found that a third of aspirants to the profession in the Court of Session would enter on the basis of having been apprenticed to an experienced professional for several years.[64] John Ford has commented that the apprentices would have spent this time

> attend[ing] the sittings of the court, running errands for their masters, assisting with the documentation required in every case, and above all listening to and learning from the oral pleadings presented at the bar. Sometimes the servitors of advocates appeared themselves as procurators in lower courts, and a few managed to gain experience as judges in other courts. More generally they acted as secretaries to the advocates they served, writing and delivering letters, drafting and witnessing formal deeds[.][65]

Similarly, from 1610, an apprenticeship of seven years was notionally required for admission as a writer to the signet for those who aspired to the upper echelons of that branch of the profession. However, Finlay's work on the community of writers in Edinburgh has suggested that there was some degree of fluctuation in this and a shorter period of three to five years was soon common.[66]

Meanwhile, two-thirds of aspiring advocates entered on the basis of their knowledge of the so-called learned laws, namely Roman law and canon law.[67] John Cairns has shown that, by at least the Restoration period, this requirement had crystallised into a trial by a panel of experienced advocates with respect to the expectant's general knowledge of Roman law and, thereafter, provision of a lecture on a topic from the books of Roman law in court before the Bench.[68] This lecture was reminiscent of the disputation required of students of law wishing to graduate at continental universities; this comparison extends as far as the traditional donning of a cap by the expectant, reflecting the doctoral cap worn as part of the law graduate's robes at continental institutions.[69]

The example of Sir James Dalrymple, later Viscount Stair and Lord President of the Court of Session, shows that it was possible to pass these exams after a period of self-study.[70] However, most aspirants would have progressed from studying the arts at one of Scotland's universities to reading law at a continental university. Schools from Italy, France, Germany and the Netherlands were fashionable at different times as new modes of scholarship developed.[71] Meanwhile, university legal education had been inconsistently available in Scotland since the Reformation, and was abolished in Aberdeen's King's College specifically for approximately 30 years before its reintroduction in 1619.[72]

The study of the learned laws became associated with the exclusivity and high status of the Edinburgh advocates.[73] This reputation can be contrasted with that of writers and other men of law, which were perceived as less noble professions.[74] It also led to a high level of reliance on the learned laws in court pleadings by advocates once they were admitted to the profession.[75] This practice, in turn, led to a significant reception of civilian jurisprudence, which contributed to the reputation of Scots law as a mixed legal system.[76]

Admission as an advocate in Aberdeen

Admission to the profession of advocate was quite different in Aberdeen. The principal source for historians of Aberdeen's advocates is John Henderson's biographical sketches of those who were admitted to the right of audience in the local sheriff court.[77] Henderson suggested that since at least the sixteenth century 'Only those of good character, education and ability were admitted'.[78] The question remained as to what that education comprised.

The Aberdeenshire sheriff court records include a note from 1633 naming 16 local advocates as having been granted the right of audience in that court. A reconstruction of the educational background of those men published elsewhere has suggested that roughly two-thirds undertook formal study in the arts at one of the local universities, and roughly half undertook an apprenticeship to an experienced local advocate. Thus the educational background of those admitted to the audience of this court included study of the arts at university, completion of an apprenticeship and a combination of both.[79] A separate reconstruction of the educational backgrounds of those who entered as advocates in the sixteenth and seventeenth centuries more generally provides additional support for this conclusion.[80] It appears that some additional prestige may have attached to those who undertook study at a university.[81]

Aberdonian advocates therefore lacked the university study of law undertaken by two-thirds of the Edinburgh community. The standards set in Aberdeen were, however, broadly consistent with those set for admission to the legal communities of other Scottish towns.[82] Indeed, Finlay has located a mid-eighteenth century case in which established procurators in Leith defended the decision not to admit a man who had completed an apprenticeship in Edinburgh to their local profession, in which they questioned whether it was for the public benefit 'that persons who have had a more eminent education in the law, should practise in the inferior courts'; it was better, they argued, for a local procurator to be educated suitably to their station and the demands of the sphere in which they were to act.[83]

It is notable that for much of the early modern period it would not have been possible for Aberdonian men to study law locally. Law teaching was abolished at King's College after the Reformation, and was reintroduced only in 1619.[84] Even after the reintroduction of law teaching at King's College, attendance at the classes of the two masters of law does not appear to have been a requirement for – or even common among – those seeking admission as an advocate.[85] This dislocation between admission as an advocate and the study of law at King's College persisted into the eighteenth century.[86] Those who did attend any such classes would likely have had a highly practical legal education, being taught by those sitting as clerks or judges in the local sheriff and commissary courts, rather than the more scholarly education in the learned laws provided at continental universities.[87]

It should be noted that not all professional pleaders in Aberdeen would have sought or been awarded the right of audience in the sheriff court. This would have included those living locally who had been admitted previously into the superior bar of the Court of Session, including Aberdeen's commissary Thomas Nicolson of Cockburnspath.[88] Moreover, Cairns has shown that in the 1680s, 'Admission [as an advocate in Aberdeen] was linked to admission to practice as a procurator before the Commissary Court'.[89] It is possible that some professional pleaders made sufficient living from pleading in such lesser courts in the area so as not to seek admission to the sheriff court. Some suggestion that this would have been possible is found in the example of the aforementioned Alexander Spalding. He entered as an advocate in 1609, but the record of his personal practice suggests that he spent much of his career in the commissary courts and undertook very little work in the sheriff court.[90] Nonetheless, it is likely that any such men would broadly have undertaken a similar pattern of education to those who sought this recognition.

The impact of legal education on local practice and the formation of legal dynasties

The pattern of education outlined here would have had a significant impact on local legal culture and its practice. Legal argumentation in the courts would, for example, have been shaped by the standard and type of knowledge expected among entrants to the profession of advocate. This is why the aforementioned knowledge of the learned laws required for attainment of audience rights in the Court of Session was a vehicle through which Scots law became a mixed legal system. That argumentation would have progressed very differently in the courts of Aberdeen is suggested by the lack of such a requirement, and the focus on practical learning, through apprenticeship and probably also at King's College.

Apprenticeship as the route of training for notaries and many advocates would also have had a wider impact on the nature of the legal community. The master-apprentice bond also often coincided with other types of relationships. A reconstruction of the apprenticeship networks of Aberdeen's sheriff and commissary courts has shown that there was 'a significant coincidence of professional and kinship relationships – through marriage and by receiving as apprentices younger relatives through consanguinity, affinity and god-parentage'.[91] One example of an apprenticeship and kinship network in Aberdeen's legal community is that of the Thomson family, which was prominent from the early seventeenth century until at least the mid-eighteenth century.[92] The aforementioned Nicolson legal dynasty, which spanned both Aberdeen and Edinburgh, likewise provides various examples of apprenticeship within the family, including the Edinburgh commissary John Nicolson of Lasswade being master to his cousin, Sir Thomas Hope of Craighall, later king's advocate.[93] Although these two networks both principally comprised those who were admitted as notaries, the same is true of that latter profession: 'the office of notary, no less than that of advocate, often descended down family lines'.[94]

Although sometimes the master-apprenticeship relationship was problematic,[95] generally the resulting bond was remarkable for its 'strength and durability' for both notaries and advocates.[96] Once established, the master-apprentice relationship 'could become a powerful mechanism for the advancement of [the professions'] members'.[97] Apprenticeship and wider kinship networks could bring legal business: Finlay has shown that the sixteenth-century Court of Session advocate, Robert Leslie, significantly benefited from such networks.[98] Such relationships might also offer the opportunity to acquire offices such as court appointments which were being promoted through the network. This might come in the form of recommendations for high-level appointments, as Sir Thomas Hope of Craighall recommended as his successor as king's advocate his former master's son, Sir Thomas Nicolson.[99] The bestowing of an office may also be arranged through a simple gift of the position, as William Anderson gifted the sheriff clerkship to his son.[100] In Aberdeen, this sharing of offices led to courts being largely run by particular networks of men who were interconnected through their apprenticeship and kinship networks.[101] Thus, the networks created through this form of educational relationship, kinship and other forms of relationship would have been a defining aspect of legal culture and communities in Aberdeen.

Men of law who became both notaries and advocates

The two professional groups of notaries and advocates should not be regarded as entirely distinct. Nineteen of the men who appear as notaries in the sheriff court records also seem to have been admitted as advocates before that court.[102] The aforementioned John Chalmer is a particularly interesting example of this group. He is mentioned four times in the sheriff court records as having worked as a notary in the 1630s, a number which indicates his business was presumably quite successful.[103] He subsequently acted as sheriff clerk depute to his brother, Patrick Chalmer.[104] He received the clerkship himself in 1646. He was therefore well established in his profession as a clerk and notary by 1649, when he was admitted as a local advocate and resigned his clerkship.[105]

This raises the question as to why these men qualified as both notaries and advocates. The biographical sketches compiled by Henderson suggest that qualification as a notary was not a prerequisite to entering as a local advocate, as it was for admission as a writer to the signet in Edinburgh.[106] Rather, as Finlay has noted, local advocates admitted by the sheriff court should be distinguished from notaries 'who were admitted centrally'.[107]

It is possible that dual recognition both as a notary for competence in drafting legal documents and as an advocate for competence in pleading cases was helpful for those trying to earn a living in Aberdeen and its environs. Indeed, several men continued to identify themselves as notaries in connection to their professional expertise both before and after their admission as advocates. For example, John Hunter was an established notary by the 1610s when he served, possibly for the first time, as sheriff clerk substitute.[108] In 1630, he was also made clerk to the lands and barony of Grandoun as well as sheriff clerk depute.[109] In 1632, however, he also entered as an advocate.[110] Yet he appears to have continued to identify himself as a notary public after his admission as an advocate, notably both in connection to his notarial work and in his own private matters.[111]

Social status and wealth of Aberdeen's men of law

Whether one chose to pursue one line of practice or to qualify as both a notary and an advocate, it seems that Aberdeen's men of law made a good living. Booton concluded that, in medieval Aberdeen, notaries maintained a 'reasonable prosperity'.[112] This observation also appears to be true of legal practice in the early modern period. With respect to the advocates, Finlay suggests that it was 'one of the strongest, and apparently most lucrative, local bars in the country',[113] albeit not as profitable as might be found in practice in the highest courts in Edinburgh.[114] Meanwhile, there is evidence of notaries also receiving good wages for their work: William Wat received eight merks 'for his fie' as town clerk in September 1643, twice the fee paid to the court's officers.[115] This standard of wealth among Aberdeen's notaries is also seen among members of that profession in other Scottish towns: Thomas has likewise indicated that most of Elgin's notaries were 'moderately wealthy', while some were among the wealthiest men of the burgh.[116]

Several notaries and advocates appear in Aberdeen's sheriff court records as cautioners for other men's debts or obligations, which indicates a good degree of wealth.[117] A particular example of this is found in the advocate Robert Paip, the patriarch of a notable local legal dynasty, who often appeared as a cautioner in the sheriff court records. This may be the reason for Henderson concluding that Paip 'conducted an extensive money lending business'.[118]

Thomas has further described Elgin's notaries as being 'amongst the burgh's social elite'.[119] This point can also be made of Aberdeen's men of law. Some notaries and advocates were, for example, admitted as burgesses of the town.[120] Some appear to have held substantial quantities of property.[121] Indeed, an examination of the god-parentage networks undertaken elsewhere has found that some advocates regarded themselves as members of the landed classes.[122] However, after the controversial provostship of the advocate John Cheyne of Fortrie in the 1590s, men of law do not appear to have served on the burgh council.[123] In this, Aberdeen can be contrasted with Elgin, in which 'the backbone of the burgh council' comprised notaries – although there is some suggestion that the town may have been exceptional in a Scottish context.[124]

Conclusion

This chapter has examined the professional groups of notaries and advocates in late sixteenth- and seventeenth-century Aberdeen, the men of law who shaped local early modern legal culture. It has examined the size of these communities, their activities and how they were trained for admission to their profession. It has shown how these professional groups differed from those in other Scottish towns, particularly those working in the capital city of Edinburgh. It has also shown that some men of law would seek admission to both professions, meaning that the town's two professional groups of men of law were not entirely distinct. Finally, this chapter has shown that by entering these professions, men of law could become members of the town's elite classes. In this, the master-apprentice bond, which was the route into the profession of a considerable number of men of law, was a long-lasting and influential mechanism to build networks and professional success.

Notes

1 See, for example, S. Koch et al. (eds) *Comparing Legal Cultures*, Bergen: Fagbokforlaget, 2017, and J.Ø. Sunde, 'Champagne at the funeral – An introduction to legal culture', in J.Ø. Sunde and K.E. Skodvin (eds) *Rendezvous of European Legal Cultures*, Bergen: Fagbokforlaget, 2010, pp. 11–28.

2 See, for example, Sunde's classification of education (or 'degree of professionalization') as one of his six criteria for understanding legal culture; Sunde, 'Champagne at the funeral'.

3 See, for example, J.W. Cairns, 'The legal education of Alexander Mylne, first president of the College of Justice' in H. Dondorp et al. (eds) *De rebus divinis et humanis: Essays in honour of Jan Hallebeek*, Göttingen: V&R unipress, 2019, pp. 15–24.

4 See, for example, a recent example of this, in addition to what is cited below; J.W. Cairns, 'John Millar's theses for admission as an advocate', *History of European Ideas* 45, 2019, pp. 304–9.

5 On the complexity of this term in the medieval period, see A. Simpson, 'Men of law in the Aberdeen Council Register? A preliminary study, circa 1450–1460', *Juridical Review*, 2019, pp. 136–59.

6 J.W. Cairns, 'Lawyers, law professors, and localities: The universities of Aberdeen, 1680–1750', *Northern Ireland Legal Quarterly* 46, 1995, pp. 304–31, at p. 305.

7 On the continental context of the lower branches of the profession, see, for example, J. Finlay, 'Lawyers and the early modern state: Regulation, exclusion, and numerus clausus', *Canadian Journal of History* 44, 2009, pp. 383–410.

8 J. Finlay, 'The history of the notary in Scotland', in M. Schmoeckel and W. Schubert (eds) *Handbuch zur Geschichte des Notariats der Europäischen Traditionen*, Baden-Baden: Nomos, 2009, pp. 393–428, at pp. 393–4; W.W. Scott, 'William Cranston, notary public c 1395–1425, and some contemporaries', in H.L. MacQueen (ed.) *Miscellany Seven*, Edinburgh: Stair Society, 2015, pp. 125–32, at p. 129; Simpson, 'Men of law in the Aberdeen Council Register?', pp. 156–7; and J. Durkan, 'The early Scottish notary', in I.B. Cowan and D. Shaw (eds) *The Renaissance and Reformation in Scotland: Essays in Honour of Gordon Donaldson*, Edinburgh: Scottish Academic Press, 1983, pp. 22–40, at p. 22.

9 E. Ewan, 'Protocol books and towns in medieval Scotland', in W. Prevenier and T. de Hemptinne (eds) *La diplomatique urbaine en Europe au moyen âge: actes du congrès de la Commission internationale de diplomatique, Gand, 25–29 août 1998*, Louvain: Garant, 2000, pp. 143–56, at pp. 144–5; Finlay, 'The history of the notary in Scotland', pp. 394–5; and Durkan, 'The early Scottish notary', p. 23.

10 *The Records of the Parliaments of Scotland to 1707*, ed. K.M. Brown et al., St Andrews, 2007–2020, <www.rps.ac.uk> (hereafter RPS), e.g. 1617/5/24, 1625/10/3, 1641/8/43.

11 RPS, 1597/11/43 (partially repealed by 1600/11/34), 1579/10/33, 1584/5/85.

12 Scott, 'William Cranston', pp. 128–9.

13 For a discussion of which in medieval Aberdeen, see H.W. Booton, 'Burgesses and landed men in North-East Scotland in the later middle ages: A study in social interaction', unpublished PhD thesis, University of Aberdeen, 1987, pp. 213–6, 224–38. See also on the activities of notaries, Finlay, 'The history of the notary in Scotland', pp. 405–7; and Durkan, 'The early Scottish notary', generally.

14 For a large collection of protocol books from Scotland, see the National Archives of Scotland, Edinburgh, NP1 series. On protocol books, their contents and their regulation, see Ewan, 'Protocol books and towns in medieval Scotland', pp. 148–56; W. Angus, 'Notarial protocol books, 1469–1700', in *An Introductory Survey of the Sources and Literature of Scots Law*, Edinburgh: Stair Society, 1936, pp. 289–300, esp. at pp. 293–6; J. Finlay, *Admission Register of Notaries Public in Scotland, 1700–1799*, 2 vols, Edinburgh: Scottish Record Society, 2012, vol. 1, pp. 12–15; and Finlay, 'The history of the notary in Scotland', pp. 397–8, 405–7. In connection to the registration of land transactions specifically, see Finlay, 'The history of the notary in Scotland', pp. 416–21.

15 RPS, 1617/5/36.

16 Durkan, 'The early Scottish notary', p. 38.

17 Booton, 'Burgesses and landed men', pp. 203–8.

18 John Kennedy was a notary public who appears from the records to have been prominent since at least 1559, and had previously served as general procurator to 'the chaplains of the college and choice of the parish kirk of Aberdeen'; the printed records do not reflect much activity on his part as clerk, and he had deceased by April 1599 [John Stuart (ed.) *Extracts from the Council Register of the Burgh of Aberdeen*, 4 vols, Aberdeen: Spalding Club, 1844–1872, vol. 2, p. 180, and David Littlejohn (ed.) *Records of the Sheriff Court of Aberdeenshire*, 3 vols, Aberdeen: for the University, 1904–1907, vol. 1, pp. 146, 196, 230, 232 (quotation), 304, 316, vol. 2, p. 20]. Mollisone, however, appears to have enjoyed significant tenure as town clerk. An entry in the council register for 1593 indicates that Mollisone had by that time become the town clerk [Stuart, *Extracts from the Council Register*, vol. 2, p. 100]. He appears to have held this capacity until at least 1618 [Littlejohn, *Records of the Sheriff Court*, vol. 2, p. 75]. By 1625, he had been succeeded in that office by Walter Robertson, who had previously been Mollisone's servitor, substitute and deputy in turn [Littlejohn, *Records of the Sheriff Court*, vol. 2, pp. 100, 139, 162, 303–4]. None of these three men appear to have entered as advocates [cf. J.A. Henderson (ed.) *History of the Society of Advocates in Aberdeen*, Aberdeen: for the University of Aberdeen, 1912]. On

the events of the 1580s, see W. Kennedy, *Annals of Aberdeen, from the Reign of King William the Lion, to the End of the Year 1818; with an Account of the City, Cathedral, and University of Old Aberdeen*, 2 vols, London: A. Brown & co., 1818, vol. 1, pp. 152, and A.M. Munro, *Memorials of the Aldermen, Provosts and Lord Provosts of Aberdeen, 1272–1895*, Aberdeen: for the subscribers, 1897, pp. 110–1.

19 Henderson, *History of the Society of Advocates in Aberdeen*, p. 86, and Littlejohn, *Records of the Sheriff Court of Aberdeenshire*, vol. 2, pp. 537–8.

20 A.L.M Wilson, 'Legal practice and legal institutions in seventeenth-century Aberdeen, as witnessed in the lives of Thomas Nicolson of Cockburnspath and his associates', *Journal of Irish and Scottish Studies* 9, 2019, pp. 93–128, at p. 101; A.M. Munro (ed.) *Records of Old Aberdeen, [1157]–1903*, 2 vols, Aberdeen: New Spalding Club, 1899–1909, vol. 1, pp. 73, 354; and Aberdeen City and Aberdeenshire Archives, OA/1/1/1, p. 161ff.

21 Munro, *Records of Old Aberdeen*, vol. 1, p. 49.

22 Ibid., p. 84.

23 Durkan, 'The early Scottish notary', p. 34.

24 Littlejohn, *Records of the Sheriff Court of Aberdeenshire*, vol. 2, pp. 121, 354, 537–8.

25 On whom, Littlejohn, *Records of the Sheriff Court of Aberdeenshire*, vol. 2, p. 537; Wilson, 'Legal practice and legal institutions', pp. 113, 118–9; and P.J. Anderson (ed.) *Officers and Graduates of University and King's College Aberdeen MVD-MDCCCLX [1495–1860]*, Aberdeen: New Spalding Club, 1893, p. 30.

26 Littlejohn, *Records of the Sheriff Court of Aberdeenshire*, vol. 2, p. 335.

27 Ibid., pp. 386–7.

28 Aberdeen University Library, MS 3361/4/88, held by the National Trust for Scotland in Crathes Castle, Aberdeenshire, fols 1r, 7r.

29 Booton, 'Burgesses and landed men', p. 202. See also on medieval Aberdonian notaries, Simpson, 'Men of law in the Aberdeen Council Register?', esp. pp. 147–8.

30 Booton, 'Burgesses and landed men', p. 202. On David Nicolson's protocol book, see ibid., pp. 215–16, 228–30.

31 On which family, see especially Wilson, 'Legal practice and legal institutions'. On the office of king's advocate, see J. Finlay, *Men of Law in Pre-Reformation Scotland*, East Linton: Tuckwell Press, 2000, ch. 7.

32 This count (and the detail provided subsequently thereupon) does not include men mentioned in pre-1600 instruments led in post-1600 cases. It is acknowledged that notaries of the same name operating at the same time may have been conflated.

33 On whom, Wilson, 'Legal practice and legal institutions'.

34 Littlejohn, *Records of the Sheriff Court of Aberdeenshire*, vol. 2, for example, pp. 121 (as a notary for a sasine), 231 (as a notary for an act of renunciation), 329 (as the recipient of wadset in Dyce, using the title of sheriff clerk), 336 (as sheriff clerk, appoints John Hunter and John Chalmer his deputes) and so on.

35 Cf. Booton, 'Burgesses and landed men', pp. 202, 242, and Simpson, 'Men of law in the Aberdeen Council Register?', pp. 147–8.

36 J.E. Thomas, 'Elgin notaries in burgh society and government, 1540–1660', *Northern Scotland* 13, 1993, pp. 21–30, at pp. 22, 23.

37 Ewan, 'Protocol books and towns in medieval Scotland', pp. 147–8.

38 RPS, 1469/20.

39 Ewan, 'Protocol books and towns in medieval Scotland', p. 146. See also Finlay, 'The history of the notary in Scotland', pp. 395–6.

40 RPS, A1504/3/108. See also Finlay, 'The history of the notary in Scotland', p. 396 and (on the punishment of false or nefarious notaries) p. 414–6, and Durkan, 'The early Scottish notary', pp. 36–7.

41 The holder of this office, William Sharp, was admitted as a burgess in Aberdeen in 23 April 1657: A.M. Munro (ed.) 'Aberdeen Burgess Register, 1631–1700', in *The Miscellany of the Spalding Club*, 2 vols, Aberdeen: for the University of Aberdeen,

1908, vol. 2, p. (409). See also on this office, *A History of the Society of Writers to Her Majesty's Signet, with a List of the Members of the Society from 1594 to 1890 and an Abstract of the Minutes*, Edinburgh: for the Society by T. & A. Constable, 1890, p. 286; Finlay, *Admission Register of Notaries Public*, vol. 1, pp. 10–13; and Finlay, 'The history of the notary in Scotland', pp. 402–3.

42 Finlay, 'The history of the notary in Scotland', pp. 398, 403.

43 This is consistent with requirements for admission of notaries during the medieval period, on which see Durkan, 'The early Scottish notary', p. 30–1.

44 RPS, 1587/7/39.

45 Finlay, 'The history of the notary in Scotland', p. 399.

46 Durkan, 'The early Scottish notary', p. 37.

47 *The Acts of Sederunt of the Lords of Council and Session, from the 15th of January 1553, to the 11th of July 1790*, Edinburgh: Neill and Co, 1790, pp. 24–5. See also Angus, 'Notarial protocol books, 1469–1700', p. 292.

48 J. Finlay, 'Pettyfoggers, regulation, and local courts in early modern Scotland', *Scottish Historical Review* 87, 2008, pp. 42–67, at p. 43, n. 4.

49 See also J. Finlay, 'The lower branch of the legal profession in early modern Scotland', *Edinburgh Law Review* 11, 2007, pp. 31–61, at pp. 47–8.

50 Aberdeen University Library (hereafter AUL), MS 558, fol. 81r. See also A.L.M. Wilson, 'The "Authentick Practique Bookes" of Alexander Spalding', in A.R.C. Simpson et al. (eds) *Continuity, Change and Pragmatism in the Law: Essays in Memory of Professor Angelo Forte*, Aberdeen: Aberdeen University Press, 2016, pp. 175–236, at pp. 185–7. See also on manuscript copying by notaries, Finlay, 'The history of the notary in Scotland', p. 407. For some examples of notaries likely educated in this manner in the fourteenth and fifteenth centuries, see Scott, 'William Cranston', esp. p. 125, 127–8 (although see also the difficulties with identifying educational patterns in this period, ibid., p. 131) and Simpson, 'Men of law in the Aberdeen Council Register?', pp. 155–6.

51 Scott, 'William Cranston', pp. 128–9.

52 Durkan, 'The early Scottish notary', p. 23.

53 Booton, 'Burgesses and landed men', p. 203, and H.W. Booton, 'John and Andrew Cadiou: Aberdeen notaries of the fifteenth and early sixteenth centuries', *Northern Scotland* 9 (first series), 1989, pp. 17–20, at pp. 17–18.

54 Henderson, *History of the Society of Advocates in Aberdeen*, pp. 85, 116 and Littlejohn, *Records of the Sheriff Court of Aberdeenshire*, vol. 2, pp. 537–8.

55 On the origin of this term, see Finlay, *Men of Law*, pp. 14–20.

56 On which professional group, see Finlay, 'The lower branch of the legal profession', p. 38 ff, and Finlay, *Men of Law*, ch. 3.

57 Finlay, 'Pettyfoggers, regulation, and local courts', p. 44.

58 Ibid., p. 43, n. 2.

59 Wilson, 'The "Authentick Practique Bookes" of Alexander Spalding', pp. 177–9.

60 Finlay, 'The lower branch of the legal profession', p. 52.

61 Wilson, 'Legal practice and legal institutions', p. 101.

62 Ibid., pp. 101–2 and Henderson, *History of the Society of Advocates in Aberdeen*, p. xi.

63 Cf. Simpson, 'Men of law in the Aberdeen Council Register?', pp. 148–9.

64 R.K. Hannay, *The College of Justice*, Edinburgh: Stair Society, 1990, p. 145. See also J.W. Cairns, 'Advocates' hats, roman law and admission to the Scots bar, 1580–1812', *Journal of Legal History* 20, 1999, pp. 24–61, at pp. 33–48, and J.D. Ford, *Law and Opinion in Scotland during the Seventeenth Century*, Oxford: Hart, 2007, pp. 2–3.

65 Ford, *Law and Opinion*, p. 3.

66 Finlay, 'The lower branch of the legal profession', pp. 46–9, and Finlay, 'Pettyfoggers, regulation, and local courts', p. 43, n. 4.

67 Hannay, *The College of Justice*, p. 145, and Cairns, 'Advocates' hats', pp. 33–48.

68 Cairns, 'Advocates' hats', pp. 34–43, and Ford, *Law and Opinion*, pp. 4–5, 8–10, 27–9.

69 Cairns, 'Advocates' hats', p. 49–52, and Ford, *Law and Opinion*, pp. 4–5.
70 See his lecture preserved as 'Scotstarvet's "Trew Relation"', *Scottish Historical Review* 13, 1916, pp. 380–92. On which, see A.L.M. Wilson, 'The sources and method of the institutions of the law of Scotland by Sir James Dalrymple, 1st Viscount Stair, with specific reference to the law of obligations', unpublished PhD thesis, University of Edinburgh, 2011, § 1.2.2 and Ford, *Law and Opinion*, pp. 7–8, 10–22.
71 J.W. Cairns, 'Lawyers, law professors, and localities: The universities of Aberdeen, 1680–1750', *Northern Ireland Legal Quarterly* 46, 1995, pp. 304–31, at p. 306, and Ford, *Law and Opinion*, p. 3.
72 Wilson, 'Legal practice and legal institutions', pp. 108–14; J.W. Cairns, 'The law, the advocates and the universities in late sixteenth-century Scotland', *Scottish Historical Review* 73, 1994, pp. 171–90; J.W. Cairns, 'Academic Feud, Bloodfeud, and William Welwood: Legal education in St Andrews, 1560–1611', *Edinburgh Law Review* 2, 1998, pp. 158–79 (part one), 255–87 (part two); H.L. MacQueen, 'The foundation of law teaching at the University of Aberdeen', in D.L. Carey Miller and R. Zimmermann (eds) *The Civilian Tradition and Scots Law: Aberdeen Quincentenary Essays*, Berlin: Duncker & Humblot, 1997, pp. 53–71; and D. Stevenson, *King's College, Aberdeen, 1560–1641: From Protestant Reformation to Covenanting Revolution*, Aberdeen: Aberdeen University Press, 1990.
73 Finlay, 'The lower branch of the legal profession', pp. 36–7, and Ford, *Law and Opinion*, pp. 4, 22–5.
74 Finlay, 'The history of the notary in Scotland', pp. 408, 413.
75 See, for example, G. Dolezalek, 'The court of session as a ius commune court – witnessed by "Sinclair's practicks", 1540–1549', in H.L. MacQueen (ed.) *Miscellany Four*, Edinburgh: Stair Society, 2002, pp. 51–84.
76 For an accessible introduction to this theme, see A.R.C Simpson and A.L.M. Wilson, *Scottish Legal History, volume one: 1000–1707*, Edinburgh: Edinburgh University Press, 2017, esp. chs 7, 9, 15, 17.
77 Henderson, *History of the Society of Advocates in Aberdeen*.
78 Ibid., p. ix.
79 A.L.M. Wilson, 'Men of law and legal networks in Aberdeen', in M. Lobban and I. Williams (eds) *Networks and Connections in Legal History*, Cambridge: Cambridge University Press, 2020, pp. 33–59, at pp. 38–45. See also, Finlay, 'Pettyfoggers, regulation, and local courts', p. 43.
80 Wilson, 'The "Authentick Practique Bookes" of Alexander Spalding', pp. 178–9.
81 Wilson, 'Men of law and legal networks in Aberdeen', p. 39.
82 Cairns, 'Lawyers, law professors, and localities', p. 305.
83 Finlay, 'Pettyfoggers, regulation, and local courts', p. 53.
84 Wilson, 'Legal practice and legal institutions', pp. 108–14.
85 Ibid., pp. 114–9.
86 Cairns, 'Lawyers, law professors, and localities', pp. 328–30. On law teaching at King's College from 1680 to 1750, see ibid., pp. 309–28.
87 Wilson, 'Legal practice and legal institutions', pp. 114–9.
88 Ibid., p. 101.
89 Cairns, 'Lawyers, law professors, and localities', p. 314.
90 AUL, MS 558, and Wilson, 'The "Authentick Practique Bookes" of Alexander Spalding'.
91 Wilson, 'Men of law and legal networks in Aberdeen', p. 44.
92 Ibid., pp. 40–45.
93 Wilson, 'Legal practice and legal institutions', p. 99; Wilson, 'Men of law and legal networks in Aberdeen', p. 48; and A. Hope, 'Sir Thomas Hope, Lord Advocate to Charles I', in MacQueen, *Miscellany Four*, pp. 145–53, at p. 147.
94 Finlay, *Admission Register of Notaries Public*, vol. 1, p. 23.
95 Finlay, 'The lower branch of the legal profession', pp. 49–51.

96 Finlay, *Admission Register of Notaries Public*, vol. 1, p. 1.
97 Wilson, 'Men of law and legal networks in Aberdeen', p. 44.
98 Finlay, *Men of Law*, pp. 136–46.
99 Wilson, 'Legal practice and legal institutions', p. 99; Wilson, 'Men of law and legal networks in Aberdeen', p. 48; and Hope, 'Sir Thomas Hope, Lord Advocate to Charles I', p. 147.
100 Littlejohn, *Records of the Sheriff Court of Aberdeenshire*, vol. 2, p. 279. George Anderson does not appear to have taken up the office, however, as it eventually passed to Patrick Chalmer (William Anderson's son-in-law). Ibid., vol. 2, p. 537.
101 Wilson, 'Men of law and legal networks in Aberdeen', pp. 45–52.
102 Notaries working as court pleaders is also seen in fifteenth-century Aberdeen (Booton, 'John and Andrew Cadiou', p. 18 and Booton, 'Burgesses and landed men', pp. 209–10), but it is unclear whether any formal recognition of their advocacy skills was required at that time. It should be noted that several other men, who were neither notaries nor advocates, also pleaded in the local courts at this time (ibid., p. 240). See also the writers in Edinburgh who further qualified as advocates in the Court of Session (Finlay, 'The lower branch of the legal profession', pp. 43–6), although there was little evidence of dual qualification as notaries and advocates in Edinburgh (Finlay, 'The history of the notary in Scotland', p. 408).
103 Littlejohn, *Records of the Sheriff Court of Aberdeenshire*, vol. 2, pp. 354, 433, 451, 476.
104 Ibid., pp. 437, 481.
105 Ibid., p. 538; Henderson, *History of the Society of Advocates in Aberdeen*, p. 116.
106 On this requirement in Edinburgh, see Finlay, 'The lower branch of the legal profession', p. 47.
107 Finlay, *Admission Register of Notaries Public*, vol. 2, p. 2.
108 Littlejohn (ed.) *Records of the Sheriff Court of Aberdeenshire*, vol. 2, p. 220.
109 Ibid., pp. 335, 336.
110 Henderson, *History of the Society of Advocates in Aberdeen*, p. 222, and Littlejohn (ed.) *Records of the Sheriff Court of Aberdeenshire*, vol. 2, p. 343–4.
111 Littlejohn, *Records of the Sheriff Court of Aberdeenshire*, vol. 2, pp. 406, 410, 501.
112 Booton, 'Burgesses and landed men', p. 211.
113 Finlay, 'The lower branch of the legal profession', p. 49.
114 Compare similar comments for a later period, Cairns, 'Lawyers, law professors, and localities', p. 312.
115 Munro, *Records of Old Aberdeen*, vol. 1, p. 73. See also on fees charged, Finlay, 'The lower branch of the legal profession', pp. 55–8.
116 Thomas, 'Elgin notaries in burgh society and government, 1540–1660', pp. 23–4.
117 See, for example, the notaries William Jack, Alexander Chalmer and Alexander Gordon, and the advocates Alexander Irving, James Irving and Andrew Clark (Littlejohn, *Records of the Sheriff Court of Aberdeenshire*, vol. 2, pp. 16, 109, 161, 166, 244, 246).
118 Littlejohn, *Records of the Sheriff Court of Aberdeenshire*, vol. 2, pp. 54, 90, 112, 142, 181, and Henderson, *History of the Society of Advocates in Aberdeen*, p. 289, n. 3.
119 Thomas, 'Elgin notaries in burgh society and government, 1540–1660', p. 27.
120 See, for example, the notary James Ross (Littlejohn, *Records of the Sheriff Court of Aberdeenshire*, vol. 2, p. 237) and the advocates William Lumsden (Munro, 'Aberdeen Burgess Register, 1631–1700', p. (371)) and Andrew Clark (Littlejohn, *Records of the Sheriff Court of Aberdeenshire*, vol. 2, p. 246). For discussion of notaries being admitted as burgesses in the medieval period, see Booton, 'John and Andrew Cadiou', pp. 17–18 and Booton, 'Burgesses and landed men', p. 208.
121 See, for example, the advocate William Lumsden, who had lands in Hedderwick, Tillocorthie, Blairton and the Chanonry of Old Aberdeen; Littlejohn, *Records of the*

Sheriff Court of Aberdeenshire, vol. 2, pp. 292, 326, 411, 435. See also on this point regarding the medieval Aberdeen legal community, Booton, 'Burgesses and landed men', pp. 217–23.

122 Wilson, 'Men of law and legal networks in Aberdeen', pp. 56–58.

123 Kennedy, *Annals of Aberdeen*, p. 163 and S. Dropuljic and A.L.M. Wilson, 'Elections and local governance in early modern Aberdeen', in A.M. Godfrey (ed.) *Miscellany Eight*, Edinburgh: Stair Society, 2020, p. 130. On Cheyne, see Henderson, *History of the Society of Advocates in Aberdeen*, p. 121, and Munro, *Memorials of the Aldermen*, pp. 118–19.

124 Thomas, 'Elgin notaries in burgh society and government, 1540–1660', pp. 24, 27–9.

INDEX

Note: Bold page numbers refer to tables and page numbers followed by "n" denote endnotes.

For Product Safety Concerns and Information please contact our EU
representative GPSR@taylorandfrancis.com
Taylor & Francis Verlag GmbH, Kaufingerstraße 24, 80331 München, Germany

www.ingramcontent.com/pod-product-compliance
Ingram Content Group UK Ltd.
Pitfield, Milton Keynes, MK11 3LW, UK
UKHW022013180926
475701UK00003B/341

* 9 7 8 0 3 6 7 2 0 6 7 9 6 *